One Family

Richard Seltzer

BookLocker
Trenton, Georgia

Published by BookLocker.com, Inc., Trenton, Georgia.

BookLocker.com, Inc.
2025

First Edition

Library of Congress Cataloging in Publication Data
Seltzer, Richard
One Family by Richard Seltzer
Library of Congress Control Number: 2024924970

Disclaimer

This book is, for the most part, a memoir. It reflects the author's present recollections of experiences over time. The truth being told is the author's truth and may not be what others recall as truth.

Epigraphs

This is not only one man, this is the father of those who shall be fathers in their turns.
In him the start of populous states and rich republics,
Of him countless immortal lives with countless embodiments and enjoyments.
How do you know who shall come from the offspring of his offspring through the centuries?
(Who might you find you have come from yourself, if you could trace back through the centuries?)"

— Walt Whitman

"Look at my arm: I've got goosebumps. To think that maybe — just maybe — through my ancestors, I may have touched the hem of Shakespeare's doublet."

— *Shakespeare: the Man who Pays the Rent*
by Judi Dench with Brendan O'Hea

Books by Richard Seltzer

Non-Fiction
One Family
Why Knot?

Trojan War Fiction
Let the Women Have Their Say
Trojan Tales
We First Met in Ithaca, or Was it Eden?
Breeze

Shakespeare Fiction
Shakespeare's Twin Sister
We All Are Shakespeare

Other Fiction
The Bulatovich Saga: The Name of Hero
Meter Maid Marion, How to Tutor a Ghost, The Third Tortoise
To Gether Tales
Echoes from the Attic (with Ethel Kaiden)
Parallel Lives
Beyond the 4th Door
Nevermind
Saint Smith and Other Stories

Children's Books
The Lizard of Oz and Other Stories
Now and Then and Other Tales from Ome
The Lizard of Oz

Jokes
Grandad Jokes

Translation (from Russian)
Ethiopia Through Russian Eyes

Business Books
Web Business Boot Camp
Shop Online the Lazy Way
The AltaVista Search Revolution, two editions
Take Charge of Your Web Site
The Social Web
The Way of the Web
Snapshots of DEC
MGMT MEMO: Management Lessons from DEC

Dedication

To my mother, Helen Isabella Estes Seltzer (1920-2010), author of *Cary-Estes-Moore Genealogy*.

Table of Contents

Part One:
Our Common Ancestry

Welcome to the Family

This is a family reunion where you're going to meet relatives you never knew were yours. You thought you were alone, but you have a vast extended family. I'll give you a sense of who they are, and why they should matter to you. This isn't a list of names and dates for you to memorize. Rather, the anecdotes I share will build paths of association. Encounters with distant cousins will help you understand their connections to you and to one another; so someday you can introduce them to your children, grandchildren, and great-grandchildren, imparting the immensity, diversity, and importance of this vast family that you didn't realize was yours.

There's a crowd. You'll be tempted to say, like T. S. Eliot (quoting Dante), "I had not thought death had undone so many."

Consider me a chatty Virgil, introducing you to all these fine and not-so-fine folks, grouped as we chance upon them, one encounter leading to another.

Why Should You Care About My Family?

You have two biological parents, four grandparents. The number of your ancestors doubles with each generation. That means you don't need to believe in Adam and Eve to conclude we're all related. Each of us could have had a quadrillion ancestors in the year 550. That's two to the power of 50: one followed by 15 zeros, or a million billion. If it took a second to count each number, it would take 31,688 million years for you to count to a quadrillion. But historians estimate that only about two hundred million people were alive at that time. What happened to your other ancestors?

Until a hundred years ago, most people lived in rural areas and seldom traveled. Families stayed in the same spot for generations. They had little contact with people in other towns, much less other countries. Unless a catastrophe — like war, plague, or famine — forced them to move and mate with strangers, they married among themselves, and everyone in a town was related. "You can be, and in fact are, descended from the same individual many times over," says Adam Rutherford in *A Brief History of Everyone Who Ever Lived: the Human Story Retold Through Our Genes.* "Your great-great-great-great-great-grandmother might hold that position in your family tree twice, or many times, as her lines of descent branch out from her, but collapse onto you... Our family trees are not trees at all, but entangled meshes" (pp. 162-163).

But, even blunted by interbreeding, the effect of doubling is so powerful that Rutherford believes "with absolute confidence" that if you're of European extraction, you are descended from Charlemagne, the eighth-century Holy Roman Emperor. You are also descended from millions of other people who lived then. The general statement, based on analysis of DNA, is that 80 percent of adult Europeans alive back then had offspring who had offspring through all the generations to today, and that every one of them is an ancestor of everyone of European descent who is alive today. (See https://www.nationalgeographic.com/science/article/charlemagnes-dna-and-our-universal-royalty)

Another statistical model, goes even further, determining that every person on Earth is at least a fiftieth cousin of everyone else (International Society of Genetic Genealogy). As Rutherford says, "It might seem that a remote tribe would have been isolated from others for centuries in, for example, the Amazon. But no one is isolated indefinitely."

My family is your family. I happen to have found the names and dates of some of our massively numerous shared ancestors. You can and should take pride in these connections, as I do.

Our ancestors include rulers of almost every country in Europe, plus Holy Roman Emperors, Byzantine Emperors, princes of Kiev, Viking chieftains, William "the Conqueror," King John (of Robin Hood and Magna Carta fame), King Alfred "the Great," and King Robert the Bruce of Scotland (who you know from the movie *Braveheart)*. Charlemagne appears 42 generations back. (That reminds me of *The Hitch Hiker's Guide to the Galaxy*, where the number 42 is the meaning of life, the universe, and everything.)

Our beliefs shape how we see ourselves and how we live our lives. What difference would it make if you knew your ancestors shaped the course of history? What difference would it make to your children if they knew that they are special in that way? How would you feel about the world and its future, if you knew you had such forebears and may have such descendants?

There are over 1600 direct ancestors listed in the Appendix at the end of this book. Whoever you are, even if you don't know the names of your great-grandparents, if you are of European descent, some part of this family tree is yours. And if you have children and your children have children for about 35 generations, a thousand years from now everyone alive on Earth, and on planets colonized by Earth, will be your descendant.

We're all one family.

The Joy of Discovery

Knowing that you are descended from famous, influential, and creative people who lived hundreds of years ago may not be enough for you. You may want to do your own research and get the joy of discovery. That's not impossible, but it will take luck as well as effort.

Few people can trace their ancestry back as many as four generations; but if you can go as far as 50 generations, you may have an experience like that of Paul Atrides ("Muad-Dib") in the novel *Dune*. Thanks to the effects of "spice," he senses the presence of all his ancestors thousands of years back. And however far back you go, building your family history may give you a pleasure like solving a massive jigsaw puzzle.

My mother was very lucky, and I couldn't have done what I did without her.

She grew up as an orphan, during the Depression, on a cobblestone street in the immigrant East Falls section of Philadelphia, in a row house crammed with seven children. She wasn't the first born, nor the baby, nor even the middle child. She was the sixth of seven — a nonentity. She got top grades in high school but couldn't afford college. She knew her father had come from Tennessee but didn't know the names or addresses of any Tennessee relatives.

Atop a nearby hill loomed the estate of the Kellys, parents of Grace, the future movie star and Princess of Monaco. Grace was nine years younger than Mom. Sometimes neighborhood kids were allowed to play tennis on their courts. Mom envied Grace and dreamed of being in High Society.

When she was 36, on a hunch, Mom wrote to Estes Kefauver. He was running for vice president with Adlai Stevenson, as a Democrat. Her maiden name was Estes, the same as his first name; and he was from Tennessee. Perhaps there could be a connection. He replied immediately, pointing her to a genealogy book published in 1939 that listed her birth and parentage.

They were third cousins.

She got a copy of the book and, with it, she found her father's sister Sallie, who was living in Brownsville, Tennessee, on what had been the family plantation. In 1959, we drove from our home in New Hampshire to Tennessee, where we met Aunt Sallie and dozens of other relatives. Little Orphan Annie had a huge extended family. We saw her father's grave. The death date was 1943.

To Mom, discovering her father's family and ancestry was a dream come true. The genealogy book *(The Cary-Estes Genealogy* by May Folk Webb and Patrick Mann Estes) provided the evidence she needed to join the Daughters of the American Revolution (DAR) as well as the even more exclusive Colonial Dames. She encouraged my Dad to look into his ancestry, and he, too, uncovered someone who had participated in the Revolution. That enabled him to join the Sons of the American Revolution (SAR). He was proud of his membership and participated in local events.

In 1979, Mom reprinted the original *Cary-Estes Genealogy* and began compiling a companion volume, covering the family since 1939. For her new book, with the zeal of someone raised as an orphan, she tried to track down everyone mentioned in the original book who was still alive. She solicited updates from them, as well as photos, anecdotes, and family history. Even after she self-published that book, *The Cary-Estes-Moore Genealogy,* in 1981, she continued to gather information for another, corresponding with and sometimes visiting hundreds of relatives all over the United States and the British Isles. Researching family history, she formed long-lasting friendships with a huge extended family. That effort also brought her the status she had craved as an orphan child. Her ancestry helped define her proper place in the world.

Ancestor Surfing

If, like me, you are fortunate enough to find an historical connection in your family history, whether by fact or tradition, start your research there. Use Wikipedia, Ancestry.com, and other online resources and see how far back those ancestral paths lead, to what people, countries, and events. Savor your personal connections to distant history. Share what you find with friends and family, and let me know, as well, by email (seltzer@seltzerbooks.com).

I always had an itch to learn about my ancestors. At the age of twelve, when visiting my Dad's parents (Pop Pop and Nana), I checked handwritten family histories compiled by my great-grandfather and by distant cousins. I took detailed notes and asked follow-up questions. Later, when Mom got the original Estes genealogy book, I did my best to decipher the formatting, the numbering system, and the abbreviations, to figure out how I fit into the overall picture. Decades later, it dawned on me that Wikipedia and other Internet resources could enable me to trace my ancestry further back.

I started with clues on pages 83-87 of *The Cary-Estes Genealogy* (which you can read online at seltzerbooks.com/ caryestescomplete.pdf). King James IV of Scotland is an ancestor. The Wikipedia entry for him shows his parents; the entries for them show their parents; and so on. I call following such a trail "ancestor surfing."

Royal marriages linked the king or heir of one country with the ruling family of another, often establishing alliances. That practice wasn't prescribed by law, but local marriages were rare. Though not the stated intent, such marriages united the ancestral pools of the most important families.

Because of the importance of the birth and health of an heir to the throne, records of ancestry were kept meticulously, like those of thoroughbred horses today. Online access to that information made it easy for me to trace many generations. Also, medieval chronicles and sagas were readily available online or in print from Amazon. And Ancestry.com often confirmed what I had found elsewhere and also provided details about non-royal ancestors.

The lists in the Appendix reveal the interconnected complexity of European royal families in the Middle Ages. I believe that our most fascinating ancestor is Eleanor of Aquitaine, mother of King Richard I "the Lion-Hearted" and of King John from the Robin Hood legends. (See more on her in Part Two: Extraordinary Women).

One line goes back 53 generations to Flavius Afranius Syragrius, who served as proconsul of Africa and prefect of Rome. He was consul in 382. His page at Wikipedia used to link to a list of the ancestors of Queen Elizabeth II, saying that he is "the earliest known ancestor of any of the royal houses of Europe." That list, which is no longer online, was identical to ours for the first 33 generations, from Flavius Afranius through King Edward III.

I became addicted, following more and more lines, further and further back; and I've just scratched the surface. I followed one line back 58 generations to a king of Armenia in 265 CE. Another line led to Odin (Norse King of the Gods) and his ancestor Thor AKA Tror, a grandson of King Priam of Troy, who was a descendant of Zeus (Greek King of the Gods). Zeus's grandmother, Gaia, Earth Goddess, was 100 generations back, at the beginning of the universe.

Internet Evangelist

Ancestor surfing came naturally to me. Working for DEC (Digital Equipment Corporation), the minicomputer maker, I was part of a small team focused on business opportunities opening on the Internet. In February 1994, soon after the Internet went public and the first web browser was released, I wrote and, together with Bertold Langer, produced a three-minute video, *A Glimpse of the Future*. The immediate purpose was to help a DEC vice president seem prophetic in a speech to his employees. But word about the video spread quickly, and the creators of Mosaic (the first web browser) and dozens of other companies, including DEC's competitors, requested and distributed thousands of copies of this video and used it to spread the word about the business potential of the Internet, which, at that time, many people found difficult to imagine. (You can see that video at youtube.com. Search for "glimpse of the future seltzer"). Soon after that, I was asked to write a speech on the same topic for Massachusetts Governor Bill Weld to deliver at the National Governors' Conference in Boston.

A year later, DEC asked me to write the first consumer-oriented book about search engines. After *The AltaVista Search Revolution* was published, they sent me around the world to deliver speeches — all over the US and Canada, plus Bogota, Buenos Aires, Rio de Janeiro, Moscow, and even Zimbabwe. This was two years before Google started, eight years before Facebook.

I believed the essence of the Internet was its ability to connect people to people. First, create a space where people can gather; then, capitalize on the business opportunities that emerge. In my many of my speeches, I highlighted nine industries that the Internet would transform over the next decade:

- publishing,
- broadcasting,
- banking/finance,
- telecommunications,
- education/training,
- manufacturing,
- government,
- healthcare,
- retail.

I had a talent for brainstorming about the impact of technology on business. The title on my business card was "Internet Evangelist." And I could speak for an hour or more, with conviction and enthusiasm, to audiences of thousands — I was preaching a new gospel, that the Internet makes it possible for people to connect closely and in unexpected, tangled ways, no matter where they live and what their backgrounds, to truly act like members of the same family.

Not Me, I'm Jewish

If, like my daughter-in-law and my girlfriend, you believe you are 100% Jewish, check your DNA. Your parents, grandparents and great-grandparents may all be Jewish as far back as anyone in your family can remember, but chances are that at least 1% of your DNA is non-Jewish. Not all putative fathers are genetic fathers. Don't be shocked at the possible infidelity of some of your ancestors. Severe penalties kept indiscretions hidden; but romance, sexual attraction, and the lure of the forbidden have always been powerful motivators. Perhaps infidelity has an evolutionary benefit, expanding the ancestral pool. Also, war and pogroms often led to rape. Jewish tradition takes those factors into account, tracing ancestry by the mother, not the father. Her contribution is certain. His is not.

One generation back, you are 50% your mother's DNA and 50% your father's; two generations, 25% of each grandparent; three generations, 12.5%; four generations, 6.25%; five generations, 3.125%; six generations, a little over 1.5% of each great-great-great-great-grandparent. So if around 200 years ago, one father-of-record was not the father-of-fact and was not Jewish, you would have about 1.5% non-Jewish ancestry. And going back 36 generations from that non-Jewish father, the number of your non-Jewish ancestors at the time of Charlemagne would be over 68 billion — two to the power of 36.

If you are less than 1% non-Jewish, that pushes the date of your first non-Jewish ancestor back further. If you are 1% of 1% non-Jewish, the anomaly happened six generations earlier, and the number of your non-Jewish ancestors at the time of Charlemagne is two to the power of 30 — over a billion.

So you, too, may be descended from Charlemagne.

"First Night" and Other Ways the Ancestral Pot Was Stirred

In medieval times in Europe, feudal lords had the right to bed any woman who was their subject, often doing so on her wedding night. It's impossible to gauge how frequently this right was exercised. But the children of such matings were raised as peasants and mated with other peasants, which spread the ancestry of nobles among the peasant population.

That practice had a long history. It was true in the days of Gilgamesh, the legendary Sumerian king. "He is king, he does whatever he wants... takes the girl from her mother and uses her, the warrior's daughter, the young man's bride" (*Gilgamesh* translated by Stephen Michael). And, according to Wikipedia, *The Babylonian Talmud* mentions a draconian decree imposed on the Jewish community that made all Jewish brides subject to rape by their Syrian-Greek oppressors before their wedding.

Religious conversion also impacted ancestral lines, changing the definition of the in-group and the out-group. In many places and for a long time, Jews were subject to serious penalties and restrictions; but if they converted, they became Christians, with all the rights of Christians, including the right to marry other Christians. The children of such marriages had both Christian and Jewish ancestors.

Also in the centuries after the fall of Rome, there were instances of mass conversion from other religions to Christianity. Several of our ancestors were credited for such events:

- Around 496, at the prompting of his wife Saint Clotilde, Clovis, the first king of France, converted to Christianity and had his troops do likewise.
- King Borivoj I (852-889) and his wife, Saint Ludmila (860-921), grandparents of "Good King" Wenceslaus, converted Bohemia (now the Czech Republic) to Christianity.
- Rollo (d. 933), the great-great-great-grandfather of our ancestor William "the Conqueror," converted his Viking warriors to Christianity as part of the treaty that gave him rule over Normandy.
- Saint Vladimir "the Great," Prince of Kiev (958-1015), made Christianity the national religion of his country.

And not all conversions were to Christianity. One of our ancestors, the Byzantine Emperor Michael II "the Stammerer" (c. 800), belonged to the Athinganoi sect, which adopted Jewish faith and rituals. According to Wikipedia, in that era, the Athinganoi were numerous in Anatolia and the Balkans and formed the backbone of the Byzantine army.

What You Believe Has Consequences

Charlemagne, your ancestor, was the seven-greats grandson of Clovis, the first king of France (see the Line of Brunhild the Valkyrie in Lines of Descent in the Appendix). Clovis was reputed to be a descendant of Mary Magdalene and Jesus Christ. (The plot of Dan Brown's *Da Vinci Code* is based on that legend). As unlikely as that story is, its implications are interesting. Apocryphal texts such as the

Gospels of Thomas, Philip, and *Mary* in *The Nag Hammadi Library* portray Mary Magdalene as a visionary and leader of the early church whom Jesus loved more than he loved his disciples. She truly understood his teachings. And according to legend, she was Jesus's wife, not a prostitute. Pregnant at the time of the Crucifixion, she fled to Gaul, where she was sheltered by the Jews of Marseille and gave birth to Sarah, an ancestor of Clovis.

By that way of thinking, everyone with European ancestry is descended from Jesus, who was Jewish, with lineage going back to King David and Abraham.

Maybe you don't consider the arguments about Charlemagne compelling. And maybe you think the legend about descent from Jesus absurd. But what would be the consequences if you believed them and if nearly everyone did? Where truth can't be determined, belief is a powerful force. This belief could help us think and act like we are all one family.

Ancestral Pool

In this mosaic of historical and personal anecdotes, fact and fiction are intertwined. I'm following threads of memory and of family history. I'm also ancestor surfing through history, looking for connections. We lie to ourselves and to one another, and coincidence shifts the paths of our lives this way and that. We believe what we're ready to believe, and what we believe is more important than what actually happens. And we all share a common ancestry, connected as one family.

I'm writing about what people believed in the past and what they believe today, independent of and sometimes in contradiction to scientific facts. For instance, without any proof one way or the other, today some of us believe in an afterlife and some of us don't. And in medieval Europe, many people had detailed ideas about what comes after death and how the dead are connected to the living. Such ideas can have a major impact on our individual lives and on the course of history.

To avoid confusion, I won't use words like "genes" and "gene pool," but rather, "ancestors" and "ancestral pool." And I'll include legends of heroes and gods and fantastical creatures that scientists would never consider but that have impact on human aspirations and reputations and notions of self-worth. And I'll try to convince you to believe that we are all one family, not because of the truth of that proposition, but because of the benefits that could redound to all of us from such a belief.

Thomas Malthus saw the dark side of population growth. He observed that human population grows faster than the food supply, until famine, war, or disease reduces it. He presumed that would always be the case, and he didn't see any benefit from it.

Undisturbed, people tend to stay put, in pockets, isolated from one another. Population growth leads to pockets colliding with one another, which triggers war, famine, pestilence, and mass migration, all of which lead to the mixing of ancestral lines, which seems to be important for the survival of the human species. But, today, large-scale mixing can occur without catastrophes.

Economic globalism, made possible by advances in communication and transportation, is bringing together previously remote and separate populations. In isolation, ideas and beliefs, as well as ancestral lines, tend to be group-specific, emphasizing differences and exclusivity rather than commonality. But now that we can mix without the need for catastrophes, we may be able to live together as one family.

More than genetics

Your connections to the past and to the future involve more than genetics. Philosophers and scientists have long debated whether nature or nurture is more important in shaping our lives. For those of us who were raised by our genetic parents, those factors are combined. But you might have been raised believing that you have one set of parents when, in fact, you were adopted. Or perhaps your mother mated with someone other than her husband. Maybe you don't know the names and dates of your grandparents or great-grandparents, but you think of yourself as part of a cultural tradition.

Also, people other than your parents may have shaped who you became, as guardians, mentors, or role models. Mom's aunts, who raised her after she became an orphan, were very important to her, especially Aunt Lil, who laid out the rules and administered punishment, protecting her and looking out for her — both feared and loved.

In ancient Rome, choice mattered more than chance. A man could adopt a child and make that child his heir even if he had birth children. Octavian/Augustus was adopted by Julius Caesar, Hadrian by Trajan, and Marcus Aurelius by Marcus Antoninus. In Plato's *Republic*, children are deliberately raised not knowing who their parents are so they will all be treated equally. Some Christian denominations revere the "apostolic succession," tracing the current ministry of the church through a chain of predecessors that leads back to Saint Peter. Some scholars see themselves as part of a chain of teachers extending hundreds of years into the past. Poets and novelists learn from those who came before them, modeling their writing on "teachers" who may have been dead for centuries.

If you build your own family history, you can choose to include adoptions, family traditions, legends, and other influences, not just genetic ties. I came across some bizarre legends. One ancestor was a sea monster, a Quinotaur (a bull with five horns). According to the seventh century *Chronicle of Flaccidus*, a Quinotaur fathered our ancestor Merovech. The historical Merovich was one of the warlords who, in alliance with the Roman general Flavius Aetius, fought against Attila and his Huns at the Battle of the Catalaunian Plains in 451, ending Attila's invasion of Gaul. (Attila, too, is our ancestor).

King John, our ancestor, by his incompetence, prompted his barons to rebel and demand he accept the terms of the Magna Carta, a foundational document of democracy in both England and America. An historian of his day, Ralph de Diceto, wrote that John was descended from Odin, king of the Norse gods, and — adding a dash of magical evil — from the demoness Melusine. With ancestors like those, no wonder I love fantasy.

Dukes of Ferrara in Renaissance Italy

Mom associated her maiden name "Estes" with the House of Este in Ferrara, Italy, which was prominent during the Renaissance. The Este family was famous for patronizing the arts and also for brutality. The poem *My Last Duchess* by Robert Browning portrays Alfonso d'Este, Duke of Ferrara, telling his new bride, Lucrezia Borgia, about his first wife, warning her that she better be faithful to him or else.

from **My Last Duchess (Ferrara)**

...

She had
A heart — how shall I say?— too soon made glad,
Too easily impressed; she liked whate'er
She looked on, and her looks went everywhere.
Sir, 'twas all one! My favour at her breast,
The dropping of the daylight in the West,
The bough of cherries some officious fool
Broke in the orchard for her, the white mule
She rode with round the terrace — all and each
Would draw from her alike the approving speech,
Or blush, at least. She thanked men— good! but thanked
Somehow — I know not how — as if she ranked
My gift of a nine-hundred-years-old name
With anybody's gift.

...

Oh, sir, she smiled, no doubt,
Whene'er I passed her; but who passed without
Much the same smile? This grew; I gave commands;
Then all smiles stopped together. There she stands
As if alive....

According to *The Cary-Estes Genealogy*, the line of descent runs as follows, going back 32 generations starting with Mom. (In my lists she appears as generation 3, I as generation 2, my children as 1, and my grandchildren as 0).

3) Helen Isabella Estes (1920-2010) married Richard Warren Seltzer
4) Smith William Estes (1881-1943) married Mae Griffith

5) Louis Powhatan Estes (1849-1902) married Lily Yates Moore (1853-1929)

6) Albert Monroe Estes (1804-1863) married Mildred Colman

7) Joel Estes (1780-1833) married Sara Langhorne Bates

8) Benjamin Estes (1753-1816) married Cecilia Thorpe

9) Abraham Estes, Jr. (1697-1759) married Elizabeth Jeeter

10) Abraham Estes, Sr. (1647-1720), emigrated from Ringwould, Kent England to St. Stephens, King Queen County, Virginia married Barbara Brock

11) Sylvester Estes (1596-1667) married Ellen Martin

12) Robert Estes (1555-1616) Ringwould, Kent, England, married Anne Woodward

13) Sylvester Estes (1522-1579) born in Deal, Kent, England died Ringwould, Kent, England, married Jone Estes

14) Nicholas Estes (1495-1533)

15) Robert Estes (1475-1506)

16) Francesco d'Este AKA Francisco Estes AKA Francisco Esteuse, born in Italy and died in England (1440-?)

17) Leonello d'Este, Marquess of Ferrara etc. (1407-1450)

18) Niccolo III d'Este, Marquess of Ferrara etc. (1383-1441)

Leonello became Marquess of Ferrara on his father's death. But when Leonello died, he was succeeded by his brother Borso, instead of his son Francesco, our ancestor. Francesco went to northern Europe, eventually settling in England. Considering the culture of violence at that time and place, he probably fled for his life. On the death of Borso, Ercole, another brother succeeded and transformed Ferrara into a cultural center. He was a patron of Leonardo da Vinci as well as the poet Ariosto. The second wife of his son and heir, Alfonso, was Lucrezia Borgia, the illegitimate daughter of Pope Alexander VI, portrayed in the Browing poem *My Last Duchess* above, and also in the Showcase series *The Borgias*.

Alexander, who became pope the year that Columbus discovered America, drew the Line of Demarcation which gave Brazil to Portugal and the rest of the Western Hemisphere to Spain. He rose to power and stayed there by murder. His illegitimate son, Cesare, commanded an army, with which he sought to control central Italy. Machiavelli addressed his infamous book *The Prince* to Cesare. It provides practical advice on how to seize power and expand it. Believing that "the end justifies the means," Machiavelli hoped that Cesare would unite Italy by conquering it.

My mother's middle name was Isabella. And one of the daughters of Ercole I was Isabella d'Este, who became the Marchioness of Mantua. Leonardo da Vinci did a portrait of her. A drawing survives, but there may have been a painting as well. *The Cary-Estes Genealogy* quotes an art critic (Raymond S. Sites) speculating that Isabella d'Este was the model for the *Mona Lisa*.

Mom believed that a family resemblance had survived for 14 generations and that her niece Joyce was a dead ringer for the Mona Lisa. To prove her point, in her genealogy book, Mom published a photo of Joyce facing a photo of the Mona Lisa.

Mom was also obsessed about Pocahontas. Her grandfather's middle name was Powhattan, so she concluded there must be a link. The connection was collateral rather than direct. A cousin married into a family that proudly traced its origins to John Rolfe and Pocahontas. But no evidence could convince Mom that she wasn't a direct descendant. She took great pride in her native American roots.

Orlando

Throughout the ages, authors have transformed family legends into inspiring tales for the many. In his epic poem *Orlando Furioso* (1516), Ludovico Ariosto, who, like Leonardo da Vinci, was patronized by our Estes ancestors, wove together fantasy, history, and Estes family legend in a romantic chivalric tale, with wizards and war and love, as well as a sea monster and a flying horse. He even included a trip to the moon. Orlando, also known as "Roland," was one of the Paladins of Charlemagne, who, like King Arthur's Knights of the Roundtable, were the subject of many medieval tales of chivalry. In this story, Orlando is obsessed with Angelica, a pagan princess who doesn't return his love, which drives him mad. The historical figure on which Orlando is based was also the subject of the eleventh century French epic, *The Song of Roland*, about a losing battle against invading Saracens in 778, during Charlemagne's reign.

In *Orlando Furioso*, Ariosto invented a common genealogy for both his legendary hero and his patron, the Duke of Ferrara.

Canto 36

LXX

"Of Trojan ancestors are we the seed,
Through famous Hector's line," (Rogero said,)
"For after young Astyanax was freed,
From fierce Ulysses and the toils he spread,
Leaving another stripling in his stead,
Of his own age, he out of Phrygia fled.
Who, after long and wide sea–wandering,
gained Sicily's shore, and in Messina reigned.

LXXI

"Part of Calabria within Faro held

> The warrior's heirs, who after a long run
> Of successors, departed thence and dwelled
> In Mars' imperial city: more than one
> Famed king and emperor, who that list have swelled,
> In Rome and other part has filled the throne;
> And from Constantius and good Constantine,
> Stretched to the son of Pepin, is their line.
> (translated by William Stewart Rose)

According to Ariosto, Astyanax, son of Hector, wasn't an infant when Troy fell and wasn't killed there. Rather, he was a young man (a "stripling"), and he left someone else to be killed in his place. He fled to Sicily, where he became the ruler of Messina. The Roman emperors Constantius and Constantine were descended from him. The "son of Pepin" is Charlemagne, who we're all descended from.

Echoes of Lancelot

Was Robin Hood real? Was King Arthur? Legend and history, faction and fact are interwoven. As Yeats put it, "How can we know the dancer from the dance?"

While William, soon to be "the Conqueror," rode toward the Battle of Hastings, a minstrel named Taillefer entertained him with *The Song of Roland* which made legend out of an historical battle in the days of Charlemagne. Taillefer sang so well that William granted him the honor of striking the first blow, and the minstrel died in battle, the teller of one legend becoming part of another.

Ripley's Believe of Not points out says that Taillefer (meaning "hewer of iron") died on October 14, and Eisenhower (which also means "hewer of iron") was born on October 14. The one invaded from Normandy, and the other to Normandy.

Chrétien de Troyes (1160-1191), author of chivalric romances, lived at the court of his patron, Marie de France (1145-1198), Countess of Champagne, another ancestor of ours. She was a daughter of Eleanor of Aquitaine and King Louis VII of France. At the age of eight, Marie was betrothed to Henry I, Count of Champagne. She married him at 14 and served as regent when he went on a crusade to the Holy Land. Shortly after his return, he died, and she became regent again. She didn't remarry.

According to the scholar Urban T. Holmes III and the novelist Roberta Kalechofsky (in her excellent, but neglected novel *The Anonymities*), Chrétien de Troyes was the pen name of a convert from Judaism to Christianity who wanted to disguise his origins. Those were the days when troubadours composed tales of courtly love. He wrote rhymed romances about King Arthur and the Knights of the Round Table. His most popular was about the adulterous affair of Lancelot and Queen Guinevere. He and Marie were close friends for years. Her husband was no love match and was often absent. One or more of her children (perhaps our ancestor) may have been fathered by Chrétien.

Another ancestor of ours, Cerdic of Wessex, 52 generations back, was the leader of the first group of West Saxons who invaded England in 495. He ruled as King of Wessex 519-534, in what is now the south of England. In the movie *King Arthur*, Cerdic and his son are portrayed as killed in battle by King Arthur and Sir Lancelot.

Odin and a Hint of Middle Earth

My research took me to the earliest recorded times, when the boundary between humans and gods was fuzzy. According to *The Ynglinga Saga* by Snorr Sturluson, written in Iceland around 1300 (the time of Dante), Odin was a king before he became a god. He reigned in Scythia, in what is now Ukraine and Russia. His capital city, Asgard, was east of the Don River, which flows into the Black Sea. He invaded and conquered Scandinavia, where his sons and their descendants reigned as kings in Sweden, Norway, and Denmark. After his death, Odin and some of his sons, like Thor, Balder, and our ancestor Njord, were worshipped as gods. Njord became associated with the sea, seafaring, wind, fishing, wealth, and crop fertility; and Asgard became the dwelling place of the gods, comparable to Mount Olympus. Sturluson listed 25 generations of Swedish kings, each the son of the one before, leading from Odin down to Olaf "Tree Feller," our ancestor.

Odin was often portrayed as a wandering one-eyed god, with a staff and a hat. He sacrificed an eye, gouging it out himself, as the price for being allowed to drink from the Well of Cosmic Knowledge. (In Marvel comics and movies, he lost his eye in battle.)

According to Sturluson, Odin was a "songsmith," speaking in rhyme. With a song he could open earth, hills, stones, and burial mounds. He was also a shapeshifter, able to make himself into fish, worm, bird, or beast. He could go to distant lands in a twinkling and could quench fire, still an ocean storm, or change the direction of the wind with words alone. He could also call the dead out of the earth. He could take strength or wit from one person and give it to another. He could blind or deafen his enemies and could make their weapons blunt. His men rushed forward without armor, like mad dogs or wolves, strong as bears or wild bulls, and could kill with a single blow. Neither fire nor iron could hurt them. They were called "Berserkers."

Another Sturluson book, *The Prose Edda*, provides a different genealogy, tracing Odin's ancestry 21 generations further back, to King Priam of Troy, saying that Troy, in what became Turkey, was the same as Asgard. Priam's grandson Tror AKA Thor travelled widely, battling giants, dragons, and other beasts. In the far north, he met and married a prophetess named Sif (our ancestor). A volcano on the planet Venus is named after her (Sif Mons), and Marvel Studios included her in the movie *Thor* and the TV series *Agents of S.H.I.E.L.D.*

That fantastical genealogy has the same starting point as the one the Renaissance Italian poet Ariosto invented for the Dukes of Ferrara (our ancestors).

There's also a connection to the fantasy world of Tolkien. According to Sturluson's *Chronicle of the Kings of Norway*, Halfdan the Black, brother of Olaf Gudrødsson (our ancestor), waged war against and defeated King Gandalf.

Should we give any credence to such legends? Sturluson recommends that we do. "Although we cannot say what truth there may be in these, yet we have the certainty that old and wise men held them to be true (*Heimskringla: Chronicle of the Kings of Norway,* p. 3)

I believe I may have seen Odin once, in the form of a hawk, in the living room of our house in Boston. When my daughter was five weeks old, a hawk flew down the chimney, alighted on a railing of her crib, and stared at her. She didn't cry. She stared back.

This was a big brown bird, clutching the railing with sharp talons. Shocked and frightened, I walked around him slowly, not wanting to scare him. I opened a window wide, then moved back, facing him, and, with hand gestures, encouraged him to fly out. He did, and was gone. The incident probably took less than two minutes, though, to me, it felt like hours. We had a bird-proof screen put on top of the chimney so that couldn't happen again.

Now I wonder what he told her and what she told him during that moment when their eyes locked.

Beowulf

Growing up, I didn't read Norse sagas or *Beowulf*. At Mom's prompting I dove into Greek myths instead. When, at age 10, I had read a dozen books on the subject, I presumed that I knew everything there was to know about Greek mythology. So I sent a letter to *Giant Step*, a quiz show where 7 to 17 year olds competed. That was the heyday of quiz shows, with the *$64,000 Question* at the top of the ratings.

One day, right before supper, I answered the phone, even though Mom and Dad were home. I had never done that before. Nobody ever called me. By chance, the caller wanted to talk to me, not them. He said he was from *Giant Step*. He wanted to know if I could compete in the broad category "mythology" rather than the narrow one "Greek mythology." Without hesitation, I said "no." I knew nothing about Norse myths and didn't want to be humiliated. End of discussion. End of opportunity.

Now, writing this book at age 78, I stumbled upon ancestors connected to *Beowulf* and finally dove into that story with gusto. I even watched the 2007 movie with Ray Winstone, Anthony Hopkins, Robin Wright, and John Malkovich.

The historical/legendary Beowulf was an ally of our ancestor Eadgils. When King Ohthere of Sweden (our ancestor) died, he was succeeded by his younger brother Onela, and his sons Eadgils and Eanmund sought refuge with Heardred, King of the Geats. When Onela went to war against the Geats and Heardred was killed, Beowulf, Heardred's first cousin, succeeded him as king. Then, with Danish help as well as help from Beowulf, Eadgils struck back, defeated Onela, and regained the Swedish throne.

In the Anglo-Saxon epic, Beowulf faces not just one but three monsters, in succession: Grendl, Grendl's mother, and a dragon. Heroes are defined by the challenges they face — the more powerful the monsters and the more of them there are, the greater the acclaim for the victor. Perhaps that's true not just in legend, but in everyday life as well. When the going gets tough, we should take pride in what we can do despite the difficulty.

Nibelungenlied and Attila the Hun

Reading the medieval German epic *The Nibelungenlied* for the first time, I didn't realize that Attila was a main character. I also didn't know that he was an ancestor of ours. (See Lines of Descent in the Appendix). In the epic, he's called "Etzel;" and he's portrayed as a civilized, honorable, and courteous European king, not a barbarian leading a murderous horde. *The Nibelungenlied* was written around 1200, over 700 years after the events purportedly occurred, by a poet who presumed that the chivalrous manners and morals of his day applied back then as well, that nothing had changed. Etzel is a High Middle German variant of the name Attila, and his people are "Huns."

The Attila of history lived from about 406 to 453. Known as "the Scourge of God," he invaded both the Eastern and Western Roman Empires and built an empire of his own in Europe. Even before he came to power, the borders were nebulous and westward moving. As the Huns advanced, they pushed Germanic tribes into territory controlled by Rome. Under Attila, the Huns battled the Romans directly and advanced inexorably, with an army estimated at over half a million, until they were stopped in 451 at the Battle of the Catalaunian Plains, near present-day Orleans, south of Paris.

As praetorian prefect of Gaul, our ancestor Tonantius Ferreolus, was instrumental in organizing the Roman defense that led to that battle. And the allied army led by Roman general Flavius Aetius included the forces of King Merovech of the Salian Franks (our ancestor) as well as those of King Gondioc of Burgundy (also our ancestor). Gondioc was the son of Gunther and Brunhild who appear in *The Niebelungenlied* as well as in Wagner's four-opera cycle *Der Ring des Nibelungen.*

Brunhild is renowned for her "vast strength and surpassing beauty" (Hatto translation). She falls in love with Sigfried "the Dragon-Slayer" and has a jealous feud with Kriemhild, who is Sigfried's wife. Brunhild has Sigfried murdered; then Kriemhild marries King Etzel (Attila) and, with his help, wreaks revenge, causing the massacre of thousands. In Norse mythology, Brunhild is a Valkyrie, a female figure who guides souls of dead warriors to Valhalla, where they enjoy fighting one another until Ragnarök, the cataclysmic battle at the end of time.

The historical Attila died of a nose bleed during revels in celebration of his last marriage. There was no wound. Like me, he may have had a blood condition that made him prone to uncontrolled bleeding. (We'll touch on that in Part Seven: Blood).

The Welsh Discovery of America

According to another legend, a Welshman named Madoc, son of Owain (an ancestor of ours), discovered America in 1170, three hundred years before Columbus. After the discovery, he returned home, recruited colonists, and made ten more trips back and forth, taking them to the New World.

Richard Haklyut, a British historian of voyages of exploration, first recorded that legend in 1582. At the time, it stirred up interest as the basis for England having an older and better claim to the New World than Spain had with Columbus.

Two hundred years later, that legend was resurrected with new forms of proof — not artifacts, but stories that could inspire more stories and become a meme. Frontiersmen in the newly opened territories along the Ohio and Missouri Rivers reported that they had encountered a tribe of light-skinned natives who spoke Welsh among themselves. They concluded that Madoc's colonists had interbred with the natives, and these were their descendants. In his book *Undaunted Courage*, Stephen Ambrose mentions that President Jefferson thought the Madoc myth might be true and instructed Lewis (of the Lewis and Clark Expedition) to look for Welsh-speaking Indians (p. 285).

When truth intersects with fantasy, sometimes they become interwoven, making cloth far stronger than that made from truth alone. Neither logic nor evidence can break it asunder. Such is the tale of the Welsh discovery of America.

The Warner Family

The trail of my associations led from Leonello to his brother Ercole to the writings of a poet patronized by Ercole. I also entertained the speculation that Chrétien de Troyes was a Jew by birth and that he fathered children of Marie de France. Professional genealogists would dismiss such tales, preferring direct genetic lines and facts without literary embellishment.

I delight in stories that have lives of their own, that get entangled with history and ancestry. I relish the coincidence that Chrétien lived in Troyes, a medieval city in what is now France, named for the ancient city of Troy, home of Hector, whom Ariosto claimed was a forebear of both the Estes family and his fictionalized hero Orlando. As Sir Walter Scott would say, "Oh, what a twisted web we weave."

If Mom had known of it before she died, she would also have loved our collateral connections with the Warner Family, which lead from indentured servant to queen.

A Warner cousin found me on Ancestry.com and generously shared with me the results of his research. He added my tree to his and assembled a chart which he printed and laminated for me. It now hangs on the wall by my desk.

The chart begins with Augustine Warner, Sr. (1611-1674). It ends with me, and includes George Washington, Meriwether Lewis of

Lewis and Clark, Robert E. Lee, and Queen Elizabeth II. Those famous people are cousins of ours, not direct ancestors, but I value the information. I hadn't realized how closely Washington, Lewis, and Lee were related to one another, much less to us.

Here are the twelve generations of descent from Augustine to Elizabeth:

12) Augustine Warner, Sr. (1611-1674) married M. Mary Townley (1614-1662)

11) Augustine Warner, Jr. (1642-1681), Speaker of the Virginia House of Burgesses married Mildred Reade (1642-1693)

10) Mary Warner (1664-1700) married John Smith (1662-1698)

9) Mildred Smith married Robert Porteus, Sr. (1679-1758)

8) Rev. Robert Porteus, Jr. (1705-1754) married Judith Cockayne (1702-1789)

7) Mildred Porteus married Robert Hodgson, Sr.

6) Rev. Robert Hodgson (1766-1844) married Mary Tucker

5) Henrietta Mildred Hodgson (1778-1844) married Oswald Smith (1794-1863)

4) Frances Dora Smith (1833-1922) married Claude Bowes-Lyon

3) Claude George Bowes-Lyon (1855-1944) married Nina Cecilia Cavendish-Bentick

2) Elizabeth Bowes-Lyon (1900-2002) married King George VI of England (1895-1952)

1) Queen Elizabeth II (1926-2022) married Prince Philip Mountbatten (Duke of Edinburgh) (1921-2021)

When Augustine Warner, Sr., the illustrious ancestor we have in common with Queen Elizabeth, emigrated to Virginia at the age of 17, in 1628, he was an indentured servant, owned by his master until his term of servitude came to an end.

The Uncertainty Principle

If you find a link to the historical past and decide to ancestor surf or to compile your own family history, don't be discouraged if you can't establish facts with certainty. Sometimes data doesn't exist or it's inconclusive or contradictory. But don't give up. The effort itself may bring joy and lead to unexpected knowledge.

Historical records are wreckage that has been picked over and rearranged by people with biases and motivations that may differ from your own. *Caveat lector!* (Reader beware!)

In your research, you are likely to use Wikipedia often. If I don't specifically say where I got information, presume it's from Wikipedia. In 2023, an estimated 4.3 billion unique visitors accessed its files, which were the equivalent of over 60 million printed pages. Currently, over 800 administrators and nearly 8000 reviewers check submitted content and propose corrections. Since it's published online, there's no need to wait years for a new print edition. Changes appear when approved. That's great for the accuracy of what's online; but, as a consequence, the entry that you read and quote might be changed or deleted without your knowing. So even if your work is published online rather than in print, you can't update what you've written every time there are changes in the Wikipedia text you relied on. Other websites you reference will also change their content or may disappear. So you should always save copies of web pages that are important to you, not just record their web addresses.

And when you write about your results, be open about your doubts and rely on your judgment rather than on the authority of supposed experts. Genealogists and historians make mistakes that, unquestioned, may be copied many times over. Raw original data, like words engraved on tombstones, are likely to be more reliable than anything you find in a book. Fortunately, databases accessible through Ancestry.com allow you to see photos of many gravestones as well as handwritten entries in record books. But negotiations over what to say on gravestones can become contentious and lead to family feuds. And sometimes the engraved words and dates are lies.

I suggest that you treat family traditions with respect, even when they seem far-fetched, like the Quinotaur and Odin. Sometimes what people believe guides their decisions and shapes the course of their lives. Sometimes beliefs are more important than facts.

Bugle Boy

In 1943, my Dad was a private in the U.S. Army, stationed in Georgia — a bugle boy waiting to be shipped to the war in Europe. The day before he was due to leave, he got orders to attend Officer Candidate School at the University of Pennsylvania in Philadelphia. His company eventually ended up at the Battle of the Bulge. He heard that they were all captured and that the train taking them to prison camp was bombed by the Allies. There was only one casualty: the bugle boy, the man who replaced him, died.

Some might see that as chance. But Dad felt he owed his life to that bugle boy, and he had an obligation to live a life that mattered; he had a personal destiny. At every decision point in his life, he remembered his debt to the bugle boy who took his place.

I'm reminded of the final scene in the movie *Saving Private Ryan*, at the cemetery near the Normandy D-Day beaches. The man who was saved stands with his children and his grandchildren at the grave of the man who saved him. Not a word is said. But you get the sense that Private Ryan's whole life was predicated on that sacrifice and that debt.

At the age of 85, Dad surfed the Web and found veterans from his old company who had been shipped to the Battle of the Bulge. He learned that the bugle boy didn't die. He got in touch with him by email, and they shared life experiences.

So there's the story that gave Dad a sense of debt and destiny; and there are the facts, which are very different. And the story that Dad believed for so long gave his life shape and meaning, in a way that the facts did not and could not.

Love at First Lie

Mom and Dad both had movie-star looks. As Dad got older, he aged like a Robert Redford. Even after his stroke, in a wheelchair and unable to speak, he kept his looks. More than 90% of the residents in his nursing home were women. And after Mom died, they all flirted with him.

Women live longer than men. Mom was three years older than Dad. Later in life, they joked that that meant they'd die at the same time. But when they met, she had no idea that she was older than he, and he wasn't about to disillusion her. He was in Officer Candidate School (OCS) at the University of Pennsylvania. That assignment had saved him from going overseas with his first unit, as a bugle boy. He was Pennsylvania Dutch and had a basic knowledge of and feel for the German language. He could improvise hilarious skits using made-up German gibberish. German training was the reason he was in Philadelphia when he met Mom at a social for servicemen at the Stage Door Canteen.

She was gorgeous. He was in seventh heaven that she would dance with him, talk to him, that she seemed as taken with him as he with her. That night, on the way back to his housing, he literally danced with the lamp posts. (They both reported that tale).

He looked mature but was only 20. He knew she was 23, soon to be 24. He was embarrassed to tell her his age. He finessed that question when she first asked. Then he was careful not to say anything that was out of sync with his adopted persona. He had no idea how she'd react when she found out. He didn't want to lose her.

They were both inexperienced and rigidly religious. Both thought sex before marriage was sinful. Both believed they were in love and wanted to marry. It was 1943, wartime. He might have to leave for Europe any day. He would probably be dropped behind enemy lines. She wanted to get married as soon as possible. This might be the only time the two of them had together. Her younger sister, Mildred, had married a fighter pilot, and after only a few weeks together, he had shipped out. He had died in the skies over Cassino in Italy. But Dad wanted to postpone the wedding until June 5, which was six months out.

He came up with lame excuses. He wanted his father as best man. He wanted this relative or that to attend. The soonest they could do it was June 5.

That made no sense to Mom. They both knew
made in Heaven. And they both wanted to get on w
side of love, pronto, while they had time and opportunity.

Dad wouldn't budge and wouldn't tell her the real reason.

He would turn 21 on June 5; and to marry before then, he would need
written permission from his parents. He was embarrassed to ask and
embarrassed to tell Mom that he had to ask. His lies weren't
plausible, but he had acting talent. With a look, a touch, he could
make her believe anything. Besides, she wanted to believe him. She
was in love.

Mom laughed when she learned of the lie and often told that story. It
became part of the fairy-tale true-love story they both told.

They were lucky. The wedding took place on June 5, 1944. The next
morning, they woke up to news of D-Day. Both invasions were
successful.

theirs was a match

ith the physical

Part Two:
Extraordinary Women

Roadmap

You're hiking on a mountain trail. Trees obscure the view. You come to a fork where both choices are obstructed by the exposed roots of a massive tree. On your left, voices sound in the distance. A dog runs by, nearly tripping you — a Dalmatian. Then another dog — a Labrador. You see a marble on the path. Bending down to pick it up, you notice a scrap of paper. It's a letter addressed to your great-uncle Charlie. You find an army bugle. When you blow on the mouthpiece, it vanishes, soundlessly.

The path forks again. You think of Frost, New Hampshire, snow, Brussels, the snows of yesteryear. You turn right this time. Will that make a difference?

You pass a cemetery and look the other way. You don't want to see the names. One might be yours.

You're old now— or in this dream you are — far beyond the middle of your life. You don't dare look behind, fearing you're on the edge of a cliff. The ground behind you might be crumbling. You close your eyes, then close them again. How many sets of eyelids must you shut in order to truly see?

You lose count, but now you see your grandparents' house with its closet full of boys' adventure books; and the house in Rockville where you fell down the hill playing pirate with Long John Silver, who lived up the street. You see your parents, young enough to be your grandchildren, dancing the jitter-bug. You see them again, older than you are now, playing solitaire — Dad in a wheelchair, Mom in a world of her own, a beam of sunlight focused on their clasped hands. You see Florence, Camelot, and Troy, all swarming with busy people. You see your granddaughters as old as you are now, and their granddaughters, and their granddaughters. You want to stop and talk to them, but you're on the path again, not in the book. Your feet can't move, but the ground is moving, carrying you with it, a treadmill speeding up. No controls in sight.

You tell yourself that this is a dream, that you'll wake up where and when you were before; that you'll dream this again, go down paths not taken, and blaze new ones. You hope the ground didn't crumble behind you, that memories will remain — your memories and the memories of others.

You wonder if this dream is yours and yours alone or if you share it with others, like the dream space of Australian aborigines.

You're in the book again. You're tempted to skim, to flip ahead, forging your own path through the pages. The book is called *One Family*. That's peculiar. Genealogy? Biography? History? Fiction? What kind of book is this?

You're dreaming again. If and when you wake this time, where will you be? Who will you be? Will you be?

You wake. You're holding the same book. It's open to "Part Two: Extraordinary Women."

Greetings, dear reader. I'm a stranger, not Odysseus. This is your life not mine. Thanks for treating me like an honored guest, a long-lost relative. I hope to read your book, too, when you write it and crave readers.

Now, go ahead. Read the next page and the next in order, or jump ahead if you prefer. The choice is yours.

A Parting Gift for Mom

I didn't discover the power of Wikipedia for genealogical research and become a true ancestor surfer until Mom was in the final stages of Alzheimer's. In her rare moments of clarity, I regaled her with anecdotes about ancestors I had uncovered. I loved sharing my surfing adventures with her.

She had always been proud of her Welsh forebears. Her grandfather on her mother's side (Griffith Owen Griffith) came to America from Llangefni, Anglesey, North Wales. I let her know that she had an ancestor on her father's side named "Helen," like her, who was a Welsh princess, daughter of Llewelyn "the Great," King of Wales.

Soon after Mom died, I assembled brief biographies of 19 strong-willed female ancestors that I'd told her about. At the memorial service, I shared those stories with the many relatives who'd gathered. I hoped that knowing they are descended from extraordinary women might inspire them to do great things.

These women were in positions of power; and their foibles, hatreds, and ambitions influenced the lives of many and affected the course of history. Often, they faced obstacles, but difficulty didn't stop them — it motivated them. Their lines of descent appear in the Appendix.

You, too, have extraordinary ancestors, some of whom could serve as role models for you, your children, and your grandchildren. Start digging!

1. Skadi, Goddess of Skiing *(Norse Line)*

In Norse mythology, Skadi was a jötunn (a non-human magical creature). She married Njord, a sea god, son of Odin, but they were incompatible. Eventually, they split up and, according to some accounts, she married her father-in-law, Odin. She was associated with bow-hunting, like the Greek goddess Artemis, and also with skiing and winter.

When Loki, the trickster god, caused the death of Balder, god of light and radiance, joy and purity, peace and forgiveness, the other gods sought revenge. They bound Loki with the tangled intestines of his children; and above him, Skadi placed a serpent which continuously dripped venom on him, making him writhe in pain. These writhings caused earthquakes. According to prophecy, Loki will eventually break free and join forces with other creatures to battle the gods during Ragnarök, when all the gods will die.

2. Basina, the Woman Who Knew What She Wanted and Got It *(Roman line)*

Basina (438-477) married a King of Thuringia, a man who was neither powerful nor ambitious. Nothing important ever happened in their insignificant little kingdom. Unwilling to settle for the life she saw ahead of her, she left him, saying, "I want to have the most powerful man in the world, even if I have to cross the ocean for him."

The greatest man of her time was Childeric I, King of the Franks. She sought him out and asked him to marry her. He accepted. Clovis was their son.

(If you are ever searching for a baby name, consider "Basina," which, in Low Franconian, means "female boss.")

3. Gormflaith, Both Beautiful and Wicked *(Line of Gormflaith)*

Gormflaith (960-1030) was "endowed with great beauty... [but] was utterly wicked," according to the Icelandic tale *Njal's Saga*. This daughter of the King of Leinster (what is now County Kildare, Ireland) married Olaf Cuaran (our ancestor), the Viking king of Dublin and York. After his death, she married the legendary Brian Boru, High King of Ireland, as part of a peace settlement. By that same agreement, her son Sigtrygg "Silkbeard," King of Dublin, married a daughter of Brian Boru. In other words, Gormflaith married the father of her daughter-in-law, and her son married his step-father's daughter. As a result, the lines of our descent from her are twisted and entangled.

Her marriage with Brian wasn't happy. She instigated a war against him that ended in the Battle of Clontarf at which he was killed.

4. Saint Itta, Sainthood was Her Family Business *(Roman line)*

Saint Itta of Metz (592-652) was the sister of two saints (Modoald of Trier and Severa) and the mother of two more (Gertrude of Nivelle and Begga of Ardenne, our ancestor). She also married a saint (Pepin of Landen). She earned her sainthood by founding churches, monasteries, and convents.

5. Saint Olga, the Vengeful Beauty *(Line of Kiev)*

When Igor, Prince of Kiev, was killed by the neighboring Drevlian tribe, his wife Olga "the Beauty" (890-969) exacted revenge. She buried some Drevlians alive and burnt others to death. Then she offered peace if they would grant a small request of hers: "Give me three pigeons ... and three sparrows from each house." She had her army attach cloth with a piece of sulfur to each bird, then set fire to the cloth and released the birds. The birds returned to their nests in the enemy city, setting fire to the thatched roofs of the houses. According to the Russian *Primary Chronicle*, "There was not a house that was not consumed, and it was impossible to extinguish the flames, because all the houses caught fire at once."

As the first Ukrainian or Russian ruler to convert to Christianity, Olga earned sainthood. She was unable to convert her husband, but her grandson, Saint Vladimir I "the Great," made Christianity the state religion.

6. Lady Ingrid Ylva, the White Witch *(Line of the White Witch)*

Lady Ingrid Ylva (1180-1250), a Swedish noblewoman, was renowned as a white witch — a master of magic used for good. This was hundreds of years before witchcraft was deemed "the Devil's work," a crime punishable by death.

During insecure times, she would live in a church tower on her estate in Bjalbo. Legend has it that when Bjalbo was attacked by enemies, she rushed to the top of the tower, ripped open a pillow full of feathers, and turned those feathers into knights in armor, who fought off the invaders.

Lady Ingrid was also known for her fortune telling. On her deathbed, she predicted that her line would succeed to the Swedish throne as long as her head was held high. Heeding those words, her son buried her standing upright, inside her tower.

7. Empress Irene Doukaina, Mother of the First Woman Historian *(Line of the Byzantine Empire)*

Irene (1066-1138) was the wife of Alexios I, the Byzantine Emperor whose appeal to the Pope started the First Crusade. She was also the great-granddaughter of a Bulgarian emperor and the mother of the next Byzantine emperor. But her most famous relation was her daughter Anna Komnena — the first woman historian ever.

In *The Alexiad*, Anna compared her mother to Athena in mortal form. "She stood upright like some young proud, always blossoming shoot, each limb and her whole body in perfect symmetry and in complete harmony... Her face shone with the soft light of the moon." (translation by E. R. A. Sewter, pp. 85-86)

On the death of her husband, Irene plotted to have Anna and Anna's husband succeed to the throne instead of her son John. When she failed, John exiled her to a nunnery where she was imprisoned for the rest of her life.

8. Alice of Jerusalem, Her Daughter and Granddaughters, Vying for Power *(Roman line)*

Alice (1110-1151) was the daughter of Baldwin II, King of Jerusalem and Count of Edessa, and the wife of Bohemond II, Prince of Antioch. Those were new countries, formed by Crusaders when they conquered the Middle East. Antioch included much of present-day

Syria. Edessa consisted of parts of present-day Syria and Turkey. Jerusalem approximated present-day Israel.

Alice's husband got his peculiar name from his father, who got it from his father, who had heard tales of a mythical giant at a dinner party (*Crusaders* by Jones, p. 54). Thus myth gets interwoven with history.

When Bohemond died in battle, Alice's father, Baldwin, tried to seize control of Antioch. Rather than sit idly by like a dutiful daughter and a woman who knew her place, Alice tried to block him by forming an alliance with the Muslim ruler of Mosul and Aleppo, offering her daughter Constance in marriage. When that ploy failed, she made peace with her father, gave up Antioch, and went into exile.

When her father died, Alice tried to retake Antioch. First, she formed an alliance against her father's successor, Fulk V, King of Jerusalem (also our ancestor). Then she sought the support of the Byzantine Emperor by offering Constance in marriage to his heir, Manuel Komnenos. When that match fell through, she married Constance to Raynald of Chatillon and helped him become Prince of Antioch. When Raynald was taken prisoner by the Moslem ruler of Aleppo, Constance claimed the throne of Antioch for herself, but the nobles supported her son, Bohemund III, instead.

Constance's daughters, Maria and Agnes, both reached positions of power by way of marriage.. Maria married the same man her mother was to have wed, Manuel Komnenos, who was then the Byzantine Emperor. And Agnes married a prince who became King Bela III of Hungary.

9. Elizabeth the Cuman, Clash of Cultures *(line of Bohemia)*
Elizabeth (1244-1290) was a daughter of Köten, Khan of the Cuman-Kipchak, a Turkic tribe from Central Asia. Köten allied with Kiev to fight against the invading Mongols, but lost at the Battle at the Kalka River (near present-day Mariupol in Ukraine). He narrowly escaped with his army. The Mongols then besieged Kiev, destroyed it, and advanced toward Poland and Hungary. Retreating in their wake, Köten appealed to the Hungarian King, converting to Catholicism and promising that his army would fight for the Hungarians against the Mongols. By that same treaty, his daughter, Elizabeth, was betrothed to the king's son Stephen, the great-grandson of Agnes of Antioch.

Despite the treaty, Hungarians assassinated Köten, suspecting he and his Cumans were in league with the Mongolians. But Elizabeth still married Stephen. They were both 12 years old.

Stephen became king on the death of his father, but he died just two years later. Elizabeth then ruled Hungary as regent for their son Ladislaus. She raised Ladislaus as a Cuman, which angered the Hungarians. But when he changed his style to appease the Hungarians, that angered the Cumans, who then murdered him.

10. Saint Ludmila, Grandmother of Good King Wenceslaus and His Murderer *(Line of Bohemia)*
Daughter of a Slavic prince, Ludmila (860-921) married Borivoj I, Duke of Bohemia, in what is now the Czech Republic. Both of them were converted from paganism to Christianity, probably by Saints Cyril and Methodius, the inventors of the Russian "Cyrillic" alphabet. When Ludmila and her husband tried to convert others, they lost the throne and were driven from the country.

Later they returned and ruled again, and their son ruled as duke after them, followed by another son of theirs, and then his eight-year-old son, Wenceslaus — the Good King Wenceslaus of the Christmas carol. His mother, jealous of his grandmother Ludmila's influence over him, had Ludmila strangled with her own veil. Later, Wenceslaus' brother Bolesaus I "the Cruel" (our ancestor), murdered him and became Duke in his stead. Despite the fratricide, Czech historians generally respect him as "an energetic ruler."

Wenceslaus is the patron saint of the Czech Republic. According to legend, when the country is in danger, his equestrian statue in Prague will come to life and awaken an army of knights asleep under a mountain, and with a magic sword he'll kill the enemies of the Czechs and restore peace and prosperity to the land.

11. Edith and Her Love Bites *(Line of Edith the Fair)*

Known as "Edith the Fair" and "Edith the Gentle Swan," this ancestor (1015-1086) was the common-law wife of Harold II, King of England. Her daughter, Princess Gytha of Wessex, married Vladimir II, Prince of Kiev

When her husband was killed at the Battle of Hastings, defeated by William "the Conqueror" (also our ancestor), Edith identified his body by markings on his chest known only to her. Heinrich Heine called those marks "love bites" in his poem "The Battlefield of Hastings."

12. Saint Margaret of Scotland *(Line of Scotland and England)*

Margaret (1045-1093) was the granddaughter of Edmund Ironside, the Anglo-Saxon king who was overthrown by Cnut "the Great," the Viking king of Denmark and Norway. Cnut sent her father and uncle to Sweden, where they were to be murdered (echoes of Rosenkrantz and Guildenstern). But they escaped and fled to the Hungarian court, where Margaret was born and raised.

In 1057, Margaret's father, Edward the Exile, was recalled to England as a possible successor to his childless uncle King Edward the Confessor. But he died soon after arrival, and Harold II became king instead. When, a few months later, Harold was killed at the Battle of Hastings, Margaret's brother Edgar claimed the throne. But the odds of his making good on that claim were slim. William "the Conqueror" was advancing on London with his Norman army.

Margaret and her family tried to escape by sailing to the Continent. But a storm blew their ship off course, and they landed in Scotland, where they sought the protection of King Malcolm III. Malcolm, a widower, married Margaret because she was one of the few remaining members of the Anglo-Saxon royal family. He then waged war against England, in support of the claims of his new brother-in-law Edgar.

In Shakespeare's *Macbeth*, Malcom succeeds to the Scottish throne after the death of Macbeth who had killed Malcolm's father Duncan.

13. Matilda of Flanders, England's Shortest Queen *(Line of Scotland and England)*
Matilda of Flanders (1031-1083), the wife of William "the Conqueror," bore him eleven children, including two kings. According to legend, when William, then Duke of Normandy, sent his representative to ask for Matilda's hand, she declined, saying she was far too high-born to marry a bastard. Learning of this response, William rode from Normandy to Bruges, found Matilda on her way

to church, dragged her off her horse by her braids, threw her on the ground, and rode off. She seems to have regarded that as a romantic gesture. When her father, Baldwin V, Count of Flanders, was infuriated at the insult, and he and William nearly went to war with one another, Matilda intervened, and despite a papal ban because they were too closely related, she married William. Through that marriage, Flanders became an ally of Normandy, enabling William to conquer Anglo-Saxon England in 1066. That was the last time England was successfully invaded.

According to the *Guinness Book of Records*, Matilda was just four feet two inches tall. She was the shortest queen in English history.

14. Urraca, First European Woman to Reign as Queen in Her Own Right *(Line of Leon and Castile)*
Urraca "the Reckless" (1081-1126) was the sole living legitimate child of the King of Leon, Castile, and Galicia (all now in Spain). When her father died, Urraca, a widow, was acknowledged as Queen in her own right, not through marriage. But soon after that, she was forced to marry Alfonso I, King of Aragon and Navarre, and he became the ruler instead of her. The marriage fell apart. He was absurdly superstitious, deathly afraid of ravens and crows; and he regularly humiliated Urraca, beating and kicking her in public. She separated from him, led a civil war against him, regained her lands, and had their marriage annulled. She reigned 1109-1126, and her son by her first husband (our ancestor) ruled after her.

15. Empress Matilda, Mistress of Disguise and the First Female Ruler of England *(Line of Scotland and England)*
Another ancestor, the Empress Matilda (1102-1167) was the first woman to rule England. Matilda was granddaughter of Matilda of

Flanders. and the last surviving legitimate child of Henry I, King of England, son of William "the Conqueror." At the age of 12 she married Henry V, the Holy Roman Emperor, thereby acquiring the title "Empress." When he died 11 years later, Matilda returned to England; and at her father's behest, the Anglo-Norman barons swore that if he died without a male heir, they would accept Matilda as ruler of England and Normandy.

Matilda then married Geoffrey, Count of Anjou, who called himself "Plantagenet" from the broom flower (planta genista) that he adopted as his personal emblem. Plantagenet became the name of the dynasty founded by their son (our ancestor), Henry II. They were in Anjou when her father died, and her cousin Stephen of Blois seized the throne in her stead. Matilda and her husband went to war against him and defeated and captured him at the Battle of Lincoln. For several months after that, Matilda was Queen of England. But on her arrival at London, where she was to be crowned, the citizens insisted that she cut their taxes in half. She refused; they closed the city gates to her; and the civil war started up again.

A year later, Stephen, who was free and once again at war with Matilda, besieged her forces at Oxford. She escaped to Wallingford, by fleeing across snow-covered fields in a white cape. Later she escaped again, disguising herself as a corpse being carried off for burial. When Stephen died in 1154, her son became King Henry II.

16. Joan, Lady of Wales, an Affair to Remember *(Line of Gormflaith)*

Joan (1191-1237), a bastard daughter of King John of England, married Llywelyn "the Great," King of Wales, the five-greats grandson of Gormflaith. Llewelyn was the last monarch to claim sovereignty over all of Wales. His power base was in North Wales, from which my Griffith ancestors came.

The Pope eventually ruled that Joan was "legitimate" even though her parents weren't married to one another at the time of her birth. I was surprised to learn that popes had the power to turn lies into truth. Apparently, he was expected to do so and probably was bribed in exchange for the favor. How different the course of history might have been if Pope Clement VII had been similarly flexible in the time of Henry VIII. He could have annulled Henry's marriage to Catherine of Aragon, and thereby delayed, if not prevented the Reformation in England.

Joan's father, King John, was forced to sign the Magna Carta, the first step toward democracy in England. He arranged for Joan to marry Llywelyn as part of a political alliance. In those days, wars between Wales and England were frequent. Llywelyn's successors faced one such challenge after another, until 1301 when King Edward I of England (our ancestor) named his son Edward II "Prince of Wales." That became the title traditionally given to the eldest son of the King of England.

In 1230, Joan and William de Braose, a prisoner of Llywelyn's, were caught making love in Llywelyn's bedchamber. William was hanged, and Joan was imprisoned for a year. She eventually reconciled with her husband. Helen, Princess of North Wales, was their daughter.

17. Joan, the Fair Maid of Kent. Two Secret Marriages *(Line of Gormflaith)*
The French historian Froissart called this Joan (1326-1385) "the most beautiful woman in all the realm of England and the most loving."

She was a great-great-granddaughter of Helen of North Wales. Her father, Edmund of Woodstock, a son of King Edward I, supported a rebellion led by Queen Isabella, which deposed Edward II. But he then conspired against the new king and for that he was executed and his wife and daughter Joan (age two) were placed under house arrest. Eventually, his daughter was reconciled with the king and was raised at court.

At the age of 12 she married Thomas Holland, Earl of Kent, in secret because she couldn't get the required royal consent. While Thomas was fighting in the Crusades, her parents, considering that marriage invalid, forced her to marry someone else. But, eventually, the Pope decreed that Thomas was her true husband.

When Thomas died eleven years later, Joan secretly married Edward "the Black Prince," her first cousin once removed. They were too closely related for the marriage to be legal. But King Edward III approved this marriage and got a dispensation from the Pope. The Archbishop of Canterbury presided over their public wedding. Since her husband was heir to the throne of England, Joan was known as the first English Princess of Wales.

The Black Prince died in 1376, and his father the king died a year later. That meant that Joan's son Richard II, a child of ten, became king. (See Shakespeare's *Richard II*). Before Richard came of age, Joan was the power behind the throne and was reputedly well-loved by the English people.

18. Marjorie Bruce, the Price of Being a King's Daughter *(Stewart Line)*

At the age of 19, Marjorie's mother died giving birth to her. Nine years later, her father, Robert the Bruce, was crowned King of the Scots. But just three months later, he was defeated at the Battle of Methven, and Marjorie and all her female relatives were captured and handed over to the English.

Marjorie spent seven years imprisoned, in solitary confinement in a convent. She was released at the age of 16, in exchange for English noblemen captured at the Battle of Bannockburn, but she had to marry Walter Stewart as his reward for his performance in that battle.

Two years later she went horseback riding while in advanced pregnancy. She was thrown, went into premature labor, delivered the child, and died soon after. That child succeeded to the throne of Scotland as Robert II, the first king of the Stewart dynasty.

19. Eleanor of Aquitaine, the Lioness in Winter *(Line of Scotland and England)*

Eleanor (1124-1204), the daughter-in-law of Empress Matilda, was one of the richest and most powerful women of the Middle Ages. At the age of 15, she succeeded her father as ruler of Aquitaine, on the Atlantic coast of what is now the south of France. Since her duchy would belong to whomever she married, she was the most sought-after bride in Europe. She married Louis VII, King of France; and with him, she took part in the Second Crusade. Having recruited her ladies-in-waiting and 300 vassals as Crusaders, she served as the leader of the troops from Aquitaine. According to some accounts, she and her ladies dressed as Amazons.

On their return to France, she asked for and was granted an annulment of her marriage to Louis, and her lands returned to her. She then married the Duke of Normandy, the son of Empress Matilda, the future King Henry II of England, who was 12 years younger than she. She bore him five sons and three daughters. The sons included the future kings Richard I and John (our ancestor).

This marriage was far from perfect. She supported her son Henry's attempt to overthrow her husband; and, for this, her husband imprisoned her for 16 years. When he died, Richard became king and freed his mother. She ruled as regent while Richard went on the Third Crusade.

She appears in the movie *The Lion in Winter* (played by Katharine Hepburn) and figures in Shakespeare's *King John*. As my sons know, she's also a leader of both the French and English civilizations in the videogame *Civilization 6*.

Why These Women?

Don't expect to see "extraordinary woman" noted in Wikipedia or on their gravestones. This is my arbitrary personal selection, not vetted like the DAR and SAR. They caught my attention and stuck in my memory.

The claim to fame of many of these women depended on the men they had to marry or the sons they bore. They sometimes served as stand-ins (regents) when their husbands were off at war or their sons were too young to reign.

Despite the paternalistic laws and traditions of their times, a few took charge of their own lives. Basina, Uracca, and Eleanor of Aquitaine cast aside the kings they were married to. Others took lovers, despite the scrutiny they were under and the consequences of infidelity. Two of them — Alice of Jerusalem and Irene Doukaina — struggled unsuccessfully for power.

Then in the twelfth century, three of these women — Uracca, Empress Matilda, and Eleanor of Aquitaine — ruled countries in their own right. It would only take another 800 years for women in general to approach parity with men.

Part Three:
History and Belief

Why Medieval History Matters

How many of those extraordinary women had you heard of before? If you didn't major in history in college, probably not many. Most American high schools skip over medieval history, or mention a few dates and make generalizations about class and social history, rather than recount details of royalty, intrigue, and war.

As you decide what to include in your own family history, you may want to revise your ideas of what is truth, and take into account that what we believe depends on the filter through which we see the world, the common assumptions of our time and place htat shape what we see and affect what we do. Looking at what people believed in medieval times can heighten our awareness of our own bias.

Genealogy is a way of telling stories held together by threads of family, and medieval history is family history. What happened then was critical in shaping the world we live in now. Before there were nation states, countries were loose confederations ruled by vassals — counts, dukes, earls, barons, margraves, princes — with shifting allegiances. Family ties determined loyalty and antipathy, war and peace, and were key to understanding what was happening. Power was local, not national. The king was only as powerful as his vassals made him. Political maps of medieval Europe that show countries in solid colors are misleading. Areas that we think of as French — such as Burgundy, Normandy, and Aquitaine — sometimes allied with England and sometimes technically belonged to the king of England by inheritance. England's Henry V claimed he was the rightful king of France. The ancestry of ruling families mattered.

We lose that flavor when we look at history through the lens of sociology and technology. In medieval times, people weren't aware of class struggle and weren't motivated by it. They assumed the king was chosen by God. You would do what your father and forefathers did. There was little or no social mobility, little or no awareness of social structure. Society was what it was. And people interested in questions of war, law, and taxes focused their attention on the decision- makers, the royal families.

Legends and poems were deemed more important than historical chronicles, which consisted of little more than lists of names, events, and dates. The poet's job was to find the real story in the details and rumors, to see the forest, to capture the essence of what happened and the true character of the participants. With no audio or video and no photography, words on paper and in memory were the only means of recording what had happened. Characters and events amplified to superhuman scale captured the imagination, and were made more memorable by meter and rhyme. Hence the importance of epic poems, many of them anonymous — for the people and by the people.

History Lessons or Education by Misdirection

Our London hotel was three blocks from the British Museum, but I turned the wrong way and was lost for hours, walking in circles. The streets changed names every few blocks, and the intersections were often curved or bent. I had my cellphone with me and could have checked Google Maps. I also could have asked for help. Instead, I enjoyed the scene and learned the neighborhood.

It occurred to me that this was an excellent teaching method — Education by Misdirection. Make the path to learning difficult rather than easy. Force students to build their own mental maps and patterns of association.

When my son, Bob, a chess prodigy, had lessons with a local master, Murray Turnbull, Murray would often make outrageous moves and challenge Bob to find ways to punish such mistakes.

My fifth-grade teacher, Robert Talbott Stevenson, deliberately included an ambiguous question in a hundred-question multiple-choice exam. "There are (many, few) gases in the atmosphere." I knew that the atmosphere consisted mostly of nitrogen and oxygen, but there were also trace amounts of many other elements. So, of course, I chose "many." I was shocked when he marked that wrong. I challenged him on that and was outraged when he wouldn't change his mind. For several weeks, every day after school I'd consult our home encyclopedia (*Funk & Wagnalls*, bought volume-by-volume in the grocery store), and the next morning I'd report my findings in show-and-tell. There were traces of dozens of gases in addition to nitrogen and oxygen. The teacher's intransigence prompted me to learn how to research and how to stand up for my ideas against authority. I got so caught up in the question that I learned a lot about the atmosphere and nearly decided to become an astronomer.

If I were a teacher, I would ask my class to do these exercises:
One — Watch videos of a sport that none of you is familiar with (e.g., for American audiences, cricket, rugby, or curling). Based solely on those videos, derive the rules of the game and come up with winning tactics and strategies.

Two — Read a substantial original work of history (such as Herodotus, Thucydides, Livy, Tacitus) and, based on the text, derive the laws and common practices of that time and place, as well as winning tactics and strategies for political and economic success.

Can we reconstruct the world view of the Middle Ages from our rambles through its history?

European Medieval World View

Common assumptions about the nature of the world and what to expect in life and death were very different in medieval Europe than they are in the West today, and ancestry was much more important than now. The social structure was God-given. There was no point in trying to change it. There was safety, stability, and predictability in the status quo. Religion and governance were linked, and much of Europe shared common beliefs. For many, the living were linked to the dead, to all their ancestors. God was real. Heaven and Hell and Purgatory were real, as well as eternal punishment and/or rewards. Life was the tip of the iceberg. The dead were always with you. Few doubted that, and those who did kept it to themselves. Religious doubt could get you killed.

Social climbing was the aim of very few and was limited in scope. Among the wealthy, the oldest son of the head of house would inherit everything. Women couldn't inherit, and younger sons were expected to pursue careers in the military or the Church. In the few places where that rule of inheritance didn't apply, such as Russia, sons inherited equal shares, estates were split at death, and inheritable wealth diminished from generation to generation, often to extinction. Where primogeniture applied, the wealth of the wealthy remained intact and could grow over time.

If you were lucky enough to have inherited wealth, the structure of Church, state, and military wouldn't change much in your lifetime. Those who held positions of power in government did so not by merit or accomplishment, but by connections with the royal family or with others who were so connected, and by exchange of favors, like in the *The Godfather*. You would want to know the personalities, loyalties, and ambitions of people with authority, and how they could be influenced or bribed. Even the Pope could be bribed, and that wasn't scandalous. It was business as usual.

Life was short. The afterlife never ended. You cared about what happened after death to you and to those you loved. The Church sold indulgences. Money paid to the Church could reduce eternal punishment or speed your journey through Purgatory to Heaven. You could also improve the lot of your dead forebears, and you hoped that those you left behind would do the same for you. You were connected to the fate of your ancestors; and after you died, your descendants would be connected to you. Ancestry was more than memories. What came next was more important than what happened during your lifetime.

That way of life was undermined by the discovery of the New World, which opened economic opportunities for those who emigrated; and, soon thereafter, by the Reformation, which questioned assumptions about the afterlife. The Middle Ages were over.

In western Europe, in the spiritual domain of the Pope, there was commonality of belief, defined and policed by the Church, which was monolithic and authoritarian. People were willing to put up with poverty and pain, because of what they expected after death. Patience and moral behavior would be rewarded.

Imagine you're standing next to Dante as Virgil explains the afterworld to him. The inventory of the dead is real, not fictive. They are related to people still living. Their experience in Hell, Purgatory, or Paradise depends in part on what their living descendants are doing now. The dead are always with us.

Dante mentions two of our ancestors. In Purgatory, he meets Hugh Capet "the Great," Duke of France and Count of Paris (898-956). Hugh laments the avarice of his descendants. Dante also sees King Philip III the Bold (1245-1285) outside the gates of Purgatory with other rulers, and identifies him not by name but by description — "the small-nosed ... father of the Pest of France." Philip was the son of King Louis IX, known as Saint Louis, for whom the city in Missouri was named. "The pest of France" was his son, Philip IV "the Fair," who was renowned for his rigid, autocratic, and inflexible personality. Bernard Saisset, bishop of Pamiers, said, "He is neither man nor beast. He is a statue."

In medieval times, history, legend, and literature were closely intertwined. Not all lying was falsehood, and sometimes facts were misleading. Sometimes fiction could string together facts in revealing ways and make events memorable even to those who couldn't read. The quality of the story was more important than its accuracy.

Shakespeare

Although Shakespeare (1564-1616) lived during the Renaissance, many of his histories and tragedies are set in the Middle Ages. His characters reflect both the worldview of his time that all men are mortal and fallible, and that of the time when the events occurred when kings were exalted and believed to have been chosen by God.

He found dramatic potential in the transition from king to ordinary man as well as that from man to king

When Richard II loses his divine right or believes he has, he realizes he's a mere man like other men:

> Cover your heads and mock not flesh and blood
> With solemn reverence: throw away respect,
> Tradition, form and ceremonious duty,
> For you have but mistook me all this while:
> I live with bread like you, feel want,
> Taste grief, need friends: subjected thus,
> How can you say to me, I am a king?

Harry was a carefree brawler and ne'er-do-well, comparable to his friend Falstaff. But once crowned as Henry V, he's awed by the thought that God chose him for this job, for which he has had no training. He has noble aims, but depends on advisors and is easily manipulated by them. He wants to do what's right if he can figure out what that is. In battle, he's bold and confident, despite the odds, because he believes he's the rightful king of France as well as England. He speaks noble words that inspire his troops to risk their lives, and they win overwhelmingly. Was God actually with him? He and his men apparently believe so, but Shakespeare may have his doubts.

In that play, Shakespeare is a stickler about the genealogy of English royalty and its implications for the legitimacy of royal succession. He begins with a lengthy discussion of the Salic Law of Succession, according to which, in places like France, if you were descended from a previous king only through a woman, you couldn't inherit the throne. That's the convoluted, questionable basis of Henry's claim to the throne of France and of his belief that God will be with him in his war for it.

To a modern theater-goer, the ending of *Henry V* — wooing a bride — feels anticlimactic. But for the historical Henry V, choosing the right queen, making the right treaty, and spawning a male heir are key to the future stability of his country.

We aren't descended from Henry V or Richard II, but we are from close relatives theirs and to other characters in Shakespeare's tragedies and histories:

- King John "Lackland" of England, son of King Henry II (Plantagenet)
- King Duncan of Scotland, who was murdered by Macbeth
- King Malcolm III of Scotland, who succeeds to the Scottish throne after the death of Macbeth
- Joan "the Fair Maid of Kent," the mother of King Richard II
- Margaret, Joan of Kent's daughter by Thomas Holland, who married John Beaufort, Earl of Somerset, a prominent character in the Henry VI plays
- John of Gaunt, close relative of multiple Shakespearean characters (uncle of Richard II, father of King Henry IV, grandfather of King Henry V, and great-grandfather of King Henry VI)
- Joan Beaufort, daughter of Margaret Holland and John Beaufort

Dynasty and the Wars of the Roses

When the king died, if his successor was a member of the same family, much would continue as before. But if the line died out or was overthrown by another dynasty, civil war could ensue, and that happened all too frequently.

In the Wars of the Roses, two competing dynasties overthrew one another repeatedly. King Henry VI ruled three separate times, which is why there are three Shakespeare plays with his name. Two streaming video series cover that period in ways that modern audiences can appreciate. *The White Queen* (BBC), starting in 1464, with the houses of York and Lancaster contending for the English throne, focuses on the lives of Elizabeth Woodville (wife of King Edward IV), Margaret Beaufort, and Anne Neville. And *The White Princess* (Starz) ends with the marriage of Henry VII and Elizabeth of York (daughter of Elizabeth Woodville), uniting the two dynasties and thereby ending the Wars of the Roses. Throughout those dramas, the mother of the king wields extraordinary power, though women at that time were officially powerless.

Our ancestors were allied with Lancaster, not York, so I'm inclined to root for them when watching those shows. We are descended from Margaret Beaufort (1385-1439) and her husband John Beaufort (1371-1410), first Earl of Somerset. Margaret was a daughter of Thomas Holland, 2nd Earl of Kent, the son of Joan the Fair Maid of Kent, granddaughter of Edward I. She was also wife of Edward the Black Prince and mother of King Richard II. John Beaufort was son of John of Gaunt, the Duke of Lancaster, and his mistress Katherine Swynford.

That Margaret Beaufort was grandmother of the Margaret Beaufort in the series (1443-1509). The younger Margaret maneuvered and colluded to make her son Henry VII, the first Tudor king.

Insight into the tangled family relationships of our ancestors may boost your enjoyment of those dramas. Ancestor surfing can enhance binge-watching.

We're also directly descended from the kings of three previous English dynasties. The details appear in Highlights in the Appendix.

Braveheart and the Kings of Scotland

You may also be familiar with Mel Gibson's *Braveheart*, a movie about battles for the throne of Scotland. We are descended from leaders on both sides of that conflict:

- Robert the Bruce, who became king by betraying William Wallace (played by Gibson),
- William "le Hardi" Douglas, a close ally of Wallace, and
- King Edward I "Longshanks" of England as well as his son the future King Edward II, and his son's wife Isabella of France.

In the movie, Edward I sends Isabella to negotiate with Wallace. The historical Edward II married Isabella a year after his father died and three years after the execution of Wallace. So the implication that she had a tryst with Wallace and that the son she bore (the future Edward III) was the son of Wallace is Hollywood fantasy. But the historical Isabella was interesting for other reasons. She led a rebellion that overthrew her husband and put her son on the throne, with her as regent. She was nicknamed "The She-Wolf of France." Perhaps it's time for a series about her.

We are also descended from all of the Scottish dynasties. For details, see the Highlights in the Appendix.

Mixing Story and History

In medieval times, history and historical romances were written at the bidding of patrons, who wanted to control how they were remembered. Lasting acclaim was more important than accuracy. They would like to be known as "The Great" or "The Bold," and they wanted their stories written in easily remembered verse.

The Dukes of Ferrara were patrons not only of Ariosto and Leonardo da Vinci, but also of Torquato Tasso, whom Pope Clement VIII crowned "king of poets." Until the 20th century, Tasso was one of the most widely read poets in Europe. His epic *Jerusalem Delivered* (1581), which plays loosely with history, tells of the conquest of Jerusalem in 1099, during the First Crusade. The main character is Godfrey of Bouillon. Historically but not mentioned in the epic, Godfrey's trusted friend was William V of Monpellier, our ancestor. Another ancestor, William IX the Troubador, Duke of Aquitaine, a leader in that same Crusade, was the first vernacular lyric poet in Provençal, the language spoken in southeastern France.

In the Fourth Crusade, a hundred years later, the western forces went astray. Instead of attacking the Saracens in the Holy Land, they conquered Christian Constantinople in 1204 and chose Baldwin, our ancestor, as Emperor. Many of our ancestors participated in the Crusades. For a list, see Ancestor Highlights in the Appendix.

The Crusaders did not just raid, then return west. They meant to stay. They built castles and forts and set up European feudal states on the shores of the Eastern Mediterranean: the County of Edessa, the Principality of Antioch, the County of Tripoli, and the Kingdom of Jerusalem. Jerusalem included historical Palestine and, at its peak, extended east of the Jordan River. The northern three states covered what is now Lebanon, southeastern Turkey, much of Syria, and eastward beyond the Euphrates River. Two of our extraordinary women played a role in their governance — Alice of Jerusalem, and Constance of Antioch.

This was a mass migration that lasted two hundred years. Unlike previous historical migrations that went from east to west and were triggered by natural catastrophes, this one went from west to east and was triggered by ideas.

Seen in a broader context, the Crusades were part of a counter-clockwise movement. In 845, Vikings besieged Paris, withdrawing on payment of a ransom. Under the leadership of our ancestor Rollo, Vikings continued to raid what is now northern France until, by treaty, they were given the region of Normandy. Two hundred years later, William "the Conqueror" (Rollo's descendant) invaded and took control of England. Over subsequent decades, other Norman ancestors of ours conquered Sicily and southern Italy. From that base, with their Crusader allies, they conquered the Holy Land.

Around the time when Rollo and his descendants headed west and south, Rurik, another Viking ancestor of ours, headed clockwise, east and south. He became the founder of a dynasty that ruled Novgorod and Kiev. Saint Vladimir I "the Great" (a descendant of Rurik) married a daughter of Byzantine Emperor Romanos II and converted the Principality of Kiev to Orthodox Christianity.

We're descended from six dynasties of Byzantine emperors, two by way of that marriage of Vladimir. Another stems from the marriage of Prince Vsevolod I of Kiev to Anastasia of Byzantium, daughter of Emperor Constantine IX Monomachos. The fourth is by way of

Eudoxia Komnena, granddaughter of John II Komenos, who married the crusader William VIII of Monpellier. (For a list, see Highlights in the Appendix.)

Two east-to-west migration invasions also involved our ancestors. We're descended from Attila the Hun (406-453) and also from Köten the Cuman. The Igor of the medieval Ukrainian epic *The Song of Igor's Campaign* was a cousin of our ancestor Prince Mstislav I of Kiev. The battle described in that poem was fought against the Cumans in 1185. Thirty-eight years later, Cumans under our ancestor Köten allied with Kiev to fight Mongol invaders and lost at the Battle of Kalka River. (See the profile of his daughter Elizabeth above).

Legends that got turned into story and epic were often about hopeless causes, bravery in the face of defeat. *Jerusalem Delivered* was an exception to that. *The Song of Roland* and *The Song of Igor's Campaign* recounted lost battles. *Beowulf* ended with both hero and dragon dead, and *The Nibelungenlied* in a massacre. *Orlando Furioso* told of unrequited love. The stories of King Arthur and the Knights of the Round Table dealt with their defeat by the invading Anglo-Saxons. Robin Hood led a futile Anglo-Saxon revolt against the ruling Normans.

The fall of the Alamo never became an epic; but in medieval times it, too, would have merited such treatment. We're connected to that indirectly. My great-great-great-grandfather, Captain Joel Estes (1780-1833), ran for Congress against Davy Crockett in 1827 and lost. And when Estes Kefauver ran for Vice President, he wore a coonskin cap as an emblem of his Tennessee ancestry.

Boccaccio's *Decameron*

When Dad took early retirement at the age of 57, he pursued acting and modeling, as he had wanted to after World War II. He got bit parts in movies and TV series — *Trading Places*, *Signs*, *Law and Order*. One of his commercials, for the Pennsylvania State Lottery, ran for more than 20 years.

When reruns came on in the middle of the night, Dad's face might appear fleetingly, and sometimes I wasn't sure if it was him. Mom, too, might appear in a chorus, singing advertising jingles to prompt viewers to buy products that weren't for sale in stores. "Call now for this limited-time TV offer!"

Rare though it was that I'd see either of them, the possibility turned late-night viewing into a family experience.

By chance (is anything by chance?) I'm reading Boccaccio's *Decameron* while writing this book. *The Decameron* is an entangled set of a hundred stories. Ten people having fled Florence during the Black Plague exchange stories with one another at a country villa. Every day for ten days each tells a story. Each teller has a personality, and each day has an assigned theme. Their stories are imbued with the mores of the time and sometimes touch upon historical figures and events connected with ancestors of ours.

For me now, immersed in medieval history and bios of our ancestors, reading *The Decameron* is like watching late-night TV in the 1970s and seeing Mom or Dad in ads and movies. Unexpectedly, I'll come across Marquis Azzo d'Este of Ferrara, King Philip II of France, or others. So my late-night reading is a family experience.

Boccaccio is lurid and detailed in his description of the plague in the introduction to his book, but the stories themselves are light entertainment, distractions from the near and imminent horror. According to modern estimates, in a few weeks in 1348, the Black Plague reduced the population of Florence from 120,000 to 50,000.

Where did the plague come from? Crimea, the scene of today's Ukraine War. The Mongolian Golden Horde was infected with the disease when they besieged a port city there. They catapulted corpses into the city to infect the inhabitants, and ships from Genoa in the harbor fled to Italy carrying the plague with them.

Dante died in 1321, 17 years before that catastrophe.

For orientation: Crusades 1095-1291, Madoc's discovery of America 1170, Mongolian Empire 13th and 14th centuries, *Canterbury Tales* 1400, Henry V's battle at Agincourt 1415, Columbus' discovery of America 1492, Luther testifying before the Diet of Worms 1521, Shakespeare's play *Henry V* 1599.

Indulgences and the Crusades

The more I read about medieval times, the more connected and comfortable I feel there. Now reading books like *Crusaders* by Dan Jones, *Guelphs and Ghibellines* by Oscar Browning, and *Heimskringla: Chronicles of the Kings of Norway* by Snorri Sturluson is like going to a family reunion packed with illustrious cousins whose names I heard before but whose stories I didn't know.

The First Crusade began in 1095. At the urgent request of Emperor Alexios I Komnenos (our ancestor), Pope Urban II sent out a call for volunteers for a religious war to recover the Holy Land from Islamic rule. But Moslems had controlled the Holy Land for four hundred years before that. Why did Urban's appeal have an immediate and massive effect after centuries of apathy?

I believe the difference was that Urban promised volunteers forgiveness of sins and eternal salvation. Without any earthly payment, between 7,000 and 10,000 knights and between 35,000 and 50,000 foot soldiers clamored for the opportunity to take part in the First Crusade. They were joined by masses of untrained, illiterate peasants who didn't even know where Jerusalem was. They gladly signed up for the long, grueling trek to the Holy Land and a war in which they might well die. Earthly pain was nothing compared to the promise of eternal salvation.

Over the course of two hundred years (1095-1291), two to six million people from Western Europe died in the Crusades, at a time when the population of Europe was only 60 to 70 million (according to the World History Project). And many who couldn't go on the Crusade begged for an alternative way to get similar after-death benefits. The Pope accommodated their wishes, accepting cash as a substitute for military service. The market for indulgences began — money paid to the Church would benefit the souls of the dead.

This wasn't a money-making scheme dreamed up by the Church. The Church didn't need to convince people of the reality of this benefit or of their ability to offer it for sale. Though the practice of indulgences began with the First Crusade, belief in its feasibility was widespread before that. The afterworld was real. The prospect of eternal punishment after death was terrifying. People wanted a way to improve their own and their forebears' eternal existence after death and hoped future generations would do the same for them. They needed a quid-pro-quo connecting the earthly world and the hereafter. They wanted to believe that salvation could be bought, and they begged for an opportunity to buy it.

Over time, the Church's pitch became more refined, with pardoners (like in Chaucer) acting as travelling salesmen, offered this benefit to peasants as well as nobles. An entire economy sprang up based on an intangible service — hard cash for after-death benefits.

The Reformation was triggered, in part, by the loss of faith in indulgences. Just as suddenly as it had been believed, it was disbelieved. It had no basis in Scripture. Buyers got nothing for their money. Yes, the soul is eternal. Yes, Heaven or the fire and brimstone of Hell await you depending on your merits and your sins. But the details of Hell and Purgatory and the business the Church had set up for selling benefits in the Beyond were nonsensical and readily subject to corruption.

The Catholic Church quickly gave up this losing battle. Pope Pius V ended the sale of indulgences in 1567. The economy of spiritual benefits which had lasted for nearly 500 years, the notion of a business relationship between the living and their dead ancestors, went poof, and was gone, as if it had never existed. Today, for many of us, it's hard to imagine how important dead ancestors were to the living and how important the living were to the dead.

Value and Belief

Does a marketplace and a currency based on an idea rather than on precious metals or other tangible objects sound unimaginable? Or is it all too familiar?

Imagine a massively parallel worldwide videogame, in which gamers pay money for tokens and health and weapons, all of which only have value in the game, creating an imaginary economy. Then the game company goes out of business, leaving you with nothing.

Remember the early days of the Internet when investors paid high prices for the "next big thing," the idea that would change the world of business. Start-ups with ambitious visions were far more valuable than established brick-and-mortar businesses. People who invested in such companies early, at the ground floor, quickly became multimillionaires. News of their success inspired others to invest. Values soared until the bubble burst.

In 2000, America Online bought Time-Warner for $182 billion in stock and debt, the largest merger in American business history. When the deal was made, Time-Warner was the world's largest media and entertainment company with annual revenues of $26.8 billion, five and a half times more than AOL's $4.8 billion (Smoak Signals/Data Analytics Blog). When the dot-com bubble burst a few months later, the Hollywood Reporter called that deal "the worst merger in history."

In 17th century Holland, rare tulip bulbs suddenly soared in value. The highest price paid for a single bulb was 5,200 guilders, 20 times the annual income of a carpenter. The boom lasted three years (1634-1637). Then the value of tulip bulbs dropped to almost nothing. Alexandre Dumas wrote a novel about that — *The Black Tulip*.

The value of stocks and bonds and even money itself depends on belief. People have agreed that certain kinds of printed paper and computer codes represent value that you can use to buy and sell goods. With inflation and deflation, the value of money itself fluctuates and, in hyperinflation, can plummet to almost nothing. Ironically, money, the basis of capitalism, is immaterial. The Great Depression was, in large part, the collapse of a belief system, like tulips, like indulgences.

The physical world changes slowly and predictably. But ideas and beliefs can change rapidly and radically, transforming who we are and reshaping our future.

Blessing or Blasphemy?

The medieval view of the dead and their relationship to the living is very different from current Christian and Jewish beliefs. Our emotional response to row after row of crosses and stars of David at Arlington and Normandy cemeteries is not from a sense of connection with the souls of those soldiers. Rather, it's from a sense of debt to them, that they sacrificed their lives for us. They are irretrievably lost. We are moved by the memory of them not because we feel connected with their immortal souls, but because their lives were cut short.

The Mormons are an exception, believing that the living can influence the fate of the souls of the dead. Joseph Smith, founder of their faith, introduced the idea of vicarious baptisms for the dead. And in 1990 nine Mormons submitted 380,000 names of Jewish Holocaust victims and posthumously baptized them. The people doing this considered it a good deed, saving souls from eternal damnation.

In response to loud and angry protests from the Jewish community (including Elie Wiesel), the Mormon Church updated their policy to prevent this from happening again. But they refused to remove the names of Holocaust victims from their International Genealogical Database and, reportedly, under special circumstances, such posthumous baptisms are still performed.

One person's blessing is another's blasphemy.

Part Four:
Truth

My intent in writing this book isn't to lecture you, to tell you my version of the "truth." Rather, I want to prompt you to think about your perspective and assumptions and to consider possibilities you might never before have entertained.

Don't just ask yourself if it's true that we're all cousins and share ancestral lines. Ask yourself, what do you mean by true?

The Russian language has two words for truth. *Istina* means absolute, religious, unchanging truth. The other word, *pravda*, was the name of the government newspaper of Soviet Russia. It implies human truth; flawed, imperfect, practical truth that will change over time and that can be changed deliberately. That's the common understanding of truth today, and there are many kinds of it.

Scientific Truth

You might presume that scientific truth has replaced religious truth. But scientific knowledge isn't absolute. It's based on experiments which depend on the accuracy of physical measurements. Results normally include an estimated error, which rarely, if ever, is zero.

On the other hand, science tends to have a bias toward simplicity, beauty, regularity, symmetry. Experiments may be designed to approximate ideal, unattainable circumstances (a perfect vacuum, a surface with no friction, an "average" person) based on the hope or expectation that the universe is fundamentally simple and orderly, as in Keats' *Ode on a Grecian Urn:*

Beauty is truth, truth beauty, — that is all
Ye know on earth, and all ye need to know.

Such a bias has guided experiments that led to discoveries with important practical implications. But wherein lies "truth"? Is it to be found in physical reality? Or are there ideas embedded in our minds that shape our experiments and our perception of the results? As scientists delve ever deeper into the frontiers of the very small and the very large, they find a far more complex and messy reality than they anticipated; and they respond by creating new concepts, new models, new truths — like anti-mater, dark matter, and dark energy.

In the Middle Ages, the rule of thumb known as "Occam's Razor" was important in setting the stage for scientific advancement. "One should not increase, beyond what is necessary, the number of entities required to explain anything." That rule made practical sense. Since you have limited time and limited brain power, you should focus your research on the most likely explanations.

In science as well as genealogy, perhaps it's time to move beyond Occam's Razor: to explore the complex, the unlikely, the redundant, and even the totally outlandish, admitting the possibility that the universe might be messy rather than systematic and beautiful. Perhaps the same laws of physics need not apply everywhere and always. Maybe there's something to be gained by studying the mess rather than sweeping it under a rug.

Presumably, our brains evolved to help us cope with everyday challenges. That ability was selected through evolution because it's essential for survival. Unaccountably, we also have the desire to know what's beyond our ability to know, to arrive at absolute as opposed to conditional truth. That's a limit we can approach but never reach. And in the absence of perfect knowledge, we have to rely on what we believe and the stories we spin to tie our beliefs together.

Historical Truth

History isn't a collection of records. It is story, with perspective and bias. The quality of the narrative — how it holds together, is meaningful and memorable — may be more important than its accuracy, which may be indeterminate.

History is either contemporaneous or after-the-fact. Eyewitnesses report what happens as it happens; historians choose what to include and exclude, what to emphasize, and what it means, after the fact, based on the outcome.

Contemporaneous accounts include newspaper reports, diary entries, letters, and records entered at the time of the event; and, in today's world, texts, emails, and video and audio recordings. But a video is made from a particular angle and distance, with a limited frame. A viewer who doesn't understand the context may misinterpret. Seeing shouldn't be believing. You need to critically examine what you see, especially now when AI and other tech tools make it possible to tamper with the original. Likewise, audio recordings may be taken out of context or modified, as well as emails and text messages. Not only is it difficult to tell if what you see and hear is the original; if changes were made, you may not know if they were deliberate. (What caused the gap in the Nixon tapes?)

Diary entries and letters and contemporaneous written records might have been forged or modified. The authors may not have wanted the truth to be known and may have withheld critical information, even if they didn't blatantly lie. An ancient epic praised for its primitive strength might be a modern forgery, like *The Poems of Ossian*. Diaries and letters reputed to be original might be modern misinformation, intended to change public and judicial opinion about the intent of the framers of *The Constitution*.

When you read your own diary or letters years later, you may have a different view of what happened, based on what you now know about the consequences. Your own words might not ring true to you. You might explore the tension between the author of the diary and the author of the book about the diary, both of whom are you. Nobel-winner Annie Ernaux exploits that technique well.

News is published in ephemeral media that are soon forgotten. It's written as events are unfolding or soon after they happened. Reporters often have a home-town bias, like announcers of baseball games. If there's a war going on, they are unequivocally on one side. Likewise, a newspaper may support one political party over another and may report on an election as if it were a sporting event. Reporters may cherry-pick facts that favor one side or the other, and embellish their stories with bias. Sometimes they might intentionally distort or invent, believing it's their moral duty to stretch the truth for a good cause. Regardless of their bias, newspaper reporters aren't prophets. They don't know which of the possible paths forward will prevail.

"What is truth" is as difficult a question today as when Pilate asked it at the trial of Jesus (perhaps our ancestor).

Writing about events years, decades, even centuries after they occurred, an historian faces daunting challenges. He's trying to assemble a massive puzzle without having all the pieces, not knowing how many are missing or what's an edge piece or a corner piece or even if the picture is rectangular or another shape, with no idea what the assembled picture will look like.

Historians who are eyewitnesses to the events they record have special knowledge but also bias. Consider Anna Komnena writing about her father the Byzantine Emperor or Julius Caesar writing about himself or Thucydides writing about a war in which he served as a general. Reading such works, you expect some embellishment and laundering, whether intended or not, and you take that into account.

Procopius was proud of his eye-witness authenticity when writing about the Byzantine Empire in the days of Emperor Justinian. Writing of himself in the third person, he bragged, "It was his conviction that while cleverness is appropriate to rhetoric, and inventiveness to poetry, truth alone is appropriate to history. In accordance with this principle, he has not concealed the failures of even his most intimate acquaintances, but has written down with complete accuracy everything which befell those concerned, whether it happened to be done well or ill by them." But Procopius wrote that book as an employee of Justinian, and in addition he wrote a "secret" history which wasn't published until a thousand years after he died. Of course, we mistrust the work written for hire, but the secret one is vitriolic, perhaps distorted by hatred and anger, seeking revenge.

Likewise, autobiographies and biographies written by the subjects' close relatives and friends may have unique details and insights, but they need to be read not as raw fact, but as narrative, selected and shaped with purpose. Whether deliberately or not, the author may be an unreliable narrator. Such ambiguity can add spice to a tell-all biography. Does the author know less about her subject than she presumes? Does she misunderstand what she thinks she knows? Is the subject more subtle and nuanced that the biographer? How close is Boswell's Johnson to the Johnson others knew? How qualified are you to write a biography of your father? How accurately could your children write about you? How well do you know yourself? And are there parts of your life that you'd like to forget and don't want anyone to know?

Inherently, writing after the fact creates bias. If you know how the sequence of events ends, that knowledge will pervade your account, as if the outcome were inevitable. This caused that. This series of events led to that one. This was brilliant. That was foolish. The importance of each event depends on how much it contributed to the known ending.

The first real historian, Herodotus, inserted himself into the story as narrator. He had personal interests and biases and was candid about them. Reading his *History* thousands of years later, in translation, we build images of how he thought and why he might have chosen to include this or that and why he wrote about it the way he did. We conclude that, in general, he was a reliable witness, and the people he relied on for information were worthy of his confidence and ours. We rejoice that, miraculously, he wrote his account at all and that what he wrote was preserved as well as it was. In his day, there was no printing press, and the materials used for writing deteriorated over time, so the entire text had to be copied by hand, repeatedly, to survive. And despite all those obstacles, the text we have today seems to be a good approximation of the original.

But is that truth?

Ken Olsen

I used to work for "the Ultimate Entrepreneur." That's the title *Fortune Magazine* gave Ken Olsen in a 1986 cover story. It's also the title of his biography by Glenn Rifkin and George Harar. I wrote MGMT MEMO, the newsletter Ken used to motivate and guide the 20,000 managers at DEC. Ken wanted to empower them to carry his messages to the company's 130,000 employees worldwide. (This was before I became the company's "Internet Evangelist.")

From humble beginnings as a tiny startup with little money but big ideas, Ken had built the second largest computer company in the world, which challenged IBM for dominance. The company culture was college-like, more focused on ideas than profits. At Ken's instigation, the first criterion for making decisions was "do the right thing." "Right" meant not just for DEC and its shareholders, but also for its customers, suppliers, and employees and the communities where they lived and did business.

DEC didn't last forever. Technology changed rapidly, and the company was getting so large that it was hard to change course. Ken compared his job to that of the captain of a aircraft carrier going down a river. You can nudge it this way, then that, but you can't steer it.

For a brief and shining moment, DEC was Camelot. It was a family, sharing common goals and ideals. We were proud to work for DEC, to work for Ken. We felt that what we did mattered, not just for us and the company, but for the world, and not just what we designed, made and marketed, but how we did it.

Product ideas started with individuals and worked their way up. Corporate management, in the role of gatekeeper, decided what to fund and support. And throughout the company, when you were in charge of a project, though you were responsible for its success, you often had no authority over the resources you needed to accomplish it. You had to convince others to support you because it was the right thing to do.

One year, when I was with the fledgling Internet Business Group, it was my job to get the company's Internet offerings displayed at trade shows. I had zero budget, but I got us into 150 shows, with recruits and resources from other parts of the company. Rather than ordering people to do what you needed done, you got them to "buy in." This system, which from the outside looked like chaos, bound us together with tangled threads of interdependence.

DEC turned an abandoned armory in a depressed section of Springfield, Massachusetts, into a manufacturing plant. They hired local people and trained them not just as assembly workers, but as managers, and the plant became an effective and productive part of the overall business. That happened not because Ken said to do it, but because the team selecting the site had internalized his values.

Local managers at a manufacturing plant in Enfield, Connecticut, initiated a team style of work. Everybody on a team knew everybody else's job as well as their own. They could fill in for one another. They could rotate. And they could take pride in what they did as a team. This was in sharp contrast to the typical assembly line, where work is divided into small meaningless tasks, that could eventually be done by machines.

A rogue computer-design team developed a major product in secret, working on their own time with borrowed resources. Instead of presenting a project plan for corporate approval, they rolled a working prototype into a meeting of the Operations Committee. The DECSYSTEM-2020 was a next-generation mainframe computer that normally would have taken years and significant investment to develop. What they did went counter to the company's product strategy, which called for abandoning that family of computers in order to focus on minicomputers with a very different design. (Yes, computers, too, have families and generations).

No one told those engineers to do that work. They were explicitly told not to. They went ahead and skunk-worked it anyway, without being noticed, much less helped by management.

For them, this was a work of love. They did what they did with gusto and pride because they felt it was the right thing to do, with no expectation of reward. For this band of brothers, the difficulty of doing it this way was an incentive. They designed that new computer in record time, with fewer engineers than was deemed feasible. And they did a great job of it. The Operations Committee approved it, and customers loyal to that family of products were surprised and delighted.

I wrote a story about the DECSYSTEM-2020 development for the company newspaper, but, at the insistence of Legal and PR, I had to rewrite it to create the appearance that management had given its blessing from the start. The outside world wouldn't have understood a corporate culture that made such a rogue project possible. What felt natural on the inside would have looked chaotic to outside observers. The company's reputation and stock price might have suffered. So, as historian, I had to modify the facts.

Now, more than a quarter century after the company went out of business, swallowed by Compaq, which was then swallowed by Hewlett-Packard, there are no Legal or PR gatekeepers to stop me from finally telling this anecdote. The DECSYSTEM-2020 was an exception, an outlier. But it epitomized the unique work environment that fostered such initiative and rewarded the team for their results rather than punishing them for breach of rules and procedures.

What I experienced at DEC was very different from the capitalism that Marx described. Ken Olsen reminded me of Robert Owen, the 19th century Scottish industrialist whose utopian values and practices Marx ridiculed as impractical. Owen's showcase factory was in New Lanark, Scotland, just 13 miles from the castle home of the Lords Fleming (our ancestors). He, like Ken, demonstrated that a work force treated like family and motivated by idealistic values can perform wonders.

The Truth, but not the Whole Truth

Soon after their wedding, Dad told Mom his true age. As I mentioned earlier, he had lied to her about that. He was afraid that she might not take him seriously if she knew he was so young. And he delayed the wedding until his twenty-first birthday because he didn't want the embarrassment of asking his parents for permission.

His insistence on the delay had seemed out of character. His excuses were trivial. She had wondered if love had blinded her. There must be some other reason, and there was. Dad had told her the truth, but not the whole truth.

At their first meeting, Nana asked about Mom's father. Mom, excited and nervous, wanting to make a good impression, gave inconsistent dates for his death. She got flustered, apologized, then insisted, too loudly, that the real date was 1932.

Nana was sure that Mom was lying about the date of death. Was he even dead? Perhaps Mom's parents had never married. Perhaps they were strangers. What kind of woman would lie to her mother-in-law-to-be when first meeting her? This Hollywood-beautiful big-city girl was telling a phony Little Orphan Annie story. The more convincingly Mom told her tale, the more that attested to her acting ability rather than to the truth of what she was saying. Nana figured that if Mom lied about that, she was lying about much more. Something so simple as a death date poisoned their relationship, permanently. Nana distrusted Mom. She hated her. She never would have given permission for the wedding,

Dad thought the inconsistency about the date of death was a simple slip of memory. His mother was jumping to wild conclusions, turning something trivial into a major issue. She was being over-protective of her son, treating him like a child with faulty judgment. He defended his choice. He would marry Mom with or without permission.

By coincidence, his mother's name was Lillian, the same as the aunt who had raised Mom. And, having lost her birth mother, Mom was hoping that his mother could be a second mother to her. Dad didn't want to let her know that his mother hated her. So he came up with excuses to delay the wedding until his twenty-first birthday. Nana was adamant — no permission. But, ultimately, she attended the June wedding. She knew Dad would go ahead with or without her blessing, and she didn't want to lose him.

Years later, Dad told Mom about his confrontation with his mother. And Mom admitted to him that, technically, she wasn't an orphan.

Her father had been arrested, convicted, and imprisoned in 1932. She didn't know if he was still in prison. She didn't know when his term would be up. She didn't know if he was dead or alive. She hadn't been allowed to visit him or write to him. Her aunts insisted that she and her siblings never talk about him, even among themselves. Everyone they knew had to believe that he was dead if they were to avoid the stigma of his crime. For decades, Dad was the only person Mom told about her father. That shared secret bonded them together even more closely than before.

So at the very start, they both lied to one another. They were a perfect match.

The History of the Siege of Lisbon by Jose Saramago

At the start of the Second Crusade, troops sailing to the Holy Land, stopped, by chance, at Lisbon and helped defeat the Moors, resulting in Portugal becoming a country and Afonso Henriques (our ancestor) its first king.

Jose Saramago (Nobel winner) wrote a novel with the title *The History of the Siege of Lisbon*, which questions historical truth in a paradoxical, philosophical, and comical style that resembles that of Borges and Lem. At the same time he tells the love story of two employees at a publishing house in modern-day Lisbon, a proof-reader and his boss.

The proof-reader, succumbing to an inexplicable urge, changes one word in a history book about the 1147 siege of Lisbon. The Crusaders say "no," instead of "yes." They sail on rather than stopping to help fight the Moors.

A woman hired to supervise proof-readers and prevent another such egregious error is intrigued by the implications of the mistake and by the proof-reader himself. She surreptitiously suggests that he write a novel that explores the possible consequences if that "no" had been historically true.

The narrative switches back and forth between present-day Lisbon and an alternative medieval past written by the proof-reader. His version of what happened is consistent with the fragmentary historical evidence, and is credibly told, with gritty texture and the addition of a love story that parallels his romance with his new boss. The Crusaders' decision, rather than creating a tornado of consequences and changing all that came after, only leads to differences in how the battle is won and who deserves credit; the outcome is the same. The rip in time caused by the change from "yes" to "no" closes as if it had never happened. The fictitious version of events, created by the proof-reader, might be closer to what actually happened than the official version.

Saramago turns what might otherwise have become an academic discourse on history, fiction, and truth into an entertaining double love story that plays out in the same city, but separated by 850 years. In this book, facts aren't as important as they're usually represented to be. There are a few well-known fixed points on a time line, and there are numerous possible story-paths from one point to another, all of which are equally valid, because they lead to the same conclusion. By looking at more than one possible path, you come to know the characters and their circumstances with the texture, ambiguity, and shading of reality, with its dynamic tensions and ever-changing possibilities, rather than with the static view of linear historical narrative. The author succeeds in showing the heroic and passionate potential of everyday people in everyday circumstances.

I wish I could achieve such a result.

Near Disasters

In plays by Aeschylus and Euripides, Iphigenia, daughter of Agamemnon, is a teenager expecting to marry Achilles but sacrificed by her father for a fair wind to speed the Greek army to Troy. The daughter's age didn't seem right to me. According to legend, Clytemnestra, Iphigenia's mother, was Helen's twin, and Helen wasn't old enough to have a marriageable daughter, wasn't grandmother age when she ran off with Paris, triggering the war. The playwrights broke with the "truth" of tradition and made Iphigenia older for dramatic effect.

In my Trojan War novel *Let the Women Have Their Say,* I portray Iphigenia as four years old and imagine what might have happened if that were the "truth." In my version, Iphigenia accidentally slits her own throat at a mock human sacrifice. Agamemnon doesn't intend to kill her. A deer will be substituted for her at the last minute, supposedly on command of the goddess Artemis, like Abraham with Isaac. But Iphigenia plays with the bright, shining, sharp blade that's intended for sacrificing the deer. She wonders if it will hurt the deer and asks if dying is changing bodies like changing clothes. She runs the blade across her own throat, unintentionally killing herself.

When I was three years old, I nearly did something similar. In the backyard at our home in Philadelphia, there was mica, a layered glass-like rock. You could peal off one thin layer after another, and each layer would be transparent. I liked playing with the glass-like pieces. And one time I ran a piece along my wrist. By chance I did it lengthwise rather than crosswise. It painlessly cut through the skin and I started to bleed. If I had cut laterally, it would have severed arteries, and I probably would have died. I still have the scar.

Twice I did other foolish things that could have cracked my skull. At the age of three, I piled cardboard boxes on the stone steps in front of our row house, building a pretend castle. When my structure was four boxes high, I climbed on top. The boxes tumbled and my face — above my chin, near my lower lip —hit the sharp edge of a step. Lots of pain. Lots of bleeding. A quick trip to the doctor for stitches. I still have the scar.

When I was seven and should have known better, on a visit to my grandparents' house, I ran out the back door onto the stone porch and was literally clotheslined. A clothesline was stretched across the porch but had no clothes on it. I didn't see it. It would have been no risk for an adult of normal height, walking. But I was running hard, and it got me on the neck, sending me to the ground, and the back of my head struck the sharp edge of a stone step. Once again I was lucky. Lots of pain and blood, but three stitches and I was fine. If I shave my head or if I go bald, the scar will show.

Considering all the hazards we face when too young to know better, it's amazing so many of us survive to adulthood. Fire burns; but until you get too close for the first time, you don't know what that means.

Children also have to survive the wisdom of adults, who strive to give them the benefits of the latest technology. In the 1950s in elementary school, teachers periodically gave us mercury to play with on our desks with our bare hands. That was a treat we looked forward to. And by law, the cloth in kids' pajamas had to include asbestos as a fire retardant. And schools had to have asbestos in the walls. And shoe stores had Xray machines that kids were free to play with to see their own bones. And pencils were covered with lead paint that tasted great when I scraped it off with my teeth.

Not that the preceding generation was much better. Before there were plastic cowboys-and-Indians, Dad played with tin-lead soldiers as well as home-made all-lead soldiers. There was a shooting gallery in the basement of the house his father had designed, so kids could have target practice and shooting matches with .22 caliber rifles. Dad and his brothers collected the spent lead, melted it, and poured it into molds, making toy soldiers with World War I style helmets. Dad passed dozens of those on to me, and they, too. tasted great.

How did I survive my childhood?

Another incident that could have turned disastrous is my earliest memory. I was in my crib, probably two-years old. In the middle of the night, I grabbed hold of a siderail, pulled myself up and over, and fell to the floor. I don't remember feeling pain, only the joy and pride of accomplishment.

Going over old notes as I write this book, I found a brief autobiography that my son Tim wrote as a school assignment when he as 12 years old. There he said, "My first memory was falling out of my crib — hard, real hard; it hurt. I was probably about two at the time."

So both Tim and I had the same experience. But he remembered the pain, and I remembered the freedom. I could crawl and roll anywhere I wanted — I was free.

Long John Silver

When I was eight and nine, my best friend was named "John" and with eye-patch and crutches he was perfect as Long John Silver from *Treasure Island*. He didn't need a costume, and it took very little imagination. He was on crutches because of polio, and he had put out an eye, not, like Odin, to drink from the Well of Cosmic Knowledge, but rather out of sheer stupidity, an object lesson for everyone who knew him, confirming what parents say about not running with scissors and not playing with knives. Holding a butter knife, he had jumped up and down on a sofa and had fallen. He liked to freak me out by popping out his glass eye and playing with it. Fortunately, he didn't do that often.

We lived in a housing development on Viers Mill Road in Rockville, Maryland. In 1950, the population was less than 7000 and there was forest all around. Now, Rockville is ten times larger than that, an urban sprawl in the DC suburbs. The development where I lived had just been built, and many of the houses had not yet been sold. The price was $12,500. Every house was identical. I recognized mine and the houses of my friends by counting buildings from the end of the block. Johnny lived three houses away.

I ran barefoot all summer. There was a black-widow spider nest under the front steps. I didn't bother them, and they didn't bother me. They were cute with the red dot on their backs. I sometimes watched them go about their chores. I had an ant farm and watched them do their chores as well. (I didn't like doing chores myself.)

The swing set on top of the hill in my backyard was our pirate ship, the Hispaniola. The hill was huge. Johnny and I would sled down it when school closed for snow — half an inch would suffice. Later, when I lived in New Hampshire, snow would be on the ground non-stop from November to April. It would accumulate up to my waist in normal conditions and over my head after a big storm. No need to shovel the walks. The town had sidewalk-size plows to do that. The paths through the snow were like World War I trenches. Snow was normal. No snow would be a disaster. The local economy depended on skiing and related tourism. And it wasn't just business. Everybody skied. My school had its own ski slope with a rope tow. If they'd known of Skadi, goddess of skiing, the people of Plymouth would have prayed to her.

In Rockville, one time when my pirate battle with Johnny got out of control, I fell down that huge hill and broke my collar bone. When I returned ten years after having moved away, that hill was about as high as my knees, and the house too, was tiny. Memory plays tricks like that. As our perspective changes, truth as we know it changes as well.

Symbolism

Sometimes you mean something other than what you say or something in addition to it. With metaphor and allegory, one thing can stand for another, enriching the narrative, making it engaging rather than preachy, showing rather than telling, triggering the reader's personal memories and associations. Aesop's *Fables* and Orwell's *Animal Farm* convey truth through the mouths of animals. Readers draw their own conclusions.

Religions often use verbal and tangible symbols to convey stories, helping believers remember dogma and imagine they are in the presence of and are speaking to saints, to Christ, to God.

Kids today reenact scenes from movies and comic books with action figures. In my day, like my classmates, I played with plastic cowboys-and-Indians, imagining clashes in the Wild West. But those cost ten cents each, a week's allowance in the 1950s. I only had a few dozen of them. Then it dawned on me: if I could make a piece of plastic a warrior in my imagination, anything would work. So I used bottlecaps instead.

Plain cork, from soda bottles, meant cavalry and cowboys. White, from ginger ale, meant officers. Aluminum, from beer bottles, meant Indians. Caps with the cork removed were major characters. On each of them, I glued a strip of paper with the character's name. When the ridged side was up, they were alive; flipped over, they were dead. Sometimes I controlled the action, deciding which to flip and when. Sometimes I shook the rug, flipped them randomly, like fate, and removed the "dead" from the battlefield before the next skirmish.

I could stage huge battles. And I wasn't limited to cowboy-and-Indian stories. I refought the Trojan War, the American Revolution, World War II. All I needed was a rug and my box of bottlecaps. I was an only child, but I had hundreds of playmates.

I'm reminded of an incident when Tim, a third grader, was in an afterschool program at the YMCA. One day Barb and I got a call to tell us they were kicking him out of the program for violation of their "zero-tolerance gun policy." It turned out that he and a friend were playing cops-and-robbers, pointing fingers at one another and shouting "Bang! Bang!" After a bizarre conversation with the instructor, Tim was let off the hook. But another such serious offense would not be tolerated.

Later, when he was a freshman at Rochester Institute of Technology, Tim was reprimanded on another gun charge. He had brought to school some of the bullet shells that Dad brought home from Army Reserves and that I had played with as a kid. I had passed them on to Tim. These were spent shells, not live ammunition, but having them on his desk in his dorm room was considered a serious offense.

Such are the risks of symbolism. Some people mistake the symbol for what it represents. Intending to reduce the likelihood of violence, they try to constrain what we think, not just what we do. But I suspect there's value in the childhood urge to fight battles and slay monsters. Our fantasies prepare us to cope with unexpected and seemingly impossible challenges.

Language

Language itself evolves over time. Slang words become standard. Common expressions drop out of use. New dialects arise.

Pronunciation changes, and words take on different meanings. Can you read Chaucer's Middle English?

How letters are represented, by hand or in print, changes. Alphabets add or subtract letters or accent marks. Such changes may happen gradually by chance or abruptly for a purpose. The Soviet government changed the Russian alphabet and rules for spelling after the Revolution. When people learned to read and write the new way in school and used the new alphabet in their everyday lives, older material became awkward to read and difficult to understand. That was a subtle but effective form of censorship, worthy of Orwell's *1984*.

As quill pens gave way to steel tip and those to fountain pens and those to ballpoint pens, the art of elaborate and careful handwriting came to an end, and what once was considered beautiful style became difficult to decipher. Handwriting used to be a matter of pride as well as a legally-accepted way of identifying who wrote a letter or signed a document. Today we sign using a finger to scribble on the screen of a payment device, or, for bigger payments and legally binding agreements, we use an online app. That's far different from the bold exuberant signature of John Hancock on the *Declaration of Independence*. When he signed, he shouted his name.

We still collect autographs of celebrities and autographed copies of printed books. And original holographic books and letters — handwritten by the author — sell for thousands of dollars. I have the Dover facsimile edition of the illustrated *Alice in Wonderland* that Lewis Carroll gave to Alice Liddell. I also have the handwritten autobiography of my great-grandfather Henry Hocker Seltzer. The personality of the author comes through in the author's hand. That's why, 50 years ago, I published my first book, *The Lizard of Oz,* handwritten rather than in type. But that's rare. Our documents, emails, and texts are all typed, and software corrects our spelling and grammar and even anticipates our words.

Now cursive handwriting is so rare that many schools no longer teach it, making it far rarer. Perhaps in the future, only a trained expert will be able to read a diary or letters from World War II, much less letters written hundreds of years earlier. If my great-grandchildren and those who come after them chance upon a handwritten page of mine, they won't know what it says.

Emojis and logos and other hieroglyphic-like symbols are now common, and you can produce them by clicking on choices. In the future, alphabet-based writing may be replaced by such pictographs enhanced by audio and video.

England had its Great Vowel Shift (1400-1700) when spoken English changed radically. We are approaching another divide now, separating the written past from the recorded future.

Obsolescence — Truth Lost and Forgotten

What was written in the distant past may be difficult or impossible for us to understand now, and what we write or otherwise record today will probably be unreadable in the future or will be lost in a gargantuan mass of saved material, including nonillions of baby, cat, and dog videos.

I wonder if alphabet-based written language was first invented in the second millennium BCE as many historians presume or if it was invented long before that and forgotten. In the millions of years that humankind has existed, maybe advances we consider modern were invented, forgotten, and reinvented many times. Today, we can't make sense of computer programs from just 50 years ago, written in coding languages that are now obsolete. The oxide on videotape flakes off after a decade or so. DVDs, too, don't last forever — they degrade and become indecipherable. And new computer designs and new versions of software make the old obsolete. How many times have you bought your entire music library over again because the dominant technology changed from 78 rpm to 45 to 33 to real-to-reel tape to 8-track to cassette to CD and now to streaming. In a couple decades, your current audio and video libraries will be useless, replaced by other formats with other devices to play them. Will everything be on clouds or stored in other ways? And when remote storage no longer exists, or when everything recorded in that mode is inaccessible or indecipherable, what evidence of our advanced civilization will remain?

I'm reminded of the ruins of the Statue of Liberty on the beach at the end of *Planet of the Apes*. Will humankind or some other rational species need to reinvent everything we have today? And was much that we consider modern today invented repeatedly in the past?

A thousand years from now, every human on Earth and even on other planets may be descended from you, but will any of your thoughts or creations survive?

Remember the horror when books printed on cheap pulp paper in the 19th century began to turn to dust on library shelves? Then came the ability to convert printed books to electronic books, saving information and creativity that would otherwise have been permanently lost. Ebooks could be duplicated in volume at no cost and distributed instantly throughout the world. The Gutenberg Project, The Internet Archive, and other volunteer projects strove to preserve and disseminate all the books of the past.

But that technological advance depends on the infrastructure of modern technology — from electricity to storage to high speed connectivity. That dependence means that all electronic books could be obliterated in a single global catastrophe, leading to a dystopian illiterate world, as often portrayed in science fiction.

Humankind may survive in flesh, android, or digital form. But what will become of all that we have wrought — our inspirations, our creations, and the record of our thoughts?

Twenty years ago, working alone in my basement on my personal computer, I assembled and manufactured, collections of electronic books on CDs and DVDs. These were books no longer protected by copyright, "public domain" books, many of them classics. I organized over 20,000 books on four DVDs — a complete library that I sold for $149. But those DVDs were useless ten years later because of market and technology changes. And, they will soon be indecipherable.

As new and better software and hardware appear and businesses you now rely on disappear, will you be able to display your family tree at Ancestry.com or your creative work elsewhere on the Internet (or on whatever comes after the Internet)? Undoubtedly, you'll be able to migrate your information to new media, like converting your super-8 home movies to VHS and then to DVD. But if your children or grandchildren don't make such conversions when they're easy to make, changing later will be expensive or impossible.

So for both human and technical reasons, historical truth is a moving target. Much of what was known before, regardless of how accurate it was, has been lost. And much that we now know will be irretrievable in the future.

Embellishment and Truth

When you tell stories about yourself and your family, it's natural to select and embellish and shape your tale to suit the audience. The story value is more important than the accuracy. No one is going to fact-check you. Unless you're running for public office or your story supports lies on your resume, a white lie doesn't matter, does it?

Embellishment in historical writing can make the events and the characters seem more important and interesting. And what's the harm in omitting negative matters that could confuse the audience or lose their attention?

What's wrong with cosmetics if they bring out your natural beauty? Doesn't time spent on such embellishment give pleasure to others? Is the well-enhanced face less true than the natural one? Who needs to see pimples, warts, moles? When a king was going to base his choice of bride on a painting, wouldn't the portrait-artist enhance her looks to the limits of credibility?

And why include the minor faults of great people in their biographies? At what point does cosmetic change become a lie? Or perhaps the author reveres the subject so much as to be blind to faults. Does colorizing black-and-white photos make them less authentic or more? Might the allegorical account of Stalin's Russia in Orwell's *Animal Farm* better convey the dynamics of dictatorship than straight history? Might a parody be more true than unadorned facts?

Sometimes a fictional story captures the essence of what could happen better than a recitation of facts and statistics. Stephen Crane was born after the Civil War and never served in the military, but his *Red Badge of Courage* is a vivid, realistic account of battlefield experience that feels more authentic than autobiographies of Civil War veterans.

I believe *The Iliad* is "true" regardless of whether the Trojan War actually took place.

Aunt Annie Jane and the Stagecoach

Mom's Aunt Lil was the disciplinarian; Aunt Agnes the breadwinner. Neither married. Though diminutive in size, both were strong-willed. Their word was law — no questions asked. As soon as their sister died, leaving a house full of children, they moved in and told the father to move out. For the two years he lived across the street, he provided no help in taking care of the family home or the children. He was incompetent and useless, as were all men.

Dad was raised to believe that women were incompetent. His mother (Nana) had an eighth-grade education. She, like the aunts, was strict and puritanical. When I knew her, Nana's hands were always in motion — straightening or dusting. "Cleanliness is next to godliness," she would say. She stood for Christian morality and insisted that the whole family attend church on Sunday. And she kept a close eye on household expenses. That was her realm. She was respected and obeyed on matters of morality, religion, and chores to keep the house in shape; but her husband made the important decisions. Only in music was there parity — mother, father, and the four boys each mastered at least one instrument, and they played together regularly in the living room, gathered around the baby grand piano. She hoped her sons would all become Lutheran ministers and marry loyal, upright, and obedient women.

When Mom and Dad fell in love, they saw their similarities, but overlooked their differences. Both had been raised Lutheran and were true believers. But Mom would not be subservient to anyone. She supported Dad throughout his career — working as secretary (to a superintendent of schools) so he could earn his doctorate in education, and typing his dissertation multiple times (in the days before personal computers, when dissertations needed to be typed with carbon copies on mechanical typewriters, with no typos and no white-out corrections). But she was itching to have her turn, which she eventually did, graduating from college and experimenting with entrepreneurial ideas.

Mom learned much from her guardian, man-hating, old-maid aunts; but she was also inspired by their feisty half-sister, Aunt Annie Jane. She saw Annie Jane rarely and at odd intervals, like a strobe light with a random pattern, but with bright, unforgettable flashes. Mom knew Annie Jane's story secondhand, never having had an opportunity for a private conversation with her; but the image was indelible.

As Mom told me decades later, Annie Jane ran away from home at the age of 15 and rode a stagecoach through the Wild West to San Francisco. Images of plains Indians and buffalo herds and gangs of bandits raced through my head. But Annie Jane was born in 1867. Just two years later, the transcontinental railroad opened up. When she was 15, in 1882, she would have taken a train and arrived in comfort after little more than two days. But "stagecoach" made for a better story. And while Annie Jane travelled alone, she had a destination — two half-brothers, Tom and Dave, had run away from home before her, and Tom claimed to have struck it rich.

She returned home a few years later, then ran away again, this time to New York City, where she got a job and lived on her own. She became a suffragette campaigning for women's rights. She met a man named Tim and encouraged him to fall in love with her. She conned him out of money to take a trip to Europe. When she returned, she refused to marry him, and he gassed himself to death. Then she fell in love with a married man; and, because of him, she never married.

When Mom felt constrained in the strait-jacket of her guardian aunts' strict regime, she must have been tempted to follow in the footsteps of her Aunt Annie Jane, though in her day there was no Wild West to run off to, no risky and exciting storied realm, no alternate life to choose.

I saw Aunt Annie Jane a couple times when she was ancient and bedridden, living with and cared for by Aunt Lil. (Agnes was dead by then). She had converted to Christian Science and although she was in continuous pain, she refused all medical care and all medication. The challenge of enduring the pain may have made her feel that God was testing her and that she was in close contact with Him. She died in 1955, at at the age of 88, of eye cancer.

Perception of Time

When my memory plays tricks on me, often the issue relates to time — the order of events and their duration. My perception of time varies with my emotional involvement in what is happening, as well as with my age. Time drags for a child and races ahead for someone as old as me. The final moments of a sporting event can remind us of the variability of time.

Because of rules that stop the clock, the last two minutes of a football game or a basketball game can go on and on, with reversal after reversal. I particularly remember the Harvard-Yale game of 1968.

It was the last game of the season, and both Harvard and Yale were undefeated. But Yale had Brian Dowling at quarterback and Calvin Hill, a future star for the Dallas Cowboys, at halfback. Undergraduate Gary Trudeau had made them two epic heroes in his *Bull Tales* comic strip in *The Yale Daily News*. We were sure to overwhelm our arch rivals.

At one point Yale led 22–0. And with 42 seconds remaining, they led 29–13. Then in a series of impossible flukes, Harvard scored 16 points. The headline in the *Harvard Crimson* the next day read "Harvard Beats Yale 29–29."

(42 seconds? In *The Hitch Hiker's Guide to the Galaxy*, that number is the meaning of life, the universe, and everything.)

A 2008 documentary brings that game to life, with actor Tommy Lee Jones, who played for Harvard in that, as himself. That movie is now available streaming on YouTube. Search for "Harvard Beats Yale 29-29."

Having endured the agony of that game (from the Yale side), my perception of time has been skewed ever since. And that distortion has been reenforced repeatedly since then by last-minute changes of fortune in critical football and basketball games. Now I see that as a good thing.

Our lives are limited. X years and it's over. But those years are made up of minutes, and minutes can miraculously expand during trauma as well as closely fought games.

I'm reminded of the race between Achilles and the tortoise, as told by the Greek philosopher Zeno. The tortoise gets a head start. Then, with a single step, Achilles covers half the distance between them. Then with every step, he cuts the distance in half again, but he never catches up with the tortoise, never passes it.

Death might be like that. In your consciousness, time expands — a minute feels like an hour, a second like a year, a nanosecond an eternity. It might be an end point you approach but never reach, as time, for you, expands.

The final minute of a Super Bowl game is a harbinger of that kind of immortality.

No wonder we become addicted to time-limited sports.

The Price of Coming of Age

What we see and what we believe depends in part on our world view, on what we take for granted because of the time and place in which we live. Our perspective also depends on our stage of life, such as child or adult.

In America today, if you're considered to be a child, you're welcome to have opinions and to express them, but they don't matter. You can't vote. You can't make legal decisions on your own. With few exceptions, if you break a law, that's considered a mistake, not a crime, and entails a much lower level of punishment.

There are several legal thresholds to adulthood, depending on the state —16, driver's license; 18, right to vote; 21, full adulthood. When I was growing up, there was another one as well — 12, when you would have to pay adult admission at a movie theater.

I looked forward to my twelfth birthday and was delighted when my Uncle Paul offered to take me to the movies that day as a gift. But when we got to the ticket window and the clerk asked how old I was, Paul said, "Eleven." I started to protest, but he silenced me with look and gesture. As we went in, he whispered to me that there was no need to pay an extra $2. No one would know. I looked young enough to be eleven. He said it was a "white lie." It didn't matter.

But it mattered to me. I was twelve, and I wanted to be twelve.

Soon after that, Dad showed me how to use our hand-pushed lawn mower. I was proud that he considered me old enough to try, and I was even prouder when I could do it with ease. He then told me that that was now my chore. He expected me to do that once every two weeks over the summer, more frequently if the grass grew faster than usual. I was outraged. Mowing to prove myself or because I felt like it was one thing. Doing so because I had to was different. Dad had trapped me. I was being penalized for being older and stronger, and there was no going back.

When I had kids of my own, I had trouble assigning them chores. Rationally, I knew that they needed to learn responsibility, and Barb and I needed help around the house. But I felt guilty every time I tried. I didn't want them to feel betrayed and trapped as I had been. That cowardice on my part was a mistake. Fortunately, the damage wasn't permanent.

Growing up in a small town in New Hampshire, a driver's license wasn't a big deal. There was no place to drive to, and there was no driver's ed program. I got a learner's permit. Dad let me take the wheel a few times. Then I took the test. There were no traffic lights. There was no traffic. All I had to do was drive around the town green without running into anything. It wasn't until years later that I had to drive on my own.

With my kids, it was a different matter. To get a driver's license was a rite of passage. And that was the scariest period of my life, even worse than the first time I let them cross the street on their own. A car is a lethal weapon, and they'd be sharing the street with total strangers who could be drunk or on drugs or distracted or simply incompetent. The contingencies were many, but it was pointless to give my kids detailed advice. They wouldn't listen, and they'd only be prepared for danger when they faced it themselves. You can tell your child over and over that fire burns and knives cut, but until they've felt the consequences, your words mean nothing.

Bob was easy. Or so I thought. The car he wanted was a stick-shift. I hadn't driven one for years. I ground the gears loudly driving it home from the seller. But Bob caught on quickly, proudly. He drove every day to and from his summer job. I thought all was well. He had successfully gone through a rite of passage; and I, as a parent, had as well. Then something broke as he got off the exit from the highway. The car spun out of control, and, by a miracle, ended up at a gas station, with the front tires pointed in opposite directions. If it had broken a few minutes earlier, on the highway, he would probably have died. The car was defective. I should have had it checked before we bought it.

My daughter, too, was excited to get her license. Unfortunately, the secondhand car she was driving had a few quirks. They weren't a problem once you got used to them, but she got into a fender bender almost immediately. Fortunately, no one was hurt.

I wish there were an inexpensive, easy way to safety-check a used car and a controlled space where young drivers could make mistakes, have minor accidents, and learn from them, without serious consequences. That would be true "Driver's Ed."

Mike was next in line, and for him a driver's license was a very big deal. He told his friends when he was going to take the driver's test and planned to celebrate. He was a good driver. I was as certain as he was that he would pass easily. But he failed. Then he had to wait months before he could take it again. And he failed again. He failed a third time. Then he finally got it. There was nothing wrong with how he drove. It was a matter of personality. He would argue with the officer giving the test about the right way to do what he was told to do. It was painful having to witness that from the backseat.

Blessedly, our youngest, Tim, who is "on the spectrum," didn't need to drive and didn't want to. For him it wasn't a rite of passage. Why should he bother to learn? Then a few years later, he needed to commute to a community college ten miles away. No license, no courses. He learned quickly and well, but after the experience with Mike and given Tim's unique personality, I dreaded the test. As it turned out, Tim struck up a conversation with the testing officer. Soon they were laughing together. And when he made a mistake, the officer encouraged him and let him try again; and that time Tim did it right. He passed the test the first time around.

It wasn't how well Mike and Tim could drive that made a difference, but how they were perceived.

My Ten Cents

Our values, too, change as we mature and age.

When I was four years old, my parents gave me ten cents a week as an allowance, and I could walk to the corner drug store and buy whatever I wanted.

The choice was between objects and experiences. If I bought plastic cowboys-and-Indians, I could play with them over and over. And if I bought comic books, I could read them over and over. In either case, I could share or trade them with friends. If instead, I bought penny candy or ice cream, while the experience would be delightful, it wouldn't last. The act of enjoying it would destroy it. I would end up with nothing. Despite temptation, I almost never opted for candy or ice cream.

When my kids were young, I hoped that they would enjoy the toys and comics I had treasured at their age and had saved for them. But they showed little interest in the old stuff, caught up as they were in the new objects of popular culture that they and their friends saw advertised.

Now I value experiences. The boxes of plastic cowboys-and-Indians and comic books just take up space. They're a burden to me, and, after I go, they'll be considered trash. At this stage of my life, I want to enjoy the moment rather than accumulate tangible goods. I value ephemeral beauty and pleasure, and it's refreshing to remember such moments writing this book.

Lawn Mowing

After freshman year of high school, lawn mowing was no longer a chore. It was a money-making opportunity, and money mattered to me. I wanted to save up for a trip to France as an exchange student. Such an experience was more important to me than anything tangible, even books.

We had a power mower so the job was easier than before; and neighbors who still had hand mowers were willing to pay me $5. One customer asked me if I would be willing to mow a cemetery and how much I would charge. I had no idea how big the cemetery was and hence how long it would take to do the job. So I asked for $5 an hour, and he agreed. It turned out it was a 90-hour task that would take me two weeks. And at the height of summer, by the time I finished, the grass would grow enough for me to start over again. To me, that was a fortune.

At first, it didn't bother me that I was mowing a cemetery. Grass was grass. Then one morning when Dad was driving me there, I heard on the radio that a friend of mine from Holderness School had died in a car accident, riding a bike on Nantucket. Death was real, and I was walking on dead bodies.

I started reading the names and inscriptions on the gravestones. One was for "Hal Pease, Jr." The lady who lived across the street from us was Charlotte Pease. She was one of my customers. She was probably in her 40s, "old" to me, as old as my Mom. I asked her if she was related to the man in the grave. She said he was her brother. He had died in the Pacific in World War II. He had received the Congressional Medal of Honor. And the Air Force base in Portsmouth, New Hampshire, was named "Pease" in his honor.

I didn't know then, but I see now on Wikipedia that he was a pilot flying a B-17 out of Queensland in Australia. On August 7, 1942, his bomber group was scheduled for a "maximum effort" mission; but his plane was grounded for repairs. Hal had a fuel tank installed in the bomb bay, rigged with a handpump to transfer fuel; and he and his crew volunteered to go on the mission. Fifty miles from the target, their group was attacked by 30 Japanese fighters. Hal and crew fought their way through to the target and successfully dropped their bombs, but their plane was heavily damaged. They were seen jettisoning their burning fuel tank and were presumed dead. In fact, Hal and one crew member bailed out. They were captured and taken to a POW camp, where they stayed until October 8, when he, three other Americans and two Australians were forced to dig their own graves, then beheaded.

The Air Force Base closed in 1991, but part of the facility continues to operate as Pease Air National Guard Base.

On the gravestone, next to Hal Pease, Jr., was engraved "Charlotte Pease," with the date of her birth. The date of death was left blank. From the birth dates, they were twins.

After mowing the entire cemetery once, I backed out of the assignment. I wouldn't have done it again at any price.

A few years after Barb died, I went on Match and met dozens of women. One of them frequently visited her husband's grave and spoke to him at length and wanted me to speak to him as well. Another lived next to the cemetery where her husband was buried and, like Charlotte Pease, had her name engraved on his gravestone, with the date of her death left blank.

After Barb's funeral, I have never visited her grave. I don't associate that stone and that plot of ground with my memory of her.

Truth and Memory

After a crime, detectives may have little physical evidence and may find it difficult to decipher what happened. Witnesses try to reconstruct the moment, but memories aren't always reliable. When there's more than one eyewitness, their accounts may contradict one another. Each may have seen the same event, but with different blind spots, insights, and prejudices. And some witnesses lie.

Sometimes criminals declare their innocence in full confidence and pass lie detector tests because they don't remember what they did or why they did it. Did Mom, in reciting what her aunts taught her to say, sometimes forget that her father was still alive and in prison?

Eyewitnesses may wrongly report what happened because of mistakes of perception. They may have been distracted or thinking of something else at the crucial, unexpected moment. And some may have Freudian moments, forgetting matters related to past trauma.

Perhaps Mom's slip-up about the date of her father's "death" falls into that category.

In the 1990s there was an outbreak of cases where daycare workers were falsely accused and wrongfully convicted of sexually abusing young children. It turned out that investigators had unintentionally planted false memories by suggestive interviewing. Mom wondered if her father might have been innocent, if his crime might have been a misunderstanding like that, an injustice. He couldn't afford a lawyer.

How good is your memory? My son Bob tells me now that, as a child, he had instances of severe abdominal pain and that his mother, Barb, did as well. I have no such recollection. I probably assumed the pain was caused by gas, gave them Tums or Alka Seltzer, maybe tried burping. But those pains could have been symptoms of a serious medical condition that later killed Barb and almost killed Bob. Now I wish I had seen those pains as alert signals and taken them seriously.

Also, over time, our memories deteriorate. We have "senior moments" when we can't find the car keys or the cellphone or the word we want. We may have early signs of senility, dementia, Alzheimer's without realizing we do.

Would you be a reliable witness? Or if you were on a jury, would you be able to determine if someone else was? Could you decide guilt or innocence beyond a reasonable doubt?

Houses and Memory

In ancient Greece and Rome, there were no printing presses. The only books were handwritten, rare, and expensive. Today, we remember where to click or how to search to get the information we want when we want it. They relied on their memories.

The Greek poet Simonides of Ceos (556-468 B.C.E.) devised a method for memorizing based on images and places, which was widely used in ancient times. As Joshua Foer explains in *Moonwalking with Einstein*, "... all one has to do is convert something unmemorable, like a string of numbers, or a deck of cards, or a shopping list, or *Paradise Lost* into a series of engrossing visual images and mentally arrange them within an imagined space, and suddenly these forgettable items become unforgettable" (p. 94). Visualize a space you know well, like the house where you live or where you grew up, and populate it with what you want to remember — one item here, another there, in sequence. Using that technique, Charmadas, a Greek philosopher (168-103 B.C.E), reputedly could memorize whole books and then recite them, as if he were reading them. Seneca the Elder (54 B.C.E. - 39 C.E.) could repeat 2000 names in the order they had been given to him.

Two houses are vivid in my memory: 4 Russell Street in Plymouth, New Hampshire, and my grandparents' house at 1234 Pinecrest Circle in Woodside Park, Silver Spring, Maryland. I can see every room in both those houses and how they connect and what is where. They are fixed elements in my memory, and I often have dreams that take place in the one or the other.

The Russell Street house had an attached barn. My Dad built a cabin cruiser on the ground floor of the barn, and the loft was a year-round basketball court, a haven for those, like me, who weren't addicted to snow sports. The barn had a cupola on top from which you could view the whole town. And there was a hole in the ceiling that gave access to crawl space leading to the house. I considered that my "secret passage" and stored personal treasures there.

Pop Pop's house, which he designed himself, had a walk-in hearth, with stone benches on either side. A musket from Daniel Boone days hung from the mantel piece. A grandfather clock near the front door played Big Ben tones on the hour. Beside the clock stood a baby grand piano, next to which there was a window the size of a picture window but made of small pieces held in place by lead, like stained glass, but with clear panes. The window looked out on a goldfish pond, to which was attached a handpump.

Though I haven't deliberately used that ancient technique, many of my personal memories and my patterns of association are tied to my images of those two houses. And when I'm in turmoil or transition, I'll dream that one or another of them is falling apart or that I'm repairing weaknesses and building extensions, making abandoned sections livable and extending my library there, making accessible books that had been stored in boxes or that were decaying from neglect. Once I dreamed an addition that extended all the way from Plymouth, New Hampshire to the Sterling Library at Yale.

But my memory of those buildings isn't always accurate, as my Uncle Paul pointed out to me when I sent him an early draft of this book. I had erred in my placement of a closet upstairs at Pop Pop's house, where books were stored and where I could immerse myself in boyhood adventures, uninterrupted. There must be other mistakes as well. *Caveat te ipsum* — beware of yourself.

Learning to Learn

We can't totally trust our memories. But maybe we might, with training and concentration, learn to remember one kind of thing exceptionally well, like the ancients memorizing entire books, or chess masters memorizing thousands of openings, or a pianist remembering every detail of an hour-long piece, or an artist remembering images, colors, and textures seen in paintings and in real life.

Are we born with our ability to learn and remember or do we build it by what we do and how we do it? I'm not considering this question from the perspective of science. It would take a lifetime to read and digest the research on that subject. I'm looking at it based on my experience and trying to make sense of it in the context of who we are and why we do what we do.

We remember best what we learn by experience — the burn on my finger, the cut on my wrist, and, later, the first fender bender. And some activities that preschoolers engage in, on their own initiative, seem to give them experiences that stretch their memory capacity and develop skills they'll need later in life. No one tells them to do those things; they simply want to. They solve puzzles, build structures with blocks, tinker toys, anything at hand. And they obsess over trivial topics, learning names and features and strengths and interactions. For Tim, it was Pokemon. For Mike, comic books. For Bob it was dinosaurs first, then baseball players, then Star Wars action figures.

When Bob was a year old, he could recognize the faces and tell the names of dozens of baseball players. He got lots of reinforcement for that. It was hilarious and miraculous to hear someone so young say "Carl Yastremski" and match the name with the card. He was learning the fundamentals of reading before he knew the alphabet and not because any adult was guiding him: that was what he wanted to do. Soon after that, he insisted that I read to him for hours every night after I got home from work. He wanted to hear the same Dr. Seuss story over and over until he knew it by heart. And before he was two, he could read one that he had never heard before.

Games, too, play an important role in pre-school learning — the ones kids learn from watching others play and asking, not the ones stores sell and parents teach. In my day, thirty years before the first home videogames, boys played with marbles and baseball cards; girls played hopscotch and jump rope; older kids played card games like fish, poker, and gin rummy, and board games like Monopoly.

Baseball cards were for playing, not for memorizing or collecting. You took turns throwing cards against a wall. The card that landed closest to the wall won. If your card ended up leaning against the wall, you won immediately. It didn't matter what player was depicted on the card or how damaged the card might be from previous games. If you "played for keeps," you owned the cards you beat. Later, baseball cards became like coins and stamps, collectors' items that you could buy and sell at stores or directly with one another; and the rarity of a particular card and its condition determined its value — early training in how to negotiate deals and how to run a business. In elementary school, Bob's first entrepreneurial venture was trading, buying, and selling baseball cards.

For me, marbles, too, were for playing. You would draw a circle on the pavement with chalk and put target marbles inside. Then you would take turns flicking shooter marbles with the back of your thumb, trying to dislodge the ones in the circle. Whatever you knocked out of the circle was yours. The target marbles were made of glass. Some had a swirl of colors. Others, called "cat-eyes," were clear glass with a dash of color on the inside. The shooter marbles were often agates, much larger than the targets and made of a natural mineral. They were rare and expensive in kids' reckoning. You wouldn't want to risk them as targets.

In addition to their role in games, marbles and baseball cards also served as currency. We learned about value and risk, how to barter and negotiate. We learned the rudiments of business and also how to gamble. Some kids learned to bully and steal, others to deal with bullies and thieves.

Dad, too, played with marbles as a kid, and I prized the agates he passed down to me. He also gave me his metal fire engine pulled by a horse and dozens of lead soldiers in World War I helmets. My kids weren't interested in those or in the hundreds of plastic cowboys-and-Indians or the thousands of bottle caps that I had played with as a kid. An heirloom is only an heirloom if the next generation values it.

If they don't already, anthropologists should study the social interactions of young children, especially the games they play, not just their rules but the underlying lessons and benefits kids get from them. Has there been a developmental change with the shift to videogames? What skills and thinking patterns do kids learn from playing them? Is there anything important that old games nourished and current games miss? And are there new skills, important in today's world, that today's kids are learning and that I missed?

Harry Lyman, an early chess mentor of Bob's, thought of a chess board as an experimental space that could enable young children to develop abstract thinking skills far earlier than Piaget deemed possible. He believed Piaget's stages of mental development were based on cultural norms rather than on nature, that young kids didn't think abstractly not because they couldn't, but because they hadn't had experience at it. He would put a few pieces on a chess board, let them know how the pieces moved, and let them experiment to solve problems. Often they'd enjoy the challenge, come back for more and more, and find solutions requiring thinking skills that Piaget would have thought far beyond their age.

The word "marbles" triggers another chess memory. 1987. Terre Haute, Indiana. I was there with Bob, who was competing in the National Elementary School Chess Championship. He was eleven, in the fifth grade. The year before, in Charlotte, North Carolina, he had won all but one game and had tied for seventh place. He was relaxed and ready. I was a nervous wreck.

Walking from our hotel to the tournament site, we found seven marbles, separately, in cracks in the sidewalk: cat-eyes, each a different color, all new with no scratches. I have no idea how those marbles got there. But finding them raised my spirits, making me feel that it was fated that Bob would win all seven of his games, which he did, winning the national championship.

By the way, as a loyal fan, I recorded every move of every one of Bob's tournament games, 951 of them. Soon after I posted them on my web site, Bob Levinson, at the University of California in Santa Cruz, found them by Internet search (AltaVista, in the days before Google) and contacted me. He paid for the right to use those games (in sequence from beginner to life master) to train his research computer chess program. That was an early attempt at Artificial

Intelligence (AI), a field that has finally come into its own. Computers, like people, need to learn how to learn. At my suggestion, he named his program "Morph," after the 19th-century American chess champion Paul Morphy and as in "metamorphosis." You can read about Morph in Wikipedia, and you can see Bob's chess games at www.seltzerbooks.com/tour1.html

Oaths

From judicial procedure, we could conclude that, unless compelled to do so, most people can't be trusted to tell the truth. In the U.S., witnesses have to swear that they will tell the truth, the whole truth, and nothing but the truth. Swearing and then lying is perjury, a felony that can land you in jail. Lying when not under oath is not a criminal offense. Authors of history books, biographies, and autobiographies don't swear such an oath and hence don't face jail time if they lie. But they are subject to defamation suits if they wrongfully damage reputations.

Oaths have played an important role in law and government since ancient times. The concept is connected with that of sacrifice. The greater your sacrifice, the more serious your appeal to the gods. The more you're willing to stake on your oath of truthfulness, the more likely you are to speak the truth. You might swear on your own life or the lives of those dear to you. The original formula for oaths seems to have been like a wager: if your words turned out to be false, you'd forfeit what you swore on.

Ironically, censorship can lend authenticity and authority to otherwise questionable historical accounts. Solzhenitsyn opposed the Soviet government and was censored and punished for his writings. He bet his life to say what he had to say; and, as a result, his *Gulag*

Archipelago, a massive collection of what otherwise would be considered hearsay, earned the highest level of credibility.

Even when you don't formally swear, the credibility of what you say and write may depend on what you're willing to stake on it. Sir Thomas More, as portrayed in *A Man for All Seasons*, was willing to die rather than betray what to him was an important principle. Likewise, Luther, when he declared "Here I stand. I cannot do otherwise," bet everything on his beliefs and thereby ignited the Reformation. Both More and Luther were authentic. At their moments of crisis, they not only spoke truth; they lived it. They embodied their beliefs. With their single-minded, unyielding devotion to their beliefs, they commanded respect and led many others to adopt those beliefs, thereby altering the course of history, without the material means to do so. This was an echo of the behavior and effect of martyrs in the early days of the Christian Church, and of sainted ancestors of ours who converted entire nations.

The phrase "famous last words" ironically echoes such moments. What a dying person says, as reported by someone who heard it, can be admissible as evidence in court, even though it's hearsay. Presumably, someone dying no longer has a reason to lie and is likely to make Pascal's gamble: if there is a God and an afterlife, there might be some benefit to speaking the truth; and if there is no God, doing so won't hurt.

"Truth" Filtered

What we consider "truth" is filtered through what we believe, through the world view of the time we live in. In the Middle Ages, people commonly assumed that the universe is static and has been so since Creation. But by the end of the eighteenth century, the physical world, society, and the types of living creatures were seen as subject to change. That new frame of mind made possible the American and French Revolutions and the Industrial Revolution as well. People were open to new ways of doing things. They didn't expect to live and work the same way their parents had, nor did they expect their children to follow in their footsteps.

Hegel articulated the general theory that change rather than stasis is the nature of reality. He saw dynamic processes at work in history and in the clash and development of ideas. Marx applied that concept to economics and the structure of society. Charles Lyell applied it to geology. Charles Darwin and his rival Charles Russell Wallace simultaneously came to the conclusion that species change over time.

Unfortunately, by twisted logic, many concluded that, if the human species is subject to change, everyone is not "created equal." Some are at "higher" stages of evolutionary development than others. Some are "low brow," others "high brow." Social class has a biological component.

The Civil War ended slavery, but didn't change the beliefs that had been used to justify it. Instead, concepts of evolution, phrenology, and eugenics provided pseudo-scientific justification for racial discrimination. And legends about Sigfried "the Dragon Slayer" and Brunhild (our ancestor), transformed by Wagner, got intertwined with beliefs about the greatness and destiny of the "Aryan race" and were used to partially justify the Holocaust.

Since then, the Zeitgeist has changed again. In the United States and most of the western world, laws support equality and suppress discrimination based on race and religion. But a residue of old beliefs still persists as prejudice. My hope is that the concept of "One Family," with its roots in religion, legend, and science, will prevail, and racism will be left in the dustbin of history.

Part Five:
Lies

Gettysburg College

Dad was the second of four boys. Their parents proudly introduced them at church each Sunday, telling everybody that all four would become Lutheran ministers. Dad's father's father, and his father, and the father before that had been Lutheran. Religion was as much a matter of family as it was of belief. Lutheran was the dominant religion of the Pennsylvania Dutch in the region around Palmyra and Gettysburg where the American branch of this Seltzer family originated. Politics, too — they all voted straight Republican, regardless of the candidates and their platforms.

Gettysburg College had a Lutheran pre-ministerial program. So that's where Dad went. He was a history buff, especially American history, and the college was near the battlefield. He loved that school and later wished that I would go there or at least one of my four children would. But he didn't push. That wasn't his nature. Often silence proved more convincing than words, but not in this case.

At the end of his freshman year, in the spring of 1942, Dad was kicked out. Once, in a rare reminiscent mood, he told me what happened.

This was the first time he had been away from home. The temptations were many, and his grades were poor; but the main reason he was expelled was a bawdy play that he wrote, directed and acted in at his fraternity.

He was expelled the semester after Pearl Harbor. He knew that if he did nothing, he'd be drafted, and he'd have to go into battle beside other draftees, ne'er-do-wells he wouldn't want to trust with his back. So he enlisted.

His older brother, Phil, enlisted as well and ended up in combat in Okinawa. Phil survived, dutifully became a Lutheran minister, and moved to Ohio, where his six children and their children continue to thrive.

When my youngest, Tim, was failing in his freshman year of college, I told him the story of his grandfather, who after getting kicked out of one college, graduated from another, and eventually became a superintendent of schools. I thought that was an inspiring tale. Important lessons learned from failure can be passed on to future generations.

Dad had had his stroke and couldn't speak. But he had written an autobiography. He intended it for the immediate family and handed out photocopies. Surely, he must have written about this critical moment in his life.

He did, but I was surprised and disappointed to find that he had sanitized the story. He said he dropped out on purpose, to enlist, as his patriotic duty. He wasn't proud to have succeeded despite his early mistakes. He was ashamed he had been kicked out. He wished it had never happened and didn't want anyone to know about it.

No one can learn from your mistakes if you bury them.

Michael Seltzer, Revolutionary Hero

Dad loved history. He taught it before he became a school administrator. The American Revolution was a specialty of his. His grandfather, Henry Hocker Seltzer, wrote an autobiography, which he updated frequently to cover new events in his life and to reevaluate what he had said before. Henry Hocker also collected information about his Seltzer ancestors.

So when Mom got into the Daughters of the American Revolution with her newly-found Tennessee family, Dad, using what his grandfather had uncovered, quickly found a Seltzer ancestor who could get him into the Sons of the American Revolution.

Dad's great-great-great-grandfather, Michael Seltzer, arrived in Philadelphia in 1752 from what is now Germany. He came with his father and settled in Pennsylvania Dutch country. In 1778 Michael signed the Oath of Allegiance to the American Colonies. In 1782, he served as a soldier of the third class in Company 7 of the 9th Battalion of Lancaster County, under Captain Bradley and Lieutenant Adam Mark. He never saw action.

Dad assembled all the necessary documentation, and his application was soon accepted.

But, as I learned decades later, using Ancestry.com and other online resources, "Seltzer" is a common Pennsylvania Dutch name. At the time of the Revolution, there were more than a dozen Michael Seltzers living in that vicinity, from different families. There is no way to know which Michael signed that document of allegiance. It could have been Dad's Michael or someone else's. Dad wasn't motivated to delve any deeper. If it was true enough for the SAR, it was true enough for him. He was proud of his revolutionary ancestor and got many years of social pleasure from his membership in the SAR.

Pebbles

In the early 1960s, *The Flintstones* was a TV sensation. In that cartoon depiction of our stone age ancestors, Fred and Wilma Flintstone and their friends Barney and Betty Rubble face modern challenges in stone-age circumstances. Much of the humor comes from the realization that the more things change, the more they stay the same. Starting in 1962, *The Jetsons*, produced a similar effect using a space-age future.

In 1963, Wilma was pregnant; and the production company, Hanna-Barbera, held a contest to name the baby. The prize would be a round-the-world trip plus $2000 in spending money. The winning name was "Pebbles." Mom, Dad, and I kicked ourselves many times. That was the name we'd given our pure-bred Dalmation. We had lost him five years before. (The breeding was important to Mom. She paid many times the price of an ordinary dog to have one with "papers" proving his line of descent).

Mom and Dad got Pebbles for me when I was seven. He was my best friend; no, closer than that — he was my brother. He slept with me, and I told him everything that mattered to me. Like Mom talking to Dad, when she had Alzheimer's and he couldn't talk at all, I had so much to say to him that it didn't matter that Pebbles couldn't reply.

Because of his breeding, Pebbles had a congenital bone problem. About once every six months, a shin bone would become detached from its thigh bone, and he would bark frantically in agony, hobbling in circles, dragging the unattached piece. The vet would put the pieces back together, like popping a dislocated shoulder into place, and Pebbles would be like it had never happened. But the problem was incurable.

In Rockville, we had a chain link fence around the backyard. That was his domain, including the huge hill with the swing set on top. When we moved to the suburbs of Baltimore we didn't have a fence. Our newly-built house was on the edge of a woods. I caught crayfish in the creek (not to keep, just for the fun of catching them) and found Indian arrowheads nearby. This was the Wild East, a boyhood paradise.

But a neighbor had a Great Dane. It was nearly as tall as I was, probably weighed three times as much as me, and was far faster than me. If I was alone on the front lawn, maybe having just biked home from school, this monster would come bounding toward me, drooling, looking like he wanted me for a snack. I'd scream. Mom would open the door, and Pebbles would rush to my rescue, making up for his lack of size with his fearlessness and determination. The Great Dane would retreat, whimpering all the way home. I would never play outside without Pebbles at my side.

One day when I was ten, Pebbles and I were on the edge of the woods, and a kid my age who I had never seen before came biking by. Seeing Pebbles, the boy yelled and waved his foot, taunting him. Pebbles responded by barking and chasing. The boy laughed and kicked at him. Then Pebbles nipped him on the thigh, and the boy stopped his nonsense and rode away at full speed.

The next day, having heard from the boy's parents, Dad took Pebbles away. He told me that he was going to give him to a nice family in the country who had lots of space for Pebbles to run around in. Pebbles would be happier there.

I suspected Dad was lying. I pleaded with him not to take Pebbles away, not to have him killed. Dad insisted that Pebbles would be fine, that this would be best for him. But I couldn't visit Pebbles — not then, not ever. And Dad wouldn't give me the address or phone number of the new owner, so I couldn't ask for photos of Pebbles in his new home. Mom told the same story. She was lying, too. I wasn't just losing my best friend, my brother, I was also losing my parents. If they lied to me about that, what else would they lie to me about?

I cried myself to sleep every night for weeks.

Panther, Thunder, and Death

I won't tell the story of the guppies and how my daughter saw one give birth, not dropping eggs, but live tiny fish swimming out of her. And I won't tell about Big Frog, who we brought back from the Cape as one of half a dozen tadpoles; how the others disappeared, and we didn't know why until one morning we saw the hind legs of the last of them sticking out of Big Frog's mouth. And I'll say nothing about the Fric and Frac, and how upstairs became an entangled maze of tubing connecting gerbil cages. (I already told that in the story "Hundreds and Hundreds of Gerbils," which you can read at seltzerbooks.com/gerbils.html.) And I won't tell you about our cats — Wally, Patches, and George — and their unique personalities. But I have to mention Panther, our black Labrador, who died at the age of 16 — 112 in dog years. (I could have sworn that he lived to 20, like

Odysseus' Argos. But the vet's records set me straight. I can't trust my memory.)

We lived in Boston, at 33 Gould Street, a house that we bought for $30,000 in 1977, when our daughter was born, and that is now listed at $993,000 at Zillow. I built a five-foot-high picket fence to keep Panther contained in the backyard. That worked fine except in thunderstorms. At the sound of thunder, he became a super creature and leaped high over that fence and ran for miles in fear. I suspect Odin deliberately targeted our neighborhood to watch Panther leap.

Normally, when the storm ended, Panther would find his way home; and we'd hear him scratching at the front door. But, once, we got a call from a passing motorist five miles away on Route One, who had run into him, head on, during a blinding cloud burst. Panther was still alive, but his skull was cracked. Miraculously, he survived, but he was more subdued after that.

He lived for a few more years; but being less active, he put on weight; until, combined with weakness from his advanced age, he could no longer stand. We took him to the vet. Nothing could be done. The vet said Panther was in agony, that we should "put him down." That was the first time that Barb and I had to confront death directly. I hadn't been with Pebbles when he died.

Barb and I were on either side of Panther when the vet gave him the lethal injection. We hugged him tightly, and I lied to him that it would be all right, that he'd get better, that he'd once again chase squirrels in the backyard, that I'd take him for frequent walks like I'd always meant to but hadn't found time for. Then he wasn't there anymore. I was still holding him, but that black body wasn't him. He didn't exist.

The Immaculate Deception

Lies need not be bad. Sometimes the end does justifies the means, and the means don't corrupt the end; not just when talking to the dying, but also during war, when victory may depend on deception.

Despite his never-tell-a-lie reputation, George Washington (cousin of our Warner ancestors) was a master of deception, and that skill of his was crucial in winning the war. He arrived in Boston in the summer of 1775, a year before the Declaration of Independence, but after Concord, Lexington, and Bunker Hill. He had nothing to do with the fighting in Massachusetts.

Most members of the Continental Congress didn't want war. They hoped and expected England would agree to reasonable terms. Assembling a make-shift army with Washington in charge was a preventive measure, to dissuade the British from punishing the colonists of Massachusetts for opening hostilities. Both sides were holding fire, waiting for diplomacy to resolve their differences.

Washington's small force of farmers and tradesmen was facing an army of professional soldiers. There was no telling how long the negotiations between the Continental Congress in Philadelphia and the British government in London would drag on. In good weather, it took six weeks for a message to go from the one place to the other.

When Washington arrived in Boston, he learned that his forces had just three rounds of gun powder per soldier. That deficiency was a closely held secret. If the British had known, they could have wiped out the colonists with ease. Washington acted as though nothing were amiss. He had his troops build fortifications on the hills around Boston and patrol the ramparts as if ready for battle.

The local farmers had little gunpowder to spare. They did their best to tool up to produce more, but that took time. The southern colonies sent some, but too little; and it took too long to arrive. Piracy helped. Privateers, empowered to prey on British shipping, captured whatever military supplies they could. But that, too, was slow and uncertain. So Washington kept up his charade, tricking the British into thinking that he was well-supplied and that they were in imminent danger.

He bluffed and won with a losing hand. The British never attacked. And they cleared out a year later, on March 17, a date that Boston still celebrates as "Evacuation Day."

Five years after that, in 1781, he did more of the same, on a grand scale. General Clinton, in command of the British forces in America, had his headquarters in New York City. Washington commanded a small force, mostly untrained recruits. Volunteers would come and go, heading home when they wanted to plant or harvest or deal with family matters. Now that France had entered the war as an ally, Washington had a French detachment as well, under Rochambeau. The French joined forces with Washington in White Plains, near New York City. A French squadron would soon set sail from Rhode Island, heading for New York as well.

Clinton intercepted dispatches from Washington confirming plans for attack and prepared accordingly. Maybe those dispatches were decoys, or maybe Washington, learning they had been intercepted, changed his plans. His army was far smaller and weaker than Clinton presumed. Moreover, news had arrived that additional Hessian mercenaries would soon join the British. So instead of attacking New York, Washington marched to Virginia — 680 miles. Meanwhile, the French squadron in Rhode Island headed south to join a French fleet already in Chesapeake Bay and to bring additional troops for Washington in Virginia.

Washington left behind a skeleton force in the outskirts of New York to keep up the appearance that his army was still there and ready to attack. Young and old marched back and forth on the ramparts of forts, carrying broomsticks or whatever else could look like guns from a distance.

The march to Virginia took fourteen weeks, but that whole time Clinton believed Washington was near at hand and ready to attack. He even sent orders to Cornwallis in Virginia to send troops north to defend New York, when, in fact, Cornwallis was about to be cut off from the sea by the French fleet and defeated on land by Washington at Yorktown.

Checkmate.

Mercy Otis Warren

That anecdote about Washington is based on a passage from *The Rise, Progress and Termination of the American Revolution* by Mercy Otis Warren, the first American woman historian. She was probably an ancestor of Jean, my college girlfriend, who recently passed away.

I chanced upon Mercy when doing research for a bicentennial play I was writing. Mercy had written a play, *The Blockheads*, as a mocking response to *The Blockade of Boston* by Burgoyne, a general with the British forces blockaded by Washington's troops in 1775. Burgoyne wrote and staged his play to occupy his idle and bored troops. In the middle of the first performance, a soldier ran into the theater shouting, "The rebels are coming!" The audience, thinking that was brilliant stagecraft, burst into applause. But, in fact, there was the threat of a skirmish. Two years later, when he lost the Battle of Saratoga and was captured, Burgoyne was allowed to return to England on "parole," having given his word, as a gentleman, that he would no longer participate in the war. He left the army and competed with Sheridan as one of the most popular playwrights on the London stage. I brought Mercy and Burgoyne together in my play *Mercy, or a Puritan Revolutionary*.

Two decades later, I typed Mercy's entire three-volume history of the Revolution (1317 pages). It had been out of print since its first and only printing in 1805. The Boston Public Library had it in open stacks. I could check it out. It was in pristine condition. It may never have been borrowed before. The antique typography (*ss* looked like *ff*), combined with outdated spelling and run-on sentences made it hard to read. I could force myself to decipher a paragraph or two, but then my mind would wander. Typing it would force me to concentrate and pay attention to every word, and I could edit for readability as I went along. The project cost me two months of my "spare time," but it was well worth the effort. I posted the book for free on my personal website and added it to my collection of books on DVD. You can read it and all her plays at seltzerbooks.com/warren

Mercy knew many of the participants in the Revolution and had unique insight into what happened and why. If her history had been widely read when first published, it might have reshaped the infant nation's self-image. It deserved an audience.

In her day, women didn't write history books, the only exception being Catherine Macaulay in England, with whom Mercy corresponded and who visited her after the war. Mercy's verbiage was pompous, perhaps deliberately mimicking Gibbon's history of Rome, the first volume of which had been published in 1776. She would rather state her conclusions than provide the first-hand accounts on which she based them. Her personal voice came through loudly toward the end, when she urgently expressed concern for the survival and future of the young republic.

She deplored Washington's dependence on his military cronies while president. And she severely criticized her life-long friend, John Adams, for losing faith in democracy and favoring monarchy instead. She came to that conclusion in 1801, just after the end of Adams' term as president. She feared that civil war might break out between those who believed in the principles of equality as stated in *The Declaration of Independence*, and those who revered aristocratic privilege, titles, and life style. In her day, the primary political divide was between those who, like her, believed in the Republic as a moral, even a religious necessity, and those who saw it as a temporary expedient. To Mercy, the American experiment in democracy was a beacon to the world, a shining example that could lead all peoples to free themselves from the tyranny that kept them in misery, poverty, and slavery.

Men like Adams responded to the French Revolution of 1789 with fear and loathing. Reports of that blood-fest convinced them that democracy is fundamentally flawed, that, at best, it's a temporary solution. Mercy cited with disdain and disappointment Adams' book *Defense of Their Constitutions*, which "drew a doleful picture of the confusion and dissolution of all republics".

In her 1317 pages, she didn't mention the undeclared war which Adams waged on the seas against republican France. She also neglected to mention his Alien and Sedition Acts which, purportedly for public security, revoked much of the Bill of Rights. Rather, she focused on what she saw as more important and more insidious — Adams' love affair with monarchy. She thought he had taken a mistress (monarchy/aristocracy) while still ostensibly sleeping with his wife (republicanism/democracy).

She felt she had to alert the young Republic of that danger and nudge it in the right direction, so it would have a chance to survive and thrive in a world dominated by monarchs and dictators. She blamed Adams' five-year sojourn in England, as a diplomat, for having led to this change in his convictions.

Mercy wrote in the third person, trying to avoid personal bias, while advocating the republicanism she so ardently believed in. She didn't spare friends like Adams, or acquaintances like John Hancock, or public idols like George Washington. She called it as she saw it, not expecting people to be consistent and predictable. She treated her immediate family with that same impartiality: her brother James Otis (early advocate of the rights of colonists), her husband James Warren (speaker of the Massachusetts House of Representatives), and her son Winslow Warren (a would-be diplomat).

If my college girlfriend, Jean, hadn't had the last name "Otis," I probably wouldn't have paid attention when I chanced upon Mercy Otis Warren in the Boston Public Library, and the world of the American Revolution wouldn't have come to alive for me, and I wouldn't have written a novel about her and Burgoyne (*Parallel Lives*)

And if I hadn't heard that Jean recently died, I wouldn't have included this chapter in this book. (More on coincidence and fate later.)

By the way, Jean, like my mother, died of Alzheimer's.

A Coincidence that Didn't Happen

In *Parallel Lives*, I speculate that a slight change at the right moment could have made a big difference not just in Mercy Warren's life but in the struggle for the rights and equality of women. She could have become Senator Warren from Massachusetts and then the first woman president.

When Catherine Macaulay, the British historian, visited America after the Revolution, from 1784 to 1785, she spent a month with Mercy, then went to New York, Philadelphia, and Virginia to meet and interview major figures in the Revolution for a projected history, which she never got around to writing, due to illness. Mercy was also writing a history of the Revolution, but she was slow about it, interrupted by family crises. She didn't publish it until 1805, after John Marshall's *Life of George Washington* had appeared and been recognized as the standard work on the subject.

Imagine if Catherine, rather than return to England, stayed in America, encouraged Mercy to finish her book and helped her with it. Say her book was published long before Marshall's, in 1786, instead of 1805, and because of the timing, her book got wide-spread recognition. Then, with the help of members of the Massachusetts Legislature who knew and respected both Mercy and her husband, their Speaker, she was named to the Constitutional Convention. There she fought hard but unsuccessfully to give women the right to vote. She couldn't even win a compromise to let women have half a vote.

Instead, in both actual history and this alternative, *The Constitution* granted to the states the power to set voting requirements. In Massachusetts, you had to be a man over the age of 21 and have been a resident for a year preceding, with an annual income of three pounds or with an estate worth 60 pounds. But nothing in *The Constitution* explicitly prevented women from running for office and serving in Congress or even as president. Its writers never imagined such an eventuality, so they didn't prohibit it. The text specifying the qualifications for office used the word "person," not "man." ("No Person except a natural born Citizen... shall be eligible to the Office of President...")

In this alternate history, Mercy, aware of that loophole, didn't bring the issue up for debate. She was then selected by the Massachusetts Legislature as the one of the first two senators from Massachusetts. At that time, she would never have been elected by the populace at large, but she had many friends in the Legislature, and the Legislature decided who would be the first senators.

Then, because of her excellent service as a senator, the people of Massachusetts reelected her repeatedly. And in 1804, when Jefferson needed a running mate who would balance the ticket North/South, he chose her instead of Governor Clinton of New York, who was his choice, historically.

In 1808, in our alternate history, Warren became the first woman President, opening a path for those who came after her.

Lie-braries

I didn't have to lie. I didn't need to say a word to succeed as an imposter, at two different libraries. The guard at the entrance presumed I was a student. He didn't ask me. It was the first day of classes at MIT, and I was carrying a Russian-English Physics Dictionary. The next day and the days after that, he recognized me, smiled, and waved me in.

This was shortly after I got out of my active duty stint in the Army, before I decided what to do and where to do it. I was living out of my car and working freelance, translating Russian books about reinforced concrete, at a penny a word — the most boring job of my life. That's why I was carrying the dictionary.

The MIT Library was a quiet place to work, and it was warm. If I wanted to take a break, I was surrounded by books on all subjects. I expected to spend an afternoon, but the library was open 24 hours, every day, and some students stayed there all night. The sofas were comfortable. Why not? That was better than sleeping in my car. I stayed there for two weeks.

Writing this, I hear echoes of Mom saying that I could be the last log-cabin president. I could also be the first library president.

A couple of years later, doing research for an historical novel, I was able to get access to the stacks at Harvard's Widener Library. Alexander Bulatovich, the target of my research, was a Russian cavalry officer who travelled in Ethiopia around 1900 and wrote about his observations and experiences. I found Solomon, a Harvard undergraduate from the part of Ethiopia where Bulatovich had travelled, and Barb and I paid him to tutor us in Oromo, his native tongue. At that time, Amharic was the official national language, and it was illegal to write in Oromo; so there were no grammars or primers. Solomon wrote lessons for us as we went along. We hoped to travel to Ethiopia so I could get first-hand impressions of the place. The Ethiopian Revolution in 1974 made that trip impossible, so we were never able to use what we had learned of the language.

But Solomon's help still turned out to be crucial to my research. He had a student job working at the checkout desk at the Widener, and he let me into the stacks, as if I were a student there. That enabled me to discover dozens of books that were shelved near related books and that I'd have never found in the card catalogue. I photocopied the complete text of dozens of them at coin-operated machines downstairs. I'm still benefitting from those copies as I write sequels to the novel I was writing then —*The Name of Hero*.

Halloween

As a kid, Halloween was my favorite day of the year. I got to be someone else for a night. Fantasy became reality. I didn't care much about the candy. I got to be an Indian chief, a pirate, or Achilles in the Trojan War. Mom and Dad never bought me costumes or accessories. They made costumes for me, and I repurposed toys that I played with all the time.

Halloween traditions fill a need to break free of the place, time, and identity we're born with, to vicariously live alternate lives. On this occasion lies are good. Masquerade is a real-world way to identify with our favorite characters, to imagine what it would be like to be someone else. Professional actors must get a feeling like that. Even if they don't win fame and fortune, they get to live more than one life, to savor the experience of seeing the world through different eyes. I believe Dad felt that way. No part was too small for him. He would dive in completely, like when he grew a beard for a year and booked up on Civil War history and his Pennsylvania Dutch to get ready for a bit part in the movie *Gettysburg*.

When my kids were Halloween-age, newspapers, magazines and television shows warned repeatedly of the dangers. There could be pins, poison, or razor blades in the candy that strangers handed out. Don't let them go trick-of-treating. Instead, take them to parties with other kids in safe venues.

I didn't want to deprive my kids of what to me had been an important part of my childhood. I made them costumes and took them around the neighborhood, not just to the homes of people we knew, but to every house we could get to in two hours. I set them a goal of a hundred houses in that time. I kept count and they delightedly ran from one house to the next. They collected lots of candy, but that wasn't the object. They were into the experience for its own sake, and they ate very little candy because it was always gone by morning. No matter what we did to keep it away from our dog Panther, he would find it while we were asleep, and all but the wrappers would be gone by morning. We laughed about that, maybe congratulated Panther. And despite all the warnings that chocolate was bad for dogs, Panther loved it and thrived.

When Bob was nine and his sister seven, I made them PACman and Ms. PACman costumes out of poster board. Three-year old Mike was more spectator than participant. The weather was perfect, and for me that was the best Halloween ever. Later, I wrote an article for my website, praising Halloween and explaining the importance of preserving the tradition. Other websites and print publications picked it up.

Bob was bold, running ahead. His seven-year-old sister held back and was reluctant to approach houses of near neighbors she didn't know well; but curiosity and pride in showing off her homemade costume won out in the end, and she'd go racing after Bob up the walk, and be just as delighted as he at the smiles and words of praise and handfuls of candy that greeted them. Three-year-old Mike wouldn't let me put him down, but he wouldn't let me take him home either, watching all the doings intently.

The same as previous years, many of the people we visited were folks we only saw at Halloween, even though they lived just a few doors away. Most of them, the elderly especially, had bought supplies of candy and were waiting. They would give out two or three times as much per kid as they originally intended, because there were so few kids trick-or-treating. And they were as delighted to see the kids as the kids were to be seen.

Halloween used to be a way to deal with fears of death and ghosts and goblins by making fun of them. And in times of rigidly prescribed social behavior, it was an occasion when mischief was condoned — a time for misrule and letting loose. But although such elements still remain, the emphasis has shifted, and the importance of the day has grown.

Today, as in the 1980s, people often don't know their near neighbors, much less the neighbors a few blocks away. For little children, those strange houses and strange people are a source of fear and anxiety. Children have been taught not to trust or talk to strangers, to beware of them. But on Halloween that prohibition is lifted; and, with fear, but impelled by curiosity and greed for candy and other loot, little ones ring doorbells at houses of strangers to find time and again that these strangers are really friendly people, like the people they know well. In the course of the evening, they gain confidence in themselves and in their neighborhood and come away not only with bags full of candy to be enjoyed for weeks after, but also a warm feeling about their neighborhood and people in general.

As for adults, especially the elderly and those who haven't had kids at home for years or never had kids, children in the neighborhood can be a source of anxiety and distrust. What mischief and vandalism might this strange new generation be capable of? On Halloween night, their fears, too, are exorcised, as wildly and imaginatively costumed kids parade to the door, a reminder of what they themselves did as children.

By a ritual act of trade, Halloween can reconfirm the social bond of a neighborhood, particularly the bond between strangers of different generations. Children go to lengths to dress up and overcome their fear of strangers in exchange for candy. And adults buy the candy and overcome their distrust of strange children in exchange for the pleasure of seeing their wild outfits and vicariously reliving their own adventures as children.

The true value of Halloween comes not from showing off costumes in front of close friends and family, but from this interchange with strangers, reaffirming our social bond with the people of the neighborhood whom we rarely, if ever, see the rest of the year. It helps preserve our sense of fellowship and community with our neighbors. It makes us feel like we're all one family.

Dad's funeral

When Dad died in 2014, at the age of 91, I didn't attend his memorial service at Arlington National Cemetery where his ashes and those of Mom were laid to rest, and he was honored with the ceremony prescribed for a full colonel. I almost didn't mention that here, which would have been an instance of lying by omission.

Dad died because he couldn't swallow. If he couldn't swallow, he couldn't eat, and if he couldn't eat, he would die.

The nursing home sent him to a rehab hospital. But after a couple weeks, he showed no progress, and they couldn't keep him any longer. They could force-feed him through a tube, but that would be painful and was only a temporary solution. He was going to die, and I had to tell him that.

Parents are supposed to explain to their children the tough facts of life and death. But this time, it was my job to tell my Dad, and I wasn't prepared for it. I had no idea what death means to the dying, only what it means to the living left behind: Barb, my wife of 39 years, had died suddenly two years before. (More on that later).

I borrowed a copy of *The Bible* from a chaplain at the hospital. I didn't believe. Dad did. I knew it pained him that I didn't. Now I needed him to believe that I believed, if that would comfort him. I needed to lie, not explicitly, but through what I did and how I did it, to convey the truth, that I loved him and would miss him, by pretending for him that the end is not the end, that there is an afterlife. Barb was unconscious in her final hours. My only experience in talking to the dying had been when Barb and I held Panther and lied to him and felt his final quiver.

Dad's brother Paul, his only remaining brother, had given comfort to the dying all his life, first as a Lutheran minister, as his parents had hoped. He had the look, the tone, and the instincts to calm and reassure his parishioners in their final hours and to help their loved ones cope as well. But Paul was in Nova Scotia. There was no way he could come in time.

My sister Sallie called the minister of the church that Dad used to attend when he could go to church. He had periodically visited Dad during the years he was in the nursing home. He came. They bonded. I could take a step back from the cliff of death.

A few years before, I had taken Barb and our son Tim to the Southwest as tourists. At the Grand Canyon, I couldn't look down. The pull and the fear were visceral. I had never felt vertigo before. Sitting in the tourist center, behind a plate-glass window, more than a hundred feet from the cliff, I felt pulled toward it, nauseous and terrified. Barb and Tim felt nothing of the kind, calmly walking to the edge and admiring the view.

Dad was returned to the nursing home by ambulance. There he received hospice care. My sister and I visited often and long. He died soon after, during the night.

Mom had died four years before that. Sallie and I were the only relatives who lived nearby. Uncle Paul and local friends came for two memorial services, one at the church, the other at the nursing home. At both services, I read a version of the Bugle Boy story that I'm including in this book. The large meeting hall at the nursing home was overflowing with people he had connected with by smile and gesture and to whom he had never been able to talk.

Months later, Sallie heard that Dad had finally reached the top of the waiting list for a funeral ceremony at Arlington National Cemetery, with all the honors and trimmings that go with the rank of full colonel. (He had stayed in the Army Reserves since World War II and had risen in the ranks over the years). I couldn't face that. I had said goodbye to him twice already. Barb had died two years before and Mom two years before that. I didn't want to go through the pangs of grief that would be triggered by seeing the rows of crosses at Arlington, a scene like at the end of *Saving Private Ryan*. Dad and I had argued often about the Vietnam War. He had wanted me to go to Cub Scouts, Boy Scouts, and West Point. I had stopped at Cub Scouts. I had served in the Army Reserves as a Russian specialist as a way to avoid Vietnam. That war was wrong, inexcusable. I wanted nothing to do with the military, including military ceremonies. Besides, it was a long haul from Boston to Virginia.

Sallie went, as did dozens of our extended family, including my son Bob, his wife, and daughters. I should have been there for them. I wasn't.

Dad had made the final arrangements and had paid for them years before he died. Mom and he were cremated, and their ashes were sent to Arlington. That was where he wanted to be buried, not in a family plot. He was proud to have served his country, to have earned the right to be buried there.

If I had a chance to do it over, I would go. That was the right thing to do. Sorry, Dad.

Why am I telling this story here in the section about lies? In part, because of that deathbed moment, when I felt I had to make Dad believe that I believed. In part, because I almost didn't include this anecdote, like Dad not wanting to admit he was kicked out of college — a sin of omission.

One memory triggers another, and I follow the tangled trails of association, like surfing the web.

Perhaps a Touch of Infidelity

After taking early retirement at age 57, before he was old enough to collect Social Security, Dad needed to supplement his income. Eventually, he would collect pensions not just from Pennsylvania as a school superintendent, but also from the Army as a full colonel, and from two actors' unions, AFTRA and SAG. But there were a few lean years before those kicked in.

Sometimes he would work as a guide on bus tours of Pennsylvania Dutch country, including the site of the Battle of Gettysburg. Though I never got to see him in action, I can easily imagine him putting on his Pennsylvania Dutch accent, singing Schnitzelbank (which teaches children the German names of body parts like the French *Allouette*), and regaling his captive audience with family anecdotes and Civil War stories.

Dad loved doing that, but Mom made him stop. She didn't like sleeping alone, and she didn't want him to go on overnight excursions with dozens of senior ladies. Likewise, she insisted that he stop acting in stage plays, ostensibly because they didn't pay enough, and they left no time for better-paying gigs. Once again, the main reason was that he would be around other women. She was jealous.

At the time, they were in their late 50s and early 60s. To me, that seemed ancient. It was hard for me to imagine people that old having sex. Mom's jealousy seemed absurd, but also quaint and sweet, a testimony to their enduring attraction to one another.

When Dad had his stroke and had to move into the nursing home, Sallie and I had to clear out his assisted-living apartment. It was difficult deciding what to keep and what to toss, reminding us both that the day would come when others would go over our stuff; what was precious to us would mean nothing to them, as if a magic wand changed everything to trash.

I wound up with a suitcase of his. From tags on the handle, I guessed it dated to his days as a bus-tour guide. In an inside pocket, I found a package of colored, party condoms. Perhaps he wasn't always faithful to Mom. Perhaps she had good cause for jealousy.

We speak of the sex "act," and much of flirtation and attraction is a matter of acting. He might have been better at that than I imagined

People are people, with weaknesses as well as strengths. That's part of our common humanity.

But one slim piece of evidence can change your idea of someone, of who they are and whether to believe them.

Alzheimer's and Handholding

When they reached their 80s, Mom and Dad's disagreements grew more intense and less resolvable. She insisted that she didn't forget this or that. Her memory was perfect. Although she couldn't afford to go to college until late in life, she was proud of what she had learned at Girl's High School in Philadelphia, particularly Latin and Elocution (memorizing and performing speeches). In her run-ins with Dad over nothing and everything, she would assert that she was smarter than he, and he would accept that like a dog who was used to being whipped. She was as proud of my straight A's as if they had been hers. They confirmed her brilliance.

As she got older, senior moments often escalated to crises. She believed Dad was gas-lighting her, moving things so she couldn't find them, making her doubt her ability to think. Whatever she didn't remember was his fault, according to her convoluted logic.

By the time she was 89 and he 86, Dad had a hard time coping with the situation. She couldn't help around the house, and she continually berated him about one thing or another.

One day the police found her in her nightgown in the middle of Main Street at 3 AM, carrying a suitcase and wanting to catch a taxi to her home in Philadelphia. They were living in Boston at the time. The diagnosis was Alzheimer's.

The two of them moved into the assisted-living wing of a nearby facility that also had an Alzheimer's wing. They would live together until the Alzheimer's advanced to the point that she needed 24/7 nursing care.

Dad was Lutheran and very religious, as he had always been. There was nothing in *The Bible* to make sense of Alzheimer's. How can life mean anything if this is how it ends? And yet in the U.S. a third of everyone over the age of 85 has Alzheimer's or a similar condition.

Soon Mom had to be moved to the Alzheimer's wing. And soon after that, Dad had a stroke and needed to be moved to the nursing wing, down the hall from the sturdy locked door leading to where Mom was. Beside that door hung a sign listing the Alzheimer's Bill of Rights, including "The right to live in a world of your own."

Every day, Dad would wheel himself down that hall, lefthanded since his right side was paralyzed. He would enter the code and visit Mom. Often I would see them playing double solitaire. They would hold hands; she would talk incessantly; and he would smile. That went on for about two years until she died. But she never knew that he was crippled and couldn't talk. She was too busy talking to notice.

Infidelity Revisited

Often, over the course of my life, I was oblivious to the implications of my decisions when I made them. I was saved by my naivete and social ineptitude from going down what I now know was the wrong path. I was tempted by other women, both before and after my marriage. That I didn't get involved with or even marry someone totally incompatible, and that I didn't stray when married wasn't a moral choice. I was self-conscious and awkward. When opportunity arose, I clammed up and backed down. I couldn't come up with the words needed to start a conversation with an attractive stranger, but I was eloquent when imagining the scene after the opportunity had passed.

I suspect that Dad was like me in that regard, that he was tempted while doing his bus tours and brought along those condoms in case he "got lucky," but never used them. And he didn't think to throw them away, because he felt no guilt for what he hadn't done.

Handholding Revisited

I now believe I was wrong in my guess that when Mom played solitaire with Dad, she was too self-absorbed to realize Dad couldn't talk.

Due to Alzheimer's, Mom was losing not just the paths of association that enabled her to recall what she wanted when she wanted, but also her ability to truly speak. She could say words, many words; but mechanically, not expressing her feelings or her current thoughts. She was similar to Dad, who after his stroke couldn't use speech or writing to express his thoughts, wishes, or needs. He could copy words with his left hand, reproducing what he saw, and make sounds that approximated words, but he couldn't articulate what he wanted to say.

He could convincingly say "Yes," in answer to questions. But he gave that answer to every question, without thought, like a reflex. He also would sometimes say "true love," in a singsong voice, approximating the tune from the movie *Friendly Persuasion*. And he would sing snippets from showtunes that he and Mom used to sing together. He could also play the accompanying notes on the piano, awkwardly, with his left hand. But he couldn't say what he was thinking. He couldn't so much as ask for water when he was thirsty. His frustration was evident.

One day I chanced upon him in the TV room when *The Miracle Worker* was playing — the scene in which the young Helen Keller realizes that the sound "water" means what she feels pouring onto her hand. Things have names. She discovers language. Dad was in tears watching that.

Mom was losing but had not yet completely lost her ability to use language as a means of self-expression. It was increasingly difficult for her to connect what she was thinking or feeling with words. But she might have been able to express herself to Dad with her eyes, with a smile, with a touch, as he could. Her endless mechanical chatter about nothing wasn't communication. Perhaps Mom and Dad connected non-verbally, "devouring one another with their eyes."

Sallie remembers that she had meaningful conversations with Mom during her increasingly rare moments of lucidity. I would say that Dad's state precluded verbal conversation with him, and that Mom shifted to eye contact and fingertip contact when they were together, perhaps not knowing she was doing so. She chattered endlessly about everything and nothing as if he weren't there; but, at the same time, they connected directly with one another without the need for words.

Is that unrealistic? Wishful thinking? Perhaps. But that's what I want to believe.

I imagine a painting by Vermeer — a beam of light streams through the window, striking their hands clasped on the card table. Their eyes are locked.

Part Six:
Fate

Claire at Christmas in Brussels

"You were devouring her with your eyes." That's what Claire's sister said in an email to me, letting me know that Claire died of diabetes. She was describing me looking at Claire in a photo taken on Christmas day 1964 at their home in Waterloo, Belgium. I had fallen in love with her the evening before, when I saw her listening to a choir in the main square of Brussels, surrounded by medieval buildings, illuminated by spotlights, as heavy first snow redecorated the world.

That snow reminds me of the refrain in a poem by Francois Villon (1431-1463) — "Where are the snows of yesteryear?" A professional thief, Villon purportedly wrote his best poetry while in jail. Some critics say that the "snow" in that poem is a metaphor for beautiful women he had known. I believe he meant that the past is irretrievable; what's done can't be undone; and our memories fade like snow melting.

I was 18. It was Christmas vacation at Brentwood School, in Essex, near London, where I had landed through vain stupidity, instead of at a college in the U.S. I was biking through Belgium; and, after that, I planned to bike, alone, through Holland.

I arrived in downtown Brussels soon after sunset. The snow had just begun. The streets were blocked with traffic and the sidewalks with pedestrians headed toward the square from which I heard Christmas music. I had to walk my bike, had no map of the city, and didn't know where the youth hostel was. I hoped to find it before it closed for the night.

The driver of a delivery van on the street beside me frantically waved to me. I deciphered that he needed help delivering coffee to a nearby restaurant. He couldn't leave his van in the middle of the road. Would I carry the boxes in for him? I helped. He was grateful. The traffic started moving. He invited me to go with him to the square up ahead where his wife and daughters were listening to the choir. Why not?

Claire caught my eye immediately; and after a few minutes of introductory chatter, the family treated me like a long-lost relative. The setting was magical. I was in a dream that I didn't want to end. But I needed to get to the hostel. I asked for directions. Instead, they invited me to spend the night, Christmas Eve, at their home in the suburbs. By morning, the blessedly heavy snow was blocking the roads. I ended up staying three days. It felt like the beginning of an alternate life.

My French was passable. Two years before I had spent a summer in Paris and Strasbourg on a student exchange. Claire didn't speak English, so soon I found myself thinking and dreaming in French.

She had a twin sister, Collette, equally cute, but in a different way, whose interests were closer to mine. But I was focused on Claire and she on me; and for most of my time there, we were together. She introduced me to poems by Jacques Prévert and Paul Valéry, especially Valéry's love poem *Les Pas*. Here's my translation of it:

Steps
Your steps, born of my silence,
blessedly and slowly,

quietly and calmly
approach the bed where I await.

Pure being, divine spirit,
how sweet are your reluctant steps.
Muse! All your gifts
come to me on your naked feet.

If by extending your lips,
you prepare to sate
my starving mind
with the nourishment of your kiss,

Don't rush,
sweetness of being and not being,
for I have lived to wait for you
and my heart has been nothing but your steps.

After I returned to school in England, I wrote to her often and long. I even wrote her a poem in the style of Prévert, in French. Here's my translation:

Together
He wandered the streets,
alone and lost.
fog inside and out,
nothing but his hands in his pockets,
nothing but his heart in his head.
He looked for nothing everywhere.

She wandered the streets,
alone and lost,

fog inside and out,
nothing but her hands in her pockets,
nothing but her heart in her head.
She looked for nothing everywhere.

They met.
Now they stroll through the streets together,
clarity inside and out,
nothing but the world in their pockets,
nothing but one another in their heads.
They look for tomorrow together.

I had wanted to become an author. Now I wanted to become a French author, like Beckett, an Irishman who wrote in French.

I had fallen in love at first sight, like my parents said they did, for which I believed I was destined.

This was like an alternate life, not just glimpsed and hinted at, but lived. It was as if the train of my life had switched from one track to another.

But her letters came less and less frequently, then stopped. My train switched back to the original track.

Chicago

I had a similar switched-track experience when I was three months old.

Early in their marriage, Mom and Dad had different ideas of their future. After leaving the active-duty Army, Dad wanted to start an acting career. He was accepted at UCLA for their drama program, and the GI Bill would pay for it. So they headed West, over Mom's objections. It had been bad enough having to go wherever the Army sent him, giving birth to me in Clarksville, Tennessee, across the border from Dad at Fort Campbell in Kentucky.

They stayed at a ramshackle hotel in Venice, California, and looked for low-cost long-term housing. But over 16 million Americans had served in World War II, and many, like Dad, hoped to start a new life in California.

After two weeks, Mom concluded they would never find a place to live. She wanted to go "home to Philadelphia," to the only security she had ever known, her safe zone, the row house where she grew up with her sisters, where her old-maid aunts raised her. At the very least, she needed to live on the East Coast, not far from Philadelphia. Dad's dream wasn't her dream, so he had to give up his.

They argued about everything. All they had in common was their child, three months old, and they lost him — me — in Chicago on the way back East. Dad wrote about this in his autobiography.

They couldn't afford Pullman accommodations, so they had to sleep sitting up. Food in the dining car was expensive. They were exhausted, hungry, and cranky when the train pulled into Chicago for an hour-long stop. At last, they'd be able to get sandwiches, snacks, and drinks. They argued over who would go and who would stay with me. A friendly porter offered to watch me while they both went; so they did, delighted to stretch their legs, and relieved that at least that argument had an ending.

When they came back, the train was gone. They had lost their baby. Who loses a baby in a train station? Who leaves their baby with a stranger? Each blamed the other, loudly, angrily, as they raced around trying to find out what had happened, how they could get word to the train that had left, when the next train would leave. For an hour, they were frantic and frazzled.

Then they learned that the train had been shunted to another track. It hadn't left yet. I was smiling and laughing in the arms of the porter when they found me.

I suspect that, early in their marriage, the rhythm of arguing and then passionately making up became an addiction. But over the course of their sixty-six-year marriage, the pain of arguing came to outweigh the pleasure of making-up.

Whatever the ostensible cause of this disagreement or that, there was an implication of betrayal, not just of one another, but of an ideal they both believed in. How could they be so at odds with one another? Theirs was love-at-first-sight, true love: fated, blessed. That it had deteriorated to the point of them making life hell for one another was a desecration of the gift they had been given.

Unpardonable Ingratitude

It hadn't occurred to me to bike through Europe. By chance, a classmate, who had never crossed paths with me but knew that I was an American, sought me out at his father's insistence and invited me to dinner. The father, Mr. Wooten, was grateful for what America did for England in World War II. He intended his kindness to me as partial payback for that. When he heard that I wanted to go to the continent over Christmas vacation but couldn't afford train or plane fare and was scared to hitch hike, he suggested biking and targeting Belgium and Holland, where the ground is flat and many residents bike everywhere. He offered to lend me his son's new bike. I accepted.

On my return from falling in love-at-first-sight with Claire, I was so wrapped up in myself that I didn't return the bike I had borrowed. It had a flat tire, and I didn't get it fixed. And I didn't tell the owner, my classmate, that I was back. And I didn't arrange to return it to him. To add to the insult, I still can't remember his first name.

I was shocked when he pounded on my door a week after I got back to school. I had completely forgotten him and my obligation to him.

Hitch Hiker's Guide to the Galaxy

Although I never met him, Douglas Adams was a student at Brentwood School when I was there. He wrote the *Hitch Hiker's Guide to the Galaxy*, a BBC radio series that became a "trilogy of five books" and was eventually made into a movie. The radio series was the best telling of the tale. I recorded the episodes on cassette tape and played them to my son Bob on our long drives to his school.

Adams also wrote episodes of *Dr. Who* and its sequel *Torchwood*. In *Torchwood*, extraterrestrial aliens first arrived on Earth in 1965. I take pride in the fact that in 1965 I was the alien at Brentwood.

Memories of Camelot

Threads of association tie together history, genealogy, literature, and personal memories.

I saw the musical *Camelot* on stage in London in the spring 1965. Richard Burton played Arthur. Julie Andrews was Guinevere. Robert Goulet was Lancelot. That was my first "real" date. I was self-conscious and clueless and paid little attention to what happened on stage.

For the first 18 years of my life, I was an only child. I had gone to an all-boys high school in New Hampshire, and was then at Brentwood, an all-boys school in England. Girls were a different species. I had no idea how they thought, how to talk to them, what they wanted, what they meant. I had a lot to learn, a lot of awkward moments to go through. I now wonder what alternate paths my life might have taken if I had grown up with a sister or many sisters, how that experience would have changed me.

I had spoken to Lindsay before, but not much. Wanting to meet girls, I had joined the Brentwood drama club. They were doing a joint production with a nearby girls school. Lindsay played the lead. I played a guard who, in a few scenes, stood in the background and didn't say a word. The play was Webster's *Duchess of Malfi.* (My only previous stage experience was as the Troll Under the Bridge in a nursery school performance of *The Billy Goats Gruff.*)

When my parents came over to tour England during my spring break (bringing my year-old sister Sallie and a babysitter for her), they offered to buy me two tickets to the play of my choice so I could take a date. I asked Lindsay. She said yes. This was a big occasion for both of us. She too had never been on a "real date." She wore a low-cut dress, probably bought for the occasion. She looked smashing, especially the parts of her I hadn't seen before.

We settled into our seats, scanned the playbill, enjoyed the overture. I remember the opening scene, but nothing else from the show on stage. Our performance in the second balcony was far more memorable.

I had "fallen in love at first sight," with Claire in Brussels four months before this. But that had faded into the distant past, like the snows of yesteryear.

Lindsay and I held hands, tingles shooting from finger tip to finger tip. For me, who had never kissed a girl, holding hands romantically was a rare sensuous experience. Our hands were resting on her left thigh when she leaned forward, far forward, so far forward that her breast brushed against the back of my hand. The balcony was dark, but lights could have been shining brightly. I was oblivious to anyone around us, to anything else in the world but the touch of her breast on the back of my hand.

Our eyes didn't meet. We didn't whisper a word to one another. We both stared fixedly at the stage, as if entranced by the show. But as she leaned still further forward, she withdrew her hand, and I cupped and caressed her breast. Then my hand was inside the cleavage of her dress, flesh to flesh, finger tip to nipple, and she continued to lean far forward, welcoming my touch. Aside from the motion of my fingertips, we didn't move for the duration of the performance, nor did we say a word to one another, even during intermission.

Afterward, I accompanied her by train to Brentwood. There at the station, we kissed, as passionately as Lancelot and Guinevere. I was 19.

Wakeup Punch

A chain of unlikely events led me to Brentwood School. I suspect that if we had full knowledge, we could trace any event that's significant to us back along a sequence of unlikely happenings, all the way to childhood, even to birth and beyond that, all the way to the beginning of humankind.

This thought echoes Thomas Aquinas' argument that everything has a cause; every event or action is the result of another; so there must have been a first cause; and God is that first cause.

For this causal sequence, let's start in Plymouth, New Hampshire. In 1958, I was a newcomer, having moved there from Baltimore. Dad, whose acting ambitions had been thwarted by Mom, had pursued a career in education and was now Dean of Instruction at Plymouth State Teachers College.

I was in the eighth grade and presumed that next fall I'd go to the high school in town, with my classmates. Mom and Dad had other ideas.

At that time, the high school in Plymouth was academically weak. Dad wanted me to go to West Point or Gettysburg. Mom was hoping for an Ivy, Princeton if possible. They both wanted me to go to Holderness, a boarding school across the river. I would be a day student, probably the only one from Plymouth.

I wasn't thinking about college. I had friends here in Plymouth, and school was easy. At Holderness, by definition, it would be hard. And that was an all-boys school — unimaginable!

My parents wanted me to sleep on it. I had. There was no way I was going to Holderness. I'd tell them that when I got home from school.

I took a shortcut through the field of uncut weeds beside an abandoned hotel, the Pemigewasset House, where Hawthorne had died nearly a hundred years before. The only other historical landmark in the town was the library building, which once served as the court house where Daniel Webster tried and lost his first case.

It was a friendly town, about the size as the one in Thornton Wilder's *Our Town*. The phone service was party-line. The phone numbers were three-digits long, and you had to go through an operator to call anywhere else. The town published a calendar once a year. For 25 cents, they'd list your birthday so neighbors would know and could celebrate with you.

I loved that town. There was no way I'd abandon it for the snobby school across the river, filled with boys from Massachusetts whose parents didn't want them at home.

I had gone for an interview and hadn't said much, but I had memorized a list of hateful details that I could throw at Mom and Dad in my impassioned defense. I wouldn't go. That was final.

Then out of nowhere, a seventh grader confronted me in the middle of the field. I had seen him around but had never spoken to him. There was nothing special about him, for good or ill. We had probably played together on empty lots, in pickup games of baseball or football. He stood in my path and didn't step aside when I got close.

Without warning, he slugged me hard in the jaw. I collapsed. He walked away. Neither of us said a word.

That was a wakeup punch.

This wasn't my town.

I was an outsider and always would be. I belonged across the river where I'd be a stranger among strangers, competing for grades, for entrance into the best colleges.

I had been a passenger in a car or on a train, going wherever it took me. Now I was in the driver's seat, with my hands on the wheel.

I didn't hear a bugle call. I didn't hit the jackpot. But because of a random act of unkindness, I would go down a different life-path.

Later I learned that my wakeup puncher was named Bob. And Bob became the name of my first child, who is now helping me edit this book. He was named for Barb's brother who died in Vietnam.

Names can lead to random associations. Mom was named Helen, as in Helen Keller.

Sometimes hearing a familiar name in a new context makes me feel like a ball in a pinball machine, bouncing from one association to another, sparking one memory after another and another.

Seeing an actor who I saw in another movie connects those movies in my mind. And the story of any movie reminds me of books with similar characters or plots. Like *Sommersby* with Richard Gere and

Jodie Foster, set in Tennessee where Mom's ancestors came from and where I, by chance, was born, reminds me of *The Return of Martin Guerre* with Gerard Despardieu, which was based on a story by Dumas. And the imposter plots of those stories call to mind Odysseus arriving home in Ithaca disguised as a beggar and toying with the idea of seducing his wife while she doesn't know who he is, as a test of her fidelity.

Everything that happens is connected to everything else that happens, like everyone having the same ancestors.

I'm reminded of the movie *Six Degrees of Separation*, with Will Smith, based on the premise that everyone on Earth is connected by acquaintance with everyone else, by a chain of at most six people.

In 1918, when the Spanish flu struck, two years before Mom was born and five years before Dad, the population of the world was 1.8 billion. Twenty-eight years later, when I was born, it was 2.3 billion. Eighteen years after that, when I graduated from Holderness, it was 3 billion. Now, in 2024, it's 8 billion. But the connections of everyone to everyone else still apply. In Disney's words, "It's a small world, isn't it?"

So by tangled patterns of association, the rapidly growing small world we live in includes all of the past and all of the future, both what we think is fiction and what we think is real.

And Thornton Wilder, who wrote *Our Town*, which captured the essence of Plymouth, which I thought was my town, went to Yale, where I went after Holderness, after Brentwood, after Claire.

How Not to Apply to College

At Holderness, I was focused, driven. If grades were what mattered in life, I would get the best, and I did. When it came time to apply for college, the adviser told me I could have my pick.

The school's regular college advisor was on leave as head alpine coach for the U.S. Ski Team at the 1964 Olympics. The stand-in knew me well. He had been my English teacher for three years. But he had no experience in college advising.

Prompted by Mom, I said I wanted to go to Princeton, which for someone from Philadelphia was the height of prestige. One student from last year's class got in there with a C average and nothing that would make his application stand out. I should have no problem. But still, I should apply to one other college as a safety. He suggested Williams.

In my interview at Williams, I was righteously honest, telling them that Princeton was my first choice.

This was in the days before early decision and early acceptance. Everybody learned their fate in late April or early May.

Both colleges rejected me.

It turned out that the C-student who got into Princeton the year before was a Dupont on his mother's side.

So I had no college to go to, and it was too late to apply anywhere else for the following fall. Somebody at Holderness suggested that I go to school in England for a year. He knew someone who arranged for Americans to do that; and, even with travel expenses, the cost would be less than a year of college in the U.S. Also, college in England was three years, not four. The final year of their secondary school would be comparable to freshman year at college in the U.S. And I could apply again to U.S. colleges from there.

I didn't hesitate when offered such an opportunity. From living with my parents in a small town in New Hampshire, I found myself in a suburb of London on my own.

And if it hadn't been for that, I wouldn't have spent Christmas vacation biking through Belgium and Holland. I'd have never met Claire and fallen in love and, ever so briefly, tasted an alternate life.

With Luck Like That

Uncle Adolph enters with a flourish — Dad's uncle, Nana's brother, the black sheep of the Daly family. He would have been a good match for Aunt Annie Jane, if they had ever met.

I never met him; but, in legend, he was bigger than life — showman, entertainer, gambler, trickster; a W.C. Fields. I imagine him as a ringmaster. I'm reminded of Dad in his role as Ringmaster in the pilot for the educational TV series *Reading Rainbow* and in his acting headshots, posed as judge, scientist, chef, cowboy, golfer.

On the wall beside my desk hangs a photo of Adolph in his World War I army uniform, sitting on a camel, with the Sphinx and Pyramids behind him. Next to that hangs a similar photo of me on camelback, in front of the Pyramids, seventy years later. And 2000 years before that, Julius Caesar probably posed for a sketch artist at that same spot.

With field promotions, probably for valor in battle, Adolph rose to the rank of captain at the age of 23. When the war ended, he toured the Mediterranean, in uniform, claiming he was on a special diplomatic mission.

Dad's brother, my Uncle Paul, called Adolph "Mr. Big," and wrote about him in *Life Lessons*, a book of memoir anecdotes that I published for him as an ebook. (His style in that book influenced my style in this). Paul recorded that the machine-gun unit Adolph was with took refuge for the night in a farmhouse. Because he was late getting back, there was no room for him, so he slept in the barn. That night a German artillery shell made a direct hit on the farmhouse, killing everyone inside. Only Adolph, in the barn, survived.

Adolph could have figured he owed his life to the sacrifice of that band of brothers who died in the farmhouse. But he wasn't predisposed for such belief. Rather, he came out of that experience with the confidence and bluster of a natural-born winner. With luck like that, no wonder he became a gambler.

Paul described him, "His voice is big. His laugh is loud and infectious. His gestures are wide and flailing. He is the 'alpha' in his pack of eight brothers and sisters. He's the consummate glad-handing-could-have-been-politician type with a quick pleasantry for everyone who comes within his range... He drives around in a big black 1936 Buick, with pull-down tasseled shades."

Paul continued, "Uncle Adolph is hard working. Family is important. He takes charge of the family summer home in Colonial Beach, Virginia. You can often see him cutting the barley grass, white-washing and pruning the fruit trees, repairing and painting, cleaning the outhouse, caulking the rowboat, frying a barrel of chicken for a big crowd, chortling while washing the dishes and having a cigar."

At the Daly summer cottage across the street from the Potomac River, the storage area preserved Adolph's memorabilia — hundreds of picture postcards from that Mediterranean trip of his, plus his military gear that I played with as a boy and that Did did, too, in his day, imagining combat, digging trenches on the beach or lying prone among the pine trees in the grove by the river, with a toy rifle or a broomstick and maybe a stack of clam shells or apples to throw like hand grenades.

After Adolph returned home from Europe in triumph, he went to the Wharton School of Business, where he was a big man on campus. And after graduation, he became a big man at race tracks — from New Jersey to Florida — a professional gambler, a smoker and chewer of expensive cigars. Generous and outgoing when luck was with him, he treated everyone at the bar and bought gifts for his nephews — wagons and pop guns, bicycles, even a goat cart with a goat to pull it. He'd join the boys in their play, digging trenches with them, teaching them how to march and about-face and salute, advising them on how to aim their toy rifles, and regaling them with anecdotes of war. Those visits were rare because good luck was rare. But his influence on Dad was strong, and on me as well, by induced personal magnetism.

According to Paul, a cousin visited Uncle Adolph in Florida in the late 1960s and found him with deteriorating health, barely surviving on Social Security. He died alone in 1973, discovered by his landlord.

I made Adolph the main character in my novel *To Gether Tales*, as the self-appointed master of ceremonies at an eight-person dinner table on a cruise ship. He orchestrates the performances of his fellow travelers, who share stories with one another, like in Bocaccio's *Decameron*. The book's narrator recounts the backstories of the diners as well as the stories they tell, nostalgically remembering the carefree socially exuberant pre-COVID way of life and wondering if it will ever return, or if it's lost, like the snows of yesteryear.

Dreams Can Be Contagious

Among the military gear that Uncle Adolph left at the summer cottage was a bugle. It now sits on my desk, behind a computer monitor. I used that bugle as a prop when I told Dad's bugle-boy story at his memorial services.

I believe Dad taught himself how to play the bugle like he later taught himself the saxophone. I imagine him running along the beach, jumping over the dead fish that had drifted ashore from the weapons testing at the Dahlgren Naval Base across the river, and practicing military bugle calls. Dad's boyhood war games, with brothers and friends, using Adolph's gear, prompted his patriotic ideas and dreams of personal heroism that shaped his response to World War II.

When the war broke out, Dad was a willing rather than a reluctant participant. By chance, he was never in combat, but he was ready for it. Instead of being shipped to Europe and captured at the Battle of the Bulge, he was trained as an officer with a German language specialty so he could be dropped behind enemy lines. ("Bulge," by coincidence, is an anagram of "bugle.")

After D-Day and his marriage, when the war in Europe was winding down, Dad's specialty switched. He began training with Nisei (Americans of Japanese descent). As a second lieutenant, he would be in charge of a team of ten or twelve Nisei in the invasion of Japan. He went through weapons familiarization — explosives, sabotage, espionage, booby traps — and studied Japanese order of battle and language. The destruction of Hiroshima and Nagasaki made that invasion unnecessary.

When I was a two-month-old fetus, over 200,000 people died horrible deaths and the Nuclear Age began; and if that hadn't happened, Dad would probably have died in the Pacific equivalent of D-Day. It just happened that way. No one I knew had anything to do with that decision, but it shaped the course of my life. I grew up with a father.

Illogically, Americans of Japanese descent were sequestered during the war, but German Americans weren't. Otherwise Dad, together with his brothers, his parents, and the extended Seltzer and Daly families, with immigrant ties to Germany extending over several generations, might have spent the war in internment camps, and he would have never met Mom, and I'd have never been born.

A few years after the war, Mom and Dad welcomed and befriended two Nisei Japanese girls who were in medical school, renting them a room in our row house in the East Falls section of Philadelphia. When I was a toddler, they were part of the family, sometimes babysitting me, sometimes providing first aid when I foolishly injured myself, like when I slit my wrist with mica. I remember them amazing me with medical magic. They would bop my knee with a little hammer, and my leg would pop up without me telling it to do so. One of them, Jane, stayed in touch with Mom and Dad and sent me Christmas gifts every year for decades. By coincidence, my youngest son, Tim, has long been obsessed with Japanese videogames, manga, and anime.

Thinking of Hiroshima, I'm reminded of Dresden and the devastation in Europe during World War II. Amid Uncle Adolph's Mediterranean postcards at the family summer cottage on the Potomac, I found a booklet of tourist photos of Dresden. It's now on a bookshelf in my apartment. Someone from the Daly family, perhaps Uncle Adolph, went there to track down relatives before the Depression made European travel too expensive for ordinary folk and before firebombing obliterated Dresden. (Echoes of *Slaughterhouse Five* by Kurt Vonnegut).

Nana's mother, Margaret, was the daughter of Adam Thor (Thour) from Coblentz and Amelia Ockert from Dresden. They met and fell in love on the ship bringing them to America. Growing up near the White House, Margaret witnessed Lincoln's funeral procession. Her grandchildren remembered her saying, "The hearse creaked along the muddy road; and, as it came close, it stopped suddenly because a mother pig and her piglets were slowly crossing the avenue in its path." As a child, Margaret performed as an extra in several productions at the National Theater, including *Rebecca of Sunnybrook Farm*.

I'm also reminded of air-raid drills at elementary school in the DC suburbs. An ear-splitting alarm would go off, signaling we had to duck under our desks and cover the back of our heads with our hands. That was supposed to protect us from a nuclear blast. And for several weeks, the *Washington Post* published excerpts from *On the*

Beach by Neville Shute every day, starting at the top of page one — describing the aftermath of nuclear war, with radioactive fallout eliminating all life on Earth, even in Australia where no bombs fell. A decade later, when, as a high school junior, I listened to radio news reports of the Cuban Missile Crisis, I wondered if I should bother to do homework, since I might not be alive in the morning. War wasn't just a possibility. It would come. The question was, when?

And the follow-up question was, how would I respond? What did I have it in me to do? Would I turn coward or be a hero? Could I shoot to kill when ordered to do so or when my life or the lives of others depended on it? If ordered to climb out of a foxhole and charge into a hail of bullets, could I do that? And could I order anyone else to?

Perhaps dreams and fantasies, like pandemics, are contagious, and Uncle Adolph was a carrier. And perhaps it's a good thing for children to imagine catastrophes and sort out what they might do in such a case. (Could today's fantasies of alien invasion prepare us for the real thing?)

Jean Therapy

A paperback copy of *The Nibelungenlied* was gathering dust on a bookshelf of mine. Writing this book and finding ancestral links to Norse legends and myths, I opened it out of curiosity; and inside the front cover, I saw an inscription. It was a gift from my college girlfriend, Jean, 56 years ago. The inscription reminded that I should say something about that chapter of my life, which also involved luck or fate.

In 1969, before the draft lottery, I was at the mercy of my local draft board. As a college student, I had a deferment that would end at graduation. I couldn't, in good conscience or as a practical matter, claim I was a conscientious objector; and I didn't want to flee to Canada. There was no point in applying for jobs because no one would hire someone likely to be drafted. I applied to grad school, knowing there would be no deferment for that, but hoping the war would end before I was called up. I wanted to write literature, not write about it or teach it. Grad school would be a stop-gap, constructive way to spend my time while I waited to learn my fate.

My roommate, Dave, was lucky. He dislocated his shoulder in a touch-football game that I played in as well. I believe the pain was excruciating, but he was in no hurry to get to the infirmary. He was smiling, not cringing. His life had been saved. He would be 4F, undraftable. Over the next few months, he lined up a job and proposed to Joyce, from Mount Holyoke, who he had been dating for two years. They got married in the fall.

I had a different kind of luck, stumbling through a fog toward my future.

Jean, like Joyce, was at Mount Holyoke; and we, too, had been dating for two years. I remember the first time we literally slept together. Yale was all-male and overnight dates typically stayed at the Taft Hotel (echoes of *The Graduate*). We would do everything short of "going all the way," and I would leave before dawn. I had never slept in the same bed with anyone, nor had she. She wanted to be able to say, in good conscience, that we didn't "sleep together."

When she relented, I was nervous and very conscious of her beside me. I was afraid that my slightest movement might wake her, and she would exile me. Finally, we did fall sleep in one another's arms, with no alarm clock and nothing we had to wake up for. That was like being together forever — ecstasy, beyond time, a touch of eternity.

Jean and I thought we were in love. It seemed inevitable that we would get married, presuming I didn't die in Vietnam before that. We both applied to grad school — she in math, me in comparative literature. She would be going to Boston University. I was still waiting to hear.

My acceptance letters all arrived at the same time, and they all made the same offer — no charge for tuition and a stipend of $1800. I would have to live on that for a year — housing, food, books, everything — which even at 1969 prices would be a challenge.

I got into Harvard. If you had asked me the day before, I would have said that was what I was hoping for. Jean and I could be together near Boston.

But I was also accepted at Yale; and without thinking, without calling Jean to talk it over, I ran to the Comparative Literature office and told them I'd be going to Yale.

I didn't consider Jean at all in making that decision. How could I think that I was in love with her?

The breakup was painful. Our identities were entangled. But it was time for us to split, and the choice of grad school was a no-fault way to do that. We were close, but not forever. She needed to get on with her life, and I with mine.

She married someone she met in grad school. Her talent in math morphed into an interest in the statistics of public health. She got a Ph.D. from Yale, then taught at the University of Texas. She recently died of Alzheimer's.

Meeting Barb

Barb and I didn't fall in love at first sight. We didn't even like one another for nearly a year after we first met in her dorm room. Rather than exchange greetings, she threw a wet washcloth at me and hit me square in the face. I laughed and ignored her.

I was dating her roommate and best friend, Anne. They were seniors at Albertus Magnus College, planning to go to Europe together in the fall. I was a grad student at Yale. Barb was savoring the trip in anticipation, going over the possibilities, not to make decisions and plan in detail — they'd be spontaneous — but to get a foretaste of places they could see and things they could do. I had wrecked that. I was monopolizing Anne's time. That was unforgivable.

The antipathy wasn't mutual. I ignored her.

In the fall, they left for Ireland on separate planes, a week apart. Together with their extended families, I saw each of them off at Logan Airport. The trip was a big deal for them, a grand adventure, going without adult supervision, without the fixed agenda of a tour. They had Eurail passes. They could go anywhere and stay as long as they liked, with no need to return home by a particular date, no responsibilities waiting for them.

Barb was beaming with pride and joy, in a big, floppy, very Irish green hat. Anne was subdued but confidant, not so much thinking ahead as relieved to finally board the plane. I later learned she had hash in her pocketbook.

I received a couple of brief, uninformative letters. Anne was enjoying herself, with little thought of what she had left behind. We might get together when she got back, but probably not. There was no way to tell who she would be after the experience — we knew it would change her. That was how we both wanted it — no commitment, but no breakup. What would be, would be.

Soon after Christmas, I phoned Barb's parents. They were more friendly to me than Anne's widowed mother. And Barb was more likely to write home than Anne was. I wanted to know where they were and when they might be coming back.

Barb answered the phone. She had ended her trip early because she wanted to be with her family at Christmas. Anne was still gallivanting, probably in Spain by now. Barb was polite, but not particularly pleased to hear from me. I suggested that we get together, so we could talk more about Anne. She hesitated. I suggested we go to a movie, *The Last Picture Show* with Cybil Shepherd. She agreed and gave me directions to her house. I should drive up Center Street in West Roxbury and turn left at the A&P. It had slipped her mind that that A&P had been torn down ten years before. Nonetheless, I found her house, which, in the days before GPS, wasn't easy without a map .

I fell for Barb slowly, unintentionally. I wasn't focused on her. I wanted to talk about Anne, and we did. It was easy talking to one another. One topic led to another, without effort. We enjoyed following one another's trails of association. The next night, we went to see the French movie *King of Hearts*. I forget what we did the night after that and the next. But we found one excuse or another to continue the pleasure of being together.

I didn't devour her with my eyes. I wasn't focused on her, and that helped me see her more clearly. I wasn't comparing her to a model of the woman I wanted to spend the rest of my life with. We stumbled forward with no idea where we were going, enjoying the journey so long as we were together.

Maybe love comes in different shapes, sizes, and colors, if it comes at all. It's difficult making sense of the tangled threads of your own life, much less deliberately connecting them to the entanglements of someone else. But they can come together, if the two of you don't work too hard at it and let yourselves discover if and how you mesh.

We married a year and a half later.

Four children and 39 years after that, she died suddenly, overnight.

Fate?

In retrospect, the chain of coincidences that brought Barb and me together seemed so outlandish that it had to have been fated. My friend Claude was driving down College Street in New Haven on the first day of spring break. We had graduated from Yale the year before. I had stayed at Yale for grad school, and he was teaching in Watts, an urban ghetto in Los Angeles. Why would he be driving down College Street and at the very moment I was walking there?

He waved and pulled over. He was hoping to find me. He was on his way to the airport, having visited his fiancée Tina, and it occurred to him that he should introduce me to an old friend of his and Tina's, a senior at Albertus Magnus College in New Haven — Anne.

I had other plans for the day, but he insisted on going to a phone booth and calling Anne. She didn't answer. Maybe he'd dialed the wrong number. He dialed again and let the phone ring over and over again. When he was about to give up, she picked up.

She was going home for spring break that day. She would have been on the road already, but her car didn't start. She headed back to her room to call for road service. As she was walking up the stairs, she heard the phone ring in her room, so she hurried. She was glad to hear from him. They hadn't spoken in more than a year. Over the phone, Claude introduced me to her. I got her number. She'd be happy to meet me when she got back from break.

If it hadn't been for my chance encounter with Claude and for Anne's broken car, I wouldn't have met Anne, and hence wouldn't have met Barb.

And Claude? How did I become friends with him? He was two years younger than me, so the odds were astronomical against us both being freshmen at Yale at the same time. But I had spent a year at school in England before college, and he had skipped his senior year of high school. He had heard from an old friend, Dave, that I was going to be a freshman at Yale when he was. Claude looked me up as soon as he got on campus.

And how did I know Dave, and how did he know I'd be going to Yale? His sister, Becky, was corresponding with me. We had almost connected romantically in the seventh grade.

My connection with Becky was the result of another absurd coincidence. When Dad, Mom, and I first moved to Plymouth, we lived half a mile from the center of town. Six months later, we moved to Russell Street, two blocks from the town green, three blocks from my school, one block from the Congregational church we attended because there was no Lutheran church, and two blocks in the other direction from the house where the Congregational minister lived.

Soon after the move, Mom got a call from one of her sisters in Philadelphia. Aunt Lil, the last remaining of the two aunts who had raised her, had died.

Mom and Dad never went to wakes and funerals. When Mom was ten, her mother died after what would have been her eighth child was stillborn. And when Mom was twelve, her father went to prison — as good as dead — leaving her an orphan. I would have thought Mom and Dad would have avoided driving all the way from New Hampshire to Philadelphia for a funeral. But this was Aunt Lil, who, together with her sister Agnes (who had years before) took care of Mom and her siblings until World War II. Mom felt compelled to go to that funeral. Dad would drive.

But what would they do with me? They'd be gone for a week, and school was in session. They didn't want me to miss that time in school. They called the Congregational minister, and he agreed that I could stay with his family.

He had a son, Dave, two years younger than me, and a daughter, Becky, who was in the same grade as me. During that week, she and I flirted and almost held hands.

Two weeks after my parents got back, Becky's father was offered a dream job in Hartford, Connecticut. He accepted, and they moved soon after.

Becky and I kept in touch by letter. Face-to-face, we were shy, but at a distance, with no chance of ever seeing one another again, our imaginations were untrammeled. Over the years, while I was at all-boys schools, our letters became passionate and explicit.

When I was in England, she let me know that she had seduced someone and did it repeatedly with him. Then she thought she was pregnant, told her parents, and was about to marry him, only to find out that she wasn't pregnant. But she married him anyway.

So the sequence of unlikely events leading to my meeting Barb stretched back to 1932, when Mom's father went to prison. If he hadn't, Aunt Lil wouldn't have taken care of Mom, and Mom wouldn't have felt obliged to go to the funeral, and I wouldn't have gotten to know Becky, and we wouldn't have corresponded, and I wouldn't have met Claude. So Claude wouldn't have introduced me to Anne, and I wouldn't have met Barb, and my life would have gone in a different direction.

The Gift of Failure

Self-confidence is necessary, but too much success at an early age could ruin your life. It could make you believe you've got it made and need not try your hardest. It would have been disastrous if I had been selected as a contestant on *Giant Step*, and even worse if I had done well in it. But perhaps that's a matter of personality, rather than a general rule.

In the seventh grade, I was a newcomer in Plymouth. Material new to my classmates was old hat to me; I had covered it two years before in Baltimore. There I had been like everyone else. Here I was considered a genius. I got swell-headed.

Our grade was going to participate in the National Spelling Bee. That would be a chance to show off my supposed brilliance. In practice sessions, I exceled. Teachers and classmates all expected me to win and go on to the next level of competition and then the next and the next — to serve as their champion.

On the day of the real competition, the words given to those ahead of me were all simple. This would be easy, I thought.

Then came my turn. The definition was "an edible seed" but the sound of the word automatically called to mind a military rank. Without hesitation, I spelled COLONEL, proud that I could easily handle such a tough word. But the correct answer was KERNEL. It took a minute for that to sink in. The word was so trivial as to be difficult. I had been knocked out in the very first round and had to spend the rest of the day watching everyone else compete.

Another failure came a few years later, in typing. Cousin Olive, Uncle Charlie's daughter, had worked at the Library of Congress for decades. She lined up a summer job for me there. I just had to pass a typing test. The job itself wouldn't involve typing, but I needed to pass the test to be eligible. I would have to type 30 words per minute on a manual typewriter. For a couple months, I went to typing sessions at Holderness School, and Mom coached me at home. (She had been a secretary and could type 120 words a minute). I always did well on tests, and typing, I was sure, didn't require much intelligence. I would ace this one. Dad drove me all the way from New Hampshire to Washington for the test, a 12-hour drive.

I failed miserably. Ten words were taken off for every mistake. My score was below zero, far below.

The shame of that failure motivated me to learn to type well, and that skill proved important to me in writing papers at Holderness and Yale and in my jobs at Benwill Publishing and DEC, and in writing books, building a website, and publishing ebooks.

In my various careers, I've never had to use anything I learned in algebra, biology, or physics. But typing has been essential.

Another Twisting Road

When I was in junior high, Dad joined the Book-of-the-Month Club, and, out of curiosity, I read their latest selection — *Dr. Zhivago* by Pasternak. After that, I read Tolstoy's *Anna Karenina* and became addicted to Russian novels.

Because of that addiction, I studied Russian in college. And because I knew Russian, when I came home from college graduation and found a letter from the draft board, I was able (with the help of Dad) to volunteer for and get into an Army Reserve unit that needed someone who knew Russian. So you could say that Pasternak and Tolstoy saved me from the Vietnam War.

I was in the Army Security Agency and got a top-secret/crypto clearance. (I later delighted in telling my kids that I used to be a spy.) There would be a delay before a training slot was open for me. In the meantime, I could start grad school.

The improbability of what happened next should serve as proof that what I'm writing is true. I couldn't have made up such a story.

My Great-Uncle Charlie (Olive's father) died that summer; and in a box of his old papers I chanced upon a letter and a related newspaper clipping from 1914.

The letter began:
> Dear Sir,
> Although I know you only from good references of your honesty, my sad situation compels me to reveal to you an important affair in which you can procure a modest fortune, saving at the same time that of my darling daughter.

The clipping said that Serge Solovieff, a banker in St. Petersburg, had embezzled over five million rubles, murdered a compatriot in Spain, been apprehended in London and extradited to Spain. The money was missing. In the letter, the embezzler was asking a total stranger to go to Santander, Spain, and retrieve his trunk from police custody. The money was hidden in a secret compartment. The letter concluded, "First of all answer by cable, not by letter, as follows: Señor Requejo, Lista Telegrafos. Santander (Spain)."

The postmark on the envelope was Madrid, which is 200 miles from Santander. There was no date on the clipping, but the item on the reverse side was a review of an issue of the *London Quarterly* dealing with the centenary of Tennyson's birth. Tennyson was born in 1809. It was hard to imagine reviewing a magazine five years after it was published. And why would anyone keep a clipping from an English newspaper for five years in a prison in Spain and then send it to a total stranger in the U.S. with a letter asking for help? Was this a hoax? What was there to gain?

Decades later, I posted that letter on my Web site, and thanks to the technique of "flypaper" (which I'll explain later), a dozen people from all over the U.S. wrote to me. They had found almost identical letters and clippings, all dated shortly before World War I. I heard from another one yesterday. You can see the originals at my website: seltzerbooks.com/solovieffseltzerfront.jpg seltzerbooks.com/solovieffseltzerletter.jpg

Before I realized this was a scam, I tried to learn more about Serge Solovieff, with the idea of writing a novel about him. A year after graduation and after basic training, while I was stationed at Goodfellow Airforce Base in San Angelo, Texas, for Russian training, the library at the local college got me microfilms of *The London Times* from 1909 to 1914. I didn't find any mention of the Russian embezzler, but I did chance upon Anthony Bulatovich.

A 1913 article reported that Russian troops had recently besieged two Russian monasteries at Mount Athos in Greece and exiled 880 monks to remote parts of the Russian Empire for believing that "the Name of God was a part of God and, therefore, in itself divine." Bulatovich — formerly a cavalry officer, who had fought in Africa and the Far East — was the leader and defender of the monks.

As portrayed by the reporter, Bulatovich was restless, full of energy, chasing from one end of the world to the other in search of the meaning of life. Ironically, when he sought quiet as a monk at Mount Athos, he found himself at the center of another conflict.

When my training ended a few months later, I moved to Boston. There I checked the reference material at Harvard's Widener Library. The Soviet encyclopedia (*Bolshaya Sovietsaya Encyclopedia*) mentioned an Alexander Bulatovich, who died in 1910. No Anthony. I would spin a fictional story based on what I knew of that period in Russian history.

Then, by chance (is anything by chance?), I returned to the Widener in the spring of 1972. They had the recently published "B" volume of a new edition of the *Bolshaya Encyclopedia,* which included a new Bulatovich entry. Alexander and Anthony were the same person. When becoming a monk, it was traditional to adopt a new name with the same first letter. And Bulatovich died in 1919, not 1910. The entry was signed by I. S. Katsnelson, a professor at the Institute of Oriental Studies in Moscow. I wrote to him, and he replied by return mail, sending me a copy of a book he had just published — a new edition of two long-out-of-print books by Bulatovich about his experiences in Ethiopia (1896-98), plus a biographical introduction. He also gave me the address of Bulatovich's sister, who was still alive, residing in Canada.

The following summer, as an Army reservist with a Russian specialty, I was assigned to the Defense Language Institute in Monterey, California, for two weeks of training. Instead of using the travel money for airfare, I bought a thirty-day go-wherever-you-want bus ticket and detoured by way of Penticton, British Columbia, where Bulatovich's sister, Princess Mary Orbeliani, was living in a nursing home.

In tape-recorded conversations and in letters before and after that visit, she told me the story of her brother's life and gave me insight into his character. At 99, she was articulate and lucid. She was still active as a water-color artist. And though, due to arthritis, she couldn't unwrap a piece of candy, her fingers came to life when she sat down at the piano and played Chopin from memory. She passed away in 1977 at the age of 103.

Back in Boston, I tracked down references to Bulatovich's participation in the Manchurian campaign of the Boxer Rebellion and his writings about the Name of God. And Princess Mary's son, Andre, sent me a copy of the handwritten official record of Bulatovich's military career, with previously unknown details about the Manchurian campaign.

I wrote an historical novel about Bulatovich, staying close to what I knew about his life, but filling in gaps, inventing other characters, and trying to visualize the scenes from within, as lived. *The Name of Hero* was published by Tarcher, a west coast subsidiary of Houghton-Mifflin, in 1981.

While researching that novel, I translated portions of Bulatovich's Ethiopian books for my own use. The more I read about Ethiopia, the more it became clear to me that experts in the field were unfamiliar with these works and could benefit from them. Prompted by Professor Harold Marcus at Michigan State University, I made the time to translate both books in full. University presses rejected the manuscript, saying that, regardless of its merit, they couldn't sell enough copies to justify publishing it. So I posted the translation on my web site; and, by the technique of "flypaper," I got an email from a graduate student in Germany. He was the great-grandson of the Ethiopian Emperor Menelik II. He said this book had to be published. Thanks to that letter, Red Sea Press published it in 2000 as

Ethiopia Through Russian Eyes. Eight years later, *Old Africa*, a journal in Nairobi, published a review of that translation, saying "this is the most important book on the history of eastern Africa to have been published for a century." (Here's a link to that review seltzerbooks.com/oldafrica.html)

The reviewer was Cynthia Salvadori, an independent scholar, who spent her life in the wilds of Kenya and Ethiopia. She had found a copy of the translation in a store in Addis Ababa and had emailed me, asking about the photos taken by Bulatovich in the 1890s. They were included in the original Russian edition, but not in the translation, because, at the time of publication, technology wasn't advanced enough to make printable copies. At her request, as a courtesy, I scanned the photos from the Russian original and sent them to her.

In correspondence with her, I learned that she was a grandniece of H. Rider Haggard, author of *King Solomon's Mines*. As a child, I had enjoyed that novel in a closet full of books at Pop Pop's house.

Second Wakeup Punch

I almost died in the summer of 2012, five months before Barb died.

I was driving back to Boston from Cape Cod, alone, in a van packed tight with stuff we had brought to the Cape for a two-week vacation. Barb was cleaning the cabin we had rented and would be following in our other car in about an hour.

Three miles from the Sagamore Bridge over the Cape Cod Canal, I realized that my brakes didn't work.

The traffic around me was travelling at 60 miles an hour. The distance between me and the car in front of me was a car length. The car behind me was also a car length away. There were cars bumper-to-bumper in the lane to the right of me. To the left of me there was a metal barrier. The car ahead of me slowed. I tapped my brakes. Nothing happened. I tapped again, harder. Nothing. A couple feet away from the car in front of me, I stomped on the brake pedal, and it went all the way to the floor with no resistance. Fortunately, the car ahead of me accelerated.

We were going downhill. I was coasting.

Options raced through my mind.

I tried to downshift, but the gears were locked.

I considered using the emergency parking brake. But if I stopped suddenly, the car behind me would slam into me, and I'd end up in a pile-up.

I considered turning off the ignition. But the van I was driving had power steering. If the engine turned off, the power steering would shut off as well.

After what felt like an hour but probably was less than a minute, around a curve, a grass median strip opened up to my left. I turned onto the grass, and the van slowed down. In what felt like another hour but was only a few seconds, it came to a stop, a hundred yards from the bridge.

My heart was racing. I saw the van, the grass, the road, the traffic, and the cloudless sky with a clarity I had never experienced before.

I didn't jump to the conclusion that I had a destiny to fulfill or that I was born lucky. But, for me, this was a second wakeup punch.

Sitting in the driver's seat didn't mean I was in control. Everything could change in an instant, regardless of what I did. I could drop dead and so could those dear to me. I should cherish those I love and savor every moment I have with them.

Highly Unlikely

The chains of events that shaped my life were highly unlikely — one coincidence leading to another. If each event hadn't unfolded precisely the way it did, my life could have ended abruptly or gone down a different track .

If you ever fell in love, think about the events leading up to that moment. After the fact, the events feel inevitable. It's difficult to imagine how your life could have turned out if everything hadn't happened exactly as it did.

The more you know about an event, the more unique it seems to you. But an outside observer, with less information, wouldn't recognize those same events as a sequence. Seen separately, what happened would appear to be ordinary.

Every time you toss a coin, the probability of heads is 50%, regardless of the results of previous tosses. But a long chain of events, such as heads, heads, tails, heads, tails, tails, tails, defies analysis. Only when you isolate a variable and simplify the context with a generalized perspective do the laws of probability apply.

A basic principle of probability, Bernoulli's Law, states that it's possible to accurately predict the average outcome of many similar events but impossible to predict the outcome of any single event. In other words, the more you know about a specific event and the circumstances that led to it, the more unique that event appears. "Average" and "random" are concepts that statisticians use to uncover order and predictability. But from your perspective, every moment of your life is miraculous, as if fated. Those contradictory views of the same events are both true.

I was born in 1946, graduated from high school in 1964, graduated from college in 1969, and for 49 years my phone number was 469-2269. Barb died 12/4/12. I now live in apartment 406 in a building numbered 146, with zip code 06460. What are the odds of that?

Eternity?

From what I said earlier, you might expect that I would encounter mythic beasts in my nightmares. Not so.

Instead my scariest nightmare was of my parents dancing. I was ten years old when I dreamt it, and I can still see it clearly. Why was it scary? I can only guess now. But, at the time, I was terrified.

I don't know where Pebbles was that night or why.

Lying in bed in the twilight before dawn, I could clearly see the room around me. I presumed I was awake. But floating near the ceiling, I saw two miniature figures dancing — ballroom style, maybe a waltz

— to music I couldn't hear. Round and round they went — near then far then near, but always small, dancing in circles in one another's arms.

I wanted to wake up. I would have pinched myself if I could. But I couldn't move. I couldn't close my eyes or look in any other direction. I couldn't scream.

I was trapped in a different reality, neither awake nor asleep. This was my room, beyond doubt, in detail. But something inexplicable was different about it, and I had no control over my body.

The image of my parents was non-threatening. They were extremely happy dancing with one another, oblivious of me. But I was shocked to find myself in this alternate world. It was very much like the world I knew, but here I was trapped and helpless.

Remembering that scene 68 years later, I would say that the Veil of Maya parted, and I had a glimpse of a reality beyond this ordinary world.

Six years later, early one morning, I had a different but equally odd vision. I was a sophomore at Holderness School. Dad had just dropped me off. I was walking across campus toward the School House building. No one was around, which was odd at that time on a school day. Total silence — no birds, no traffic, no chatter. And grass, bushes, everything living and growing and the sky as well had a peculiar green aura, as if the green were streaming from within, rather than the result of reflected light.

I wasn't scared. I was delighted. It felt like a religious experience. For a few minutes, I sensed I was in touch with a different reality that underlay the normal. Beautiful, peaceful.

I was reminded of a poem by Coleridge that I had recently read, *Dejection: An Ode.*

> …
> All this long eve, so balmy and serene,
> Have I been gazing on the western sky,
> And its peculiar tint of yellow green ...
> **III**
> My genial spirits fail;
> And what can these avail
> To lift the smothering weight from off my breast?
> It were a vain endeavour,
> Though I should gaze for ever
> On that green light that lingers in the west:
> I may not hope from outward forms to win
> The passion and the life, whose fountains are within.

But I wasn't "dejected." I was elated, ecstatic.

I was also reminded of the Wordsworth poem: "The world is too much with us late and soon. In getting and spending we lay waste our powers…" I was that pagan having "glimpses that would make me less forlorn," seeing Proteus rising from the sea and hearing Triton blow his wreathèd horn.

That night I dreamed the opening lines of a poem of my own:
> I caught a glimpse of eternity,
> and it winked back at me.

Excited that had written something poetic in my sleep (like Coleridge writing *Kubla Khan)*, I told my English teacher. He dismissed it immediately, saying I must have read those lines somewhere and remembered the words but not the source. A common trick of memory. Nothing of importance.

That stroke of disillusionment hurt me more than the wakeup punch that prompted me to go to Holderness. For a brief shining Camelot moment I had felt a special and intimate connection to all of reality. Then it was gone, irretrievable. I've never had such a moment again, but the possibility of a special state of mind or of being, of sensitivity to powers beyond human ken still intrigues me.

My girlfriend tells me that last night I talked and screamed in my sleep. She says I spoke in a Scandinavian language. But I don't know any Scandinavian language. Was that Snorri? Maybe Odin himself speaking through me?

When a Gravestone Tells the Future

In the summer of 1963, after my junior year of high school, I spent a few weeks in Strasbourg, France, as an exchange student. The town of Seltz was nearby, across the Rhine in West Germany. My host family took me there to check the cemetery, in hopes of finding clues to the origin of my family name "Seltzer."

In that part of Europe, graves and gravestones are only preserved if the family keeps paying a maintenance fee. Otherwise, the plots are recycled; new dead replace old. The oldest graves in this cemetery dated back to the late 19th century. I wasn't likely to find the graves of any direct ancestors of mine, since my Seltzer forebears emigrated to Pennsylvania in the 18th century. But I did find one Seltzer gravestone. The name on it was "Barbara Seltzer."

My wife, whom I first met eight years later, was named Barbara.

When I met her, did her name trigger that memory?

Dad, like his grandfather before him, kept detailed diaries throughout his life. In his final years, he turned his diary entries into an autobiography. Reviewing that as I write this, I see that before Dad met Mom, he thought he was in love with someone else and was seriously thinking about marrying her. The other woman was named Barbara.

A Final Word on Fate

As I get older, I have moments when, walking into a room, I realize I don't know why I'm there. Did I forget? Or was there no reason?

Sometimes when writing this book, looking back at my life, I have a similar disorienting doubt. Why was I born? Why am I here? Is there a reason?

Other times, the disparate events of my life seem to fall into place, as if they were pieces of a complicated jigsaw puzzle magically assembling themselves, as I watch.

Part Seven:
Blood

Medical History

We know that we inherit physical traits from parents and grandparents. We recognize similarities looking in the mirror. And relatives admiring newborns see Aunt Mary's button nose, Cousin George's cleft chin. He's the spitting image of his father. Like father, like son. The apple doesn't fall far from the tree.

We expect the color of eyes and hair to be passed along; beauty and athletic ability; baldness and obesity. And as they grow up, our babies develop resemblances to other relatives.

On your first visit to a new doctor, you're asked for your family medical history. Do/did your parents or grandparents have diabetes, stroke, heart problems, cancer, a disease of the lungs? At the emergency room, you're asked the same questions.

Dad told me that both his parents died of colon cancer in their 80s. When I told my doctor that, he scheduled me for frequent colonoscopies. After Dad died, in his papers, I found his father's obituary: he died of a stroke instead. No need for so many colonoscopies.

Vulnerabilities, immunities, longevity, and robust health, too, can be inherited. If you know members of your immediate family have an inherited medical problem, you can take preventive action, such as changes in lifestyle or diet or a regimen of medications. Also, if you need a transplant, you will want to know which, if any, of your relatives might be a match.

Considering the clear benefits, it's strange that laws and practices prevent us from learning about the health conditions of our close relatives. What we do know is largely anecdotal — what someone told us, what we guessed. There's no automatic and accurate way for us to share health information with our relatives and their doctors. On the contrary, HIPPA laws restrict the dissemination of health information, for the sake of privacy.

Family medical history could be part of your identity, together with your DNA data. The more detailed, accurate, and accessible the data is, the better for you and your close relatives. Does privacy make sense here, when sharing could provide enormous benefits?

It's also important to know for certain who your father is. That shouldn't be hidden to avoid shame. You should have a right to that information, and it should be based on a paternity test rather than on what your parents tell you (and one another). And if you are adopted, you should have medical information about your birth parents, if possible.

Why, with the medical technology available today, do our attitudes about paternity echo those of the Middle Ages? Why should children born out of wedlock — either before marriage or to someone other than the husband — be labeled "bastard," stigmatized for life through no fault of their own.

The criminalization of incest may have originated from repulsion at taking advantage of helpless children. It could also be rooted in the observation that closely-related couples are prone to having children with mental and physical defects. Both church and state codified the traditional prohibition, with varying definitions of how close was too close. Still in effect, such laws are not based on science.

Inherited Immunity?

Mom's mother had nine siblings. I've mentioned five of them — the guardian aunts Lillian and Agnes, and the runaways Annie Jane, Tom, and David. What happened to the other four?

- Elizabeth Rachel, the oldest, had a nervous breakdown in her teens. Mom told me that Elizabeth had her first period at school. No one had explained to her what was going to happen. Suddenly, blood was running down her legs and puddling on the floor. She freaked out, screamed, and wouldn't stop screaming. She was put in an insane asylum, and there she remained, until she died 70 years later.
- Griffith Owen, named after his father, was hit by a pipe as a young man, and he, too, spent rest of life in an insane asylum.
- George Bogan died of typhoid fever at the age of 19.
- Stanley caught measles when he was young and was blind in one eye after that. He died of alcoholism.

Those are horrible fates, but accidental, not inherited. What apparently was inherited by all ten children was an important immunity.

In 1918, the Spanish flu infected about 500 million people — a third of the world's population — and caused the deaths of 50 million people. Echoes of the Black Plague.

Mom's mother was one of ten children, her father one of seven. Four of her siblings were born before 1918. Dad's mother was one of nine children, his father one of three. That's a total of thirty-three close relatives alive in 1918 and (as far as I can tell) none of them caught the Spanish flu.

Perhaps they had natural immunity and I inherited it from both Mom and Dad. And perhaps that provided some protection during the COVID-19 pandemic. I've not yet contracted even a mild case of it. And I don't believe anyone in my extended family has had a serious case. Knock on wood.

Sallie's Birth

Mom was raised as an orphan. She knew her father was in prison, but her aunts insisted that she tell everyone she was an orphan. They wouldn't talk about what had happened. They forbade her and her siblings from talking about it to one another. She was supposed to forget it, and she tried hard to do so. But when she walked to and from school, she had to pass the huge, castle-like prison where he was incarcerated and where she could never visit him. So until she was 36, when she, by chance, discovered his relatives in Tennessee, she knew nothing about the health of his side of the family.

Hence it was natural for her mother's fate to loom large for her. Mom had watched her mother go through the discomforts of pregnancy, heard her screams during delivery at home, seen the still-born body of what would have been her brother, and watched her mother painfully decline in the aftermath.

Mom's mother was cared for at home, not at a hospital. This was the Depression. With such a large family, it was hard making ends meet. Her father was lucky to have any job at all. They didn't have health insurance. And when death mercifully ended her mother's pain, the body was laid out on the kitchen table for friends and relatives to view.

Mom wanted lots of children. Having grown up with six siblings; that was normal, expected. All children should have such companionship. She and Dad were delighted when she got pregnant with me, but she was also anxious that she might die from childbirth, like her mother. She didn't share that fear with Dad. She didn't want to admit it. Admitting it would make it more real, and sharing her concerns with Dad would dampen his joy. She had had lots of practice concealing what she knew and feared.

When the doctor had their blood tested — not just hers, his as well — I imagine she asked him, "Why?" He would have explained that not all blood is the same. There are several types — O, A, B, and AB. Each of those has an Rh factor, either positive or negative.

Dad's was AB negative, as he'd learned when he enlisted in the Army. It was rare and valuable. It was the only type that could be used to treat everyone in a blood transfusion. If he were ever down-and-out, he could sell his blood — an amusing and reassuring discovery. And at one point later in life, he did resort to that.

Mom was O positive. She probably expressed concern that their Rh factors didn't match. Could that be bad for the baby or for her?

The doctor would have said she should be fine. If she were negative and her husband positive, that would be risky. But since she was positive, it shouldn't matter whether he was positive or negative.

"You're sure of that?" I imagine her asking.

"This is new, discovered just a few years ago. There's lots we don't know."

"So there is some risk?"

"No need to fret. This is your first child, so whether your Rh matches your husband's doesn't matter. Problems only arise on a second pregnancy. Then antibodies from the mother could pass into the baby's bloodstream. But you're Rh-positive. That doesn't apply to you. You don't have to worry about that."

"But you're not absolutely sure?"

"For a first birth, you have no need for concern."

From this, Mom probably concluded that she was okay for the moment, but if she had a second baby there might be problems. The risk was small, but she didn't want any risk. And the pain she felt in childbirth was far greater than she'd expected. She didn't want to go through that again. In any case, because of her mother's fate, she might have a proclivity for complications following childbirth. Best to scale back their plans for having children.

So she told Dad that the mismatch of their Rh factors meant it would be dangerous for them to have a second child. They should avoid another pregnancy.

He believed her. They were careful. So I grew up as an only child.

I didn't miss having siblings. I never thought about it. I had my parents' full attention, and they competed with one another for my affection. I was special.

Shortly before my parents moved from New Hampshire to Philadelphia, Mom's doctor told her that she was post-menopausal. She was 43. Dad had been offered a job as superintendent of schools in Bristol, Pennsylvania, near Philadelphia. I stayed at Holderness as a boarder for my senior year. When she and Dad came back up for my graduation, they chanced upon the doctor who had said she was beyond the possibility of becoming pregnant. Mom was holding the baby he had thought she could never have.

They named her "Sallie," after the aunt Mom had recently found in Tennessee, her father's sister.

Sallie's birth, 18 years after mine, was uncomplicated. We could have had a dozen siblings. Instead, although we had the same parents, we were each raised as an only child.

Cosmetic Surgery

Physical resemblance isn't always a matter of heredity. Sometimes cosmetic surgery plays a role, either restoring looks or transforming them.

Mom was hit by a truck when she was six. Her jaw bone shattered. That was in 1926, when reconstructive surgery was primitive, but surgeons successfully repaired the damage by grafting the jaw bone of a sheep. There was no visible scar; and as she grew, the bone grew, so her face stayed symmetrical and beautiful. She joked that her sheep's bone jaw gave her the gift of gab.

Our son Mike was born with cleft lip and cleft palate. There was a gaping hole above his mouth to his nose. And there were no teeth in his upper mouth where there was no bone into which teeth could grow. And there was no palate — the barrier between the top of the mouth and the nose. He went through a series of operations in his first year, closing the gap, giving him a palate, and cosmetically reshaping what was visible on the outside. But he still had no upper teeth in the center of his mouth. When he was 13, after his other adult teeth had come in and the bones of his head had grown, he was scheduled for another surgery in the summer, so the recovery wouldn't interfere with school. As it turned out, it conflicted with Little League. He had earned a spot in the all-star game. The surgery meant he had to miss it.

The surgeon took bone from his hip and grafted it into his mouth, where his upper teeth should have been. And over the following months, teeth grew through the graft, straight and strong. It was miraculous.

The surgeon talked in terms of sculpting in four dimensions, taking into account the effects of growth and scarring, imagining what the face would look like ten, twenty, thirty years in the future.

Restoration

Cosmetic surgery is forward-looking. For Mom and Mike, repair was necessary. How they looked affected what people thought of them. A hideous or disproportioned face would have changed the course of their lives, like a bad reputation. People who turned out to be important to them wouldn't have tried to get to know them. Dad wouldn't have asked Mom to dance at the Stage Door Canteen, and I wouldn't be here to write this book.

Artwork and architecture are also four-dimensional. But in those cases, restoration is intended to undo the ravages of time rather than shape the future. I believe in preserving them as they have aged rather than making them look new. I believe in savoring and appreciating the effects of change over time.

I cringe when I see Renaissance or medieval paintings "restored" with vibrant colors. A temple and its statues from the days of Pharoah Rameses II were disassembled and reconstructed on high ground to save them from submersion during building of the Aswan Dam. At the new site, bright-colored seemingly pristine murals look unreal, as if they were the work of Disney artists.

If you want to see a work of art as it might have looked when it was first created, make a copy and "restore" that, but keep the original with the palimpsest effects of natural aging, one layer on top of another.

I'm reminded of the four-dimensional experience made possible by streaming and the ready availability of movies and TV shows. You can, in a short time, see the same actors or actresses at all stages of their careers; and, with image search, you can find photos of well-known people at all ages of their lives.

My favorite view of Boston is from a courtyard of the Boston Public Library. You can sit on a stone bench, surrounded by a 19th century structure with Italianate columns, and above it, a few blocks away, you can see the Prudential and John Hancock Towers in sharp modern contrast. And you can see far more salient contrasts when you walk through London, with buildings from the days of Dickens next to McDonald's and futuristic office buildings.

I carry that appreciation to a wide variety of experiences — including history, with its layers of mistakes, lies, and misinterpretations. I savor change as an important part of existence, rather than consider it a fault that needs to be fixed through "restoration."

Against All Odds

Two of my sons, Mike and Tim, have been fighting demons since birth, and even before that. Beowulf would be proud of them.

Mike's umbilical cord was abnormally large. The doctor and nurses in attendance were shocked — they'd never seen anything like it. Prior to his birth, we were told Mike was going to be large, over ten pounds. (This was when ultrasound was less accurate than now). Instead, his birth weight was six pounds five ounces. The extra bulk was the umbilical cord, which restrained his movement while he was in the womb. That reminds me of the Norse god Loki, bound with the intestines of his children and tortured by our ancestor Skadi.

The four operations that Mike went through in his first year to correct his cleft lip and cleft palate were absolutely necessary and brilliantly done, but the recovery had unintended consequences. After each operation, he had to be restrained in a "straitjacket" for a period of about four weeks, so he wouldn't tear out his stitches and reopen the wounds. This restraint was imposed on him during the time when babies normally practice and develop their fine-motor skills. He was later diagnosed with "sensory integrative dysfunction," for which he had physical therapy throughout elementary school to improve his handwriting.

It's easy to imagine the nightmares he must have had, imprisoned or in the clutch of a dragon, fighting to break free.

The Cost of Misdiagnosis

Tim's umbilical cord broke during delivery, leading to a rapid scramble by nurses and doctors. His brothers and sister and I were all in the birthing room, witnessing this moment of frantic anxiety, not knowing what was going on, unable to do anything to help. There was a delay of more than a minute before Tim made his first cry.

He was born with a narrow trachea. So when he got a cold, swelling of the lining of his throat could obstruct his breathing, leading to croup. He would breath roughly and cough. The danger was that his breathing passage would close completely. Sometimes steam from hot water in the shower would alleviate the issue, or driving with the windows open on a cool night on the way to the emergency room. During his first year of life, half a dozen times the problem persisted until we got to the hospital, where they gave him medicine to reduce the swelling. We would take him home a few hours later.

One time, he needed intensive care for three days and underwent a series tests and imaging that indicated that in addition to a narrow trachea, he had a "malrotated intestine," meaning that his intestines were not in their normal position. We were also told that he probably had Opitz Syndrome, a birth defect that could mean poor motor skills, speech delay, and learning disabilities. That assessment was based on his eyes being relatively far apart and the fact that he laughed and smiled a lot.

For nearly a year, Barb and I worried about Opitz Syndrome. What should have been our joy at our newborn's smiles and giggles was transformed into fear that his happiness was a symptom of an incurable condition that could limit his ability to think, to function, to enjoy life. A year later, we found out the diagnosis was wrong. And another doctor looking at the imaging concluded that the intestine wasn't malrotated either. Instead, the ligaments were attached in an unusual way, which shouldn't be a problem.

Tim had other issues, but not those.

Uniquely Unique

Current medicine is built around norms and averages and has difficulty dealing with the rare and unique. Tim is uniquely unique. The monsters he has had to fight may never have been seen before.

Tim was labelled as having "Asperger's Syndrome," which later was renamed "on the autism spectrum." We needed that diagnosis when he was in school so his different ways of doing things wouldn't be treated as misbehavior but rather as a "disability," and so he could later qualify for social services that he needed. But he defies all definition. Tim is Tim. He's a category of one and proud to be so.

In high school when doing math homework and tests, Tim would often write the correct answer without showing how he arrived at it. Trying to change his behavior, his teachers gave him no credit for those answers. He wasn't being rebellious and disobedient. He didn't know how he arrived at the answers. Then as the problems got more complex, sometimes he didn't know the answers; and, without seeing his steps, teachers couldn't figure out where he went wrong, so they couldn't help him. That was a losing battle. He thinks differently by nature, not because he wants to. That's who he is.

He's also hypersensitive to sound. When he was sitting in a classroom, noises from several blocks away that no one else noticed would distract and annoy him, preventing him from focusing on what the teacher said.

He can't stand sweets of any kind. They taste revolting to him. He has never willingly tasted ice cream or candy. He never drinks soda.

If someone wanted to be friendly and offered to share a chocolate bar, he would pull away in disgust.

He also had severe nearsightedness. If someone he knew was walking toward him, he wouldn't recognize that person until under ten feet away. If someone waved to him from afar, he wouldn't notice and hence wouldn't respond. Glasses strong enough to correct that made it difficult for him to see close up; and he would trip on stairs or on irregularities in the pavement. He couldn't adjust to bifocals. His vision seems to have improved over the years. And he reads well without glasses.

Many of the generalizations about Asperger's/autism don't apply to Tim. Kids "on the spectrum" typically don't have a sense of humor, lack common sense, and can't handle abstractions. Tim's teachers unanimously praised him for his sense of humor and for his ability to see through BS and get to the heart of a matter. He has no interest in team sports but shows no signs of clumsiness and excels at karate, which he performs with ease and grace.

Kids on the spectrum often have excellent rote memory but little ability to understand what they memorize. Tim has terrible rote memory, but great ability to understand and develop abstract concepts. He remembers ideas, not details. He's inclined to see the forest and not the trees.

Articles with advice for parents presume that kids on the spectrum are mentally rigid, and only feel comfortable in predictable environments. They suggest micromanaging — laying out in great detail how tasks should be performed. But Tim bristles when anyone treats him that way. He works best when the goal is clear and he's free to find his own path. He stresses out in rigid environments and thrives when given flexibility and freedom.

Given an assignment to write a tanka (Japanese five-line poem) for English class in high school, Tim dashed off dozens of them in an hour, several of which his English teacher published in the school literary magazine. Here's a sampling:

 Darkness and light fight.
 Each represents hope and fears,
 and is eternal.
 Though any light can breach the dark,
 there must be someone to light it.

 Many movies come,
 showing the greatest actors,
 that we learn to love.
 Yet we see actors all the time,
 in the mirror and around us.

 The old Ninja,
 they are present in our lives,
 as cheesy villains.
 But do we really understand
 the shadow's way of life?

 Common sense is rare,
 with few ever thinking of it,
 and fewer knowing.
 Since so many confuse it
 why call it common sense?

The wind is free,
as are the birds that ride it,
going wherever.
A pilot stares and wonders,
"Why can't I be that free?"

Life is no easy track
and we have to run through the woods,
blind to mistakes.
If we can't find the right path
we'll just have to improvise.

For the last twelve years, Tim has lived on his own, near his sister who keeps an eye on him and treats him like he's her son. She has done a much better job with him than I did. He comes to visit me by train once a month and sleeps over. We have great conversations.

He has grown out of some of his issues or has learned to adjust. When he lived with me, he couldn't cook anything for himself. He insisted that if he boiled hot dogs they tasted like ashes. If I cooked them the same way for the same duration, they tasted good. He now has no problem cooking for himself. I can't explain why.

When he was 16, Tim wrote, "If you ask someone 'who are you?' and get a simple answer, either they're lying or they're not too bright. Some people have so many twists and turns in their personalities that if a maze were made, a poor fool would get dizzy and give up halfway out the entrance."

A World of His Own

I frequently took Tim to meetings of the Anime Club at MIT. He was a devoted fan of Japanese anime, and the club was open to any and all. I pointed out to him that "MIT" is "Tim" spelled backwards, trying to motivate him to study hard in hopes of going there for college. I don't think my words had any effect.

He got into Rochester Institute of Technology, on early acceptance. He wanted to study game design; but, instead, they put him in general computer programming, with a fixed curriculum, no choice of courses. Freshman Discrete Math was a prerequisite for everything that followed. He lasted less than two months. He was given the choice of withdrawing before mid-terms and coming back to try again the following fall. He had the text books and knew what was expected of him. He could study on his own and return well prepared. He did that, and the second time he only lasted one month.

Barb and I took him with us on a five-week guided tour of China. He loved the experience. Then Barb and I visited Uncle Paul (Dad's brother) in Nova Scotia. My cousin John (Uncle Phil's son) and his wife Joyce were visiting there at the same time. They mentioned that they both had gone to Wittenberg College in Ohio and that all six of Phil's children had gone there and met their future spouses there. When we got home, I suggested that Tim look at the Wittenberg web site. That day they were featuring their East Asian Studies major. We visited the campus. He loved it. He got in on early acceptance.

He seemed to be doing well until his mother died in December, a week before first semester final exams.

He flew home. He could take the tests later. After Christmas vacation, I drove him back to school. He reported that all was well. But a few months later, I got a call from the school administration saying that he hadn't been attending classes, hadn't turned in homework, and was failing all his courses. They understood that the shock of his mother's death was the issue. They said that if he dropped out before final exams and took incompletes, he could return and start over. But if he took the tests and failed, he wouldn't be able to return.

He needed time to grieve and heal. I signed him up for courses at a nearby community college the following fall, so he could ease back into school work. He'd probably be able to transfer credits. He could start at Wittenberg in January. To do that, he needed to get his driver's license so he could drive himself to school. He hadn't wanted to do that before. Now he had good reason and did fine.

All seemed to be going well. He reported that he was enjoying his classes at the community college and was doing well in them. Then in early December, I got a call from one of his teachers. He hadn't been to class for a long time. He had been leaving for school in the morning and coming home at the expected time, but he hadn't been going to his classes. In the presence of his therapist (whom he saw weekly), I asked him what he was doing during that time. He didn't know. He sincerely thought that he had been going to class. He wasn't lying. He was delusional. He agreed that he shouldn't go back to Wittenberg. He needed to explore other life choices. He would find his own path forward.

Barb's Death

Twelve years have passed since Barb died.

Her intestines twisted, cutting off the flow of blood — a condition known as "volvulus." Apparently, when she was born, her intestines were untethered, not fully held in place. They were prone to getting tangled. She sometimes suffered from stomach pain. We thought it was gas, but she might have had twists, leading to pain, that randomly untwisted.

A volvulus is dangerous because it can block blood flow to parts of the intestines. Those parts may die and get gangrenous. Barb's volvulus could have happened any time in her life. A sneeze while leaning one way or another could have triggered a fatal twist. It was amazing she lived so long.

A few years before, Barb had had appendicitis. She had severe abdominal pain. I took her to the emergency room. The doctors didn't think it was appendicitis because the pain was on her left side, not her right, where the appendix is. I insisted that they make sure. They did an MRI. The appendix was on the wrong side and was about to burst. It ruptured while they performed emergency surgery. She came through, but there were lingering fears of infection. We were lucky. She was fine. But those doctors said nothing about why the appendix was in the wrong place or what the implications of untethered intestines might be.

By coincidence, the first pains from her fatal condition came the day after Dad was sent to the ER by ambulance because of swelling in his right leg, a possible sign of a blood clot. I joined him there and sat with him all night, only to find out it was a false alarm. So when

Barb got her pains, I thought that, too, might be something minor. She took Tums for gas and Tylenol for pain, as she always did. Maybe she could sleep and feel better in the morning. It was easy to convince myself of that, and easy for Barb to believe it as well. But that was a mistake.

When we woke up the next morning, Barb called her doctor and explained her symptoms. He told her to come to his office so he could exam her. She decided to take a shower first and told me to check my email in my office downstairs until she was ready.

While she was in the shower, she must have realized she was dying. She walked back into the bedroom and lay down calmly in the narrow space between the bed and the wall. She couldn't have fallen to get into that position.

Lying on her back, stretched out on the floor beside our bed, stark naked, she was smiling. Her eyes were glazed over. She was barely breathing and non-responsive, but she looked happy.

I called 911, and the EMTs arrived at the door in less than two minutes. They presumed she had had a heart attack. When they were ready to carry her to the ambulance, her heart stopped. They resuscitated her and then took her away. Her heart stopped again in the ambulance, and again they resuscitated her. In the emergency room, it stopped for a third time, and she was brought back again. At that point, the doctor on duty concluded that she must be brain dead. He said that if it were his wife, he wouldn't resuscitate her again. It was over.

I told him that our son Bob had had volvulus a few years before – an important detail that I describe in the next chapter. I thought she might have the same condition. The doctor explained that intestinal volvulus is very rare in adults — one in a million. He also said that he was familiar with it, having dealt with several cases over the last year. He could operate, but that would be pointless. Why put her through agony for nothing? I told him that if there was any chance, however small, that she might be saved, please do it. If she was brain dead, she wouldn't feel it.

He performed the operation. It was indeed a volvulus. But it was far too late to save her. She had been as good as dead that morning, when she lay down after the shower. The volvulus had restricted blood flow. The lining of her intestines was compromised and toxins had escaped into her blood stream. Her organs were shutting down. She was 62. We had been married for 39 years.

She went gently into that dark night.

I should have suspected twisted intestine when she first had abdominal pain. I should have taken her straight to the emergency room instead of presuming that the pain was from gas and would soon go away. I should have told the doctor right away that our son had had twisted intestine and this might be that. If I had, she might be alive today. The guilt and regret from that still weigh heavily on me twelve years later.

They kept her on life support for a few hours so our children and her extended family could gather, hold her hand, and say goodbye to her while her heart was still beating. This was a total shock. She had been fine the day before. The surgeon explained what had happened to all of us. He assured us that this isn't hereditary, that her near family shouldn't worry; they weren't at risk.

Blood, Fate, and Coincidence

Our oldest, Bob, had a volvulus four years before that. Despite excruciating pain, he was able to drive himself to a local hospital in Princeton, where he worked. A doctor with experience in performing this rare kind of surgery happened to be on duty. She correctly diagnosed it and operated immediately. She saved his life. It was a one-in-a-million condition. What were the odds that the attending ER doctor would have performed this procedure before? The right doctor at the right place at the right time.

Unknown to us, Bob was born with a malrotated bowel, which means that he, like Barb, was predisposed to a volvulus. Like Barb, he had massive stomach pains over the years. I remember staying up with him at night, giving him Tums or Alka Seltzer, burping him. He remembers those incidents better than I do. I thought it was indigestion. Who would suspect a child's stomach pain could be serious? When I comforted him, and put him to bed, he might never have woken up. Maybe by burping him I jostled him enough to untwist his intestines.

Doctors said that Barb's untethered intestine and Bob's malrotated bowel were unrelated. But like Barb, Bob's appendix was on the wrong side of his body. That seems like an unbelievable coincidence.

And now, going over old records as I write this book, I'm reminded that as an infant Tim was diagnosed with a malrotated intestine. Maybe that diagnosis wasn't wrong. Maybe the problem resolved itself. Tim never complained of abdominal pain, so there's no reason to believe he has that condition now. But that's further reason to suspect a genetic connection.

When Bob was seven, I made the mistake of taking him to the horror film *Poltergeist*. It gave him nightmares. When the videotape became available, I rented it and played it in slow motion, so he could see that the monsters were fake, made of papier-mâché. That didn't help. The boy in the story was Bob's age, looked like him, and was named Robbie. The sister was played by Heather O'Rourke who looked very much like Bob's sister. By bizarre and tragic coincidence, that promising actress died at the age of 12 of a congenital intestinal issue that restricted blood flow — perhaps this same "extremely rare" condition.

Endgame Tactics

My appendix was where it should be, on the right side, and it hurt worse than anything I'd felt before. I was nine years old. If the doctor had told me I was dying, I'd have believed him. But what I remember best is what I did during the recovery, home from school and confined to bed for two weeks. Paradise.

I focused on the game Hi-Q (peg solitaire). It's played on a board with holes arranged in a cross formation: nine holes in a square at the middle, and two rows of three holes on each arm of a cross, for a total of 33 holes. In the initial position, there are pegs in every hole except the one in the middle. You move by jumping one peg over another (horizontally or vertically, not diagonally) to land in an open hole. As in checkers, when you jump over a piece, you remove it from the board. You keep jumping until there are no more legal moves. The object is to end up with as few pegs left as possible. Ultimate mastery is ending up with one peg left in the middle.

I didn't want to just play the game repeatedly and get random results. I wanted to solve it, to figure out how to end up with one peg in the middle hole every time.

So I started with the end position and worked backwards, checking all the positions that could lead to that, and all the positions that could lead to those positions, and keeping notes on the possibilities that I had tried, until, when my two-week vacation was almost up, I had a complete solution. It wasn't the only solution, but it worked, and following my notes I could do it repeatedly.

Decades later, I put the solution on my web site to share it with others (seltzerbooks.com/hiq.html). Many people wouldn't want to know, because then the game is no longer fun to play. But for me, the satisfaction from solving the game was enormous.

Now I realize that my approach to that game resembles the best way to play endgame in chess, when all that remains are the kings and a few pawns, the kinds of positions that Harry Lyman would show young kids to exercise their abstract thinking. Instead of planning forward (this move, then that, then that), you plan backward, visualizing the ideal position you want to get to and figuring out how to go from there to here, and, hence, here to there.

Perhaps that's a good strategy for end of life as well. Where do you want to be at the end, and what paths could lead from there to here and here to there?

Risk of Pain Killers

The night before she died, Barb thought her problem was pain. She needed to stop it, and Tylenol wasn't enough. We went to bed. I slept soundly, but she probably got up repeatedly. It wasn't until the morning after she died that I noticed empty pill containers on the bathroom floor — Vicodin, Codeine, and others. She must have had bouts of severe pain before that or she wouldn't have had a supply of those meds.

Pain is the body's alarm system, telling you, loudly, that something is seriously wrong, and you better do something about it. Painkillers don't treat the condition causing the pain. They just shut off the alarm.

If you know what's wrong and you're doing something about it, of course you should do what you can to minimize the pain. But Barb didn't know what was wrong, and the pills helped her to sleep when she needed to seek urgent care.

I wish I knew then how intense her pain was. I could have gotten her to the hospital sooner. Maybe she could have survived.

Public Health Data

I wonder how this surgeon, who by chance was on duty in the emergency room when Barb arrived, could have seen several cases over the last year if it was a one-in-a-million occurrence. I suspect that the frequency of this condition has been underestimated. If the surgeon hadn't operated, her death would have been recorded as "heart failure."

He said there was no record of another parent and child both having this condition. He was adamant about that, but how could he have known? And were the data accurate?

I've encouraged Bob to have his daughters tested. He hasn't. He says the test for a congenital intestine condition comes at the cost of exposure to radiation, and neither of them has had intense stomach pain. But he says that every time one of them has a tummy ache, he wonders.

Statistics on cause-of-death are important in determining where to invest research funds and medical training. Heart disease and cancer are typically at the top of the list.

Often, a dying patient has multiple issues, and it may not be clear which proved fatal. The statistics should include more detail and should be based on more than the anecdotal observations of the attending physician. Conditions that are considered rare may be more common than we appreciate. They may have gone undiagnosed. Conditions that can lead to twisted intestine may, in fact, be inherited.

Because so few autopsies are performed, (and primarily when the death is deemed suspicious), cause-of-death health data tend to be incomplete, faulty, anecdotal. Such imprecision means that relatives of the deceased might not know their health risks. And the distribution of health resources and the focus of medical education, which depend on morbidity data, may be inaccurately skewed toward heart disease and cancer, with other conditions getting short shrift.

Imagine setting up an experiment to see if the systematic gathering of accurate data might prove valuable. Randomly select a sample of deaths caused by illness or medical condition (not accident or murder) and perform autopsies to determine what happened. Compare those results with what was reported on death certificates.

If there's a huge discrepancy, mandate that a percentage of all deaths be autopsied and use that data to recalculate frequencies and risks.

I don't understand why this hasn't been done already.

Why was she smiling when I found her?

Barb was Catholic. She only went to Mass on special occasions, but she believed in God and Heaven and Hell. She probably prayed, but silently. The brother she was closest to had died in Vietnam. He was a medic. Reportedly, he stepped on a mine. We named our first born "Bob" after him. Barb's sister Ann was bipolar. Ann was fine until she reached college age. Then she started having manic high-energy episodes, followed by low energy and depression. Doctors put her on lithium, which dealt with the symptoms but gradually destroyed her kidneys. Eventually, she needed dialysis, and, in her 60s, she needed a kidney transplant; but she was low on the donor list. Barb wanted to donate one of hers. I didn't want her to. I was afraid of losing her. She went ahead and got tested without telling me. She wasn't a match.

Barb's father, who had a pacemaker for many years, died of heart failure in 1992 at the age of 81. When Barb's mother needed 24/7 care, she was admitted to the nursing home where her daughter Ann then lived. She died in 2005 at the age of 91. Ann died in 2007.

The Heaven that Barb believed in was fully populated with people she knew and loved.

Premonitions

Sitting together on the sofa watching television the night before she died, Barb couldn't have had any idea that she would be dead in twelve hours. But over the two days before, she had taken a series of uncharacteristic steps that helped those she would be leaving behind.

She finished her Christmas shopping long before she normally did. She designed our annual Christmas card. That was an important tradition — one which she had always delayed, sometimes to as late as the following Easter. And, for the first time, she designed and printed 15 copies of another card, intended to accompany a Christmas gift of a compass that she had bought for friends and relatives.

She had all of the Christmas gifts organized in stacks, gifts for nearly thirty people, weeks earlier than in any other year. Did she know she wouldn't be around to give them out?

When she passed, while trying to deal with the grief and shock, I stared at that stack of gifts. There was no way that I or the assembled family and friends could tell what was for whom. I searched for a master list and finally found one tucked in a notebook she'd never used before, on a rarely-used desk. With that, I was able to sort the gifts and distribute them at her wake.

The gifts weren't wrapped, so someone ran to the store to buy gift bags. Meanwhile, we found a bag full of gift bags in the same room as the gifts.

Barb had never mentioned the cards with the message about the compass. The picture on the front and the product description came from Amazon. But I couldn't find the original of the message anywhere on the Internet. She may have written it herself or have stumbled upon it and loved it so much that she made it hers. Those words helped me through that day and the day after. She must have meant them to serve as inspiration for her friends and relatives.

To Help You Find Your True North
to find north
one must know where south is
to find south
one must be willing to dive
sinking
to
the
watery
depths
where
monsters
of
the
mind
thrive
to navigate
not by sight
but by sound
to discern
not by fact
but by mystery
dive, dive deep
for therein lies the way
of the spirit.

The Compass
Essential to guide a man's travels,
In journeys o'er sea and land.
Its needle, a simple reminder
O' the Power inside every man.
If each could only remember,
The Compass of the mind is the heart,
So quiet it speaks, if you listen
Love is its passionate art.
Compass roses are little assistance,
Seeking Truth each man must find,
If drive for Success tears the man's heart
He's lost his moral compass of mind.

She also left what seemed like farewell messages. On the first page of the same notebook where I found the Christmas list, I found a poem that Barb had copied two years earlier by hand:

Miss me, but let me go
When I come to the end of the road
And the sun has set for me,
I want no rites in a gloom filled room!
Why cry for a soul set free!
Miss me a little, but not too long
And not with your head bowed low!
Remember the love that we once shared.
Miss me, but let me go.

For this is a journey we all must take
And each must go alone.
It's all a part of the Master's plan

A step on the road to home.
When you are lonely and sick of heart
Go to the friend we know
And bury your sorrows in doing good deeds,
Miss me, but let me go.

That poem is by Christina Rossetti (1830-1894). It's often read at funerals.

Another notebook on the same table had just two entries: the address of a friend and a list of goals from September 9, 2005:

Find what you love to do
Do what you love
Spend time with people you like
Surround yourself with things you like
Be discrete — don't tell everything!

The Concept of an Afterlife

There's no unanimity about the meaning of death even within the same religion and during the same time period. Nothingness? Existence without consciousness or activity? Or another mode of being, with eternal pleasure or pain?

Ecclesiastes says, "Whatsoever thy hand findeth to do, do it with thy might; for there is no work, nor device, nor knowledge, nor wisdom in the grave, whither thou goest." That image of death is reflected in the phrase "rest in peace," which is echoed in the Latin *requiscat in pace*, having the same initials, "R.I.P.," and dating back before the 5th century C.E.

In contrast, Dante's dead, whether in Hell, Purgatory or Heaven, did not rest. Their pleasure or pain after death was more important than what happened to them on Earth, and they could benefit from the prayers and payments of the living.

I don't have an answer. I wish I did. I wish that with the power of belief I could make Heaven real and give Barb a place there, in company with those she loved on Earth, and ancestors as well — extraordinary women and extraordinary men, and friendly regular folk, too. And I might join her there, and find her among the nonillions of entities from Earth and from the rest of this universe and from others as well. (I hope there's a real *Hitch Hiker's Guide* to help with that challenge.)

Despite Barb's premonitions, I don't believe that's the case.

I hope I'm wrong.

Dad's Stroke

Mom died in 2010, Barb in 2012, Dad in 2014, five years after his stroke.

Early one morning, I got a call from a nurse in Dad's assisted living facility. He was in an ambulance on his way to the ER. I joined him there, where the doctor in charge asked me when the stroke had occurred. All I knew was what the nurse had told me: early that morning, a janitor heard him groaning in his apartment and found him on the floor. They called for an ambulance.

The doctor explained that if a clot is blocking blood flow to the brain, a medicine (tissue plasminogen activator or tPa) can break it up. That treatment often leads to complete recovery. But if the stroke is caused by a leakage of blood into the brain (instead of a clot) or if this medicine is given after three hours have passed, the shot would probably kill him.

Dad might have fallen the night before, in which case this was long after the three-hour limit. And I had had a stroke nine years before. I had been lucky. There was no permanent damage. But it had been the bleeding, hemorrhagic kind of stroke, without a clot.

Hemorrhagic strokes are rare. Nearly nine out of ten strokes are caused by clots (ischemic strokes). But my susceptibility to the bleeding variety might have been inherited from Dad. So I decided not to give him the shot. I have no way of knowing if I was right, but the doctors weren't able to find a clot.

His right side was completely paralyzed. He couldn't speak. And that wasn't going to improve. He had to move from his assisted living quarters to the nursing home in another wing of the same building, where he could get 24/7 care. There was no room for his belongings in his new room, nor was he ever going to use them again. Sallie and I had a few days to clear everything out, sorting through all of what had been treasures to him, deciding what we could store and what we had to discard. Difficult. Painful.

Apparently, the left side of his brain, the seat of analytical thought, which also controls the right side of the body, was irrecoverably damaged. But the right side of his brain, the seat of sensitivity and creativity, was intact.

Before the stroke, Dad was rational and authoritarian, a school administrator. He also was judgmental. He looked down on people in wheelchairs, as if that were a sign of moral as well as physical weakness.

The stroke caused a personality change. He became more empathetic and emotional. Now, unable to say a word, he could speak with his eyes and facial expressions. He became more sociable. I believe he made many friends. That was probably, in part, a benefit of his acting experience. I remember seeing him, in preparation for a play, in front of a mirror practicing control of his facial expressions.

He had check-marked "do not resuscitate" on his entry form at the assisted living facility a couple years before. I was shocked to see those words, in large type, taped to the door of his room. Someone fit and healthy should never be asked to make such a decision. There's no way for you to know what you'll want when faced with the possibility of imminent death. Without words, Dad made it clear that he wasn't ready to die. As his medical proxy, I had that sign taken down. He should be given whatever care he might need. He lived another four years — possibly some of the happiest years of his life.

His baseline of expectations changed. Rather than being depressed, comparing his present state to what it had been before, he compared today to yesterday, and set his expectations for tomorrow accordingly. Some days were good, and others were very good. He never said a word to anyone in the nursing home. He couldn't. But he seemed to know everyone, and everyone knew him; and he was all smiles and glad-handing.

I lived within walking distance. I visited for half an hour a day, every day. Sallie went once a week, every week, and spent the day.

I remember the first time I held his hand. I had never done so as an adult before his stroke. It would have seemed odd to hold my father's hand, like I was a five-year-old out for a walk with him. But when he was in a wheelchair and couldn't speak, it felt natural to touch, to squeeze as part of our connecting and communicating.

I tried experiments meant to teach him how to write or draw with his left hand. They didn't work, but he seemed to appreciate my enthusiasm and creativity. I felt closer to him than I had ever felt before. We had our routines. He seemed happy. Sallie told me that she, too, felt closer to Dad in his last four years, when he couldn't speak, than she had at any other time.

Then one day, he couldn't swallow anymore. He was doing fine in other ways. I wouldn't have been surprised if he lived to a hundred, like his Uncle Gus. But this was going to be the end for him.

The stroke hadn't affected his ability to swallow. But after four years of not speaking, the muscles of his throat atrophied, and there was nerve deterioration as well. (I described the end and his funeral above).

In the aftermath, I wondered about the relationship between speaking and swallowing.

Maybe humans evolved the ability to make sounds through the throat because that exercised muscles needed for swallowing. Then the ability to generate a wide range of sounds made it possible to use sound for communication. But in the beginning was the need to eat and drink. The Word came later.

My Stroke

I had my stroke in 2000, at the age of 54. Fortunately, no deficits resulted.

I was at the dining-room table eating salad. Suddenly the room started spinning around me. I couldn't keep my balance. Was I in a tornado? The spinning stopped. No one else had felt it. I didn't know what to make of it.

The next morning, going down to my home office, I was severely dizzy again and had to grab hold of furniture to stay on my feet. When I recovered, I went to see my doctor. He put me through cognitive tests and checked my walking and hand-eye coordination. He didn't detect any problems, but sent me to get an MRI to see if I had had a stroke. The film showed a black spot, about the size of a golf ball, in the cerebellum. He concluded that, yes, I had had stroke, and I was lucky not to have deficits. He put me on coumadin, a blood thinner, to deal with possible clots.

Shortly before my stroke, Barb lost her temper with her boss, who was mistreating a colleague friend of hers. She stormed out and quit. That was out of character and unexpected. It meant that, after a grace period, we had to change health plans. We joined an HMO, Harvard Community Health Plan. I took a copy of the film from the MRI to my new doctor, Dr. Krohn, and he gave it to a neurologist who was part of the same HMO. The neurologist concluded that blood had leaked from my left carotid artery into my cerebellum. It was a major stroke, but there was no clot. This was a hemorrhagic stroke. Dr.

Krohn immediately took me off coumadin. My problem was bleeding, not clotting. The coumadin could have killed me. He also put me on a regimen of meds appropriate for my condition, and I've been on them ever since, for 24 years, with no recurrence of the problem. In addition, follow-up tests indicated that I had a low platelet count, meaning my blood might not clot properly.

This rare condition was called "idiopathic thrombocytopenic purpura." "Idiopathic" was a fancy way of saying that doctors hadn't a clue what caused it. The name was later changed to "immuno," keeping the abbreviation — ITP — the same. The immune system mistakenly attacks platelets, which are necessary for blood to clot, and does so intermittently, so your platelet count may go down, then up, then down again. If it goes too low, a minor cut or nose bleed could lead to serious loss of blood, and a bruise might lead to uncontrolled internal bleeding.

I began seeing a hematologist (blood specialist), who monitored my platelet count. When the count went seriously low, doctors tried several treatments, none of which worked. Finally, they removed my spleen, believing that it was zapping my platelets, as if they were foreign invaders. In other words, I nearly died from an internal case of mistaken identity.

Ever since my spleen was removed in 2005, my platelets have stayed safely high. They are now normal. But I'm still tested periodically to make sure the problem hasn't recurred. In rare instances, a new spleen can grow.

By quitting her job and forcing us to change doctors, Barb saved my life. And my stroke was a stroke of luck. If I hadn't had it, I'd have never known I had ITP and could have died from that.

ITP and Rasputin

Before I was diagnosed with ITP, I had never heard of that condition. The only bleeding disease I knew of was hemophilia, and I associated that disorder with the story of Rasputin and Alexei, the son and heir of the last Russian Tsar. My experience made me realize that a posting I had stumbled upon on the Internet might be true — misdiagnosis may have, in part, caused the Russian Revolution.

Alexei had periodic bouts of internal bleeding. It was believed that he had hemophilia, for which there was no cure. It was known to be hereditary and was called the "royal disease." Eight of his royal cousins died of it. Queen Victoria and Prince Albert, through their daughters Alice and Beatrice, passed the mutation for hemophilia to the royal houses of Spain, Germany, and Russia. Normally, the disorder afflicts only men. Women are carriers. Alexei's four sisters didn't have it. Alexei through his mother was a great-grandson of Queen Victoria.

Doctors couldn't help Alexei. But a peasant monk named Rasputin apparently stopped the bleeding with prayer. Because of this seemingly magical, presumably God-given power, Alexei's father, Tsar Nicholas II, came to depend on Rasputin's advice. And that advice prompted decisions that led to the Russian Revolution.

But the symptoms of hemophilia don't come and go. That's characteristic of ITP, which I had and which is not hereditary. The hemophilia diagnosis was never confirmed by laboratory tests because they didn't exist at that time. If it were ITP, Rasputin's success may have been a coincidence. He happened to be at the right place at the right time. John Kendrick makes that case in "Russia's Imperial Blood: Was Rasputin Not the Healer of Legend?" (National Library of Medicine, 2004.)

Perhaps ITP might also explain how Attila the Hun died of a nosebleed.

Part Eight:
Talent

Talent isn't fate. Slaying a dragon doesn't mean you have to make a career of it. You have choice. Instead of doing what comes easily to you, you might want to pursue something that's a challenge.

Do you inherit your inclination to follow one path or another? Or is it more a matter of nurture, growing up believing you can become such a person — entrepreneur, actor, writer — and you become what you believe you can become?

And having one talent doesn't mean you don't have others. Sometimes one leads to another, and that to yet another, in a twisting path you never imagined.

Student Council Election

Did I lose by one vote or two? I don't remember. I was the new boy in Plymouth, a town of 2500. For no apparent reason, I became popular. Before I knew the names of more than three of my seventh-grade classmates, they nominated me for vice president of the Student Council. My opponent would be Becky, in the other seventh-grade class. I had never met her. She had lived in Plymouth her whole life, and her father was the Congregational minister. The odds against me were enormous; but spontaneously, without telling me they were going to do so, a dozen girls in my class came up with cheerleading moves and slogans and put on a show supporting me in the schoolyard every day at lunchtime and before and after school.

The two seventh-grade classes each got to nominate the candidates for vice president. Becky and I had to deliver campaign speeches to an assembly of the whole school (K to 8). I wrote out every word on 3 x 5 cards and stared at the cards as I read them, not daring to look at the audience. My opening line was, "I was born in a hospital in Clarksville, Tennessee."

Becky won; but I still thought I might be destined for a career in politics.

That was the Becky I got to know when Mom and Dad went to Aunt Lil's funeral, the Becky with whom I almost held hands and carried on a steamy correspondence, a necessary link in the chain of events leading to my meeting and marrying Barb.

Politician?

Soon thereafter, Mom told me that Estes Kefauver, the esteemed senator from Tennessee who had run for vice president of the United States, was her third cousin and that we, when I was one, lived in a log cabin in someone's backyard in Silver Spring, Maryland. That meant I could be the last "log-cabin president."

But there might be a problem. There was a skeleton in the family closet. Her father, who I thought had died when she was young, actually went to prison, convicted of a serious crime. She told me because she didn't want me to be caught off guard if a political opponent learned of that and tried to smear me with it.

That was more than I could handle at the age of 13. I had never met her father. He died before I was born. How could what he did affect me?

In high school, I was a Goldwater Republican, like my parents. I loved his *Conscience of a Conservative,* and I proudly shook hands with him when he visited Plymouth in advance of the 1964 primary. That was soon before my sister was born. My parents were living near Philadelphia, and I was a boarder at Holderness for my senior year.

The following summer, the Democratic National Convention was held in Atlantic City, and I volunteered because I wanted the experience, despite my Republican allegiance. Birch Bayh, a senator from Indiana, was in charge of the hundreds of volunteers from all over the country. He promised that if we showed up on the boardwalk in front of the Convention Hall at 5 AM, he would give us passes to go inside on nomination day. We showed up but weren't let in. The morning TV news and talk shows, like *Today*, focused cameras on us repeatedly. The angrier and louder we got at our betrayal, the more it looked to the national audience as if the youth of America were wildly enthusiastic for Lyndon B. Johnson.

None of us had slept that night. Bayh told us the printer had screwed up and wouldn't deliver the signs for the crowd to wave during the nomination. This was a PR nightmare. He asked us to make original signs with materials he supplied. We would carry some and delegates would carry others on the convention floor. Both exhausted and disappointed, we waved those signs angrily when the cameras turned on us. It made for great theater, at our expense. None of those signs ever made it inside the convention hall.

I told myself that maybe it was just the Democrats who were underhanded and manipulative, or maybe just Birch Bayh. Surely, the Republicans couldn't be that bad.

In high school, I had toyed with the idea of becoming a Congressional page as the first step in a political career. And, at the prompting of Dad, I considered going to West Point. I was a fan of the *West Point* TV series. It looked challenging and for me at that time, the more difficult the better. If we went to war and I served in it, that would look good on my record when I ran for office. A minor wound would be good, too.

In the fall of 1965, after my year in England, I started at Yale and immediately joined the Young Republicans Club. There were over a thousand members, a quarter of the student body. The president of the club visited me in my dorm room soon after the massive first meeting. He was recruiting volunteers to go to New York City and stand on street corners, handing out leaflets for John Lindsay, who was running for mayor. He didn't say anything about Lindsay and what Lindsay stood for. He didn't care if his volunteers were knowledgeable. He just wanted lots of them to show up so he'd get credit for having recruited them. I'd never heard of Lindsay and knew nothing about New York politics. I was disgusted by this recruiting effort. I quit the Young Republicans. That was the end of my political aspirations. For that, I thank the Young Republican whose name I don't remember.

Dad

Dad went from acting to education and back to acting. His parents first groomed him and his three brothers to become Lutheran ministers. Such a career resonated with him. He looked forward to delivering sermons. He reveled in public performance. When he was at Gettysburg College preparing for such a career, that talent prompted him to write, direct, and act in a bawdy play which was acclaimed by his frat brothers, but got him expelled.

After the war, Dad's first objective was to go to the UCLA Drama School. When the housing shortage and his wife's impatience made that impossible, he decided to become a teacher, who, like a minister, performs in front of an audience.

Money was tight for the years when I was a toddler. While earning an M.A. at the University of Pennsylvania, Dad taught in junior high, coached tennis and track, worked part-time as a cab driver, went to Army Reserves meetings, and periodically sold his rare AB-negative blood. Mom and Dad also rented an attic room to a pair of Nisei Japanese women who were medical students.

Then we moved to Rockville, Maryland, where Dad got a job as vice principal in a high school, while he was earning a Doctor of Education degree at the University of Maryland. Eventually, he rose through the ranks of education until he became a superintendent of schools.

His success as an administrator derived in part from a skill he had learned from acting — using silence. He would sit quietly and smile, and the student who was a discipline problem or the teacher with an issue would squirm and talk on and on, filling the silence with words, incriminating himself or herself or backing down with an apology. No need for him to raise his voice, to say a word.

That approach was effective at home as well. I thought of Mom as Charybdis, the whirlpool Odysseus faced. She would praise me no matter what I did, no matter how little I tried, pulling me down by making it easy for me to make no effort. Dad was the cliff where the monster Scylla lived — unscalable, with expectations I could never meet.

Dad was proud of his accomplishments over ten years as superintendent of schools in Lower Moreland Township, in the Philadelphia suburbs. The district had 200 teachers and 3300 students. The new high school building that he championed included a planetarium, and he added a TV studio so the music director could teach via closed circuit, eventually recruiting and training a 40-piece symphony orchestra.

While at that job, when he was in his 50s, Dad also studied Physical Anthropology at the University of Pennsylvania. He completed all course work needed for a Ph.D., but didn't write a dissertation. He wanted to study the effects of lead-poisoning on the learning ability of children. But to do the research, he would have had to take a year off from work.

Meanwhile, he stayed in the Army Reserves and rose to the rank of full colonel (a far cry from the bugle boy). After Vietnam and before the Gulf Wars, his specialty was Civil Affairs, building scenarios for the unlikely event that we conquered and occupied another country. How could we apply knowledge of the local culture and political situation to deal with issues of governance and diplomacy? In that capacity, Dad was able to combine his military service with his interest in history and anthropology. He was sometimes a student and sometimes an instructor. His team focused on the Middle East, around Iraq.

While he was proud to be a superintendent of schools, he took early retirement at 57, even though that meant family finances would be tight. He wanted to act, and, finally, he could and did. He got bit parts in movies and TV shows, modeled for ads, and acted in stage plays.

He was proud to be picked for a bit role in the movie *Gettysburg*, which would be filmed on the actual battlefield. He would be a Pennsylvania Dutch elder. For a year, he grew a beard to be authentic in the part. When they filmed his scene, the director's wife was in it, so he felt confident that it would make the final cut. He anxiously awaited the release. But that scene wasn't included. He doesn't appear anywhere in the movie. Close, but no cigar.

In parallel, he had a love for music. He took violin lessons as a child, and his siblings learned instruments as well. The family would gather at the piano and play and sing together, often hymns. He taught himself the piano, a chord method that sufficed for after-dinner singalongs, one tune merging into another, like on the *Mitch Miller Show*. Sometimes Mom and he sang together in harmony. He taught himself the saxophone as well, and while Dean of Instruction at Plymouth State, he moonlighted playing with a dance band. Dad wanted to teach me the saxophone. I now wish I had let him.

When he was in his late 80s, before his stroke, he played violin in two community orchestras. And after his stroke, when he couldn't talk, he could still sing. (Oliver Sacks discusses that phenomenon in his book *Musicophilia*). The therapist at the nursing home who encouraged him dubbed him "The Music Man." There's a two minute video clip of him singing on YouTube. (Search for "musicman seltzer").

Dad also had artistic talent. He painted murals on the walls of the houses we lived in. At Christmas, he painted winter scenes on the windows. And later in life, he did oil paintings. A couple of those now hang in my apartment.

He learned handyman skills from his father, but I didn't learn from him. He could fix anything. I don't remember him ever hiring anyone to do work around the house. If he didn't know already, he'd learn how to do it.

His biggest project was a 19-foot cabin cruiser he built in our barn in New Hampshire, with the help and guidance of Uncle Walt, Mildred's second husband, a shipbuilder by trade. I was fascinated watching them warp the wood and apply the fiber glass. But I never willingly helped, and I learned nothing.

Dad was proud of what he could do with his hands. In that, he took after his grandfather's brother, Uncle Gus, who was born the year after the Battle of Gettysburg and lived to the age of 101, near the site of that battle. In the 19th century, Uncle Gus was a harness maker with a creative streak. He could design and carve toys and gadgets of all kinds. In his old age, he made "authentic" antiques. Experts couldn't distinguish between what he made yesterday and furniture made a hundred years before. He used old wood, old methods, old tools. In my bedroom I have a desk he built in 1935. I wrote some of this book sitting at that desk. I remember playing with a chain he had carved from a single block of wood and seeing him catch a fly in flight with his bare hand at the age of 100.

Henry Hocker Seltzer

As I write this book, I often check a brown, three-ring University of Maryland binder that Dad used in his college days. It's stuffed with notes I made in pencil when I was a teenager, interviewing Nana and Pop Pop about family genealogy. Uncle Gus's brother, my great-grandfather Henry Hocker Seltzer probably did the same with his grandparents when he was a teenager.

Born in 1856, Henry Hocker was determined to prove himself; and I believe that trait passed down to Dad and to me.

I have his handwritten autobiography, his family genealogy, his unpublished textbook *Book-Keeping on the Farm,* a register of all the books he owned, and a detailed record of his activities as a teacher. He loved making lists and keeping records. I also have several of his diary-like journals. He often noted the weather. On the day when his son, my grandfather, was born, he only mentioned the rain.

I got his obsession for making lists and organizing information, though neither my father nor my grandfather had that. I've kept a list of every book I've read for the last 66 years. The 4000 books on the shelves that cover every wall of my one-bedroom apartment are carefully organized. And at the end of this book, you'll find a list of over 1600 ancestors, organized by a system of my own devising.

Henry Hocker grew up on a farm near Gettysburg. His family spoke Pennsylvania Dutch at home. English was his second language, putting him at a disadvantage when he first went to school. But he did well and was proud of his accomplishments. As soon as he graduated from his one-room school, he began teaching in another, in a nearby town. There was no need to go to college to get teaching credentials. County school boards each held their own competitive tests to determine who was qualified to teach. Over his ten years of teaching, he handled, alone, as many as 65 students at a time, ranging in age from 5 to 21, for a wage of $33 per month. He had to deal with the usual challenges of rural schools — behavior problems, parents who had little respect for book learning, and arbitrary decisions by county-level school administrators. During corn-husking season, only 3-5 students would show up.

Each year he took the teaching test of another nearby county, not because he wanted to change jobs, but to prove he could do well. One year, for the same reason, he took the federal Civil Service test. To his surprise, he did so well that the Treasury Department offered him a bookkeeping job in Washington, DC. He took it. That's where he got married and raised three sons.

At the age of 40, he got an M.D. degree from what later became George Washington University. But he practiced medicine very little, having gotten the degree to prove that he could.

Henry Hocker Seltzer died in 1925 at the age of 68. The obituary doesn't mention the cause of death. The longest paragraph in his will dealt with how his books should be divided among his children "as equitably as possible." His books were his most valued possessions. He would probably agree with Ashleigh Brilliant who wrote, "The closest you will ever come in this life to an orderly universe is a good library."

Sallie

My sister, Sallie, like me, seems to have followed in Henry Hocker's footsteps. She has many talents, and has periodically felt the urge to start afresh and prove herself in a new field. She says I influenced her interest in writing as well as in French and Russian literature. She remembers me reading *Le Petit Prince* to her in French when she was two and on her swing. And she went to Mount Holyoke College, in part, because my girlfriend Jean had gone there.

After graduating with a major in Russian, she moved to the West Coast and earned an M.A. in Cinema-TV at U.S.C. She made a full-length movie, *The Magazine*, on her own, paying for it by credit card and working with volunteer friends from Paramount, where she was a production assistant and then a paralegal. That was in the days when independent films were shot in 16-mm. Afterward, based on that experience, she wrote a post-production manual, with advice on how to make low-budget movies. A publisher bought the rights to it but set her up with an editor who had no experience in film. The project ground to a halt. Sallie got to keep the advance, but the book was never published.

Then she moved to New York, went to Studio One, worked as a paralegal for Showtime and wrote more movie scripts, submitting them to film festivals and winning prizes.[*]

Next she became a writer and singer of folk songs, performing in coffee houses around Boston, recording two albums, and selling CDs of her music. After that, she got extensive training in yoga and became a yoga therapist and instructor. She wrote and published the book *Back to Balance: Heal Your Life, Heal Your Spine*, a 30-day do-it-yourself program using yoga and ayurveda (traditional medicine native to India). Then she earned a masters degree and, at the age of 58, a doctorate in acupuncture.

Sallie was briefly married to a brother of my wife Barb. She was in her early 40s, like Mom was when she was born. She wanted children, but that didn't work. They divorced. She didn't remarry.

---

[*] Her *Eugene Onegin* won Best Adapted Screen play at the 1995 WorldFest Houston. *Ghost Fish* AKA *Crazy Baby* won the 1999 Hudson Valley Film Festival prize for Best Original Screenplay. And she was a finalist for the Eugene O'Neill Theater Center Award in 1999, and also a semi-finalist for the Nicholl Fellowship Awards in 1994 with *The House on Conrad Street* AKA *An East Falls Story* (inspired by Mom's childhood). In addition, she was a National Endowment for the Arts Fellow twice, winning month-long sabbaticals to work on screenplays.

Now, at the age of 60 and single, she's in the process of adopting a preteen girl, who will be a wonderful addition to the family — my one and only niece.

Flypaper

My daughter, like Dad and Sallie, has an acting/entertainment streak. I vividly remember her first performance — at a ballet recital held in a packed high-school auditorium. She was four years old, dancing solo, wearing a hula skirt. Confident and proud, she loved being on stage in front of an audience. She got a standing ovation.

In high school she played the lead in *The Diary of Anne Frank*. She went to Sarah Lawrence College because of its reputation for drama and dance. She spent the summer of 1997 on the west coast with Sallie and acted in her movie *The Magazine*. While there, she got an audition for a part in a TV series. That came about in a twisted, roundabout way, like much in my life.

While I was the Internet Evangelist at DEC, I built a personal web site and populated it with lots of text, including my list of every book I had read since 1958. I had stumbled upon a principle that I called "flypaper." Old friends I hadn't heard from for decades started sending me emails —about half a dozen of them each month. At first I was flattered. Isn't it amazing that those people were looking for me? Then it dawned on me — why would they look for me?

With a few quick queries, I figured out that they were actually looking for themselves or something that was important to them. They had entered their own name or their obsession in a search engine. Since I had lots of content at my Web site, many of my old friends were mentioned there. If I had wanted to find them, I could have worked long and hard and never succeeded. But because their search words appeared on web pages of mine and those pages were well indexed by search engines, they found me.

While my daughter was with Sallie on the west coast, I got an email from Lee Aronsohn, the TV writer and producer (*Two and a Half Men, The Love Boat, Murphy Brown, The Big Bang Theory,* and *Cybil*). He was a fan of the cartoonist Gary Trudeau, creator of the *Doonesbury* cartoon strip. A search had brought him to the list of books I had read, which included *Bull Tales,* self-published by Trudeau while an undergrad at Yale, when I was there. It was based on his cartoon strip about the Yale football team, published in the *Yale Daily News.* Aronsohn wanted that rare book for his collection and was willing to pay handsomely for it. We negotiated over the phone, and, instead of money, I asked him to give my daughter an audition for one of his shows. He agreed and did. She didn't get a part, but she did get the opportunity and experience, which I thought was well worth a book that was gathering dust on my shelf.

Now, decades later, my daughter is returning to that life path. She's writing, directing and producing a series of educational videos for children and distributing them through YouTube. She's also writing a screenplay based on her brother Bob's unpublished novel *Cynk*.

Why don't I use her name? That's her choice. I don't understand it, but I'll honor it.

Bob and Chess

How did Bob, a child chess prodigy, end up writing a novel?

Before he was two, he could read Dr. Seuss books (not just memorize them). Soon he was doing 100-piece puzzles and his drawings were complex and colorful. Barb and I sought advice on school options. I wrote to David Henry Feldman, a child expert at Tufts University who later wrote the book *Nature's Gambit* about prodigies. He was particularly impressed by Bob's artwork.

I taught Bob the moves of chess when he was three, sometimes adding action figures and inventing rules for how they would move. Then he lost interest and moved on to other challenges, until he was eight; and, unprompted, he asked me to play a game of chess. He beat me, and I haven't beaten him since.

I took him to tournaments and got him lessons with Murray Turnbull, who played speed chess outside Au Bon Pain in Harvard Square. His sign read: "Play the Chess Master for $1." Murray wasn't a professional chess teacher — he was a street player, a scrapper, who delighted in winning from losing positions. And Bob wasn't an ordinary student. He didn't memorize openings and didn't study endgames. He could see the board differently than others. One time, he played and beat three people at the same time blindfolded (three different boards, with everyone shouting out their moves). Bob says that's like in the streaming series *Queen's Gambit* where Beth Harmon sees pieces floating in the air. Top players don't need to look at a chessboard to analyze moves.

I kept Feldman at Tufts updated on Bob's progress. He was impressed not that Bob was a chess prodigy, but that unlike any of the prodigies he had known, Bob's brilliance wasn't limited to a single field.

Bob thrived. He was national chess champion for his age group five times. He represented the U.S. in the World Under 12 Championship in Puerto Rico and the World Under 14 in Timisoara, Romania (in the days of the Iron Curtain). At the Cadet invitational, among the eight top-rated players under the age of 16 in the U.S., he placed first, winning all seven of his games. (Second place had just three wins and a draw). In that tournament, he beat Josh Waitzkin, subject of the book and movie *Searching for Bobby Fisher,* prompting *The Boston Globe* to write a feature about him entitled, "Searching for Bobby Seltzer." He became a Master at the age of 14.

Thanks to his notoriety, Bob was invited to play chess simultaneously against three stars from the Boston Celtics (Kevin McHale, Bill Walton, and Danny Ainge) at a charity event. They were known for playing chess at halftime in their basketball games to help them relax and focus. Then, thanks to recommendations from Feldman, Bob got invitations to appear on television. On *Live With Regis and Kathy Lee*, he played two dozen adults from the Manhattan Chess Club simultaneously and beat all but one of them. And once, when I was flying back from a meeting in Atlanta, the overhead video monitors displayed a CNN news clip about Bob and his chess victories.

When he reached Life Master at 15, he decided that he had had enough. He loved the game, but he didn't want a career as a professional chess player. He had the talent, but that wasn't the life he wanted. Instead, he would use the skills he learned from chess in other endeavors. Several of his chess-playing friends have become very successful in finance and investing. Chess may be a good training ground for that pursuit.

Bob majored in molecular biophysics and biochemistry at Yale, where he met his future wife, who had the same major and got an M.S. at the same time as her B.S. They got starter jobs in management consulting, then founded an Internet company during the boom. When the bubble burst, they went to Wharton School of Business for M.B.A.'s, then both got jobs in venture capital, where they quickly rose to become partners in their respective firms. Now he's an entrepreneur again, building veterinary practices and focusing on specialties like cardiology and eye care.

Over the course of two years, while working as a venture capitalist, he wrote a dystopian scifi novel, *Cynk*. He didn't tell anyone until he finished the first draft, which was 164,000 words long. It was an unexpected urge. He tracked his efforts in Excel and spent over 2400 hours. He had never written fiction before and hasn't since.

Pop Pop

When we lived in Rockville, just ten miles from Silver Spring, we would visit Nana and Pop Pop once a month, and I would crawl into a storage closet on the second floor and explore books that weren't deemed worthy of the library bookshelves — historical novels and adventure stories published around 1900 and targeted at young boys. When Pop Pop died, none of his sons wanted those books, so some trickled down to me. They're part of my library now, but, due to limited shelf space, some once again have been relegated to a closet. (Sorry, books. I shouldn't have done that to you.)

Seven historical novels by G.A. Henty made the cut and are on my shelves. They brought to life for me some of the historical events I've mentioned here. Henty published 122 historical novels for boys. Typically the narrative centers on a teenage boy who finds himself in battle. Identifying with him, I imagined myself in that time and place. His experience was my experience, expanding my world. In particular, I enjoyed *The Dragon and the Raven*, about the siege of Paris by Vikings, who I now know we're descended from. The label on the flyleaf indicates "Book number 16 of Warren Ray Seltzer's private library."

Dad probably got his artistic bent from his father, but that seems to have skipped my generation and the generation of my children, except for Bob. He showed talent as a toddler, but didn't pursue it. Now one of his daughters is artistically inclined, and also loves music, acting, and creative writing. His other daughter is more into athletics (competing internationally in synchronized skating) and already, as a high-school student, is helping with important research on deep brain stimulation at Mount Sinai Hospital. She probably gets that from her mother's side — both her maternal grandparents have Ph.D.'s in science and technology. The doubling mathematics of ancestry works in both directions. Only half my children's genes come from me and only a quarter of my granddaughters'; but we share common ancestry.

The Lizard of Oz

Pop Pop and his brother, Uncle Charlie, were both architects. The house Dad grew up in was Pop Pop's creation. In the basement, there was a pedal-driven printing press. Benjamin Franklin probably used one like that.

Franklin's *Autobiography* was one of the first books I read. My name is "Richard" as in *Poor Richard's Almanac*, and I imagined myself printing books on Pop Pop's press. In the fourth grade, I "published" several issues of a "newspaper," typing it with carbon paper (before the days of copy machines). No one bought it, but I was proud to have done it.

The floor-to-ceiling bookcases in the library at Pop Pop's house reflected his love of books. The walls of the house were adorned with his calligraphy and his drawings of ancient buildings. One piece of calligraphy, a quote from Francis Bacon's *Essays*, now hangs in my apartment:

> Some books are to be tasted, others to be swallowed, and some few to be chewed and digested; that is, some books are to be read only in parts; others to be read, but not curiously; and some few are to be read wholly, and with diligence and attention.

I was itching to publish books, not just write them. And in 1974, I did both.

After I had received dozens of rejections for my book *The Lizard of Oz*, Barb asked, "Why don't we do it ourselves?" That was all the encouragement I needed.

We had no experience in book publishing and no money. College had instilled in me a respect for the editorial judgment of established publishers. I saw the role of the writer as an extension of the role of the student: you submit your work and patiently await judgement. But *The Lizard of Oz* had evolved in ways that gave me confidence that it should be published, regardless of what professionals said.

The story of the story began when I visited the elementary school class of a friend, Judy Morgan, to read to them stories I had written. When I finished reading, they swarmed me with questions. One asked what I was going to write next. I made up a few titles: *The Quest for the Holy Mackerel, The Lizard of Oz*. They clambered to hear *The Lizard of Oz*. So I started writing a story with that title with the kids in Judy's class as characters. I went back a few times to read them new chapters; then school ended, but the story kept growing, and became a fable for all ages. That summer I went to coffee houses in the Boston area, reading the story aloud to audiences of strangers, getting encouraging reactions to new chapters and revisions.

When I was at the University of Massachusetts, earning a master's degree in comparative literature, I saw an artist's request on a bulletin board. Christin Couture needed a book to illustrate for a course. I got in touch with her; and once she drew the characters, it was hard for me to imagine them any other way. The Humbug, the Redcoats, the Witch, Mr. Bacon, Sir Real, Prince Frog, the Weatherman, the Mothers of Fact, Joan of Noah's Ark, and the Lizard himself all took on new life in her drawings. So copies of the illustrations accompanied the manuscript in its rounds from publisher to publisher, until my wife and I decided to go ahead and start our own company.

At that time, I was working for Benwill Publishing, writing for and editing *Circuits Manufacturing* and other technical trade magazines. I brainstormed with my old college roommate, Dave Gleason. He had recently earned an MBA from Harvard Business School and was in the habit of evaluating business ideas. He also had experience dealing with printers and had done some silk-screen printing himself.

Hand lettering, I thought, would suit the child-like tone and anti-machine content of the story. It would also enable me to put the words where I wanted on the pages, ending a page where a thought ended and shaping the words to fit the shape of the illustrations. But, as Dave pointed out, production costs depend largely on the number of pages, and normal hand lettering would leave a lot of wasted space. He suggested that I make the letters and pages large and have the printer photographically reduce them. So long as the reduction was the same on each page, the printer could do the book with a single camera setting and there would be no extra charge. I settled on a reduction to two-thirds, which brought my lettering down to about the size of 12 point type.

I used a felt-tip pen and typing paper, cutting off strips when I made mistakes. Barb lined up and pasted the pieces together on large sheets of paper. Working nights and weekends, we got the camera-ready copy together and delivered it to the printer in two weeks.

Dave designed the cover starting with Christin's line drawing of the Lizard. And he hand-silkscreened the covers for the first printing. Silkscreening 1200 covers with two colors of ink isn't easy. I wouldn't advise anyone to do it to save money. We did it this way because *The Lizard* was our first book, and we wanted the first copies to be collector's items.

We kept the production cost of 1000 copies (128 pages each) under $1000, which we borrowed from a bank as a personal loan. We had decided to start a company on August 15. On October 4, we picked up the finished books at the printer and dashed into the Boston Globe Book Festival, where we had rented an exhibit table for $50.

We named our company The B&R Samizdat Express. B = Barbara. R = Richard. Samizdat means "self-published" in Russian. The name sounded so much like a train that we called it "Express" instead of

"Press." This unusual name, with its explanation, as well as the unusual title of the book, prompted potential buyers and reviewers to give it a second look.

A month after we received the first copies, we saw we would run out of books soon. So we ordered a second printing of 3000. By the time we received those copies, demand had dried up. We had printed and distributed thousands of promotional fliers. We had also sent out 200 copies of the book to reviewers. But we had reached a dead end.

Then a form letter arrived from *Library Journal*. At first it looked like an ad. Then I realized that a clipping was attached. *The Lizard* would be reviewed in the January 15 issue. A few days later a similar letter arrived rom *The Booklist*, a publication of the American Library Association. Their review would appear February 1. Both reviews were favorable and both treated *The Lizard* as a book intended for adults.

I sent follow-up letters to other reviewers whom we had sent copies, asking if they had scheduled or already published reviews. The book editor at *The Philadelphia Bulletin* replied with a question: "Tell me something about your business — who you are, what you are, and where did you get that name?" I replied with a lengthy letter, and on January 26 the lead review in the Sunday *Bulletin* was a very favorable commentary on *The Lizard* and our company. That review led to others in half a dozen local papers in Pennsylvania and New Jersey. Then, thanks to the *Library Journal* and *Booklist* reviews, we started getting library and book-jobber orders from all over the US and Canada. Reviews also appeared in alternative newspapers — *The Valley Advocate* (western Massachusetts), the *Lancaster Independent*

Press, and *Aspect* (a bimonthly literary magazine published in the Boston area).

We started going to small-press book fairs, where we met and talked to other amateur publishers. We weren't alone. Others were running up against similar obstacles and were trying to find solutions. They, too, were publishing what they wanted the way they wanted. Our individual efforts were part of a "movement."

Returning to the Globe Book Festival in the fall of 1975, I was one of the scheduled speakers and had an opportunity to talk to an audience of about a hundred. WBUR-radio interviewed me there, and one of the broadcasters took an interest in *The Lizard.* At his prompting, I wrote a radio script of *The Lizard*, but nothing came of that.

In 1976, when the second printing was running out, we ordered a third printing of 5000. But the expenditure in time and money far exceeded the income. This was a hobby, not a business. We had made friends and learned about book publishing, but it was time to move on.

So I continued to work as an editor of high tech magazines and shifted my focus to our growing family and to writing an historical novel, *The Name of Hero.* A couple of decades later I set up a web site samizdat.com to promote my writing and then to publish ebooks.

Forty years after the start of The B&R Samizdat Express and twenty years after the launch of the web site, I was offered $20,000 for the domain name, for which I had paid $20. By chance, that name appears in the novel *Infinite Jest* by David Foster Wallace, and an avid fan wanted to set up a web site with that name.

Quotes from reviews of The Lizard of Oz:

"an intriguing and very entertaining little novel" *Library Journal*

"a snappy hip fable" *Booklist*

"a commentary on our times done delightfully" *Philadelphia Bulletin*

"Carroll and Tolkien have a new companion" *Aspect*

"a work so saturated that the mind is both stoned with pleasure and alive with wonder" *Lancaster Independent Press*

"a gallery of figments of contemporary culture that could take its place on the library shelf of memory along with classic figures of children's fiction" *Valley Advocate*

Ebooks

I, like Mom, Sallie, and Bob, have an entrepreneurial streak. If one venture doesn't work, sooner or later, I'll try another. Twenty years after publishing *The Lizard of Oz*, while still working as "Internet Evangelist" at DEC, I became a publisher of ebooks.

I met the editor of National Braille Press at a conference. She let me know that, while thousands of public domain books (classics no longer under copyright) were available in electronic form on the Internet, they were formatted in a way that made them difficult for the blind to read with the devices they used to convert electronic text to voice. Reformatting those books was relatively simple. So, rather than waste time and effort applying for grants, I did the work in my spare time, putting the books on 3-1/2 inch disks, one book per disk. I sold them on consignment through National Braille Press, pricing them so I didn't make a profit but didn't lose money either.

After DEC was sold to Compaq, I turned my ebook sideline into a business, gathering public domain books into collections on CDs and DVDs and selling them through eBay and a Yahoo store as well as to the blind. My largest collection had over 20,000 books, in plain-text format, on four DVDs. You clicked on links in a cascading series of tables of contents, and the full text of the book (unembellished, text and only text) appeared on your computer screen. The complete set sold for just $149. I did the work alone on my PC in my home office.

Then technology and the marketplace morphed again. Collections of books on CD and DVD never took off, but individual books downloaded from Kindle and other ebook stores quickly became popular. I converted my books to their format and sold them through Kindle. In the early days of Kindle, 4% of the books they had for sale came from me. Amon my best sellers were *The Babylonian Talmud* and *Lincoln's Complete Writings*, including his telegrams to his generals. (The generals must have been outraged by Lincoln's micromanagement.) For a while, *The Complete Works of Mark Twain* alone (as a single file which sold for 99 cents, of which I got 50 cents) brought in over $100 a day. I had no costs for production, warehousing, marketing, or distribution. The books were classics. Readers searched for them, with no need for me to prompt them.

When Amazon decided to publish public domain books themselves and to make them available for free, I sold my versions through other vendors. I also built my own online store ("Quench," as opposed to Kindle), and found ways to make the books more readable and to sell bundles of related books, rather than just single titles.

Barb, Mike, and Tim helped me. Bob advised me. For a few years, I made good money from this business, and we were able to travel to

Europe, Egypt, and China. But the competition became intense. We were on a treadmill, working harder and faster but getting nowhere. Those ebooks are still available through Barnes & Noble, Google Play, Kobo, and other ebook stores; but I don't make new ones.

Mom and My Teachers

It feels strange writing about my parents, my late wife, my kids, my sister, myself, and others as if we were characters in a novel. I've never done that before. I'm used to writing fiction. Now I'm remembering rather than inventing, discovering rather than creating. And, for the first time, I'm seeing the threads that tie together the pieces of our lives, how disparate activities stem from similar impulses and talents.

I didn't realize until recently how much my mother and a handful of teachers had influenced me. Now I wonder what effect I may have had on my children. Perhaps not much.

I tried to encourage Bob to love literature. When Barb was pregnant with him and he was restless, I would read aloud from *War and Peace* and that would settle him down. I doubt that had any effect on him, but it made me feel like I was a conscientious father-to-be. Maybe what I conveyed was more general than that — a love for ideas and brainstorming.

When I was two, Mom tried to teach me the *Lord's Prayer*. She would read it aloud repeatedly. Then she would focus on a single phrase, like "Our Father," and try to get me to repeat that phrase after her. I wouldn't say a word. Then one night, after a month or two, before she could prompt me, I recited the whole thing on my own.

She also read to me every night at bedtime, long after I could read for myself.

In the second grade, my teacher, Mrs. Radcliffe, would test us every day on our reading homework. She'd put a series of questions on the blackboard with multiple-choice answers. I soon realized that the answers always followed the same pattern — 1-A, 2-B, etc. So instead of reading the assignment, and without even reading the questions, I wrote down the answers and turned them in. She thought I was a genius, and she never caught on. My self-confidence soared. I got used to straight A's and worked hard to keep up my undeserved reputation. That same year, I wrote my first story, "How the Parakeet Got Purple Cheeks," in the style of Kipling's *Just So Stories*.

By the third grade, I was writing stories frequently and reading them in show-and-tell at school. They were very short and based on characters in TV shows, like today's fanfiction. I loved sharing my ideas and performing in front of an audience. That same year, Mom gave me her beginning Latin book and helped me through the opening chapters. I took it with me to school and would sit with it under the oak tree for which the school was named. I would show off to the girls how brilliant I was by trying to teach them. In retrospect, I'm not sure what they thought, but at the time, I assumed they were duly impressed.

In the fifth grade, encouraged by Mom, I memorized Mark Antony's funeral oration and recited it for show-and-tell — not just the opening lines— the whole speech.

The next year, my teacher, Mrs. Jean Wohlfert, wrote a letter to my parents saying that I had exceptional talent as a writer and encouraging them to foster that. She said she had never written such a letter before. But what I most remember from that year is how I let her down.

She had a shelf of books for independent reading. She wanted us to record how many hours it took us to finish each book so we'd increase our reading speed. Because I had memorized Mark Antony's speech, she presumed I was familiar with Shakespeare's plays, but I had only read that one speech because Mom pointed me to it. Mrs. Wohlfert suggested that I read *Tales from Shakespeare* by Charles and Mary Lamb. She thought I'd breeze through it. I took it home and forgot about it. A month later when she asked me about the book, I was embarrassed to admit that I had barely opened it. I lied. She asked me which plays sounded most interesting. I lied very badly, and she soon realized that I didn't know what I was talking about. She didn't challenge me or reprimand me but she looked very disappointed. I had lost her good opinion of me. That hurt deeply. I never wanted to let anyone down like that again.

In the eighth grade, I typed up a list of my personal beliefs, in imitation of Luther, and delivered them to my Sunday school teacher, much to his dismay. What I had to say wasn't outlandish or unreasonable or even original. These were my personal conclusions based on what I had heard and read and what little I had experienced. My self-confidence had no bounds. A sampling:

- A superior being (God) created the universe and is constantly recreating life.
- The entire universe, with only the exception of life, works systematically.
- Only the actions of living things and their results are unpredictable.

- Lies are usually unnecessary and almost always lead to complications.

The next year, at Holderness, I wrote an expanded version of that list of beliefs for Sacred Studies (Religion) class. I began, "Life is a continuous process of building, wrecking, and building again." I had a running battle with my teacher, Mr. Payne. I believed in the literal truth of *The Bible*. I had read it cover-to-cover in church on Sundays, rather than pay attention to the service or the sermon. No one would reprimand me for reading *The Bible* in church. I was shocked when Mr. Payne pointed out that the first two chapters of *Genesis* contradicted one another. I was outraged that he talked rationally and critically about matters of faith. He was the debate coach. I joined. It was a revelation that you could and should be able to argue both sides of the same issue without hypocrisy. When on the affirmative, you could come up with a plan good enough to make a dubious proposition feasible. And when you liked a proposition, you could argue against it by proving your opponent's plan wouldn't work.

Entrepreneurs

You become an entrepreneur because you have a business idea that you're passionate about. You also want to be your own boss, and you're willing to accept the risk of that. But you need to know how to turn your idea into a profitable business model, and you have to take care of all the details. Your workday never ends.

At one time or another, many in our family have been entrepreneurs: Sallie with her yoga and acupuncture practices, Bob and his businesses, and me with *The Lizard of Oz* and my ebook business. That probably started with Mom's example.

Mom's first ventures involved little or no investment. She made lampshades with designs made from autumn leaves, preserved under see-through plastic. She sold those on consignment in shops throughout New Hampshire. Dad made lamps to go with them from old jugs or whatever else was at hand, one from an antique rifle.

Then she set out to design, make, and sell sexy nightware for housewives. Unfortunately, she didn't know how to run a fashion business. She named her company "P.J. Zebra," after her favorite animal. Its tagline was "The Last Word," and the theme was zebra stripes. She believed she could do anything, but wound up with a warehouse full of merchandise and no sales outlets. She lost all the money that she and Dad had saved for years. Mom had the will, but not the way.

Later, she started an armorial jewelry business. Dad would research coats of arms for customers and would draw the designs so a jeweler could engrave them on gold signet rings and other jewelry. She sold those through ads in publications of the DAR and the Colonial Dames. Though she didn't make much money at that and had no employees, she took pride in having her own business and made many friends through the endeavor.

In contrast, Bob's Trenza, was a serious operation, with 27 employees and a vision that could have changed the Internet. They had a way to make the Web a 3D experience for better, quicker, and more effective navigation. They built a working prototype but couldn't get the second-round financing they needed, because the Internet investment bubble had burst.

Bob is an entrepreneur to the core. He started in elementary school, trading baseball cards, both as a collector and for the profit. Some were worth hundreds of dollars. In high school, rather than apply for summer jobs at places like McDonald's, I suggested that he start a chess school; and he did so with gusto and creativity. Rather than pay for a venue, he taught at the homes of students and encouraged parents to invite their children's friends to participate. He wrote a syllabus with detailed lesson plans, and the second summer he hired several of his chess-player friends and trained them as teachers. He even incorporated the business — Masters of the 21st Century. With the profits, he treated the whole family to a vacation in the Cayman Islands.

In college, during the early Internet boom, he was tempted to drop out to do an ecommerce startup. Fortunately, I talked him out of that. After graduation he became a management consultant, started Trenza, then, for twelve years, was a venture capitalist, using his skills in finance and negotiation to help others build companies. Now, again, he has a company of his own, managing and growing a collection of veterinary clinics.

Global Education Motivators

Mom's entrepreneurship also inspired her nephew Wayne, son of her sister Virginia, He had gone straight from high school to a job with an insurance company. When he realized that wasn't what he wanted to do for the rest of his life, he turned to Mom and Dad for college advice. They invited him to live with us in Plymouth, and Dad helped him get into Plymouth State.

Like Dad, Wayne became interested in history and government; and like Mom, he showed entrepreneurial talent and ambition. Those impulses combined in 1981 when, while a high school history teacher in the Philadelphia suburbs, he founded a non-profit company, Global Education Motivators (GEM), which became an NGO of the United Nations. To promote mutual understanding and world peace, GEM arranged for high school classes to make videos about themselves and to share those with other classes around the world. After retiring as a teacher, Wayne has put all of his energy into GEM. Its activities have evolved to take advantage of Internet technology to help students from diverse backgrounds recognize their common interests and pursue them.

Tim

One summer during high school, Tim, my youngest, "on the spectrum," was an intern at a nearby computer company. On the first day, when he arrived with half a dozen other interns, the foreman pointed to an old clunky printer in the corner and asked if anyone would like to try to fix it. Tim volunteered. He had never so much has held a screw driver before that, but he immediately got to work, taking it apart. At lunchtime the foreman asked him if he wanted to see the schematics. Tim replied, "With a machine like this, the problem's probably a broken mechanical part. No need for schematics." He found the broken part. They could easily replace it.

On the final day, they gave him a dozen broken PCs. Tim took them apart and used the pieces to assemble half a dozen working ones.

He has fixer instinct and talent, but instead of working on electronics, he applies it to words and videogames.

Tim started with fanfiction, a subculture that few parents and teachers are aware of. Many preteens and teens who seem lost in the worlds of videogaming devote long hours to reading and writing stories based on their favorite characters from movies, TV shows, videogames, comic books, and graphic novels (particularly Japanese manga). Many of these stories grow to novel length. The authors share them online with no intention of making money from them — simply for the pleasure of writing them and interacting with others of similar bent. They typically ignore issues of copyright and trademark. The fact that they are operating in a gray zone that adults don't approve of makes this activity all the more tempting.

In middle school and high school, Tim read hundreds of fanfics, picked the best, then worked online with the authors to edit and improve their work. When he deemed they were ready, with the permission of the authors, he posted those fanfics at his web site to make them easy for others to find and read. No money exchanged hands.

As the web expanded from text and static images to video, he started making Let's Plays — video commentaries on videogames. While playing, he records the action and overlays his comments, sometimes friendly humorous chatter, sometimes insightful critiques with advice for both players and game designers. Over the years, he's developed a unique style and voice. He has posted over four thousand videos on YouTube. He has a thousand subscribers, and his videos have had nearly a million views. He doesn't get paid for any of that. It's a labor of love.

In addition, he has started writing dozens of novels. He always has one in the works.

Tim has narrative instinct, quickly recognizing the heart of a story and the true nature of its characters. He could be a developmental editor for fiction or a story consultant for movies and videogames. But he prefers to do what he wants when he wants. He's happy being who he is and doing what he loves.

Mike

My son Mike has talent in using computers and the Internet. He worked as a volunteer tech guru in his high school's Computer Department. But instead of following that bent, he majored in English in college and wrote two novels while there. Then, rather than rewrite, edit, and polish them to make them publishable, he went in other directions.

In the best scene of his *Behind Locked Windows,* the protagonist is strapped to a table, enduring great pain. To me, that was an echo of his experience before birth, entangled in an umbilical cord that was monstrous like a dragon's tail, or as an infant, straight-jacketed for weeks at a time, at the doctor's insistence, so he wouldn't tear out stitches after facial surgery.

Now he's back in tech, but he's having experiences that may once again trigger his novel writing. He's working in computer security, preventing online bank fraud and identity theft.

Mom's Writing

Mom craved a college degree as a symbol of status; so after I graduated from Yale, she earned a B.A, from Goddard College in Vermont. They had a program that gave credit for life experience and that only required her to be on campus a few weeks a year. In between, she did independent projects. This program, a forerunner of today's distance education, enabled her to be certified to teach high-school English in Pennsylvania. She did a few gigs as a substitute, but mainly she wanted validation.

Mom, like me and my children, had a writing itch. And she had the gift of the gab (thanks, of course, to her sheep's bone jaw). She could tell a mundane tale in a way that captivated her audience.

She also believed she was clairvoyant.

One night she dreamed about a classmate from Philadelphia she hadn't seen in thirty years — Genevieve Baker. She described the dream in detail at breakfast, then later that day at a county fair in New Hampshire where she was selling her lampshades, Mom bumped into Genevieve and her artist-farmer husband Jimmy Fortune. One of his paintings now hangs in my bedroom.

While at Goddard, Mom wrote an excellent short story about Jimmy Fortune. She had talent. I expected that any day she'd write a best-selling novel, like the mother in John Irving's *The World According to Garp* who outshines her author son.

She showed flare in her genealogy book, including a motley assemblage of family anecdotes and photos rather than just listing who married whom, with what offspring.

The closest Mom came to writing a creative book was assembling someone else's autobiography from scattered notes. In her genealogical research, she came across Virginia Bradford (1899-1995) a distant cousin who was a silent film star in the 1920s. She met Virginia in England, when visiting other distant relatives, in the aftermath of publishing her genealogy book. Later Mom threw a party for her in Philadelphia.

Virginia gave her a stack of notes for an autobiography she had never gotten around to writing. With Virginia's blessing, Mom tried to make it readable. Then she tried to get an agent to handle the project. That didn't go anywhere, but I loved the opening lines:

> My age? Ninety. I was born in Memphis, Tennessee, on November 18, 1900, although my sister Grace, and my son, Billy, insist I was born in 1899. I never had a birth certificate. Maybe I wasn't born at all. Maybe I'm immortal. Funny thing about age. I was three years older than Grace growing up, now she's older than I am.

This Book

Writing this book is a matter of memory rather than invention. I'm creating a context for understanding the scattered pieces of my life.

I've led a pinball life, and this book that began as an essay about genealogy now feels like a memoir, with quirky digressions, told in a tangled way.

Perhaps this winding tale, following multiple paths of association, reflects my concern about the possibility of Alzheimer's, which Mom suffered from and died of. If one path to a particular memory fails, I have many other ways to get there.

The process of writing is my reason for writing. There is no final conclusion that I know already and want to convince you of. There are no solidly proven facts here to be added to the structure of human knowledge, no firm foundation on which to build other truths. I'm learning by exploring these threads of association.

I write not to tell what I know, but to find out if there might be answers to seemingly unanswerable questions, and, if so, what they might be. I'd like to know what truth is, if there is fate, and where I fit in the overall scheme of things.

Part Nine:
Identity

When I was 13 and Mom told me her father was a convicted criminal, she also told me that the crime was incest and that the victim was her sister Mildred. Friends of Mildred might also have been abused. Mom provided no details. Mildred had never told her about it, on strict orders from the aunts. Mom also said she believed her father was innocent, that his conviction was a mistake, a misunderstanding spawned by the sexual repression of that time. Perhaps an overzealous detective or prosecutor unintentionally planted false memories in the minds of the supposed victims, as was the case in false convictions of daycare providers in recent years.

When I wrote *Nevermind*, a novel inspired by events from my parents' lives, the scene where they left me on a train in Chicago became a starting point for alternate realities. They didn't find me. Each blamed the other. They broke up, and each, separately, set out to track me down. Then they each, separately, found a version of me and raised me, in parallel worlds.

In that novel, I gave her father the benefit of the doubt.

> Father had done something to Emily [Mildred] and her friends. Years later, from the few clues she had gathered, she guessed that he somehow talked them into undressing and getting into the bathtub and gave them an intimate washing. Maybe it was nothing more than that. Maybe people over-reacted, maybe he was given an unjustly harsh sentence. Then again, maybe it was something horrible, and he deserved even worse.

In one alternate world, Mom met her father after his release from prison, at his family's home in Tennessee. They got to know one another. He was a different person than she had remembered. He told her a version of his life story in which there was no crime, no prison. She didn't know if he was delusional, but she wanted to believe him, and he may have been telling the truth.

I couldn't write those passages today, knowing what I now know.

Mom remembered her father as the manager of an A&P store across the street from the family's row house, after her mother died in 1930 and the aunts moved in to take care of the children. He lived alone above the store. Sometimes his youngest, Mildred, came to visit. Sometimes she brought friends. That's where the crime took place. The involvement of Mildred's friends probably explains why it was reported to the police and quickly prosecuted.

Coached by her aunts, Mom told everyone the orphan story. She knew it wasn't true, but she lived the part she was playing as if it were. She had talent as an actress. Everyone but her mother-in-law believed her and based their image of her on what she said. She only confided in Dad who kept her secret.

This reminds me of the Alzheimer's Bill of Rights, in particular the right to live in a world of your own. Mom grew up having to say that her father was dead while knowing he was in prison. The lie must have been hard to sustain. It led to a lifetime feud with her mother-in-law. And there must have been other instances when she slipped up, or almost did. She must have felt ashamed, as if she were somehow to blame for what he had done and guilty for lying about it over and over. It was hard to walk the tightrope of deception. When she succumbed to Alzheimer's, that conflict came to an end. She could live in the reality she wanted and feel no qualms about doing so.

Her mother-in-law had sensed that something was wrong at their first meeting, and Mom never told her the truth. Only after Nana died in 1973 did Mom feel she no longer had to lie about the date of her father's death. So in her genealogy book, she recorded that he died in 1943, the date she had seen on his gravestone, not 1932, the year he went to prison. She felt no need to mention he was a convict. Later, when the death certificate was posted on the Internet, that confirmed 1943. Story over.

But now, 14 years after Mom died, the prison record is online, affirming that her father's crime wasn't a matter of touching or something innocent that might have been misconstrued as sexual abuse. "William Smith Estes" (first two names reversed), Convict 7820, was convicted of "rape, incest, fornication" and served his full 15-year-sentence at Eastern State Penitentiary in Philadelphia. He got out of prison in 1947.

The 1943 gravestone and the death certificate were for someone else, whose name we don't know. And we have no idea what happened to the real Smith William Estes after he left prison — where he went, what he did, when he died.

According to the death certificate, Smith William Estes died in Brownsville, Tennessee, of chronic endocarditis, contributed to by hypertension and chronic interstitial nephritis. Medical websites explain that as "a nonspecific diagnosis of a pattern of kidney injury." But because I now know that an imposter and not my grandfather died of that, I don't have to worry about having inherited a kidney condition. And I don't have to worry about lung disease, either, which Mom had guessed was her father's cause of death.

When I first saw the prison record, I thought that maybe his family had faked his return home. Perhaps, because he was the oldest son, they needed for him to be officially dead to resolve inheritance issues. In any case, they would have wanted to hide his crime, not to be associated with it. They were wealthy, respected, and influential. Perhaps, they filed for his Social Security registration in 1940, a friendly doctor issued a death certificate in 1943, and they put a fake gravestone over an empty grave.

Then a more logical answer occurred to me. His identity was valuable, and Smith William may have generously given it to a friend, probably a cellmate. He had hoped to be released in 1939, after serving half his sentence. That was his "early release date," which the records show was denied; his appeal was denied as well. He couldn't afford a lawyer. There would be no appeal beyond that. So he was going to have to serve another seven and a half years. If a friend was due to be released soon and had no family to go to, that friend was as good as dead. This was the Depression. It was hard for anyone to find a job, impossible for an ex-con. Smith Williams' family hadn't seen him in over 35 years. If this friend was approximately the same height, his family wouldn't notice the difference. My grandfather could have coached this man for months, teaching him everything he'd need to know to become a successful imposter.

This scenario sounds like the plot of the movie *Sommersby* with Richard Gere and Jodie Foster. Set in Tennessee in the years following the American Civil War. In that film, a farmer returns home from the war, and his wife begins to suspect that he's an impostor. But in that case, the husband and the imposter weren't friends. The one stole the identity of the other, like in the online identity thefts my son Mike now deals with. This was an identity gift, a life-saving gift.

I wish I could find out the names and crimes of his cellmates 1932-1939, and who among them was released after March 4, 1939, when Smith William's early release was denied and before October 1940, when someone with his name filed for Social Security in Tennessee. That's probably the imposter. But such records don't exist. A few handwritten lines mark his arrival, the denial of early release, and his final release after serving the full term. That's all. There's no mention of his behavior or his health or what work he did over those 15 years of imprisonment. No mention of cellmates.

There's also no record of the death of the real Smith William Estes after 1947. Death certificates and obituaries for the U.S. for those dates are online and searchable now. And there's no Pennsylvania resident with that name in the 1950 Census. Perhaps when he was released in 1947, someone did for him what he had done for someone else — gave him a new identity.

Now I wonder why he left his family home in Tennessee when he was in his early twenties and went to Philadelphia where he had no relatives and probably no friends. Was he banished? What might he, the eldest son, have done to deserve that? In that case, he might have felt wronged, been bitter about it, and deliberately not talked about them and not contacted them.

But his marriage and the births of his children were recorded in the genealogy book published in 1939. Some people in Tennessee knew he lived in Philadelphia, was married, and had a family. But, apparently, none of them tried to help or even contact his new family either before or after the trial and incarceration.

He had married the daughter of Welsh-Irish immigrants and settled in East Falls, an immigrant neighborhood. He had little education, though his father was a doctor as well as a wealthy landowner. And his uncle, too, was a doctor. His uncle, William L. Estes, was the founding director of St. Luke's Hospital in Bethlehem, PA. There's no indication that Smith William was ever in touch with this illustrious uncle. His wife and children in Philadelphia didn't know he had living kin in Tennessee, much less in nearby Bethlehem.

I once speculated that he went to Philadelphia to go to college but flunked out or was kicked out. But Census records indicate he had little or no education. There was no high school in Haywood County when he was growing up. He probably went to a one-room school, like the one that Henry Hocker Seltzer taught in, with no formal graduation. In the 1910 Census, he was a policeman, in 1920, a tool maker — probably at Leeds & Northrop from a photo of him at work.

Eastern State Penitentiary was near the row house where Mom grew up. She had to walk past it on her way to and from school, and she knew that's where he was. An older sister of hers was married to one of the guards. It was a high-security prison. It held the bank robber Willie Sutton, and for nine months it held Al Capone on the charge of carrying a concealed weapon, before his arrest by Elliot Ness for the more serious crime of tax evasion.

The prison was shut down in 1971. Today it's open to the public as a tourist site, with free daytime admission and special members-only experiences. Built in 1829, it covers 11 acres and has 450 cells. The walls are 30 feet high. It looks like a medieval castle. (For an online video tour see easternstate.org).

I'm reminded of Edmond Dantes' imprisonment and escape in *The Count of Monte Cristo* and of the long imprisonments of Eleanor of Aquitaine and Marjorie Bruce. What would my grandfather have done during such a long incarceration?

In 1932 Mildred, his victim, was 10 years old, the seventh and youngest child. (Mom was the sixth.) Mildred had to testify against her father in court. But on orders from their aunts, she never told Mom what had happened. And later, she didn't tell her own children.

Her daughters, who I hadn't seen in decades, were shocked when I shared what I knew with them at Mom's memorial gathering. Mildred had died 13 years before, and I had presumed that they knew. They were glad that I told them. The truth relieved their anxiety. Mildred had had multiple nervous breakdowns, and her children had feared that proclivity might be hereditary.

Mom, Mildred, and siblings told everyone they were orphans. They said it so often that it almost became true to them, and their memory of what had happened faded and became dream-like, which was the aunts' well-meaning idea of healing, and which also protected their reputations, giving them the gift of a new identity. As orphans, they inspired sympathy and were protected from the stigma of being the offspring of a convicted incestuous rapist.

Mom was grateful to her aunts for saving her from the shame of her father's crime. And in gratitude for that, she and Dad drove from New Hampshire to Philadelphia for Aunt Lil's funeral. And I stayed at Becky's house and almost held her hand. And six years later I met Becky's brother's friend Claude. And five years after that, Claude introduced me to Anne, whose roommate Barb I fell in love with and married, and had four wonderful kids and a full life.

I thank Aunt Lil, who created the lie that shielded Mom and her siblings from scorn, and who did all she could to maintain their identity as orphans, regardless of how difficult that was, believing it was the right thing to do. I thank her for the identity gift that started the chain of events that shaped my life, because I couldn't have dreamed of or wished for such a wonderful family and such a wonderful life.

Afterthought

I wrote this book in a month, from first conception to the end of the first draft. I was halfway through writing a novel, *The Name of Man*, a sequel to *The Name of Hero*, when the idea for this started waking me in the middle of the night.

That was unlike anything I had experienced before. Rather than creating, I was remembering, following entangled threads of association. It was like taking dictation. One idea led to another. The pieces fit together. Sparks flew.

I got up and scribbled on pads of paper for several hours in the middle of the night, not by plan or choice. I had to write these thoughts down because they were buzzing in my head and I couldn't sleep until I recorded them. The next day, I would edit, polish, rearrange. I sometimes struggled over the order of the pieces and how to segue from one to the next. But often what I wrote at night — sometimes long-forgotten anecdotes — fit smoothly, verbatim. I then rewrote the book twenty times — adding, deleting, and moving pieces around — once again prompted by my dreams.

This book had to be written. I had no choice. The internal logic kept pulling me forward in unexpected directions. I started writing a genealogy book, but it morphed to become memoir.

Halfway through, the phrase "identity gift" occurred to me. The discrepancy between the date on my grandfather's gravestone and the date of his release from prison drove me to that. An impostor had received an identity gift from my grandfather.

Then tears came to my eyes, tears of joy, as I realized that the important act, the difficult task of building and sustaining the lie that he was dead, not in prison, was also an identity gift. Mom's aunt had protected her from the stigma of her father's crime, enabling her to lead a normal life.

While writing the book, I misremembered her name as "Gladys." The night after finishing the first draft, it finally dawned on me that the gift-giver, the aunt who raised Mom was "Aunt Lil." It occurred to me that very few people who knew her, other than me, are still alive, and in a few years there will be none. But without her, my life wouldn't have been as it has been. I wouldn't even have been born. I hope this book preserves for a little longer the memory of her gift and of my gratitude to her.

By coincidence, one of my two granddaughters has a name very similar to Lillian. I never mentioned Aunt Lil to Bob, nor did Bob know that my Dad's mother (Nana) was also named Lillian. He and his wife arrived at that name through family connections on her side. This tale is packed with coincidences.

We are all tied together in ways we don't know or can't fathom. Hence the title — *One Family*.

Appendix

Acknowledgements

To Mom, who encouraged my earliest writing efforts and built my confidence so I'd think independently and express my thoughts without depending on the authority of experts.

To my late wife Barb, who indulged and supported me in my writing and in my entrepreneurial efforts.

To Dad, who set unattainable standards for me so I would always strive to do better. He often did that silently, which made his wishes all the more loud and authoritative.

To my son Bob for his detailed feedback and suggestions, helping to make this a much better book than it would have been.

To Nancy, for her insightful critiques.

To my sixth grade teacher Jean Wohlfert, who thought I had talent as a writer.

To my Uncle Paul, my sister Sallie, my cousins Wayne and Joyce.

To my beta readers for their feedback: Rochelle Cohen Sexton, Larry Polin, and Gabi Coatsworth.

To Steve Felson, and Judy Duchan.

Thanks also to David Quammen, Jared Diamond, and Steven Pinker for their brilliant books which prompted some of these thoughts, and to readers who love this book and tell others, who will tell others, so it can touch the lives of many.

And thanks to Todd Engel, the brilliant cover designer at Booklocker. I love the family tree.

I also want to thank My Unconscious, who has been with me at every stage of writing and rewriting this book, waking me in the middle of the night with insights and associations, and not letting me sleep until I write them down. Homer would have called it his Muse. I wish I could hear that voice as well as he did and that my words, like his and Odin's, could sing.

Internet Links

My email address — seltzer@seltzerbooks.com (feedback welcome)

My web site — seltzerbooks.com

My author page at Amazon — www.amazon.com/stores/Richard-Seltzer/author/B000APBTAA

My Ancestry.com handle — seltzer146

Searchable version of the 1600 ancestors listed below — seltzerbooks.com/1600.pdf

List of all books I've read since 1958 — seltzerbooks.com/readall.html

A Glimpse of the Future (three-minute video) — youtube.com/watch?v=cRfq3SLCVeM or search for glimpse of the future seltzer

The Music Man (two-minute video) — youtube.com/watch?v=IHK_bGnzpVo or search for music man seltzer

Dad's autobiography — seltzerbooks.com/lifeandtimes.html

Dad's doctoral dissertation — seltzerbooks.com/humanrelations.html

Autobiography of Henry Hocker Seltzer, my great-grandfather — seltzerbooks.com/hockercomplete.pdf

The Cary-Estes Genealogy published in 1939 — seltzerbooks.com/caryestescomplete.pdf

The Cary-Estes-Moore Genealogy by Mom — seltzerbooks.com/moorecomplete.pdf

Video tour of Eastern State Penitentiary — easternstate.org

Sergei Solovieff letter — seltzerbooks.com/solovieffseltzerletter.jpg

Sergei Solovieff clipping —
seltzerbooks.com/solovieffkepplefront.jpg

Source documents about Alexander/Anthony Bulatovich
seltzerbooks.com/sourcesandrelateddocuments.html

Review of *Ethiopia Through Russian Eyes* from *Old Africa* —
seltzerbooks.com/oldafrica.html

Solution to the game Hi-Q or Peg Solitaire —
seltzerbooks.com/hiq.html

Documentary movie Harvard Beats Yale 29-29 —
https://www.youtube.com/watch?v=rtKj67kh9L4

"Hundreds and Hundreds of Gerbils" —
seltzerbooks.com/gerbils.html also at medium.com

Bob's chess games — seltzerbooks.com/tour1.html

Life Lessons by Uncle Paul, an ebook — search for it at Barnes &
Noble or Google Play

Article about the pilot episode of Reading Rainbow, in which Dad
was the Ringmaster — https://tomorrow.is/features/reading-rainbow-
check-it-out-30-years-on/

Lines of Descent

The names of ancestors mentioned in Extraordinary Women and other major figures are in bold.

Norse and Greek Gods

according to Hesiod:

100) Gaia

99) Uranus mated with Gaia, his mother

98) Cronus mated with Rhea

according to Homer:

97) Zeus, king of the gods

96) Dardanus, founder of the city of Dardania

95) Erichthonius

94) Tros, founder of the kingdom of Troy

93) Ilus, founder of the city of Troy

92) Laomedon, king of Troy

91) Priam, king of Troy, married Hecuba

according to *The Prose Edda* by Snorri Sturlson:

91) Priam, king of Troy, which is also known Asgard

90) Troan, daughter of Priam, married Munon AKA Mennon or Memnon, king of Troy

89) Tror AKA Thor married Sif. Tror was raised in Thrace by King Loricos, who he murdered. Tror then ruled Thrace. Later he travelled north.

88) Lordi

87) Eiridi

86) Vige

85) Vingerif

84) Moda

83) Magi

82) Seskef

81) Bedrig

80) Athra

79) Acnar

78) Itrmann

77) Heremod

76) Skjaldun AKA Skjold

75) Biaf AKA Bjar

74) Jat

73) Gudolf

72) Fin

71) Friallaf AKA Fridleif

70) Voden

69) **Odin** married Frigida AKA Frigg. According to Snorri Sturluson, "Each member of his family is divine."

according to *Saga of the Ynglings* by Snorri Sturluson

70) Bür, father of all other gods

69) **Odin**, king of the gods married Frigg AKA Frigida

68) Njord of Noatum, sea god and sole sovereign of the Swedes married **Skadi**, ski goddess and jötunn

67) Yngve Frey, god of peace, fertility, prosperity, and fair weather; sovereign of the Swedes

66) King Fjölner of Sweden

65) King Sveigde of Sweden

64) King Vanlande of Sweden

63) King Visbur of Sweden

62) King Domalde of Sweden

61) King Domar of Sweden

60) King Dyggvi of Sweden

59) King Dag of Sweden

58) King Agne of Sweden

57) King Alaric of Sweden

56) King Yngvi of Sweden

55) King Jorund of Sweden

54) King On or Aun the Old of Sweden

53) King Egill or Ongentheow of Sweden, mentioned in *Beowulf*

52) King Ohthere or Ottar of Sweden, mentioned in *Beowulf*

51) King Eadgils of Sweden, mentioned in *Beowulf*

50) King Eysteinn AKA Östen of Sweden

49) King Ingvar Harra of Sweden

48) King Onund or Anund of Sweden

47) King Ingjald III of Sweden

46) King Olaf Tree Feller or Olof Tratalja of Sweden

45) Halfdan Hvitbeinn "Whiteshanks,"petty king in Norway

43) Eystein Halfdansson, King of Romerike and Vestfold in what is now Norway

42) Halfdan the Mild, King of Romerike and Vestfold in what now in Norway

41) Gudrød the Hunter king in southeast Norway

40) Olaf Gudrødsson AKA Olaf Geirstad-Alf, Norwegian king, brother of Halfdan the Black who fought King Gandalf

39) Ragnvald (or Rognvald) "the Mountain-High" Olafsson, king of Vestfold in what is today Norway

38) Ascrida Rognvaldsdatter married c. 819 Eystein Ivarsson b. 788, a king in Norway

37) Rognvald Eysteinsson, Earl of More in Western Norway, and founder of the Earldom of Orkney

36) Rollo (860-932) founder and first ruler of the Viking principality that became Normandy married Poppa

35) William I "Longsword" (893- 942), Second Duke of Normandy

34) Richard I "The Fearless" (933-996), Duke of Normandy

33) Richard II "The Good" (963-1027), Duke of Normandy d. 1026

32) Robert I "The Magnificent" (1000-1035), Duke of Normandy

31) **William I "the Conqueror"** King of England (1027-1087) reigned 1066-1087 married 1053 **Matilda of Flanders** (c. 1031-1083

30) Henry I, King of England "Beauclerc" (1068/1069-1135) reigned 1100-1135) married **Matilda of Scotland** AKA Edith, (c. 1080-1118) daughter of Malcolm III King of Scotland, who succeeded to the Scottish throne after the death of Macbeth and who was the son of Duncan I, King of Scotland, who was murdered by Macbeth

29) **Empress Matilda** (1102-1110), briefly (contested) the first female ruler of England in 1141, widow of Henry V Holy Roman Emperor) married Geoffrey V "the Handsome," Plantagenet, Count of Anjou and Maine and Duke of Normandy

28) King Henry II of England (1133-1189) married **Eleanor of Aquitaine**

27) King John I "Lackland" of England (1166-1216) married Isabella of Angouleme

26) King Henry III of England (1207-1307) married Eleanor of Provence

25) King Edward I "Longshanks" of England (1239-1307) married Eleanor of Castille

24) King Edward II of England (1284-1327) married Isabella "the She-Wolf of France"

23) King Edward III of England (1312-1377) married Philippa of Hainault

22) John of Gaunt, First Duke of Lancaster (1340-1399) married Katherine Swynford

21) John Beaufort, First Earl of Somerset (1371-1410) married Margaret Holland

20) Joan Beaufort (1404-1445) married King James I of Scotland

19) Joan Stewart (1428-1486) married James Douglas, First Earl of Morton

18) John Douglas, Second Earl of Morton (1459-1513) married Janet Crichton

17) Agnes Douglas married Alexander Livingston, Fifth Lord Livingston of Callandar, guardian of Mary Queen of Scots

16) William Livingston, Sixth Lord Livingston of Callandar (1528-1602) married Agnes Fleming

15) Alexander Livingston (1561-1621) married Eleanor Hay

14) Margaret Livingston married John Fleming (1589-1650)

13) Alexander Fleming (1612-1668) emigrated from Scotland to Virginia married Elizabeth Anderson

12) John Fleming (1627-1686) emigrated with his father from Scotland to Virginia) married Mary

11) Charles Fleming (1659-1717) married Susannah Tarleton

10) Susannah Tarleton Fleming married John Bates

9) James Bates (1721-1786) married Winnifred Grymes

8) Daniel Bates (1756-1801) married Elizabeth Cary Bell

7) Sarah Langhorne Bates (1781-1825) moved from Virginia to Tennessee, married Joel Estes

6) Albert Monroe Estes (1804-1863) married Mildred Colman

5) Louis Powhatan Estes (1849-1902) married Lily Yates Moore

4) Smith William Estes (1881-1943) moved from Tennessee to Philadelphia, married Mae Griffith

3) Mom, Helen Isabella Estes (1920-2010) married Dad, Richard Warren Seltzer

2) Me

1) My children

0) My grandchildren

Line of Brunhild the Valkyrie and Clovis, First King of France who by Legend was a Descendant of Jesus and Mary Magdalene

56) Gibicca, King of Burgundy (c. 407)

55) Gunther, King of Burgundy (d. 437) married **Brunhild**, a Valkyrie, probably from Iceland, *Nibelungenlied*

54) Gondioc (420-473) fought in alliance with the Romans against Attila

53) Chilperic II, King of Burgundy (450-493)

52) Saint Clotilde (44-541) married **Clovis**, first King of the Franks (c. 466-Nov. 27, 511)

58) Teutomer, French general in service to Rome

57) Richomeres (d. 393) married Ascyla. Richomere was Roman consul in 384. Supreme commander in the Eastern Empire 388-393. Uncle of General Arbogast.

56) Theodemer, a Frankish king.

55) Chlodio (c. 392/395-445/448)

54) **Merovech** AKA Meroveus or Merovius (411-457) Semi-legendary founder of the Merovingian dynasty of the Salian Franks. He is said to be one of several barbarian warlords and kings that joined forces with the Roman general Aetius against the Huns under Attila in the Battle of the Catalaunian Plains, .

53) Childeric I (c. 440-c. 481) married **Queen Basina of Thuringia** (c. 438-477)

52) **Clovis**, first King of the Franks (c. 466-Nov. 27, 511) married Saint Clotilde (44-541) married

51) Chlothar I, King of the Franks (497-561)

50) Blithilde (c. 538-c. 603) married Ansbertus

49) Arnoald, Bishop of Metz and Margrave of Schelde (560-611)

48) **Saint Itta of Metz** (592-652) married Saint Pepin of Landen the Elder, Mayor of the Palace of Austrasia

47) **Saint Begga** (615-693) married Ansegisel

46) Pepin II (the Middle) of Herstal, Mayor of the Palace of Austrasia 635-714) mated with Alpaida

45) **Charles Martel** (the Hammer), Mayor of the Palace of Austrasia, (688-741), commander of the European army that defeated the Moors at the Battle of Tours in 732 married Rotrude of Tier

44) King Pepin of the Franks "the Short" (d.768) married Bertrada of Laon

43) **Charlemagne**, Holy Roman Emperor (742-814) married Hildegarde of Vinzgouw

42) King Pepin (Carloman) of Italy (777-810) married Bertha

41) King Bernard of Italy (797-818) married Cunigunda

40) Count Pepin of Vermandois, Lord of Senlis Peronne and Saint Quentin (b. 815)

39) Count Herbert I of Vermandois, Lord of Senlis, Peronne and Saint Quetin (848-907) married Bertha de Morvois

38) Beatrice of Vermandois (880-931) married King Robert I of France and Marquis of Neustria

37) Duke Hugh Capet of France "the Great," Count of Paris (898-956) married Hedwige of Saxony

36) King Hugh Capet of France (939-996) married Adelaide of Aquitaine

35) King Robert II of France (972-1041) married Constance of Arles

34) King Henry I of France (1008-1060) married Anne of Kiev

33) King Philip I of France "the Amorous" (1052-1108) married Bertha of Holland

32) **Alice of Jerusalem** (1110-after 1151) married Prince Bohemond II of Taranto and Antioch, Crusader (1108-1130)

31) **Constance of Antioch** (1127-1163) married Prince Raynald of Antioch, Crusader

30) **Agnes of Antioch** (1154-1184) married King Bela III of Hungary AKA Caesar Alexius of the Byzantine Empire

29) King Andrew II of Hungary, Crusader (1177-1235) married Gertrude of Merania

28) King Bela IV of Hungary and Croatia and Duke of Styria (1206-1270) married Maria Laskarina

27) King Stephen V of Hungary, Dalmatia, Croatia, Rama, Serbia, Galicia, Lodomeria, Cumania, and Bulgaria, also Duke of Styria (1239-1272) married **Elizabeth the Cuman**

26) Mary of Hungary (1257-1323) married King Charles II "the Lame" of Naples and Sicily, King of Jerusalem, Prince of Salerno

25) Eleanor of Anjou AKA Eleanor of Naples (1289-1341) married King Frederick III of Sicily

24) Elisabeth of Sicily AKA Isabel of Aragon (1310-1349) married Duke Stephen II of Bavaria

23) Duke Frederick of Bavaria (1339-1393) married Maddelena Visconti

22) Elizabeth of Vabaria-Landshut (1383-1442) married Frederick I, Hohenzollern, Elector of Brandenburg and Burgrave of Nuremberg

21) John Hohenzollern (the Alchemist), Margrave of Brandenburg-Kulmbach (1406-1464) married Barbara of Saxe-Wittenberg

20) Dorothea of Brandenburg AKA Dorthea of Hohenzollern, AKA Dorothy Achilles (1431-1495) married Christian I King of Denmark, Norway and Sweden, also Count of Oldenburg and Delmenhorst

19) Margaret of Denmark (1456- 486) married James III, King of Scotland

18) King James IV of Scotland (1473-1513) married Agnes Stewart

17) Janet Stewart, "Lady Janet" (1505-1563) married Malcolm Fleming, 3rd Lord Fleming

16) John Fleming, 5th Lord Fleming (1537-1572) married Elizabeth Ross

15) John Fleming, 6th Lord Fleming and 1st Earl of Wigton (1567-1619) married Lilias Graham

14) John Fleming (1589-1650) married Margaret Livingston

13) Alexander Fleming (1612-1668) emigrated from Scotland to Virginia married Elizabeth Anderson

12) John Fleming (1627-1686) emigrated with his father from Scotland to Virginia) married Mary

11) Charles Fleming (1659-1717) married Susannah Tarleton

10) Susannah Tarleton Fleming married John Bates

9) James Bates (1721-1786) married Winnifred Grymes

8) Daniel Bates (1756-1801) married Elizabeth Cary Bell

7) Sarah Langhorne Bates (1781-1825) moved from Virginia to Tennessee, married Joel Estes

6) Albert Monroe Estes (1804-1863) married Mildred Colman

5) Louis Powhatan Estes (1849-1902) married Lily Yates Moore

4) Smith William Estes (1881-1943) moved from Tennessee to Philadelphia, married Mae Griffith

3) Mom, Helen Isabella Estes (1920-2010) married Dad, Richard Warren Seltzer

2) Me

1) My children

0) My grandchildren

Attila's Line

45) Mundzuk

44) **Attila the Hun** (406-453)

43) Caba AKA Ernak

42) Almos

41) Ugyek

40) Arpad, start of Arpad dynasty of Hungarian rulers

39) Zoltan

38) Taksony, Grand Prince of the Hungarians

37) Michael

36) Vazul

35) Bela I of Hungary (1015-1063)

34) Geza I of Hungary (1049-1077)

33) Almos of Hungary (1070-1127)

32) Bela II "the Blind" of Hungary (1110-1141)

31) Geza II of Hungary (1130-1162)

30) Bela III of Hungary (1148-1196)

29) Andrew II of Hungary (1177-1235) Crusader

28) Bela IV of Hungary (1206-1270)

27) Stephen V of Hungary (1239-1272) married **Elizabeth the Cuman**

26) Mary of Hungary (1257-1323) married King Charles II "the Lame" of Naples and Sicily, King of Jerusalem, Prince of Salerno

25) Eleanor of Anjou AKA Eleanor of Naples (1289-1341) married King Frederick III of Sicily

24) Elisabeth of Sicily AKA Isabel of Aragon (1310-1349) married Duke Stephen II of Bavaria

23) Duke Frederick of Bavaria (1339-1393) married Maddelena Visconti

22) Elizabeth of Vabaria-Landshut (1383-1442) married Frederick I, Hohenzollern, Elector of Brandenburg and Burgrave of Nuremberg

21) John Hohenzollern (the Alchemist), Margrave of Brandenburg-Kulmbach (1406-1464) married Barbara of Saxe-Wittenberg

20) Dorothea of Brandenburg AKA Dorthea of Hohenzollern, AKA Dorothy Achilles (1431-1495) married Christian I King of Denmark, Norway and Sweden, also Count of Oldenburg and Delmenhorst

19) Margaret of Denmark (1456- 486) married James III, King of Scotland

18) King James IV of Scotland (1473-1513) married Agnes Stewart

17) Janet Stewart, "Lady Janet" (1505-1563) married Malcolm Fleming, 3rd Lord Fleming

16) John Fleming, 5th Lord Fleming (1537-1572) married Elizabeth Ross

15) John Fleming, 6th Lord Fleming and 1st Earl of Wigton (1567-1619) married Lilias Graham

14) John Fleming (1589-1650) married Margaret Livingston

13) Alexander Fleming (1612-1668) emigrated from Scotland to Virginia married Elizabeth Anderson

12) John Fleming (1627-1686) emigrated with his father from Scotland to Virginia) married Mary

11) Charles Fleming (1659-1717) married Susannah Tarleton

10) Susannah Tarleton Fleming married John Bates

9) James Bates (1721-1786) married Winnifred Grymes

8) Daniel Bates (1756-1801) married Elizabeth Cary Bell

7) Sarah Langhorne Bates (1781-1825) moved from Virginia to Tennessee married Joel Estes

6) Albert Monroe Estes (1804-1863) married Mildred Colman

5) Louis Powhatan Estes (1849-1902) married Lily Yates Moore

4) Smith William Estes (1881-1943) moved from Tennessee to Philadelphia married Mae Griffith

3) Mom, Helen Isabella Estes (1920-2010) married Dad, Richard Warren Seltzer

2) Me

1) My children

0) My grandchildren

Roman Line

55) Afrianus Syagrius (c. 345-384), Roman politician and administrator whose family originated in Lyon. 380-382 praetorian prefect of Italy, 381 praefectus urbi of Rome, 382 consul.

54) unnamed daughter

53) Tonantius Ferreolus, praetorian prefect of Gaul (390-475) married **Papianilla** (born 415).

52) Tonantius Ferreolus, Gallo-Roman senator married Industria)

51) Ferreolus of Rodez, Gallo-Roman senator married Saint Dode of Reims

50) Ansbert or Ansbertus, Gallo-Roman senator married Blithidle

49) Bishop Arnoald of Metz and Margrave of Schelde (560-611)

48) **Saint Itta of Metz** (592-652) married Saint Pepin of Landen the Elder, Mayor of the Palace of Austrasia

47) **Saint Begga** (615-693) married Ansegisel

46) Pepin II (the Middle) of Herstal, Mayor of the Palace of Austrasia 635-714) mated with Alpaida

45) **Charles Martel** (the Hammer), Mayor of the Palace of Austrasia, (688-741), commander of the European armies that defeated the Moors at the Battle of Tours in 732 married Rotrude of Tier

44) King Pepin of the Franks "the Short" (d.768) married Bertrada of Laon

43) **Charlemagne,** Holy Roman Emperor (742-814) married Hildegarde of Vinzgouw

42) King Pepin (Carloman) of Italy (777-810) married Bertha

41) King Bernard of Italy (797-818) married Cunigunda

40) Count Pepin of Vermandois, Lord of Senlis Peronne and Saint Quentin (b. 815)

39) Count Herbert I of Vermandois, Lord of Senlis, Peronne and Saint Quetin (848-907) married Bertha de Morvois

38) Beatrice of Vermandois (880-931) married King Robert I of France and Marquis of Neustria

37) Duke Hugh Capet of France "the Great," Count of Paris (898-956) married Hedwige of Saxony

36) King Hugh Capet of France (939-996) married Adelaide of Aquitaine

35) King Robert II of France (972-1041) married Constance of Arles

34) King Henry I of France (1008-1060) married Anne of Kiev

33) King Philip I of France "the Amorous" (1052-1108) married Bertha of Holland

32) **Alice of Jerusalem** (1110-after 1151) married Prince Bohemond II of Taranto and Antioch, Crusader (1108-1130)

31) **Constance of Antioch** (1127-1163) married Prince Raynald of Antioch, Crusader

30) **Agnes of Antioch** (1154-1184) married King Bela III of Hungary AKA Caesar Alexius of the Byzantine Empire

29) King Andrew II of Hungary, Crusader (1177-1235) married Gertrude of Merania

28) King Bela IV of Hungary and Croatia and Duke of Styria (1206-1270) married Maria Laskarina

27) King Stephen V of Hungary, Dalmatia, Croatia, Rama, Serbia, Galicia, Lodomeria, Cumania, and Bulgaria, also Duke of Styria (1239-1272) married **Elizabeth the Cuman**

26) Mary of Hungary (1257-1323) married King Charles II "the Lame" of Naples and Sicily, King of Jerusalem, Prince of Salerno

25) Eleanor of Anjou AKA Eleanor of Naples (1289-1341) married King Frederick III of Sicily

24) Elisabeth of Sicily AKA Isabel of Aragon (1310-1349) married Duke Stephen II of Bavaria

23) Duke Frederick of Bavaria (1339-1393) married Maddelena Visconti

22) Elizabeth of Vabaria-Landshut (1383-1442) married Frederick I, Hohenzollern, Elector of Brandenburg and Burgrave of Nuremberg

21) John Hohenzollern (the Alchemist), Margrave of Brandenburg-Kulmbach (1406-1464) married Barbara of Saxe-Wittenberg

20) Dorothea of Brandenburg AKA Dorthea of Hohenzollern, AKA Dorothy Achilles (1431-1495) married Christian I King of Denmark, Norway and Sweden, also Count of Oldenburg and Delmenhorst

19) Margaret of Denmark (1456- 486) married James III, King of Scotland

18) King James IV of Scotland (1473-1513) married Agnes Stewart

17) Janet Stewart, "Lady Janet" (1505-1563) married Malcolm Fleming, 3rd Lord Fleming

16) John Fleming, 5th Lord Fleming (1537-1572) married Elizabeth Ross

15) John Fleming, 6th Lord Fleming and 1st Earl of Wigton (1567-1619) married Lilias Graham

14) John Fleming (1589-1650) married Margaret Livingston

13) Alexander Fleming (1612-1668) emigrated from Scotland to Virginia married Elizabeth Anderson

12) John Fleming (1627-1686) emigrated with his father from Scotland to Virginia) married Mary

11) Charles Fleming (1659-1717) married Susannah Tarleton

10) Susannah Tarleton Fleming married John Bates

9) James Bates (1721-1786) married Winnifred Grymes

8) Daniel Bates (1756-1801) married Elizabeth Cary Bell

7) Sarah Langhorne Bates (1781-1825) moved from Virginia to Tennessee married Joel Estes

6) Albert Monroe Estes (1804-1863) married Mildred Colman

5) Louis Powhatan Estes (1849-1902) married Lily Yates Moore

4) Smith William Estes (1881-1943) moved from Tennessee to Philadelphia married Mae Griffith

3) Mom, Helen Isabella Estes (1920-2010) married Dad, Richard Warren Seltzer

2) Me

1) My children

0) My grandchildren

Line of Dukes of Bohemia

40) Borivoj I, Duke of Bohemia (852-889) married **Saint Ludmila** (c. 860-921) daughter of Slavibor a Sorbian prince

39) Vratislaus I, Duke of Bohemia (888-921) married Drahomira

38) Boleslaus I, "the Cruel", Duke of Bohemia (d. 967) married Biagota. Boleslaus was a brother of "**Good King Wenceslaus**" and killed Wenceslaus to get his throne.

37) Dobrawa (940-977) married Mieszko I, King of Poland

36) Boleslaw I, Duke of Poland, "the Brave" (967-June 17, 1025) the married Emnnilda of Lusalia

35) Mieszko II Lambert, King of Poland (990-May 10/11, 1034) married Richeza of Lotharingia (995/1000-March 21, 1063)

34) Casimir I (July 25, 1016-Nov. 28, 1058) the Restorer married Maria Dobroniega (1012-Dec. 13, 1087), daughter of Vladimir "the Great," Grand Duke of Kiev.

33) Vladislav I Herman, Duke of Poland (1044-June 4, 1102) married Judith, daughter of Vratislaus of Bohemia

32) Boleslaw III (Aug. 20, 1086-Oct. 28, 1138) Wrymouth, a duke of Lesser Poland, Silesia and Sandomierz married Zbyslava of Kiev (1085/1090-1114)

31) Vladislav II (1105-May 30, 1159) Duke of Poland married Agnes of Babenberg, daughter of Margrave Leopold II of Austria and half-sister of King Conrad III of Germany

30) King Alfonso VII of Castile (March 1, 1105-Aug. 21, 1157) by his second queen, Richeza of Poland (1140- June 16, 1185)

29) Sancha of Castile (Sept. 21, 1154 or 1155-Nov. 9, 1208) married Alfonso II of Aragon the Chaste or the Troubadour (1157-1196) reigned 1162 to 1196 [We are also descended from Alfonso II Count of Provence, another son of Alfonso II of Aragon]

28) Peter II of Aragon (1174- Sept. 12, 1213) married Marie of Montpellier (1182-April 18, 1213)

27) King James I of Aragon "the Conqueror" (Feb. 2, 1208-July 1276) married Violant or Yolanda (c. 1212-1253) daughter of Andrew II of Hungary

26) Isabella of Aragon (1247-1271) married King Philip III "the Bold" of France (Capet) (1245-1285), reigned 1270-1285. Philip appears in Dante's Divine Comedy. Dante does not name him directly, but refers to him as "the small-nosed" and "the father of the Pest of France."

25) Charles of Valois (1270-1325) married Marguerite of Anjou and Maine (1273-1299)
their son became Philip VI King of France, their nephews became Louis X, Philip V, and Charles IV, kings of France

24) Jeanne of Valois (1292-1342) married William I Count of Hainault (1286-1337)

23) King Edward III of England (1312-1377) married Philippa of Hainault

22) John of Gaunt, First Duke of Lancaster (1340-1399) married Katherine Swynford

21) John Beaufort, First Earl of Somerset (1371-1410) married Margaret Holland

20) Joan Beaufort (1404-1445) married King James I of Scotland

19) Joan Stewart (1428-1486) married James Douglas, First Earl of Morton. Known as "the deaf princess," Joan used sign language.

18) John Douglas, Second Earl of Morton (1459-1513) married Janet Crichton

17) Agnes Douglas married Alexander Livingston, Fifth Lord Livingston of Callandar, guardian of Mary Queen of Scots

16) William Livingston, Sixth Lord Livingston of Callandar (1528-1602) married Agnes Fleming

15) Alexander Livingston (1561-1621) married Eleanor Hay

14) Margaret Livingston married John Fleming (1589-1650)

13) Alexander Fleming (1612-1668) emigrated from Scotland to Virginia married Elizabeth Anderson

12) John Fleming (1627-1686) emigrated with his father from Scotland to Virginia) married Mary

11) Charles Fleming (1659-1717) married Susannah Tarleton

10) Susannah Tarleton Fleming married John Bates

9) James Bates (1721-1786) married Winnifred Grymes

8) Daniel Bates (1756-1801) married Elizabeth Cary Bell

7) Sarah Langhorne Bates (1781-1825) moved from Virginia to Tennessee married Joel Estes

6) Albert Monroe Estes (1804-1863) married Mildred Colman

5) Louis Powhatan Estes (1849-1902) married Lily Yates Moore

4) Smith William Estes (1881-1943) moved from Tennessee to Philadelphia married Mae Griffith

3) Mom, Helen Isabella Estes (1920-2010) married Dad, Richard Warren Seltzer

2) Me

1) My children

0) My grandchildren

Line of Princes of Kiev

37) **Saint Olga** (890-969) married Prince Igor of Kiev

36) Prince Sviatoslav I of Kiev (935-972) married Malusha

35) Saint, Prince **Vladimir I "the Great"** of Kiev (958-1015)

34) Prince Yaroslav of Kiev "the Wise" (978-1054) married Ingegerd Olafsdottir. We are descended from him at least four ways: from his daughter Anne of Kiev, his son Izaslav I of Kiev, and his daughter Anastasia, as well as his son Vsevolod, as shown below.

33) Prince Vsevolod I of Kiev (1030-1093) married Anastasia

32) Prince Vladimir II Monomakh of Kiev (1053-1125) married Gytha of Wessex

31) Prince Mstislav I of Kiev "the Great" (1076-1132) married Christina Ingesdotter

30) Ingeborg of Kiev married Canute Lavard

29) King Valdemar I of Denmark "the Great" (1131-1182) married Sofia of Minsk

28) Helen of Denmark (1177-1233) married William of Winchester, AKA William Longsword, Lord of Luneburg

27) Duke Otto of Brunswick-Luneberg "the Child" (1204-1252)

26) Duke Albert I of Brunswick-Luneberg "the Tall" (1236-1279) married Adelheide

25) Duke Albert II of Brunswick-Luneberg "the Fat" (1268-1318) married Rixa

24) Duke Magnus I of Brunswick-Luneberg "the Pious" (d. 1369) married Sophie Brandenburg

23) Duke Magnus II of Brunswick-Luneberg) (1324-1373) married Catherine Anhalt-Bernburg

22) Katharina Elisabeth of Brunswick (1385-1423) married Count Gerhard VI of Holstein

21) Hedvig of Schuaenburg, Duchess of Schleswig and Countess of Holstein (1398-1436) married Dietrich AKA Theodoric the Lucky, Count of Delmenhorst and Oldenburg

20) King Christian I of Denmark, Norway and Sweden, also Count of Oldenburg and Delmenhorst (1426-1481) married Dorothea of Brandenburg AKA Dorothea of Hohenzollern

19) Margaret of Denmark (1456- 486) married James III, King of Scotland

18) King James IV of Scotland (1473-1513) married Agnes Stewart

17) Janet Stewart, "Lady Janet" (1505-1563) married Malcolm Fleming, 3rd Lord Fleming

16) John Fleming, 5th Lord Fleming (1537-1572) married Elizabeth Ross

15) John Fleming, 6th Lord Fleming and 1st Earl of Wigton (1567-1619) married Lilias Graham

14) John Fleming (1589-1650) married Margaret Livingston

13) Alexander Fleming (1612-1668) emigrated from Scotland to Virginia married Elizabeth Anderson

12) John Fleming (1627-1686) emigrated with his father from Scotland to Virginia) married Mary

11) Charles Fleming (1659-1717) married Susannah Tarleton

10) Susannah Tarleton Fleming married John Bates

9) James Bates (1721-1786) married Winnifred Grymes

8) Daniel Bates (1756-1801) married Elizabeth Cary Bell

7) Sarah Langhorne Bates (1781-1825) moved from Virginia to Tennessee married Joel Estes

6) Albert Monroe Estes (1804-1863) married Mildred Colman

5) Louis Powhatan Estes (1849-1902) married Lily Yates Moore

4) Smith William Estes (1881-1943) moved from Tennessee to Philadelphia married Mae Griffith

3) Mom, Helen Isabella Estes (1920-2010) married Dad, Richard Warren Seltzer

2) Me

1) My children

0) My grandchildren

Line of Gormflaith

36) **Gormflaith** (960-1010) married (1) Olaf, King of York and Dublin (2) Brian Boru, High King of Ireland

35) King Sigtrygg "Silkbeard" of Dublin (d. 1042) married daughter of Brian Boru, High King of Ireland

34) Olaf of Dublin

33) Raignaillt married King Cynan ab Iago of Gwynedd in Wales (1014-1063)

32) King Gruffydd ap Cynan of Gwyedd in Wales (1055-1137) Wales married Angharad ferch Owain

31) King Owain Gwynedd of Gwynedd in Wales (1100-1170) married Gladys ferch Llywarch

30) Iorwerth ab Owain Gwynedd "the Broken-Nosed" (1145-1174) married Mared ferch Madog

29) Prince Llywelyn "the Great" of Wales (1173-1240) married **Joan of Wales**, 1191-1237, daughter of King John of England

28) Helen of North Wales (1207-1253) married Robert de Quincy, Lord of Ware

27) Hawsie de Quincy (1250-1295) married Baldwin Wake, Lord of Bourne, d. 1281

26) John Wake (d. 1300) married Joan de Fiennes

25) Margaret Wake (1297-1349) married Edmund of Woodstock, Earl of Kent, executed for treason in 1330

24) **Joan, Countess of Kent "the Fair Maid of Kent"** (1327-1385) married Thomas Holland, First Earl of Kent, 1314-1360), also married Edward the Black Prince (1330-1376)

23) Thomas Holland, (1350-1397) Second Earl of Kent, councilor of his half-brother King Richard II of England

22) Margaret Holland (1385-1439) married John Beaufort, First Earl of Somerset

21) Joan Beaufort (1404-1445) married King James I of Scotland (1394-1437). We are descended from their daughter Annabella and from their daughter Joan Stewart as well as from their son King James II of Scotland.

20) King James II of Scotland (1430-1460) married Mary Gueldres

19) James III, King of Scotland married Margaret of Denmark (1456-486)

18) King James IV of Scotland (1473-1513) married Agnes Stewart

17) Janet Stewart, "Lady Janet" (1505-1563) married Malcolm Fleming, 3rd Lord Fleming

16) John Fleming, 5th Lord Fleming (1537-1572) married Elizabeth Ross

15) John Fleming, 6th Lord Fleming and 1st Earl of Wigton (1567-1619) married Lilias Graham

14) John Fleming (1589-1650) married Margaret Livingston

13) Alexander Fleming (1612-1668) emigrated from Scotland to Virginia married Elizabeth Anderson

12) John Fleming (1627-1686) emigrated with his father from Scotland to Virginia) married Mary

11) Charles Fleming (1659-1717) married Susannah Tarleton

10) Susannah Tarleton Fleming married John Bates

9) James Bates (1721-1786) married Winnifred Grymes

8) Daniel Bates (1756-1801) married Elizabeth Cary Bell

7) Sarah Langhorne Bates (1781-1825) moved from Virginia to Tennessee married Joel Estes

6) Albert Monroe Estes (1804-1863) married Mildred Colman

5) Louis Powhatan Estes (1849-1902) married Lily Yates Moore

4) Smith William Estes (1881-1943) moved from Tennessee to Philadelphia married Mae Griffith

3) Mom, Helen Isabella Estes (1920-2010) married Dad, Richard Warren Seltzer

2) Me

1) My children

0) My grandchildren

Line of Edith the Fair

33) **Edith the Fair** married King Harald II of England

32) Gytha of Wessex married Prince Vladimir II Monomakh of Kiev

31) Prince Mstislav I "the Great" of Kiev (1076-1132) married Christina Ingesdotter

30) Ingeborg of Kiev married Canute Lavard

29 King Valdemar I "the Great" of Denmark (1131-1182) married Sofia of Minsk

28) Helen of Denmark (1177-1233) married William of Winchester, AKA William Longsword, Lord of Luneburg

27) Duke Otto "the Child" of Brunswick-Luneberg (1204-1252)

26) Duke Albert I "the Tall" of Brunswick-Lunebuerg (1236-1279) married Adelheide

25) Duke Albert II "the Fat" of Brunswick-Luneberg (1268-1318) married Rixa

24) Duke Magnus I "the Pious" of Brunswick-Luneberg) (d. 1369) married Sophie Brandenburg

23) Duke Magnus II of Brunswick-Luneberg (1324-1373) married Catherine Anhalt-Bernburg

22) Katharina Elisabeth of Brunswick (1385-1423) married Count Gerhard VI of Holstein

21) Hedvig of Schauenburg, Duchess of Schleswig and Countess of Holstein (1398-1436) married Count Dietrich AKA Theodoric "the Lucky" of Delmenhorst and Oldenburg

20) King Christian I of Denmark, Norway and Sweden, also Count of Oldenburg and Delmenhorst (1426-1481) married Dorothea of Brandenburg AKA Dorothea of Hohenzollern

19) Margaret of Denmark (1456- 486) married James III, King of Scotland

18) King James IV of Scotland (1473-1513) married Agnes Stewart

17) Janet Stewart, "Lady Janet" (1505-1563) married Malcolm Fleming, 3rd Lord Fleming

16) John Fleming, 5th Lord Fleming (1537-1572) married Elizabeth Ross

15) John Fleming, 6th Lord Fleming and 1st Earl of Wigton (1567-1619) married Lilias Graham

14) John Fleming (1589-1650) married Margaret Livingston

13) Alexander Fleming (1612-1668) emigrated from Scotland to Virginia married Elizabeth Anderson

12) John Fleming (1627-1686) emigrated with his father from Scotland to Virginia) married Mary

11) Charles Fleming (1659-1717) married Susannah Tarleton

10) Susannah Tarleton Fleming married John Bates

9) James Bates (1721-1786) married Winnifred Grymes

8) Daniel Bates (1756-1801) married Elizabeth Cary Bell

7) Sarah Langhorne Bates (1781-1825) moved from Virginia to Tennessee married Joel Estes

6) Albert Monroe Estes (1804-1863) married Mildred Colman

5) Louis Powhatan Estes (1849-1902) married Lily Yates Moore

4) Smith William Estes (1881-1943) moved from Tennessee to Philadelphia married Mae Griffith

3) Mom, Helen Isabella Estes (1920-2010) married Dad, Richard Warren Seltzer

2) Me

1) My children

0) My grandchildren

Line of the Byzantine Empire

33) Alexios I, Byzantine Emperor (1056-1118) married **Irene Doukaina**, their daughter **Anna Komnena** (1083-1153) was the first woman historian ever.

32) Theodora Komnene (b. 1096) married Konstantinos Angleos

31) Andronikos Angelos

30) Alexios III Angelos, Byzantine Emperor (1153-1211) married Euphrosyne Doukaina Kamatera

29) Angelina Komnene (1176-1212) married Theodore I Laskaris, Emperor of Nicaea

28) Maria Laskarina married King Bela IV of Hungary and Croatia and Duke of Styria (1206-1270)

27) King Stephen V of Hungary, Dalmatia, Croatia, Rama, Serbia, Galicia, Lodomeria, Cumania, and Bulgaria, also Duke of Styria (1239-1272) married **Elizabeth the Cuman**

26) Mary of Hungary (1257-1323) married King Charles II "the Lame" of Naples and Sicily, King of Jerusalem, Prince of Salerno

25) Eleanor of Anjou AKA Eleanor of Naples (1289-1341) married King Frederick III of Sicily

24) Elisabeth of Sicily AKA Isabel of Aragon (1310-1349) married Duke Stephen II of Bavaria

23) Duke Frederick of Bavaria (1339-1393) married Maddelena Visconti

22) Elizabeth of Vabaria-Landshut (1383-1442) married Frederick I, Hohenzollern, Elector of Brandenburg and Burgrave of Nuremberg

21) John Hohenzollern (the Alchemist), Margrave of Brandenburg-Kulmbach (1406-1464) married Barbara of Saxe-Wittenberg

20) Dorothea of Brandenburg AKA Dorthea of Hohenzollern, AKA Dorothy Achilles (1431-1495) married Christian I King of Denmark, Norway and Sweden, also Count of Oldenburg and Delmenhorst

19) Margaret of Denmark (1456- 486) married James III, King of Scotland

18) King James IV of Scotland (1473-1513) married Agnes Stewart

17) Janet Stewart, "Lady Janet" (1505-1563) married Malcolm Fleming, 3rd Lord Fleming

16) John Fleming, 5th Lord Fleming (1537-1572) married Elizabeth Ross

15) John Fleming, 6th Lord Fleming and 1st Earl of Wigton (1567-1619) married Lilias Graham

14) John Fleming (1589-1650) married Margaret Livingston

13) Alexander Fleming (1612-1668) emigrated from Scotland to Virginia married Elizabeth Anderson

12) John Fleming (1627-1686) emigrated with his father from Scotland to Virginia) married Mary

11) Charles Fleming (1659-1717) married Susannah Tarleton

10) Susannah Tarleton Fleming married John Bates

9) James Bates (1721-1786) married Winnifred Grymes

8) Daniel Bates (1756-1801) married Elizabeth Cary Bell

7) Sarah Langhorne Bates (1781-1825) moved from Virginia to Tennessee married Joel Estes

6) Albert Monroe Estes (1804-1863) married Mildred Colman

5) Louis Powhatan Estes (1849-1902) married Lily Yates Moore

4) Smith William Estes (1881-1943) moved from Tennessee to Philadelphia married Mae Griffith

3) Mom, Helen Isabella Estes (1920-2010) married Dad, Richard Warren Seltzer

2) Me

1) My children

0) My grandchildren

Line of Leon and Castile

28 Raymond, Count of Galicia (c. 1070-May 2, 1107) married **Urraca, Queen of Leon and Castile** (1081-1126)

29) Alfonso VII of Leon and Castile (March 1, 1105-Aug. 21, 1157) married Berenguela of Barcelona

28) Ferdinand II of Leon (c. 1137-Jan. 22, 1188) married Urraca of Portugal

27) Alfonso IX of Leon (1171-1230) married Berengaria of Castile

26) Fernando III, King of Castile and Leon married Jeanne, Countess of Ponthieu

25) Eleanor of Castile (1241-1290) married Edward I, King of England (Plantagenet) (1239-1307) reigned (1272-1304)

24) King Edward II of England (April 25, 1284- Sept. 21, 1327?) reigned 1307-1327 married Isabella of France AKA She-Wolf of France (c. 1295- Aug. 22, 1358), 23) King Edward III of England (Nov. 13, 1312-June 21, 1377) reigned 1327-1377 married Philippa of Hainault (1314-1369)

22) John of Gaunt (Plantagenet), First Duke of Lancaster (1340-1399) married Katherine Swynford (1350-1403)

21) John Beaufort, first Earl of Someset (1371-1410) married Margaret Holland (1385-1439)

20) King James I of Scotland (Stewart) (1394-1437), reigned 1406-1437 married 1424 Joan Beaufort (1404-1445)

19) Joan Stewart (1428-1486) deaf-mute married James Douglas, First Earl of Morton. Known as "the deaf princess," she used sign language.

18) John Douglas, Second Earl of Morton (1459-1513) married Janet Crichton

17) Agnes Douglas married Alexander Livingston, Fifth Lord Livingston of Callandar, guardian of Mary Queen of Scots

16) William Livingston, Sixth Lord Livingston of Callandar (1528-1602) married Agnes Fleming

15) Alexander Livingston (1561-1621) married Eleanor Hay

14) Margaret Livingston married John Fleming (1589-1650)

13) Alexander Fleming (1612-1668) emigrated from Scotland to Virginia married Elizabeth Anderson

12) John Fleming (1627-1686) emigrated with his father from Scotland to Virginia) married Mary

11) Charles Fleming (1659-1717) married Susannah Tarleton

10) Susannah Tarleton Fleming married John Bates

9) James Bates (1721-1786) married Winnifred Grymes

8) Daniel Bates (1756-1801) married Elizabeth Cary Bell

7) Sarah Langhorne Bates (1781-1825) moved from Virginia to Tennessee married Joel Estes

6) Albert Monroe Estes (1804-1863) married Mildred Colman

5) Louis Powhatan Estes (1849-1902) married Lily Yates Moore

4) Smith William Estes (1881-1943) moved from Tennessee to Philadelphia married Mae Griffith

3) Mom, Helen Isabella Estes (1920-2010) married Dad, Richard Warren Seltzer

2) Me

1) My children

0) My grandchildren

Line of the White Witch

27) **Ingrid Ylva** (1180-1250) married Magnus Minneskold (d. 1210)

26) Birger Magnusson, founder of Stockholm (1210-1266) married Ingeborg Eriksdotter of Sweden

25) King Valdemar I of Sweden (1239-1302) married Sophia of Denmark, know for her ability in playing chess.

24) Ingeborg of Sweden married Count Gerhard III of Holstein-Ploen

23) Count Gerhard IV of Holstein-Ploen married Anastasia of Wittenberg

22) Ingeborg of Holstein-Ploen married Count Conrad I Count of Oldenburg

21) Count Christian V of Oldenburg (1347-1423) married Agnes Honstein

21) Count Dietrich of Delmenhorst and Oldenburg, "Theodoric the Lucky" (1398-1440) married Hedwig Schauenburg

20) King Christian I of Denmark, Norway, and Sweden (1426-1481) married Dorothea Hohenzollern

19) Margaret of Denmark (1456- 486) married James III, King of Scotland

18) King James IV of Scotland (1473-1513) married Agnes Stewart

17) Janet Stewart, "Lady Janet" (1505-1563) married Malcolm Fleming, 3rd Lord Fleming

16) John Fleming, 5th Lord Fleming (1537-1572) married Elizabeth Ross

15) John Fleming, 6th Lord Fleming and 1st Earl of Wigton (1567-1619) married Lilias Graham

14) John Fleming (1589-1650) married Margaret Livingston

13) Alexander Fleming (1612-1668) emigrated from Scotland to Virginia married Elizabeth Anderson

12) John Fleming (1627-1686) emigrated with his father from Scotland to Virginia) married Mary

11) Charles Fleming (1659-1717) married Susannah Tarleton

10) Susannah Tarleton Fleming married John Bates

9) James Bates (1721-1786) married Winnifred Grymes

8) Daniel Bates (1756-1801) married Elizabeth Cary Bell

7) Sarah Langhorne Bates (1781-1825) moved from Virginia to Tennessee married Joel Estes

6) Albert Monroe Estes (1804-1863) married Mildred Colman

5) Louis Powhatan Estes (1849-1902) married Lily Yates Moore

4) Smith William Estes (1881-1943) moved from Tennessee to Philadelphia married Mae Griffith

3) Mom, Helen Isabella Estes (1920-2010) married Dad, Richard Warren Seltzer

2) Me

1) My children

0) My grandchildren

Line of Scotland and England

40) Alpin mac Echah (778-834), king of Da Riata, which included parts of Ireland and Scotland

39) King Kenneth I (810-858) of Scotland

38) King Constantine I (836-877) of Scotland

37) King Donald II (died 900) of Scotland

36) King Malcolm I (897-954) of Scotland

35) King Kenneth II (932-995) of Scotland

34) King Malcolm II of Scotland (954-1034)

33) Bethoc of Scone married Crinan of Dunkeld AKA Grimus, Mormaer of Atholl, Lay Abbot of Dunkeld (b. c. 975 in Athoil, Perthshire,Scotland killed in battle in 1045 at Dunkeld)

32) Duncan I, King of Scotland (c. 1001-1040) reigned 1034-1040 (murdered by Macbeth)

31) King Malcolm III of Scotland married **Saint Margaret of Scotland** (1045-1093).

30) Matilda of Scotland (1080-1118) married King Henry I of England (1068-1135), son of **Matilda of Flanders** 1031-1083 and King William "the Conqueror" of England

29) **Empress Matilda** (1102-1110) married Duke Geoffrey Plantagenet "the Handsome" of Normandy

28) King Henry II of England (1133-1189) married **Eleanor of Aquitaine**

27) King John I "Lackland" of England (1166-1216) married Isabella of Angouleme

26) King Henry III of England (1207-1307) married Eleanor of Provence

25) King Edward I "Longshanks" of England (1239-1307) married Eleanor of Castille

24) King Edward II of England (1284-1327) married Isabella of France

23) King Edward III of England (1312-1377) married Philippa of Hainault

22) John of Gaunt, First Duke of Lancaster (1340-1399) married Katherine Swynford

21) John Beaufort, First Earl of Somerset (1371-1410) married Margaret Holland

20) Joan Beaufort (1404-1445) married King James I of Scotland

19) Joan Stewart (1428-1486) married James Douglas, First Earl of Morton. Known as "the deaf princess," she used sign language.

18) John Douglas, Second Earl of Morton (1459-1513) married Janet Crichton

17) Agnes Douglas married Alexander Livingston, Fifth Lord Livingston of Callandar, guardian of Mary Queen of Scots

16) William Livingston, Sixth Lord Livingston of Callandar (1528-1602) married Agnes Fleming

15) Alexander Livingston (1561-1621) married Eleanor Hay

14) Margaret Livingston married John Fleming (1589-1650)

13) Alexander Fleming (1612-1668) emigrated from Scotland to Virginia married Elizabeth Anderson

12) John Fleming (1627-1686) emigrated with his father from Scotland to Virginia) married Mary

11) Charles Fleming (1659-1717) married Susannah Tarleton

10) Susannah Tarleton Fleming married John Bates

9) James Bates (1721-1786) married Winnifred Grymes

8) Daniel Bates (1756-1801) married Elizabeth Cary Bell

7) Sarah Langhorne Bates (1781-1825) moved from Virginia to Tennessee married Joel Estes

6) Albert Monroe Estes (1804-1863) married Mildred Colman

5) Louis Powhatan Estes (1849-1902) married Lily Yates Moore

4) Smith William Estes (1881-1943) moved from Tennessee to Philadelphia married Mae Griffith

3) Mom, Helen Isabella Estes (1920-2010) married Dad, Richard Warren Seltzer

2) Me

1) My children

0) My grandchildren

Stewart Line

23) **Marjorie Bruce** (1296-1316) married Walter Stewart, 6th High Steward of Scotland

22) Robert II, King of Scotland, first king of the Stewart Dynasty (1316-1390) married Elizabeth Mure

21) Robert III, King of Scotland (1337-1406) married Annabella Drummond

20) James I, King of Scotland (1394-1437) married Joan Beaufort

19) Joan Stewart (1428-1486) married James Douglas, First Earl of Morton

18) John Douglas, Second Earl of Morton (1459-1513) married Janet Crichton

17) Agnes Douglas married Alexander Livingston, Fifth Lord Livingston of Callandar, guardian of Mary Queen of Scots

16) William Livingston, Sixth Lord Livingston of Callandar (1528-1602) married Agnes Fleming

15) Alexander Livingston (1561-1621) married Eleanor Hay

14) Margaret Livingston (1586-1634) married John Fleming

13) Alexander Fleming, emigrated from Scotland to Virginia (1612-1668) married Elizabeth Anderson

12) John Fleming, emigrated with his father from Scotland to Virginia) (1627-1686) married Mary

11) Charles Fleming (1659-1717) married Susannah Tarleton

10) Susannah Tarleton Fleming married John Bates

9) James Bates (1721-1786) married Winnifred Grymes

8) Daniel Bates (1756-1801) married Elizabeth Cary Bell

7) Sarah Langhorne Bates, moved from Virginia to Tennessee (1781-1825) married Joel Estes

6) Albert Monroe Estes (1804-1863) married Mildred Colman

5) Louis Powhatan Estes (1849-1902) married Lily Yates Moore

4) Smith William Estes, moved from Tennessee to Philadelphia (1881-1943) married Mae Griffith)

3) Helen Isabella Estes (1920-2010) married Richard Warren Seltzer

2) Me

1) My children

0) My grandchildren

Ancestor Highlights

Movies

The Lion in Winter. King Henry II of England, Queen Eleanor of Aquitaine, and their son King John I.

Braveheart. King Robert the Bruce of Scotland, William "le Hardi" Douglas, ally of William Wallace. King Edward I of England, his son the future Edward II and his son's wife Isabella of France. In the movie, King Edward sends Isabella, his daughter-in-law, to negotiate with Wallace. But in history, Edward II married Isabella a year after his father died and three years after the execution of Wallace. So the implication that she had a tryst with Wallace and her son was Wallace's is simply Hollywood fantasy. But Isabella was an interesting character in her own right, leading a rebellion that overthrew her husband and put her young son Edward III on the throne, with her as regent. She was nicknamed "The She-Wolf of France."

King Arthur. Cerdic of Wessex (d. 534) and Cynric of Wessex, his son, who ruled as King of Wessex. Cerdic was leader of the first group of West Saxons to come to England in 495. The movie shows he and his son killed in battle by King Arthur and Sir Lancelot.

The Da Vinci Code. Both the novel and the movie propose the theory that Clovis, King of France, was a direct descendant of Jesus Christ and Mary Magdalene. Wikipedia says about that novel, "Mary Magdalene was of royal descent (through the Jewish House of Benjamin) and was the wife of Jesus, of the House of David. That she was a prostitute was slander invented by the Church to obscure their true relationship. At the time of the Crucifixion, she was pregnant. After the Crucifixion, she fled to Gaul, where she was sheltered by the Jews of Marseille. She gave birth to a daughter, named Sarah. The bloodline of Jesus and Mary Magdalene became the Merovingian dynasty of France."

Dante
Hugh Capet "the Great," Duke of France and Count of Paris (898-956). Hugh laments the avarice of his descendants.
King Philip III the Bold (1245-1285), seen outside the gates of Purgatory.

The Decameron
Marquis Azzo d'Este of Ferrara
King Philip II of France

Operas
Tannhäuser by Wagner: Hermann I, Landgrave of Thuringia
Lohengrin by Wagner: Henry the Fowler
The Ring Cycle by Wagner: Gundahar AKA Gunther, King of Burgundy and his wife Brunhild

Poets
Marie of France
Chretien de Troyes (possible)
William IX, the Troubadour, Duke of Aquitaine

Gods and Mythical Monsters
Greek
Gaia
Uranus
Cronus
Zeus

Norse

Odin AKA Woden, king of the gods (Wednesday)

Frigg, goddess of marriage, motherhood, and clairvoyance (Friday)

Njord, sea god

Skadi, ski goddess

Yngve Frey, god of peace, fertility, prosperity, and fair weather; sovereign of the Swedes

Brunhild, valkyrie, lover of Sigfried the dragonslayer

Gothic, Frankish, Germanic

Quinotaur, a bull with five horns

Melusine, a demoness

Crusaders

King Fulk V of Jerusalem (1089-1143)

King Louis IX of France (Saint Louis) (1214-1270)

King Philip III "the Bold" of France (1245-1285)

Isabella of Aragon, wife of Philip III; accompanied him on the Eighth Crusade, against Tunis (1247-1271)

Emperor Baldwin I of Constantinople (1172-1205)

Baldwin II, Count of Edessa and King of Jerusalem (1075-1131)

Bohemond I of Antioch (1054-1111)

Bohemond II, Prince of Taranto and of Antioch

Raynald of Chatillon, Prince of Antioch (1124-1187)

King James I of Aragon, father of Isabella (1208-1276)

King Louis VII of France (1120-1180)

Count Ramon Berenguer IV of Barcelona (1114-1162)

Duke Eudes I of Burgundy (1060-1101)

James, Lord of Avesnes (1152-1191)

Duke Welf I of Bavaria (1035-1101)

Alan fitz Flaad, Breton knight (1060-after 1120)

Eleanor of Aquitaine, queen of France then queen of England (1124-1204)
Alexander Stewart, 4th High Steward of Scotland (1210-1282)
Alan fitz Walter, Second High Steward of Scotland (1120-1204)
Emulf of Hesdin, knight, took part in Norman conquest of England (died 1097)

Saints

King Louis IX of France (Capet) "Saint Louis" King Louis IX of France, Crusader (1214-1270)
Saint Margaret (1045-1093)
Saint Irene AKA Piroska of Hungary (1088-1134)
Saint Vladimir "the Great," Prince of Kiev (958-1015)
Saint Olga of Kiev (c. 890-969)
Saint Adelaide of Italy (931-999)
Matilda of Ringelheim AKA Saint Matilda or Saint Mathilda (895-968)
Saint Ludmila (860-921), grandmother of "Good King" Wenceslaus
Saint Clotilde, wife of Clovis (475-545)
Saint Begga (615-693)
Saint Itta of Metz (592-652)
Saint Doda of Reims (born before 509)
Saint Anulf of Metz (born around 582)
Saint Leudwinus, Count of Treves (660-772)
Saint Clodulf of Metz (605-697)

Kings of England

House of Wessex

Egbert, first king of England (770-839)
Ethelwulf, (died 858)

Alfred "the Great" (886-899
Harold II Godwinson (1022-1066)

House of Normandy
William I "the Conqueror" (1028-1087) conquered England 1066
Henry I "Beauclerc"(1068-1135)

House of Plantagenet
Henry II (1133-1189)
John I "Lackland" (of the Magna Carta) (1166-1216)
Henry III (1207-1272)
Edward I "Longshanks" (1239-1307)
Edward II (1284-1327)
Edward III (1312-1377)

Kings of Scotland
House of Alpin
Kenneth I (810-858) conqueror of the Picts, first king of the Scots
Constantine I AKA Causantin mac Cinaeda (836-877)
Donald II (died 900)
Malcolm I (897-954)
Kenneth II (943-995)
Malcolm II (954-1034)

House of Dunkeld
Duncan I (1034-1040) killed by Macbeth
Malcom III (1031-1093) killed Macbeth
David I (1084-1153)

House of Bruce
Robert I "the Bruce" (1274-1329)

House of Stewart
Robert II (1316-1390)
Robert III (1337-1406)
James I (1394-1437)
James II (1430-1460)
James III (1451-1488)
James IV (1473-1513)

Kings of Wales
Llywelyn "the Great" (1173-1240)
Rhodri "the Great" (820-878)

Kings of Dublin
Sigtrygg II "Silkbeard" (970-1042)
Olaf AKA Amlaib Cuaran (died 980)
Brian Boru, High King of Ireland (941-1014)

Kings of France
Merovingian Dynasty
Chlothar I (died 561)
Clovis I (466-511)
Chlideric I (died 481)
Merovech·(411-458)

Carolingian Dynasty
Charles Martel (688-741)
Pepin "the Short" (714-768)
Charlemagne (748-814)
Louis the Pious (778-840)
Charles the Bald (823-877)

Capet Dynasty
Robert II (972-1031
Henry I (1008-1060)
Philip I (1052-1108)
Louis VI (1081-1137)
Louis VII (1120-1180)
Philip II "Augustus" (1165-1223)
Louis VIII (1187-1226)
Louis IX "Saint Louis" (1214-1270)
Philip III (1245-1285)

Kings of Aragon and Pamplona and Counts of Barcelona

Garcia Jimenez of Pamplona (late 9th century)
Sancho I of Pamplona (860-925)
Garcia Sanchez I of Pamplona (919-970)
Sancho II of Pamplona (938-994)
Garcia Sanchez II of Pamplona (died 1000)
Sancho III Garces of Pamplona (992-1035)
Ramiro I of Aragon (1007-1063)
Sancho Ramirez of Aragon and Pampona) (1042-1094)
Ramiro II "the Monk" of Aragon (1086-1157)
Ramon Berenguer IV, Count of Barcelona and Aragon (1114-1162)
Alfonso II of Aragon and Barcelona (1157-1196)
Peter II of Aragon and Barcelona (1178-1213)
James I of Aragon and Barcelona (1208-1276)

Kings and Queen of Castile, Leon, Pamplona

Urraca (1081-1126) first European queen to reign in her own right
Alfonso VII "the Emperor" (1105-1157)
Ferdinand II (1137-1188)

Alfonso IX (1171-1230)
Ferdinand II (1137-1188)
Alfonso IX (1171-1230)
Fernando III (1199-1252)
Alfonso VI "the Brave" (1040-1109)
Ferdinand I "the Great" (1015-1065)
Sancho Garaces III (992-1035)
Garcia Sanchez II (died 1000)
Sancho II "the Strong" (1036-1072)
Sancho I "the Fat" (932-966)
Ramiro II (900-951)

Kings of Portugal
Sancho I "the Populator" (1154-1211)
Afonso I Henriques "the Conqueror (1106-1185), first king of Portugal

Kings of Hungary
Bela I "the Boxer" (1015-1063)
Bela II "the Blind")1109-1141)
Geza II (1130-1162)
Bela III (1148-1196)
Andrew II (1177-1235)
Bela IV (1206-1270)
Stephen V (1239-1272) married Elizabeth the Cuman
Taksony (931-970s)
Zoltan (880 or 903-950)
Arpad (845-907) founder of Arpad Dynasty
Almos (820-895)
Attila the Hun (406-453)

Dukes of Bohemia

Boleslaus I (915-972) brother of Good King Wenceslaus, who killed Wenceslaus to get his throne
Vratislaus I (888-921)
Borivoj I (852-889)

Dukes and Kings of Poland

Mieszko I (930-992)
Boleslaw I "the Brave" (967-1025)
Mieszko II Lambert (990-1034)
Boleslaw III "the Wry-Mouthed" (1086-1138)
Vladislav II AKA Wladyslaw II "the Exile" (1105-1159)

Princes of Kiev

Mstislav I Vladimirovich "the Great" of Kiev (1076-1132)
Vladimir II Monomakh (1053-1125)
Vsevolod I of Kiev (1030-1093)
Yaroslav I the Wise (978-1054)
Saint Vladimir I "the Great" (958-1015)
Prince Igor, reigned (912-914)
Prince Sviatoslav I (c. 942-March 972)
Sviatopolk II (1050-1113)
Iziaslav I (1024-1078)

Kings of Denmark

Christian I of Denmark, Norway, and Sweden Christian I of Denmark, Norway, and Sweden, reigning 1448-1481
King Valdemar I of Denmark (1131-1182)
King Valdemar II of Denmark
King Eric I of Denmark (c. 1060-1103)

Kings of Sweden

Valdemar I of Sweden (1239-1302)
Olof Skotkonung (980-1022)
Eric "the Victorious" (945-995)

Holy Roman Emperors

Otto I "the Great" (912-973)
Otto II "the Red" (955-983)
Lothair III (1075-1137)
Frederick I Barbarossa (1122-1190)
Charles the Bald (823-877)
Louis the Pious (778-840)
Charlemagne (748-814)

Byzantine Emperors

Macedonian Dynasty

Romanos II (938-963)
Constantine VII (905-959)
Leo VI "the Wise " (868-912)

Amorian Dynasty

Michael III "the Drunkard" (840-867)
Theophilos, Byzantine Emperor (812-842)
Michael II the Stammerer (770-829)

Monomachos Dynasty

Constantine IX Monomachos (c. 980-1055)

Komnenos Dynasty

John II Komnenos (1087-1143)

Alexios I Komnenos (1057-1118) father of Anna Komnene, the first woman historian

Angelos Dynasty
Alexios III Angelos (1153-1211)

Latin Dynasty
Emperor Baldwin I of Constantinople (1172-1205)

Emperor of Bulgaria
Ivan Vladislav (died 1018)

Kings and Princes of Armenia
Ashot II Bagratuni (died 690)
Smbat I (850-912)
Ashot I (820-890)
Smbat VIII "the Confessor" (9th century)
Ashot Msaker AKA Ashot IV Bagratuni (8th century)
Smbat VII Bagratuni (died 775)
Ashot III Bagratuni "the Blind" (690-762)
Varaztirots II Bagratuni (590-645)

1600 Ancestors

Since, historically, a son keeps the surname of his father and a daughter adopts the surname of her husband, I trace from son to father to his father, as far back as I can go. And I trace the ancestry of a mother by her maiden name, from her father to his father, as a separate family. Hence, by this convention, my father's ancestors are under the Seltzer family; my mother's are under Estes; my father's mother's are under Daly; mother's mother's are under Griffith; and so on. In the Middle Ages, before surnames came into common use, the place of origin, the region ruled, or a nickname distinguishes one John from another. And when a given name is repeated from one generation to the next, they are numbered: John I is the father of John II, the father of John III.

The standard practice in American genealogy books is to designate the generation of the first immigrant with the number one and count from there forward to the present. But I needed a way to add newly-found ancestors from long before immigration, and I wanted a way keep track of hundreds or thousands of direct ancestors.

Hence, I number the generations starting at the present and counting backwards. "Seltzer 0-13 Germany" means that the Seltzer family list starts with the present (0) generation (my granddaughters) and extends 13 generations back to when our ancestors were in Germany. Similarly, "Estes 3-32 Italy" means that starting from the third generation (my mother's), the Estes family list extends back to the 32nd generation in Italy.

I assign everyone a number. Each digit represents a generation. 1 = male, 0 = female. You read from left to right, starting at the period.

0.1 means Bob, the father of my granddaughters, who are in the present (0) generation

0.11 means me, their father's father

0.111 means my Dad, their father's father's father

0.0 means their mother

0.1001 means four generations back, their father's mother's mother's father

0.10110 means five generations back, their fathers mother's father's father's mother.

With these numbers, you can tell at a glance the number of the generation (the number of digits) and whether the connection in each generation is by the mother or father (zero or one).

I will post a pdf of this list at my website so you can download it and search it. Go to seltzerbooks.com/1600.pdf

Seltzer 0-13 Germany

<u>Generation 0</u>

Adelaide

Lillian

daughters of

<u>Generation 1</u>

0.1 Robert Richard Hartley Seltzer (b. July 29, 1975), Milton Academy, B.S. Yale, M.B.A. and M.S. Wharton married Aug. 10, 2002 in Boston, MA **0.0 Stacey Denenberg** (b. July 18, 1976), B.S. and M.S. Yale, M.B.A. Wharton

Bob's siblings =

Mike

Tim

Unnamed sister

Bob = son of

<u>Generation 2</u>

0.11 Richard Warren Seltzer, Jr. (b. Feb. 23 1946 Clarksville, TN) B.A. Yale 1969, M.A. University of Massachusetts 1973 married July 28, 1973 Boston, MA **0.10 Barbara Ann Hartley** (Feb. 20 1950-Dec. 4 2012) B.A. Albertus Magnus 1971, M.A. Boston State. Richard's sibling = Sallie

Richard = son of

<u>Generation 3</u>

0.111 Richard Warren Seltzer, Sr. (June 5, 1923 Washington, DC-June 14, 2014) married June 5, 1944 in Philadelphia, PA, **0.110 Helen Isabella Estes** (Jan. 31, 1920 Philadelphia, PA-Dec. 28, 2010 West Roxbury, MA). **See Estes Family.** Helen B.A. Goddard College. Richard B.A. University of Maryland.; M.S. University of Pennsylvania; Ed.D. University of Maryland; superintendent of schools Bristol Township, Lower Moreland Township, and Columbia, PA. His autobiography seltzerbooks.com/lifeandtimes.html, his dissertation seltzerbooks.com/humanrelations.html

Richard's siblings =

Charles Philip Seltzer

James Henry Seltzer

John Paul Seltzer (Uncle Paul)

Richard = son of

<u>Generation 4</u>

0.1111 Warren Ray Seltzer (April 20, 1891 Washington, DC-April 13, 1978, Washington, DC) architect, married June 19, 1918 **0.1110 Lillian Leona Daly** (Oct. 6, 1890-April 15, 1973) **See Daly Family**

Warren's siblings =

Charles W. Seltzer (Uncle Charlie), daughter = Olive

Edgar Arnold Seltzer

Warren = son of:

Generation 5

0.11111 Henry Hocker Seltzer (Aug. 28, 1856-Aug. 7 1925), physician, married (1) 1877 **0.11110 Susan Arnold** (April 1859-Dec. 1916), daughter of Peter Arnold married (2) Oct. 18, 1918 Sarah L. Behm (1856-). His autobiography *Henry Hocker Seltzer, Pennsylvania Dutch Teacher, Civil Servant, and Physician-Memories of 1856-1915* is online at seltzerbooks.com/hockercomplete.pdf

siblings of Henry Hocker Seltzer =

John P. Seltzer (1851-1922)

Martin Seltzer (1852-1934)

James M. Seltzer (1854-1855)

Elizabeth E. Seltzer (1859-1934)

Benjamin F. Seltzer (1861-1949)

Charles Augustus Seltzer (Uncle Gus) (1864-1965), daughter = Violet

Harvey L. Seltzer (1866-1936)

Henry Hocker = son of

Generation 6

0.111111 Henry Uhland Seltzer (June 15 June, 1824-Nov. 25, 1897) married **0.111110 Anna Hocker** (May 10, 1827-Jan. 10, 1914) **See Hocker Family**

Henry Uhland = only son of

Generation 7

0.1111111 Philip Seltzer (Dec. 6, 1772-April 19, 1847) died of tuberculosis in Annville, PA married March 25, 1800 **0.1111110 Maria Uhland** (Aug. 10, 1784-Feb. 25, 1860) died of cancer. Philip was a stone mason He also cultivated a small farm which he owned in Bellegrove, PA.

Philip's siblings =

Anna Maria Seltzer (b.1771)

Abraham L. Seltzer (1773-1863)

Jacob Seltzer (1776-1846)

Barbara (1777-1875)

Michael Seltzer (1780-1863)

John Seltzer (1783-1856)

John George Seltzer (1813-1899)

Philip = son of

Generation 8

0.11111111 Johann Michael Seltzer (March 23, 1740 Lutheran, Parchim, Mecklenburg-Vorpommern, Germany-1815 Mount Zion, Lebanon, Pennsylvania) married **0.11111110 Barbara Gasser** (b. 1748). Michael arrived in Philadelphia with his father in 1752. He may have served in the American Revolution.

Johann Michael's siblings =

Georg Christian

Johann Jacob

Johann Phillip

Maria Eva

Johann Michael = son of

Generation 9

0.111111111 (Johann or Hans) Jacob Seltzer (Feb. 15, 1711-1772) married 1733 **0.111111110 Anna Maria Welsen** (d. 1769) Johann was a cooper and farmer. He arrived in Pennsylvania from Germany in 1752 with his wife, his daughter Maria Eva, his sons Johann Michael, Johann Philipp, Georg Christian, and Johann Jacob.

Jacob = son of

Generation 10

0.1111111111 Wyerich Seltzer (1661 Michelfeld, Amberg-Sulzbach, Bayern, Gemany-1742 Michelfeld, Amberg-Sulzbach, Bayern, Germany) married 1683 **0.111111110 Anna Catherina Neff** (1666 Michelfeld, Ostalbkreis, Baden-Wuerttemberg, Germany-1759 Michelfeld, Heidelberg, Baden-Wuerttemberg, Germany) **See Neff**

Wyerich = son of

Generation 11

0.11111111111 Erasmus Seltzer (1640, Michelfeld, Amberg-
Sulzbach, Bayern, Germany-1703, Michelfeld, Germany) married
1658 **0.11111111110 Margaretha Donner** (Dec. 27, 1638 Sundgau,
Germany-June 26, 1667 Michelfeld, Amberg-Sulzbach, Bayern,
Germany)

Erasmus = son of

Generation 12

0.111111111111 Georg Seltzer (1604 Michelfeld, Amberg-Sulzbach,
Bayern, Germany-Nov. 22, 1669, Michelfled, Amberg-Sulzbach,
Bayern, Germany) married 1662 **0.111111111110 Anna Baur** (1605
Germany-1654 Laimen, Baden-Wuerttemberg, Germany)

Georg = son of

Generation 13

0.1111111111111 Ulrich Seltzer (1572 Michelfeld, Amberg-
Sulzbach, Bayern, Germany-1607 Michelfeld, Heidelberg, Baden-
Wuerttemberg, Germany) married 1600 Michelfeld, Amberg-
Sulzbach, Bayern, Germany **0.11111111111110 Margaretha** (b.
1576)

Estes 3-32 Italy

Generation 3

0.110 Helen Estes (Jan. 31, 1920 Philadelphia, PA-Dec. 28, 2010,
West Roxbury, MA) married June 5, 1944 at Redeemer Lutheran
Church, Philadelphia, PA, **0.111 Richard Warren Seltzer, Sr.** (June
5, 1923 Washington, DC-June 14. 2014. West Roxbury, MA) **See
Seltzer.** Helen was the compiler and author of *Cary-Estes-Moore
Genealogy* seltzerbooks.com/moorecomplete.pdf
her siblings =

John Griffith Estes (Jack) (Sept. 27, 1908-Nov. 30, 1961) died of cancer of lungs and bone

Lewis Stanley Estes (March 31, 1911- Aug. 9, 1978, Philadelphia)

Jean Brulinski (b. June 18, 1922)

Lillian Margaret Estes (b. Dec. 12, 1909) married 1929 William Norris Moyer, Jr.

Virginia Griffith Estes (b. Jan. 13, 1914-2000) married June 12, 1937 Edward Robert Jacoby, Jr. (June 27, 1914-Jan. 1, 1974)

Agnes Griffith Estes (b. August 20, 1915 Philadelphia) married Sept. 3, 1938 George John Meyers, Jr. (b. May 23, 1916 Philadelphia)

Mildred Elizabeth Estes (b. July 20, 1922 Philadelphia-April 13, 1997 Somers Point, NJ) married (1) March 3, 1943 in Philadelphia James Glisson Brinton (1920-1944) killed in action at Cassino, Italy), married (2) 1947 Walter Taney Rowland (b. Dec. 30, 1917 Prospect Park, PA d. Sept. 16, 1969 Somers Point, NJ), married (3) 1973 James Kleiner

Helen = daughter of

Generation 4

0.1101 Smith William Estes (June 17, 1881 Brownsville, Haywood, TN-after 1947) married Nov. 29, 1906, Philadelphia, PA **0.1100 Mae Griffith** (May 27, 1883 Philadelphia, PA-May 27, 1930 Philadelphia, PA) **See Griffith**

his siblings =

Mary Moore Estes (b. 1876)

Mildred C. Estes (1879-1938)

Belle Estes (1883-1938)

Laurence B. Estes (1885-1962)

Sallie ("Aunt Sallie") Estes (1888-1981)

Warner W. Estes (b.1890)

Smith William = son of

Generation 5
0.11011 Louis (Lewis) Powhatan Estes (Nov. 22, 1849-Sept. 6, 1902) physician and land owner married Oct. 30, 1875 **0.11010 Eliza "Lilly" Yates Moore** (1853-1929) **See Moore**
his brother = William Lawrence Estes (1855-1940) Bethel College, KY 1872; Medical Dept. U. of VA 1877; Univ. College of NY 1878; Surgeon in Chief, St. Luke's Hospital, Bethlehem, PA from 1881 until retirement in 1920, author of *Treatment of Fractures.*
Louis = son of

Generation 6
0.110111 Albert Monroe Estes (Nov. 19, 1804-Dec. 22, 1863) married (1) Nov. 22, 1832 in Haywood County, TN, Elizabeth Alston Pickett (Dec. 16, 1811-Nov. 16, 1843), married (2) Nov. 17, 1848 **0.110110 Mildred Colman** (1823-Nov. 30, 1849), married (3) Dec. 20. 1854 Margaret Owen Burton daughter of Dr. William Owen of Henrico County, VA. Albert enlisted in the Confederate Army May 23, 1862, Seventh (Duckworth's) Cavalry Regiment. Rank at enlistment = private. Final rank = captain. He owned about 150 slaves at the start of the Civil War.
his siblings =
Moreau Pinckney Estes (Nov. 14, 1806-Oct. 17, 1871)
Henry Carey Estes (Jan. 9, 1808-winter of 1835)
Virginia Thorp Estes (May 11, 1811-1860)
Eliza Jane Estes (b. Nov. 15, 1815)
Cornelia Sarah Rebecca Estes (b. Feb.14, 1818)
Judith Bell Estes (March 10, 1821-June 28, 1903)
Sarah Ann Estes (Nov. 24, 1823-June 30, 1848)
Albert = son of

Generation 7
0.1101111 Joel Estes (Jan. 22, 1780-Aug. 16, 1833) married Oct. 13, 1801 **0.1101110 Sarah Langhorne Bates. See Bates** Joel was a

captain in War of 1812. He commanded a company of volunteer riflemen from the 43rd Regiment of Virginia Militia and which was later attached to the 4th Regiment. Began service Sept. 16, 1813.

his siblings =

Triplet Thorpe Estes (1778-1852)

John H. T. Estes, first lieutenant of light artillery July 1, 1808, captain September 1809

Benjamin Estes. (d.1868), captain

Thomas Estes (d. in St. Louis, MO)

William Estes (lived in Petersburg, VA, d. in Mississippi)

Edward Estes (d. in Campbell Co., VA)

Elisha W. Estes (d. in KY)

Thorp Estes (d. in TN)

Nancy Estes (b. in VA, d. in KY)

Elizabeth Estes (b. in VA, d. in Kanawaha Co., WV)

Lucy Estes (b. in VA, d. in Shelbyville, KY)

Cecilia Estes (b. in VA, d. in MO)

Sarah Ann Estes (b. in VA, d. in MO)

Martha Estes (b. in VA, d. in Bedford Co. VA)

Joel = son of

Generation 8

0.11011111 Benjamin Estes (1753 probably in Spotsylvania County, VA-July 22, 1816) married 1777 **0.11011110 Cecelia Rebecca Thorp (Thorpe)** (1750-1816)

son of

Generation 9

0.110111111 Abraham Estes, Jr. (1697-1759) married **0.110111110 Elizabeth Jeeter**

son of

Generation 10
0.1101111111 Abraham Estes, Sr. (1647-1720), emigrated from Ringwould, Kent, England to St. Stephens, King Queen County, Virginia married **0.1101111110 Barbara Brock**
son of
Generation 11
0.11011111111 Sylvester Estes (1596-1667) married **0.11011111110 Ellen Martin**
son of
Generation 12
0.110111111111 Robert Estes (1555-1616) Ringwold, Kent, England married **0.110111111110 Anne Woodward**
son of
Generation 13
0.1101111111111 Sylvester Estes (1522-1579) born Deal, Kent, England died Ringwould, Kent, England married **0.1101111111110 Jone Estes**
son of
Generation 14
0.11011111111111 Nicholas Estes (1495-1533) married **0.11011111111110 Anny**
son of
Generation 15
0.110111111111111 Robert Estes (1475-1506)
son of
Generation 16
0.1101111111111111 Francesco or Francisco Estes AKA Francesco or Francisco Esteuse, born in Italy and died in England (b. 1440)
son of

Generation 17
0.11011111111111111 Leonello d'Este, Marquess of Ferrara etc.
(1407-1450)
son of
Generation 18
0.1101111111111111111 Niccolo III d'Este, Marquess of Ferrara
(1383-1441)
son of
Generation 19
0.1101111111111111111 Alberto I d'Este, Marquess of Ferrara
(1347-1393)
son of
Generation 20
0.11011111111111111111 Obizzo III d'Este, Marquess of Ferrara
(1294-1352)
son of
Generation 21
0.110111111111111111111 Aldobrandino II, Marquess of Ferrara
(d. 1326)
son of
Generation 22
0.1101111111111111111111 Obizzo II d'Este, Marquess of Ferrara
(1247-1293)
son of
Generation 23
0.11011111111111111111111 Rinaldo I d'Este
son of
Generation 24
0.110111111111111111111111 Azzo VII d'Este
son of

Generation 25
0.110111111111111111111111111 Azzo VI d'Este, Marquess of Este
(1170-1212)
son of
Generation 26
0.110111111111111111111111111 Azzo V d'Este (d. 1190)
son of
Generation 27
0.110111111111111111111111111 Fulco I (d. 1128) [We are also
descended from Welf I, another son of Alberto Azzo II]
son of
Generation 28
0.110111111111111111111111111 Albert Azzo II of Este (c. 997-c.
1097), Margrave of Milan and Liguria, Count of Gavello and Padua,
Rovigo, Unigiana, Monselice, and Montagnana; founder of the
House of Este (named for a town in Padua), around 1073 he made a
castle at Este his residence from which the House of Este takes its
name married around 1035 **0.110111111111111111111111110**
Kunigunde or Chuniza of Altdorf (c. 1020-Aug. 31, 1054), daughter
of **0.110111111111111111111111101** Welf II Count of Altdof.
Albert = son of
Generation 29
**0.110111111111111111111111111 Alberto Azzo I, Margrave of
Milan** (d. 1029)
son of
Generation 30
0.110111111111111111111111111 Oberto II, Margrave of Milan
(d. after 1014) married **0.110111111111111111111111110** Railend
son of

Generation 31
0.1101111111111111111111111111111 Oberto I, Margrave of Milan
(d. 975) (d. Oct. 15, 975), founder of the Obertenghi family, Count of
Milan from 951
son of
Generation 32
0.1101111111111111111111111111111 Adalbert, Margrave of Milan
(KA Obertenghi or Adalbertnii) (b. c. 970, d. before 1018 or in 1029)
Frankish nobility who settled in Lombardy

Daly 4-9 Ireland
Generation 4
0.1110 Lillian Leona Daly (Oct. 6, 1890-April 15, 1973 married
June 19, 1918 **0.1111 Warren Ray Seltzer** (April 20, 1891
Washington, DC-April 13, 1978, Washington, DC) architect. **See
Seltzer**
her siblings =
John Milton (6) Daly died at 94 years old
Mabel May (6) Daly b. 18 January 1888, d. August 1947; married
Wood
Harry Wesley (6) Daly b. 29 September 1883, d. 27 June 1959
William Washington (6) Daly, Jr. (6) b. 7 September 1884, d. 10 July
1938
Edwin Earl (6) Daly b. 1889, d. 1973
Adolph A. (6) Daly b. 29 January 1895, d. 1 March 1973 (Uncle
Adolph)
Margaret Adele (6) Daly b. 20 January 1897, d. 27 May 1995 (98
years); married Miller
Amy A. (6) Daly b. 6 October 1885, d. 14 April 1888
Edna E. (6) Daly b. 17 November 1886, d. 8 July 1888
Lillian = daughter of of

Generation 5

0.11101 William Washington Daly, Sr. married **0.11100 Margaret Matilda Thor (Thour). See Thor**

William = son of

Generation 6

0.111011 John Michael Daly b. 23 May 1830 in Dublin, Ireland, d. 4 February 1904 in Norfolk, VA; married (1) **0.111010 Amanda Baker** of Philadelphia (b. 20 October 1835 in Philadelphia, d. 1884) daughter of **0.1110101 Thomas Baker** married (2) Mary Quinen.

his siblings =

John died young

James b. 21 September 1826 in Dublin

Alice b. 28 October 1828 in Kilbeggan

Jane b. 5 October 1833 in Kilbeggan

Agnes b. 7 June 1835 in Dublin

William died young

Thomas b. 18 September 1839 in Philadelphia married Sept. 19, 1860 Carolline M. Wilson

Mary Jane died young

Margaret died young

William Hudson b. 11 July 1842 in Indiana County

Patrick died young

Mary Ellen b. 29 June 1848 in Wilmington, Delaware

John Michael = son of

Generation 7

0.1110111 Thomas Daly (Feb. 20, 1792-1858) at the Gibsonton distillery near Charleroi, PA married 18 June 1822 in St. Paul's Catholic Church, Arran Quay, Dublin, by Rev. Gormley, **0.1110110 Mary Maher**.

his siblings =

Catharine Daly b. 7 March 1791, died young

Thomas Daly b. 20 February 1792,

Jane Daly b. 24 July 1793,

James Daly b. 3 December 1794, died young

Alice Daly b. 16 December 1797, d. September 1811.

Thomas = son of

Generation 8

0.11101111 John Daly d. 22 May 1806; married **0.11101110 Alice Wheeler** 25 June 1789.

son of

Generation 9

0.111011111 Patrick (1) Daly, b. 13 May 1724, Athlone, Ireland

Griffith 4-6 Wales

Generation 4

0.1100 Mae Griffith (May 27, 1883 Philadelphia, PA-May 27, 1930 Philadelphia, PA) married Nov. 29, 1906, Philadelphia, PA **0.1101 Smith William Estes** (b. June 17, 1881 Brownsville, Haywood, TN, d. after 1947) **See Estes**

siblings, children of Isabella Bogan Griffith =

Elizabeth Rachel Griffith born in Cork, April 27, 1869 (had nervous breakdown in teens, put in insane asylum where she died in the 1950s)

Isabella Agnes Griffith, born in Cork, July 18, 1870, never married, with sister Lillian raised the children of her sister Mae.

Thomas Owen Griffith, born in Philadelphia April 21, 1873, ran away from home

Lillian Griffith, born in Philadlephia, Nov. 9, 1875, never married, with sister Agnes raised the children of sister Mae after her death (Aunt Lil)

Griffith Owen Griffith, born in Philadlephia, Aug. 28, 1877 (hit by pipe, spent rest of life in insane asylum)

David Griffith, born in Philadelphia Jan. 3, 1879 died of heart trouble married Florence Van Hart (daughter of mayor of Camden, New Jersey)

George Bogan Griffith, born in Philadelphia, Jun 1, 1885, died 1904 of typhoid fever

Stanley Griffith, born in Philadelphia, Aug. 6, 1890, measles caused one eye to be closed, died of alcoholism

half-sibling, daughter of Ann Jane Williams Griffith =

Annie Jane (b. Jan. 28, 1867, d. 1950s) (Aunt Annie Jane)

Mae = daughter of

Generation 5

0.11001 Griffith Owen Griffith (b. Sept. 22, 1837 in Pen y Crag, Llengefni, Anglesey, North Wales) married (1) April 3, 1866 at Bangor Cathedral, North Wales, Ann Jane Williams (b. Sept. 23, 1837 at Bearnmaris d. Feb. 18, 1867) married (2) **0.11000 Isabella Bogan** (1848-1914) **See Bogan.** Griffith and Isabella emigrated together to Philadelphia where Griffith became manager of a tea company store.

Griffith = son of

Generation 6

0.110011 Owen Griffith (1795-1888) married **0.110010 Ann Humphreys** (1796-1887) (daughter of **0.1100101 David Humphreys**)

Thor 5-6 Germany

Generation 5

0.11100 Margaret Matilda Thor (Thour) married **0.11101 William Washington Daly, Sr.**

daughter of

Generation 6
0.111001 Adam Thor (Thour) from Coblentz married **0.111000 Amelia Ockert** from Dresden. They met and fell in love on the ship bringing them to America

Bogan 5-6 Ireland
Generation 5
0.11000 Isabella Bogan (1848-1914) married at Wesley Chapel, Patrick St., Cork, Ireland Feb. 18, 1868 **0.11001 Griffith Owen Griffith** (b. 1837) **See Griffith**
siblings =
James Lillian Bogan married Elizabeth H.
William Mullins Bogan married Agnes
Amos Frederick Bogan d. 1905 married Annie Vearian
Isabella = daughter of
Generation 6
0.110001 James Bogan silk manufacturer married **0.110000 Elizabeth A. Lillie** (1805-1870)
Elizabeth = daughter of
Generation 7
0.1100001 John Lillie (1780-1856)

Moore 5-7 Wales, Maryland, North Carolina
Generation 5
0.11010 Eliza "Lily" Yates Moore (1853-1929) married Oct. 30, 1875 **0.11011 Louis (Lewis) Powhatan Estes** (Nov. 22, 1849-Sept. 6, 1902) **See Estes**
daughter of

Generation 6
0.110101 Smith William Moore (Nov. 1, 1818-Feb.2, 1872) married
0.110100 Mary Ordelia Yates (Dec.29, 1820-July10, 1906) **See
Yates**
Generation 7
0.1101011 Shields Moore, immigrated to Maryland from Wales in
1725 married **0.1101010 Blandana Risdon**, They moved to North
Carolina.

Yates 6-9 Virginia

Generation 6
0.110100 Mary Ordelia Yates (b. 1820) married **0.110101 Smith
William Moore** (1815-1888) **See Moore**
daughter of
Generation 7
0.1101001 Warner Minor Yates (April 27, 1795-1861) married (1)
Mary Mason (by family tradition, the niece of George Mason of VA
1725-1792, author of the Declaration of Rights, which was the basis
for the Bill of Rights), married (2) Dec. 30. 1819 **0.1101000 Mildred
J. Menefee** (b. 1803 d. c. 1880)
son of
Generation 8
0.11010011 Charles Lewis Yates (1752-1807) married **0.11010010
Mary Goodloe** (1756-1824)
son of
Generation 9
0.110100111 George Yates IV (1727-1777) married **0.110100110
Frances Fielding Lewis** (1731-1777) **See Lewis**

Hocker 6-8 Pennsylvania

Generation 6

0.111110 Anna Hocker (May 10, 1827-Jan. 10, 1914) married
0.111111 Henry Uhland Seltzer (June 15 June, 1824-Nov. 25, 1897)
See Seltzer
daughter of
Generation 7
0.1111101 Martin Hocker (1768-1862) married (1) Christina
Beinhower (1777-1808) married (2) **0.1111100 Barbara Smith**
(1787-1878)
Martin = son of
Generation 8
0.11111011 John Adam Hocker, arrived in America in 1749 married
0.11111010 Christina

Bates 7-10 Virginia, Kentucky

Generation 7

0.1101110 Sarah Langhorne Bates married Oct. 13, 1801 married
0.1101111 Joel Estes (Jan. 22, 1780-Aug. 16, 1833) **See Estes**
daughter of
Generation 8
0.11011101 Daniel Bates (July 6, 1756-c. 1801) married May 21,
1776 in Chesterfield County, VA **0.11011100 Elizabeth Cary Bell** (
b. about 1758 in Virginia, d. 1825 in Kentucky) daughter of David
Bell and Judith Cary **See Bell**
son of
Generation 9
0.110111011 James Bates (March 7, 1721-Nov. 9, 1786) married
Nov. 11, 1746 in Goochland County, St. James Wortham parish, VA
0.110111010 Winnifred Grymes or Grimes or Hix (b. Jan. 18, 1729
in Goochland)

son of
Generation 10
0.1101110111 John Bates (1685-1723) married about 1709
0.1101110110 Susannah Tarleton Fleming. See Fleming

Bell 8-9 Virginia

Generation 8
0.11011100 Elizabeth Cary Bell (b. about 1758 in Virginia, d. 1825 in Kentucky) married **0.11011101 Daniel Bates** (July 6, 1756-c. 1801) married May 21, 1776 in Chesterfield County, VA **See Bates**
daughter of
Generation 9
0.110111001 David Bell (c. 1716-Nov. 8, 1806) of Belmont on the James River in Buckingham Co. VA married 1744 in Henrico County, VA **0.110111000 Judith Cary** (b. Aug. 12, 1726 in Henrico County, VA-April 16, 1798) David was a captain in the French and Indian War. **See Cary**

Cary 9-16 England

Generation 9
0.110111000 Judith Cary (b. Aug. 12, 1726 in Henrico County, VA-April 16, 1798) married 1744 in Henrico County, VA **0.110111001 David Bell** (c. 1716-Nov. 8, 1806) of Belmont on the James River in Buckingham Co. VA **See Bell**
daughter of
Generation 10
0.1101110001 Henry Cary (1675-1749) married (1) Sarah Sclater (c. 1695-before 1719) married (2) **0.1101110000 Anne Edwards** (d. c. 1740) daughter of **0.1101110000 1 John Edwards of Surrey** married (3) 1741 Elizabeth Brickenhead. Henry was one of the earliest students at William and Mary College. As s a contracting builder, he

constructed the President's house and the chapel of William and Mary College, 1729-1732.

son of

Generation 11

0.11011100011 Henry Cary (c. 1650-1720). As contracting builder, he such public buildings as the court-house of York County, 1694; the fort on the York River, 1697, the first capitol at Williamsburg, 1701-1703; William and Mary College (reconstruction after the fire of 1705); and the Governor's palace, 1705-1710.

son of

Generation 12

0.110111000111 Miles Cary (1622-1667) immigrated to Virginia from Bristol, England in 1640 or 1645. He was killed by the Dutch during their foray upon Hampton Roads in June 1667."

son of

Generation 13

0.1101110001111 John Cary (1583-1661) draper of Bristol married (2) c.1617 **0.1101110001110 Alice Hobson,** daughter of **0.11011100011101 Henry Hobson**, mayor of Bristol

son of

Generation 14

0.11011100011111 William Cary (1550-1633) draper, sheriff of Bristol 1599 and mayor, 1611. We are descended from his first wife, name unknown. After she died of old age, when he was over 80, he married his servant and had a son, when his living sons were nearly 60 years old.

son of

Generation 15

0.110111000111111 Richard Cary (c. 1515-1570) married (1) **0.110111000111110 Anne** (d. before 1561), draper

son of

Generation 16
0.1101110001111111 William Cary (b. 1500 or 1492 d. March 28,
1572), draper, sheriff of Bristol 1532, Mayor, 1546, temp. Henry
VIII.

Stewart 9-32 Scotland, France

Generation 19
0.110111011011011110 Joan Stewart (1428-1493) deaf-mute
married **0.110111011011011111 James Douglas** (1426-1493) First
Earl of Morton **See First Douglas**
daughter of
Generation 20
0.1101110110110111101 King James I of Scotland (Stewart) (1394-
1437), reigned 1406-1437 married 1424 **0.1101110110110111100
Joan Beaufort** (1404-1445) **See Beaufort** [We are also descended
from James I through the Graham line from his sister Lady Mary
Stewart]
son of
Generation 21
0.11011101101101111011 King Robert III of Scotland (1340-1406),
reigned 1390-1406 married 1367 0.**11011101101101111010
Annabella Drummond** (1350-1401) **See Drummond**
[We are also descended from her brother Sir John Drummond, 12th
of Lenox]
son of
Generation 22
0.110111011011011110111 King Robert II of Scotland (1316-1390),
reigned 1371-1390 married **0.110111011011011110110 Elizabeth
Mure** (later legitimized with formal marriage 1349)
Robert = son of

Generation 23

0.110111011011011101111 Walter Stewart, 6th High Steward of Scotland (d. 1326) married **0.11011101101101111101110 Marjorie Bruce** (1296-1316), daughter of **0.110111011011011111011101 King Robert I of Scotland See Bruce**

Walter = son of

Generation 24

0.110111011011011111011111 James Stewart, 5th High Steward of Scotland one of the six Regents of Scotland (1243-1309) married **0.110111011011011111011110 Cecilia**, daughter of **0.110111011011011110111101 Patrick Dunbar**

James = son of

Generation 25

0.1101110110110111110111111 Alexander Stewart, 4th High Steward of Scotland (1214-1283) married **0.1101110110110111110111110 Jean**, daughter of **0.1101110110110111110111110 Angus or James Macrory, Lord of Bute.** Alexander accompanied King Louis of France on the Crusade in 1248.

Alexander = son of

Generation 26

0.110111011011011110111111 Walter Stewart, 3rd High Steward of Scotland (d. 1246) married **0.110111011011011110111110 Bethoc**, daughter of 0.110111011011011110111101 **Gille Crist, Earl of Angus**

Walter = son of

Generation 27

0.1101110110110111101111111 Alan fitz Walter, 2nd High Steward of Scotland married **0.1101110110110111101111110 Alesta**, daughter of **0.1101110110110111101111101 Morggan Earl**

of Mar. Alan accompanied Richard the Lionheart on the Third
Crusade. He was a patron of the Knights Templar.
Alan = son of
Generation 28
**0.110111011011011110111111111 Walter Fitzalan, 1st High
Steward of Scotland**, held that post c. 1150-1177 (d. 1177) Norman
by culture and by blood a Breton married
**0.110111011011011110111111110 Eschyna de Londoniis of Molla
and Huntlaw**
Walter = son of
Generation 29
0.1101110110110111101111111111 Alan fitz Flaad, Breton knight (c.
1078-1121) d. after 1114) married **0.1101110110110111101111111110
Avelina,** daughter of **0.1101110110110111101111111101 Emulf of
Hesdin**, who was killed on crusade at Antioch
Alan = son of
Generation 30
0.11011101101101111011111111111 Flaad
Flaad = son of
Generation 31
Alan = son of
Generation 32
0.110111011011011110111111111111 Alan, a crusader in 1097,
Dapifer to the Archbishop of Dol, near Mont Saint-Michel

Fleming 10-25 Scotland
Generation 10
0.1101110110 Susannah Tarleton Fleming married about 1709
0.1101110111 John Bates (1685-1723). **See Bates**
daughter of

Generation 11

0.11011101101 Charles Fleming (b. 1667) (of New Kent County, VA) married **0.11011101100 Susannah Tarleton** (d. 1687) daughter of **0.110111011001 Stephen Tarleton**

son of

Generation 12

0.110111011011 John Fleming (b. 1627 Cumbarnauld, Lanarkshire, Scotland d. April 27, 1686 in New Kent County, VA

son of

Generation 13

0.1101110110111 Alexander Fleming (b. 1612 Cumbernauld, Lanarkshire, Scotland d. Dec. 30, 1668 Rappahannock Co., VA) married **0.1101110110110 Elizabeth (AKA Elspet) Anderson** (b. 1614, Glasgow, Lanarkshire, Scotland d. Oct. 6, 1656 Rappahannock Co., VA)

Generation 14

0.11011101101111 John Fleming (b. Dec. 9, 1589 Kincardine, Perth, Scotland d. May 7 1650 Cumbernauld, Lanarkshire, Scotland) married **0.1101110110110 Margaret Livingsto**n (b. about 1587 Callendar, Stirlingshire, Scotland d. 1634) **See Livingston**

son of

Generation 15

0.110111011011111 Lord John Fleming (1567-1619) 6th Lord Fleming, first Earl of Wigton in Scotland from 1606 married 0.110111011011110 Lilias Graham. **See Graham**

son of

Generation 16

0.1101110110111111 John Fleming, 5th Lord Fleming (b. 1537 Biggar, Lanarkshire, Scotland d. Sept. 6, 1572 Biggar, Lanarkshire, Scotland) [We are also descended from his sister Margaret] married May 10, 1562 **0.1101110110111110 Elizabeth Ross** (b. 1541

Halkhead, Lanarkshire, Scotland d. April 14, 1578, Scotland), daughter of **0.11011101101111101 Robert Ross** married **0.11011101101111100 Agnes Moncrieff**

John = son of

Generation 17

0.11011101101111111 Malcolm Fleming Third Lord Fleming (c. 1494-Sept. 10, 1547) 3rd Lord Fleming married **0.11011101101111110 Lady Janet Stewart** (1502-1562) illegitimate daughter of **0.11011101101111110 1 King James IV** of Scotland. **See Second Stewart**. Lady Janet Stewart served as governess to her niece, Mary, Queen of Scots, and was briefly a mistress to Henry II of France.

Malcolm = son of

Generation 18

0.110111011011111111 John Fleming, Second Lord Fleming (b. 1465 Biggar and Cumbernauld, Lanarkshire, Scotland d. Nov. 1, 1524) Lord Chamberlain of Scotland in 1524 married **0.110111011011111110 Eupheme Drummond** (b. 1467 Cumbernauld, Lanarkshire, Scotland d. May 1502 Perthshire, Scotland), daughter of **0.1101110110111111101 John Drummond** (1438-1519) married **0.1101110110111111100 Elizabeth Lindsay** (1445-1519)

John Fleming = son of

Generation 19

0.1101110110111111111 Malcolm Fleming, First Lord Fleming (b. 1437 in Biggar, Lanark, Scotland d. 1477) married **0.1101110110111111110 Euphame Livingstone**

son of

Generation 20

0.11011101101111111111 Robert Fleming 1st Lord Fleming (1414-1491) married 1436 in Biggar, Lanarkshire, Scotland

0.11011101101111111110 Janet Douglas (1420-1437) **See Second Douglas**

son of

<u>Generation 21</u>

0.110111011011111111111 Sir Malcolm Fleming of Biggar and Cumbernauld (1383-1440, executed) married before June 28, 1413 **0.11011101101111111110 Elizabeth Stewart** daughter of **0.11011101101111111101 Robert Stewart** 1st Duke of Albany married **0.11011101101111111100 Muriel Keith**

Malcolm = son of

<u>Generation 22</u>

0.110111011011111111111 David Fleming (b. 1343 in Biggar, Lanarkshire, Scotland, d. Feb. 14, 1406 in Edinburgh, Mid-Lothian, Scotland) married **0.11011101101111111110 Isabel Strathechin** (1347-1382)

son of

<u>Generation 23</u>

0.110111011011111111111 Malcolm Fleming (b. 1312 in Biggar, Lanarkshire, Scotland d. Sept. 1, 1382 in Biggar, Lanarkshire, Scotland) married **0.11011101101111111110 Christian Fleming** (b. April 1323 in Biggar, Lanarkshire, Scotland, d. 1400 in Biggar, Lanarkshire, Scotland)

son of

<u>Generation 24</u>

0.110111011011111111111 Patrick Fleming (1286-1306) married **0.11011101101111111110 Joan Fraser** (1290-1312)

son of

<u>Generation 25</u>

0.110111011011111111111 Robert Fleming (b. 1252 in Bratton, Scotland d. 1314 in Biggar, Lanarkshire, Scotland) married

0.11011101101011111111111110 Joan Douglas (b. 1258 in Hermiston, Midlothian, Scotland d. 1307)

Lewis 9-11
0.11010010 **Frances Fielding Lewis** (1731-1777) married
0.110100111 George Yates, IV (1727-1777). **See Yates**
daughter of
Generation 10
0.110100101 Colonel John Lewis, IV married **0.110100100 Frances Fielding** (1702-1731)
His brother Charles Lewis married Mary Howell, and their son Charles Lewis (1721-1782) married Mary Randolph, and their son Charles Lilburn Lewis married Lucy Jefferson, sister of Thomas Jefferson). And another brother of his, Colonel Robert Lewis (1704-1765) married Jane Meriwether (1705-1753, and their son William Lewis (1735-1779) married Lucy Meriwether (1751-1837), and their son Captain Meriwether Lewis was the Lewis of the Lewis and Clark Expedition/
John = son of
Generation 11
0.1101001011 John "Councillor" Lewis II (1669-1725) married
0.1101001010 Elizabeth Warner (1672-1730). **See Warmer**

Neff/Naf 10-17 Switzerland
Generation 10
0.111111110 Anna Catherina Neff (1666) Michelfeld, Ostalbkreis, Baden-Wuerttemberg, Germany-1759 Michelfeld, Heidelberg, Baden-Wuerttemberg, Germany) married 1683 Michelfeld, Ostalbkris, Baden-Wuerttemberg, Germany **0.111111110 Wyerich Seltzer** (1661 Michelfeld, Amberg-Sulzbach, Bayern, Gemany-1742 Michelfeld, Amberg-Sulzbach, Bayern, Germany) **See Seltzer**

daughter of

Generation 11

0.1111111101 Rudolf Neff (1622 Hausen am Albis, Canton of Zurich, Switzerland-1677 Michelfeld, Heidelberg, Baden-Wuerttemberg, Germany) married 1648 Affoltern, Canton of Zurich, Switzerland, **0.1111111100 Regina Zimmerman** (1629-1679) **See Zimmerman**

Rudolf = son of

Generation 12

0.11111111011 Felix Naf (1587 Hausen, Bern, Switzerland-1649 Affoltern, Am Albis, Zurich, Switzerland) married 1607 Heish, Se, Canton of Zurich, Switzerland **0.11111111010 Anna Ringger** (1591-1628) **See Ringger**

son of

Generation 13

0.111111110111 Ulrich Naf (1550 Heisch, Hasen am Albis, Canton of Zurich, Switzerland-1591 Hausen, Canton of Zurich, Switzerland) married Hausen, Se, Zurich, Switzerland **0.111111110110 Verena Huber**

son of

Generation 14

0.1111111101111 Max Naf (1500 Vollenweid, Canton of Zurich, Switzerland-1571 Heisch, Hausen Am Albis, Canton of Zurich, Switzerland)

son of

Generation 15

0.11111111011111 Hans Naf (1467-1531) married **0.11111111011110 Katherina Huber** (1470-1504)

Hans = son of

Generation 16
0.111111110111111 Hans Naf (1430 Hausen, Canton of Zurich, Switzerland-1500 Rengg, Switzerland) married 1467
son of
Generation 17
0.1111111101111111 Heinrich Neff (1388 Rengg Langnau, Canton of Zurich, Switzerland-1448 Rengg, Switzerland) md 1429 Switzerland, **0.1111111101111110 Verena** (1388-1455)
son of
Generation 18
0.11111111011111111 Hans Neff (1366 Langnau, Zurich, Switzerland-1406 Rengg, Switzerland)

Zimmerman 11-12 Switzerland

Generation 11
0.1111111100 Regina Zimmerman (b. Dec. 13, 1629 Affolturn, Zurich Canton, Switzerland d. Sept. 3, 1679 Duhren, Switzerland) married 1648 Affoltern, Canton of Zurich, Switzerland, **0.1111111101 Rudolf Neff** (1622 Hausen am Albis, Canton of Zurich, Switzerland-1677 Michelfeld, Heidelberg, Baden-Wuerttemberg, Germany) **See Neff**
Regina = daughter of
Generation 12
0.11111111001 Caspar Zimmerman (b. July 9, 1594 Albis, Zurich Canton, Switzerland d. Dec. 2, 1681 Affolturn, Zurich Canton, Switzerland) married Nov. 20, 1627 **0.11111111000 Anna Lussi** (b. Nov. 30, 1608 Affolturn, Zurich Canton Switzerland d. April 9, 1644, Affoltern, Am Albis, Zurich Canton, Switzerland) **See Lusi**

Warner 11-13 Virginia

<u>Generation 11</u>

0.1101001010 Elizabeth Warner (1672-1730) married **John "Councillor" Lewis II** (1669-1725)

her sister =

Mildred Warner (1671-1701) married Major Lawrence Washington (1659-1698), their son = Captain Augustine Washington (1694-1743) married Mary Ball (1708-1789), their son = President George Washington (1732-1799) married Martha Dandridge Custis (1731-1802) **See Fleming**

Elizabeth = daughter of

<u>Generation 12</u>

0.11010010101 Colonel Augustine Warner II (1642-1681) married **0.11010010100 Mildred Reade** (1642-1695)

his sister =

Sarah Warner married Lawrence Townley, their daughter Alice Townley married John Grymes, their son = Charles Grymes (1696-1753) married Frances Jennings (1694-1743), their daughter = Lucy Grymes married Henry Lee of Leesville, VA, their son Henry Lee ("Light Horse Harry") (1756-1818) married Anne Hill Carter, their son = General Robert E. Lee (1807-1870)

Augustine = son of

<u>Generation 13</u>

0.110100101011 Colonel Augustine Warner (1611-1674) married **0.110100101010 Mary Townley** (1614-1662)

Lusi 12-13 Switzerland

<u>Generation 12</u>

0.11111111000 Anna Lussi (b. Nov. 30, 1608 Affolturn, Zurich Canton Switzerland d. April 9, 1644, Affoltern, Am Albis, Zurich Canton, Switzerland) married Nov. 20, 1627 **0.11111111001 Caspar**

Zimmerman (b. July 9, 1594 Albis, Zurich Canton, Switzerland d. Dec. 2, 1681 Affolturn, Zurich Canton, Switzerland) **See Zimmerman**
Anna = daughter of
<u>Generation 13</u>
0.1111111110001 Heini Lusi (b.1580, Affoltern, Zurich Canton, Switzerland) married Sept. 28, 1606 Affoltern, Zurich Canton, Switzerland, **0.111111110000 Barbeli Vollenweider** (b. 1581, Affoltern, Zurich Canton, Switzerland), daughter of **0.1111111100001 Heini Vollenwider** (b. 1565, Affoltern, Zurich, Switzerland) married 1597 Affolturn, Zurich Canton, Switzerland, **0.1111111100000** Anna Schurpin (b. 1565)

Tarleton 11-13
<u>Generation 11</u>
0.11011101100 Susannah Tarleton (1663-after 1717) married
0.11011101101 Colonel Charles Fleming (1659-1717) (of New Kent County, VA) **See Fleming**
Susannah = daughter of
<u>Generation 12</u>
0.110111011001 Stephen Tarleton (1637-1688) married
0.110111011000 Susanna Bates (1635-1717) daughter of
0.1101110110001 John Bates (May 23,1598-before Jan. 24, 1667) b. Canterbury, Kent, England, d. Virginia and **0.1101110110000 Elizabeth Winston** (Aug. 12, 1605-March 30, 1701) b. Yorkshire, England, d. Middletown, Bruton Parish, York, VA
Stephen = son of
<u>Generation 13</u>
0.110111011001 John Tarleton (1610-1677) married **0.110111011009 Ursula**

Ringger 12-21 Switzerland

<u>Generation 12</u>

0.1111111100 Anna Ringger (1591 Affoltern, am Albis, Canton of Zurich, Switzerland-1628 Affoltern, am Albis, Canton of Zurich, Switzerland) married 1607 Heish, Se, Canton of Zurich, Switzerland, **0.1111111101 Felix Naf** (1587 Hausen, Bern, Switzerland-1649 Affoltern, Am Albis, Canton of Zurich, Switzerland) **See Neff/Naf**
Anna = daughter of

<u>Generation 13</u>

0.11111111001 Oswald Ringger (1565 Hausen Se, Canton of Zurich, Switzerland-1630 Hausen, Canton of Zurich, Switzerland) married **0.11111111000 Anna Blickenstorfer** (b. 1573 Stalikon, Canton of Zurich, Switzerland)
son of

<u>Generation 14</u>

0.111111110011 Rudolf Ringger (1520 Maschwanden, Canton of Zurich, Switzerland-1587 Hausen Am Albis Canton of Zurich, Switzerland) married 1542 Canton Zurich, Switzerland
0.111111110010 Barbara Egli
son of

<u>Generation 15</u>

0.1111111100111 Jorg Ringger (b. 1480 Maschwanden, Canton of Zurich, Switzerland)
son of

<u>Generation 16</u>

0.11111111001111 Werner Ringger (1456 Schwamendingen, Canton of Zurich, Switzerland-1480 Hoff, Canton of Zurich, Switzerland)
son of

Generation 17

0.111111110011111 Hans Ringger (1412 Schwamendingen, Canton of Zurich, Switzerland-1487 Maschwanden, Canton of Zurich) **married 0.111111110011110 Kathrinen** (b. 1426 Switzerland)

son of

Generation 18

0.1111111100111111 Heini Ringger (1385 Osd, Canton of Zurich, Switzerland-1453)

Heini = son of

Generation 19

0.11111111001111111 Rudolf Ringger (1350 Canton of Zurich, Switzerland-1385)

son of

Generation 20

0.111111110011111111 Uli Ringger (1333 Canton of Zurich, Switzerland-1370)

son of

Generation 21

0.1111111100111111111 ? Ringer (b. 1288) married ? (b. 1292)

Livingston 14-17 Scotland

Generation 14

0.1101110110110 Margaret Livingston (b. about 1587 Callendar, Stirlingshire, Scotland d. 1634) married **0.1101110110111 John Fleming** (b. Dec. 9, 1589 Kincardine, Perth, Scotland d. May 7 1650 Cumbernauld, Lanarkshire, Scotland) **See Fleming**

daughter of

Generation 15

0.11011101101101 Alexander Livingston (1561-1621) married **0.11011101101100 Eleanor Hay** (1565-1630)

son of

Generation 16

0.110011011011011 William Livingston (1528-1502), 6th Lord Livingston of Callandar married **0.1101110110110110 Agnes Fleming** (1535-1597)

son of

Generation 17

0.1101110110110111 Alexander Livingston (1500-1551), 5th Lord Livingston of Callandar married **0.1101110110110110 Agnes Douglas. See First Douglas** Guardian of Mary, Queen of Scots, during her childhood and his sister Mary Livingston was one of the four attendants of Mary, Queen of Scots.

Graham 15-24 Scotland

Generation 15

0.110011011011110 Lilias Graham (b. 1568 Montrose, Lanarkshire, Scotland d. 1605 Perth, Perthshire, Scotland) married Jan. 13, 1585 in Montrose, Angus, Scotland **0.110111011011111 Lord John Fleming** (1567-1619) 6th Lord Fleming, first Earl of Wigton in Scotland. **See Fleming**

daughter of

Generation 16

0.1101110110111101 John Graham, third Earl of Montrose (1547, Montrose, Lanarkshire, Scotland-Nov. 9, 1608, Forfar, Angus, Scotland), Chancellor of the University of St. Andrews 1599-1604 married **0.1101110110111100 Jean Drummond** (1548, Machany, Perth, Scotland-1595, Scotland)

son of

Generation 17

0.11011101101111011 Robert Graham, Master of Montrose (1515-Sept. 10 1547, Musselburgh, Midlothian, Scotland) married **0.11011101101111010 Margaret Fleming** (1528, Boghall castle,

Biggar, Lanarkshire, Scotland-Jan. 1587 Auchterarder, Perthshire, Scotland) [we are descended from her brother John as well]. **See Fleming**

son of

Generation 18

0.110111011011110111 William Graham, second Earl of Montrose (1492-1571) married Dec. 1515 **0.110111011011110110 Lady Janet Keith Graham (**1495 Kincardinshire, Scotland-Aug. 27, 1547, Scotland) **See Keith**

son of

Generation 19

0.1101110110111101111 William Graham, (1447 Perth, Perthshire, Scotland-Sept. 9 1513 Flodden Field, Branxton, Northumberland, England) first Earl of Montrose married Nov. 25, 1479 **0.1101110110111101110 Annabella Drummond Graham,** (1463 Innerpeffray, Crief, Perthshire, Scotland-March 17, 1505 Stobhall, Cargill, Perthshire, Scotland) daughter of **0.11011101101111011101 John Drummond, 1st Lord Drummond** married **0.11011101101111011100 Lady Elizabeth Lindsay. See Drummond** [We're also descended from her brother William Drummond, Master of Drummond]

William = son of

Generation 20

0.11011101101111011111 William Graham, 2nd Lord Graham (1433 Dunning, Perthshire, Scotland-1472 Perth, Perthshire, Scotland) married before 1460 **0.11011101101111011110 Helen or Elene Douglas** (1425 Mar, Aberdeenshire, Scotland-1476 Graham, Scotland) daugther of **0.110111011011110111101 William Douglas** (Feb. 24, 1398 Mar, Aberdeenshire, Scotland-Oct. 1437 Mar, Aberdeenshire, Scotland) 2nd Earl of Angus married

0.11011101101111011110 0 Margaret Hay (1404, Locharret, Scotland-April 22, 1484 Mar, Aberdeenshire, Scotland) William Graham = son of

Generation 21

0.110111011011110111111 Patrick Graham, 1st Lord Graham and Archibishop of St. Andrews (1417, Angusshire, Kincardineshire, Scotland-June 24, 1466) married **0.11011101101111011110 Christian Erskine** (1497, Glenesk, Angusshire, Scotland-1479, Mugdock Castle, Stirlingshire, Scotland), daughter of **0.1101110110111101111101 Sir Robert Erskine,** (1370 Sinton, Selkirksshire, Scotland-Nov. 6, 1452 Sinton, Selkirkshire, Scotland) 1st Lord Erskine and **0.1101110110111101111100 Christian Stewart** Patrick = son of

Generation 22

0.1101110110111101111111 Alexander Graham (1396 Angusshire, Kincardineshire, Scotland-1420, Scotland) married **0.1101110110111101111110 Lady Mary Stewart,** daughter of **0.110111011011110111101 King Robert III of Scotland** married **0.110111011011110111100 Annabella Drummond** (1350-1401 [We are also descended from Annabel's brother King James I of Scotland who married Joan Beaufort]. **See Stewart** Alexander = son of

Generation 23

0.110111011011110111111111 Sir William Graham (1376 Angusshire Kincardineshire, Scotland-1424 Kincardine, Perthshire, Scotland) md (1) .**0.110111011011110111111110 Gille Stewart** (1358, Scotland-1388, Scotland) daughter of .**0.1101110110111101111111101 Sir John Stewart,** son of **0.110111011011110111111111011 Walter Stewart, 6th High Steward of Scotland** married (2) Isabella Graham, daughter of Sir John Graham (b. before 1285) William = son of

Generation 24
0.110111011011110111111111 Patrick Graham (1350 Kincardine, Aberdeenshire, Scotland-Aug. 10, 1413 Dunduff, Kincardineshire, Scotland)

Second Drummond 16-31 Scotland

Generation 16
0.1101110110111100 Joan Drummond married**0.1101110110111101 John Graham, third Earl of Montrose** (1548- Nov. 9, 1608), Chancellor of the University of St. Andrews 1599-1604 **See Graham 15**
Joan = daughter of
Generation 17
0.11011101101111001 David Drummond, Second Lord Drummond in 1519 married before Dec. 7, 1543 **0.11011101101111000 Lilias Ruthven**
David = son of
Generation 18
0.110111011011110011 Walter Drummond, Master of Drummond (d. 1518) married Feb. 1513/1514 **0.110111011011110010 Lady Elizabeth Graham**, daughter of **0.1101110110111100101 William Graham, 1st Earl of Montrose** married **0.1101110110111100100 Janet Edmonstone** (b. before 1483), daughter of **0.11011101101111001001 Sir Archibald Edmonstone**
Walter = son of
Generation 19
0.1101110110111100111 William Drummond, Master of Drummond (d. 1490) [We're also descended from his sister Annabella Drummond, who married William Graham] married **0.1101110110111100110 Isabel Campbell,** daughter of **0.11011101101111001101 Colin Campbell, Earl of Argyle**

William = son of
Generation 20
0.11011101101111001111 John Drummond, 1st Lord Drummond
(1440 Stobhall, Perthshire, Scotland-Dec. 18, 1519 Drummond
Castle, Strathearn, Scotland) 1438, d. about 1519) married 1462
0.11011101101111001110 Lady Elizabeth Lindsay, (1445 Crawford,
Lanarkshire, Scotland-Nov. 22, 1509 Stobhall, Cargill, Perth,
Scotland) daughter of **0.110111011011110011101 Sir Alexander
Lindsay,** (b. Glenesk, Angusshire, Scotland-Sept. 13, 1453 Finhaven
Castle, Angusshire, Scotland) 4th Earl of Crawford married
0.110111011011110011100 Margaret Dunbar (1425 Cockburn,
Benwickshire, Scotland-Jan. 1499 Cockburn, Berwickshire,
Scotland)
John = son of
<u>Generation 21</u>
0.110111011011110011111 Sir Malcolm Drummond (d. 1470)
married **1445 0.110111011011110011110 Mariot Murray**
son of
<u>Generation 22</u>
0.1101110110111100111111 Sir Walter Drummond married
0.1101110110111100111110 Margaret Ruthven, daughter of
0.11011101101111001111101 Sir William Ruthven, who lived at
Ruthven, Scotland.
Walter = son of
<u>Generation 23</u>
0.11011101101111001111111 Sir John Dummond
son of
<u>Generation 24</u>
0.110111011011110011111111 Sir John Drummond, 12th of Lenox
(1356-1428) married **0.110111011011110011111110 Elizabeth
Sinclair** (b. 1363) daughter of **0.1101110110111100111111101 Henry**

Sinclar, 1st Earl of Orkney married **0.1101110110111001111111010 Jane Holyburton** [We're also descended from Sir John's sister Annabella Drummond who married King Rober III of Scotland]
John = son of
<u>Generation 25</u>
0.110111011011110011111111 Sir John Drummond 11th of Lennox (1318-1373) married **0.110111011011110011111111 Mary Montifex** (b. 1325)
son of
<u>Generation 26</u>
0.1101110110111001111111111 Sir Malcolm Drummond, 10th Thane of Lennox (b. after 1295, d. 1346) married
0.1101110110111001111111110 Margaret de Graham
Malcolm = son of
<u>Generation 27</u>
0.11011101101111001111111111 Sir Malcolm Drummond, 9th Thane of Lennox (b. after 1270 d. 1325) married
0.11011101101111001111111110 Margaret Graham, daughter of
0.11011101101111001111111101 Sir Patrick Graham of Kincardine
Malcolm = son of
<u>Generation 28</u>
0.110111011011110011111111111 Sir John Drummond, 8th Thane of Lennox married **0.110111011011110011111111110 Elena Stewart**, daughter of **0.110111011011110011111111101 Walter Stewart, Earl of Menteith** married
0.110111011011110011111111100 Mary of Monteith, Countess of Menteith
John = son of

Generation 29

0.11011101101111001111111111111 Sir Malcolm Drummond, 7th
Thane of Lennox (b. after 1209 d. 1278)

Generation 30

0.1101110110111100111111111111111 Malcolm Beg Drummond, 6th
Thane of Lennox (b. after 1169 d. 1259) married
0.1101110110111100111111111111110 Ada of Lennox
Malcolm = son of

Generation 31

0.11011101101111001111111111111111 Sir Malcolm Drummond, 5th
Thane of Lennox_(b. before 1153 d. 1200)

Second Stewart 17-32 Scotland

Generation 17

0.11011101101111110 Lady Janet Stewart (1502-1562) married
0.11011101101111111 Malcolm Fleming, 3rd Lord Fleming (c.
1494-Sept. 10, 1547) **See Fleming**
Janet served as governess to her half-niece Mary, Queen of Scots.
Janet was briefly a mistress of King Henry II of France, by whom she
had a legitimated son: Henri d'Angoulême. Her daughter, Mary
Fleming, was one of the young queen's *Four Marys*.
Janet = daughter of

Generation 18

0.110111011011111101 King James IV of Scotland (1473-1513)
reigned 1488-1513 mated with **0.110111011011111100 Lady Isabel
Stewart,** daughter of **0.1101110110111111001 James Stewart, 1st
Earl of Buchan**
James = son of

Generation 19

0.1101110110111111011 King James III of Scotland_ (c. 1451/1452-
1488) reigned 1460-1488 married 1469 **0.1101110110111111010**

Margaret of Denmark (1456-1486), daughter of
0.11011101101111110101 King Christian I of Denmark, Norway and Sweden. See Oldenburg
James = son of
<u>Generation 20</u>
0.11011101101111110111 King James II of Scotland (1430-1460)
reigned 1437-1460 married **0.11011101101111110110 Mary of Guelders** [We are also descended from his sister Annabela Stewart]
James = son of
<u>Generation 21</u>
0.11011101101111101111 King James I of Scotland (1394-1437)
reigned 1424-1437 married **0.11011101101111110110 Joan Beaufort** (1404-1445) **See Beaufort**
son of
<u>Generation 22</u>
0.11011101101111101111 King Robert III of Scotland (1340-1406), reigned 1390-1406 married 1367 **0.11011101101111101110 Annabella Drummond** (1350-1401) **See First Drummond**
son of
<u>Generation 23</u>
0.11011101101111110111111 King Robert II of Scotland (1316-1390), reigned 1371-1390 married **0.11011101101111110111110 Elizabeth Mure**
son of
<u>Generation 24</u>
0.11011101101111101111111 Walter Stewart, 6th High Steward of Scotland (d. 1326) married **0.11011101101111101111110 Marjorie Bruce** (1296-1316), daughter of King Robert I of Scotland See **Bruce or Brus**
son of

Generation 25

0.1101110110101111011111111 James Stewart 5th High Steward of Scotland one of the six Regents of Scotland (1243-1309) married **0.1101110110101111011111110 Cecilia Dunbar** (1278, Dunbar Castle, East Lothian, Scotland-Oct. 26, 1327 Cullen Banffshire, Scotland) daughter of **0.110111011011111110111111101 Patrick Dunbar**

James = son of

Generation 26

0.110111011011111110111111111 Alexander Stewart, 4th High Steward of Scotland (1214-1283) married **0.110111011011111110111111110 Jean**, daughter of **0.110111011011111110111111101 Angus or James Macrory, Lord of Bute**. Alexander accompanied King Louis of France on the Crusade in 1248.

Alexander = son of

Generation 27

0.11011101101111110111111111 Walter Stewart, 3rd High Steward of Scotland (d. 1246) married **0.11011101101111110111111110 Bethoc**, daughter of_**0.11011101101111110111111101 Gille Crist, Earl of Angus.** Walter was the first to use the Stewart name.

Walter = son of

Generation 28

0.11011101101111110111111111111 Alan fitz Walter (1150, Paisley, Renfrewshire, Scotland-1204, Dundonald, Kyle, Aurshire, Scotland) 2nd High Steward of Scotland a married **0.11011101101111110111111110 Alesta Stewart** (1150 Carrick, Ayrshire, Scotland-Sept. 22, 1182, Paisley, Renfrewshire, Scotland) daughter of **0.110111011011111110111111101 Morggan Earl of Mar** (1115, Dunfermline, fife, Scotalnd-March 30, 1182, Mar,

Aberdeenshire, Scotland. Alan accompanied Richard the Lionheart on the Third Crusade.

Alan = son of

<u>Generation 29</u>

0.1101110110011111101111111111111 Walter Fitzalan, 1st High Steward of Scotland held that post c. 1150-1177 (d. 1177) Norman by culture and by blood a Breton married

0.1101110110011111101111111111110 Eschyna de Londoniis of Molla and Huntlaw (1106, Roxburghshire, Scotland-1209, Paisley Abbbey, Renfrewshire, Scotland)

son of

<u>Generation 30</u>

0.110111011011111101111111111111 Alan fitz Flaad, Breton knight and lord of Oswestry (d. after 1114) married

0.110111011011111101111111111110 Avelina, daughter of

0.110111011011111101111111111101 Emulf of Hesdin, who was killed on **crusade** at Antioch

Alan = son of

<u>Generation 31</u>

0.11011101101111110111111111111 Flaad

Flaad = son of

<u>Generation 32</u>

0.11011101101111110111111111111 Alain, a crusader in 1097, Dpaifer to the Archbishop of Dol, near Mont Saint-Michel

First Douglas 17-24 Scotland

<u>Generation 17</u>

0.1101110110110110 Agnes Douglas married **0.1101110110110111 Alexander Livingston** (1500-1551), 5th Lord Livingston of Callandar. **See Livingston**

daughter of

Generation 18

0.11011101101101111 John Douglas, 2nd Earl of Morton (1459-1512) married **0.11011101101101110 Janet Crichton** (1461-1493) son of

Generation 19

0.110111011011011111 James Douglas (1426-1493) married **0.110111011011011110 <u>Joan Stewart</u>** (1428-1493) **See Stewart** son of

Generation 20

0.1101110110110111111 James Douglas (1407-1458) married **0.1101110110110111110 Elizabeth Gifford** (1409-1456) son of

Generation 21

0.11011101101101111111 James Douglas (1383-1441) married **0.11011101101101111110 Elizabeth Stewart** (1387-1411) daughter of **0.11011101101101111101 Robert III King of Scotland** (1337-1406)_ married **0.11011101101101111100 Annabella Drummond** (1350-1401)

James = son of

Generation 22

0.110111011011011111111 James Douglas (1350-1420) married **0.110111011011011111110 Agnes Dunbar** (1350-1378) 4th Countess of Moray (AKA Black Agnes of Dunar)

John = son of

Generation 23

0.1101110110110111111111 John Douglas (1320-1350) married **0.1101110110110111111110 Agnes Munfode** (1320-1377)

John = son of

Generation 24

0.11011101101101111111111 James Douglas (1300-1323) married **0.11011101101101111111110 Joan of Scotland** (1278-1337)

Oldenburg 19-31 Denmark, Germany

Generation 19

0.1101110110111111010 Margaret of Denmark (1456-1486) married 1469 **0.1101110110111111011 King James III Stewart of Scotland** (c. 1451/1452-1488). **See Stewart**

daughter of

Generation 20

0.110111011011111110101 King Christian I (1426-1481) King of Denmark 1448-1481, Norway 1450-1481 and Sweden 1457-1464, also Count of Oldenburg and Delmenhorst married

0.110111011011111110100 Dorothea of Brandenburg (1430/1431- 1495), AKA Dorothea of Hohenzollern and Dorothy Achilles. **See Hohenzollern**

son of

Generation 21

0.1101110110111111101011 Count Dietrich of Oldenburg (1398- 1440) AKA Derrick of Oldenburg and Theoderic of Oldenburg and Theoderic the Lucky, Count of Delmenhorst and Oldenburg married **0.1101110110111111101010 Hedwig of Schauenburg** (1398-1436) AKA Helvig of Schauenburg. **See Schauenburg**

son of

Generation 22

0.1101110110111111010111 Count Christian V of Oldenburg, became count 1398 (b. before 1347 d. 1423) married **0.1101110110111111010110 Agnes of Holstein. See Holstein-Ploen**

son of

Generation 23

0.1101110110111111010111 Count Conrad I of Oldenberg (d. appox. 1368) married **0.1101110110111111010110 Ingeborg von Braunschweig**

son of

Generation 24

0.1101110110111110101111 Count John II of Oldenburg married
0.1101110110111110101110 Hedwig of Diepholz

John = son of

Generation 25

0.11011101101111101011111 Count Christian III of Oldenburg
married **0.11011101101111101011110 Hedwig of Oldenburg**

son of

Generation 26

0.110111011011111010111111 Count John I of Oldenburg (1204-
1270) married **0.110111011011111010111110 Richeza of Hoya-
Stumpenhausen**

son of

Generation 27

0.1101110110111110101111111 Count Christian II of Oldenburg
(d. 1233) married **0.1101110110111110101111110 Agnes of Altena-
Isenburg**

son of

Generation 28

0.11011101101111101011111111 Count Maurice of Oldenburg
(1145-1211) married **0.11011101101111101011111110 Salome
Wickerode**

son of

Generation 29

0.110111011011111010111111111 Count Christian I of Oldenburg
(d. 1167) married **0.110111011011111010111111110 Kunigunde**

Christian = son of

Generation 30

0.1101110110111110101111111111 Count Elimar II of Oldenburg
ruled 1108-1142 married **0.1101110110111110101111111110 Eilika**

von Werl-Rietberg, daughter of
0.110111011011111101011111111101 Count Heinrich von Rietberg
Elimar = son of
Generation 31
0.110111011011111101011111111111 Count Elimar I of Oldenburg
(1040-1112) married 1102, **0.110111011011111101011111111110**
Richenza daughter of **Henry, Count of Rietberg** daughter of
0.110111011011111101011111111100 Dedi or Adalger

Keith 20-21 Scotland

Generation 20
0.110111011011110110 Lady Janet Keith (1495, Kincardineshire,
Scotland-Aug. 27, 1547, Scotland) married Dec. 1515
0.110111011011110111 William Graham, second Earl of Montrose
(1492-1571) **See Graham**
daughter of
Generation 21
0.110111011011110111 11101 William Keith, Marischal of Scotland (d.
1463) married **0.110111011011110111 0111 00 Lady Elizabeth or Eliza**
Gordon See Gordon

Beaufort 20-34 England, France

Generation 20
0.110111011011011 0111 100 Joan Beaufort_(1404-1445) married 1424
0.110111011011011 0111 101 King James I of Scotland (Stewart)
(1394-1437), reigned 1406-1437 **See Stewart**
daughter of
Generation 21
0.110111011011011 0111 1001 John Beaufort, first Earl of Someset
(1371-1410) married **0.110111011011011 0111 1000 Margaret Holland**
(1385-1439) daughter of **0.110111011011011 0111 0001 Thomas**

Holland, 2nd Earl of Kent, who was the son of
0.110111011011011110011110 Joan "the Fair Maid of Kent,"
granddaughter of Edward I of England, wife of Edward the Black
Prince and mother of Richard II of England **See Holland**
John = son of

<u>Generation 22</u>

**0.110111011011011110011 John of Gaunt (Plantagenet), First
Duke of Lancaster** (1340-1399) married **0.110111011011011110010
Katherine Swynford** (1350-1403) daughter of
0.1101110110110111100101 Payne de Roet a Flemish herald from
Hainault. Richard II was John of Gaunt's nephew. King Henry IV
was his son.
John = son of

<u>Generation 23</u>

0.1101110110110111100111 King Edward III of England (Nov. 13,
1312-June 21, 1377) reigned 1327-1377
married **0.1101110110110111100110 Philippa of Hainault** (1314-
1369) **See Hainault**
son of

<u>Generation 24</u>

0.11011101101101111001111 King Edward II of England (April 25,
1284- Sept. 21, 1327?) reigned 1307-1327 married
**0.11011101101101111001110 Isabella of France AKA She-Wolf of
France** (c. 1295- Aug. 22, 1358), daughter of
0.110111011011011110011101 King Philip IV of France (1268-
1314) and **0.110111011011011110011100 Joan I of Navarre** (d.
1305) **See Second Capet, Navarre**
Edward = son of

<u>Generation 25</u>

0.110111011011011110011111 Edward I, King of England
(Plantagenet) (1239-1307) reigned (1272-1304) married

0.1101111011011011110011110 Eleanor of Castile (1241-1290) daughter of **0.11011101101101111100111101 Fernando III, King of Castile and Leon** and his second wife, **0.11011101101101111100111100 Jeanne, Countess of Ponthieu See Castile**

[We are also descended from Edward by way of his first wife, Isabella of Angouleme, Plantagenet family]

Edward = son of

<u>Generation 26</u>

0.11011101101101111100111111 Henry III, King of England (Plantagenet) (1207-1272) reigned 1216-1272) married **0.11011101101101111100111110 Eleanor of Provence** (c. 1223-1291) daughter of **0.110111011011011110011111101 Ramon Berenguer V count of Provence and Beatrice of Savoy. See Provence**

Henry = son of

<u>Generation 27</u>

0.110111011011011111001111111 John I, "Lackland," King of England (Plantagenet) Magna Carta (1166-1216) reigned 1199-1216) married **0.110111011011011111001111110 Isabella of Angoulême** (1187-1246) daughter of **0.1101110110110111100111111101 Aymer Taillefer, Count of Angouleme**

John = son of

<u>Generation 28</u>

0.1101110110110111100111111111 Henry II, King of England (Plantagenet) (1133-1189) reigned 1154-1189) married **0.1101110110110111100111111110 Eleanor of Aquitaine** (1122-1204) daughter of **0.11011101101101111001111111110 1 William X, Duke of Aquitaine**, and **0.110111011011011110011111110 Aenor de Châtellerault. See Aquitaine, Normandy, First Saxony, Champagne** [We are also descended from Eleanor's marriage to the King of France]

Henry = son of

Generation 29

0.110111011011011110011111111111 Geoffrey V Count of Anjou and Maine from 1129 by inheritance, from from 1144 also Duke of Normandy by conquest (Plantagenet) AKA "the Handsome" (Aug. 24, 1113-Sept. 7, 1151) married **0.110111011011011110011111111110 Empress Matilda** (1102-1110), briefly the first female ruler of England in 1141 (widow of Henry V Holy Roman Emperor)

Geoffrey = son of

Generation 30

0.11011101101101111001111111111 Fulk V of Anjou AKA Fulk the Younger, (1089/1092-Nov. 13, 1143) Count of Anjou 1109-1129 and King of Jerusalem 1131-1143 went on Crusade in 1120 and became a close friend of the Knights Templar married **0.11011101101101111001111111110 Eremburga of La Fleche**, daughter of **0.11011101101101111001111111101 Elias I of Maine** and **0.11011101101101111001111111100 Matilda**, daughter of **0.1101110110110111100111111111001 Gervais, Lord of Chateau-du-Loir**

Fulk = son of

Generation 31

0.1101110110110111100111111111111 Fulk IV AKA le Réchin (1043-1109) Count of Anjou 1068-1109 married **0.1101110110110111100111111111110 Bertrade de Monfort** (c. 1070-Feb. 14, 1117), who later deserted her husband and bigamously married King Philip I, she was the daughter of **0.1101110110110111100111111111101 Simon I de Monfort** (c. 1025-Sept. 25, 1087) married (2) **0.1101110110110111100111111111100 Agnes d'Evreux** (b. 1030) **See Rouen**

Fulk = son of

Generation 32

0.11011101101101111100111111111111 Geoffrey Count of Gatinais AKA Aubri (d. 1043 or 1046) married

0.11011101101101111100111111111110 Ermengarde of Anjou (c. 1018- March 18, 1076_, daughter of

0.11011101101101111100111111111101 Fulk the Black, Count of Anjou married **0.11011101101101111001111111111100 Hildegarde of Sundau**

Geoffrey = son of

Generation 33

0.11011101101101111001111111111111 Hugues du Perch Count of Gatiais married **0.11011101101101111001111111111110 Beatrice de Macon,** daughter of **0.11011101101101111001111111111101 Aubry II de Macon**

son of

Generation 34

0.11011101101101111001111111111111 Fulcois Count of Perche (10th century) married **0.11011101101101111001111111111110 Melisende**

Second Douglas 20-28 Scotland

Generation 20

0.11011101101111111110 Janet Douglas (1420-1437) married 1436 in Biggar, Lanarkshire, Scotland, **0.11011101101111111111 Robert Fleming** 1st Lord Fleming (1416-1491) **See Fleming**

daughter of

Generation 21

0.110111011011111111101 Sir James Douglas, 7th Earl of Douglas (1394-1494) married **0.110111011011111111100 Beatrice Sinclair** (1398-1462)

son of

Generation 22

0.110111011011111111011 Sir George Douglas (1376-1402)
married **0.110111011011111111010 Stewart Douglas Kennedy**
(1380-1465)

son of

Generation 23

0.110111011011111111110111 William de Douglas (1313-1384)
married **0.110111011011111111110110 Margaret Sewart** (1325-1418)
son of

Generation 24

0.110111011011111111101111 Archibald Douglas (b. 1297 in
Douglas, Lanarkshire, Scotland d. July 19, 1333 Haliden Hill,
Nurthumberland, England) married **0.110111011011111111101110
Beatrice De Lindsay** (1291-1352) See the historical novel *Castle
Dangerous* by Sir Walter Scott

son of

Generation 25

0.110111011011111111011111 William "le Hardi" Douglas (1255-
1298) married **0.110111011011111111011110 Eleanor de Lovaine**
See the movie *Braveheart* with Mel Gibson.

son of

Generation 26

0.110111011011111111110111111 William Longleg, Lord of Douglas
(1220-1274) married (2) **0.110111011011111111110111110 Constance
Battail of Fawdon**

son of

Generation 27

0.110111011011111111101111111 Archibald I, Lord of Douglas
(before 1198-c. 1238) married **0.110111011011111111101111110
Margaret**, daughter of **0.110111011011111111011111101 Sir John
Crawford of Crawfordjohn**

Archibald = son of

Generation 28

0.110111011011111111101111111l William of Douglas (d. 1214) lived in Clydesdale, under the King of the Scots married **0.110111011011111111101111110 Margaret**, sister of Freskin of Kerdal, a Flemish laird from Moray

Schauenburg 21-30 Germany

Generation 21

0.110111011011111101010 Hedvig of Schauenburg (1398-1436) AKA Helvig of Schauenburg married **0.110111011011111101011 Count Dietrich of Oldenburg** (1398-1440) AKA Derrick of Oldenburg and Theoderic of Oldenburg and Theoderic the Lucky, Count of Delmenhorst and Oldenburg **See Oldenburg**

daughter of

Generation 22

0.110111011011111101010101 Count Gerhard VI of Holstein married **0.110111011011111101010100 Katharina Elisabeth of Brunswick** (1385-after 1423) **See Brunswick**

son of

Generation 23

0.11011101110111111101011 Henry II of Holstein-Rendsburg, Duke of Schleswig married **0.11011101110111111101010 Ingeborg of Mecklenburg**

son of

Generation 24

0.110111011011111101010111 Gerhard III of Holstein-Rendsburg Duke of Holstein-Rendsburg (c. 1292-April 1, 1340) married **0.110111011011111101010110 Sofie of Werle**

son of

Generation 25

0.110111011011111010101111 Henry I, Count of Holstein-Rendsburg (1258-1304) married **0.1101110110111111010101110 Heilwig of Bronckhorst**

son of

Generation 26

0.1101110110111111010101011111 Gerhard I Count of Holstein-Itzehoe (1232-1290) married **0.1101110110111111010101011110 Elizabeth of Mecklenburg**

son of

Generation 27

0.11011101101111110101011111 Adolf IV of Holstein (before 1205-1261) married **0.11011101101111110101011110 Hellwig of Lippe** (c. 1200-c. 1248/1250)

son of

Generation 28

0.1101110110111111010101111111 Adolf III Count of Schauenburg and Holstein (1160-1225) married **0.1101110110111111010101111110 Adelheld of Querfurt**

son of

Generation 29

0.11011101101111110101011111111 Adolf II of Holstein (1128-1164) married **0.11011101101111110101011111110 Mechthild of Schwarzburg-Kafernburg** (d. 1192)

Generation 30

0.110111011011111101010101111111 Adolf of Holstein (d. Nov. 13, 1130) First Count of Schuenburg and Second Count of Holstein married **0.110111011011111101010111111110 Hildewa**

Gordon 21-24 Scotland

Generation 21

0.1101110110111101100 Lady Elizabeth (Eliza) Gordon married
**0.1101110110111101101 William Keith 2nd Earl Marischal. See
Keith**

daughter of

Generation 22

0.11011101101111011011 George Gordon, Earl of Huntly (before
1455-1501), Chancellor of Scotland (1498-1501) married
0.11011101101111011010 Annabella Stewart (1433-1471) **See
Second Stewart**

son of

Generation 23

**0.110111011011110110111 Alexander Seton, later Alexander
Gordon,** 1st Earl of Huntly, Lord of Badenoch and Cluny, knighted
1439/40 (d. 1470) married **0.110111011011110110110 Elizabeth
Crichton**, daughter of **0.110111011011110110110 0.1101110110111101101101 William
Crichton,** Chancellor of Scotland

Note -- change of surname from Seton to Gordon

Generation 24

Alexander = son of

0.110111011011110110111 1 Alexander Seton (d. 1440) married
0.110111011011110110111 0 Elizabeth (d. 1439) daughter and heiress
of **0.1101110110111101101101 Sir Adam Gordon**

Holland 21-25 England

Generation 21

0.1101110110110 1111000 Margaret Holland (1385-1439) married
0.1101110110110 1111001 John Beaufort, first Earl of Someset
(1371-1410) **See Beaufort**

daughter of

Generation 22

0.110111011011011110001 Thomas Holland, 2nd Earl of Kent (1350-1397), councillor of his half-brother King Richard II married **0.110111011011011110000 Alice FitzAlan**, daughter of **0.1101110110110111100001 Richard FitzAlan,** 10th Earl of Arundel and **0.1101110110110111100000 Eleanor of Lancaster**

Thomas = son of

Generation 23

0.<u>1101110110110111100011</u> Thomas Holland, 1st Earl Earl of Kent (c. 1314-Dec. 26, 1360) military commander during the Hundred Years' War married **0.<u>1101110110110111100010</u>** Joan "the Fair Maid of Kent" (1328-1385), granddaughter of Edward I of England. **See Plantagenet** At the Battle of Crécy, Thomas was one of the principal commanders in the van under the Prince of Wales.

Thomas = son of

Generation 24

0.<u>110111011011011110001</u>11 Robert de Holland 1st Baron Holland (c. 1283-1328, beheaded for treason) = ancestor of George Washington, Thomas Jefferson, Louis XVI, and Winston Churchill, knighted 1305 married about 1308 **0.<u>110111011011011110001</u>10** Maud De La Zouche, daughter of **0.<u>110111011011011110001</u>101** Lord Alan la Zouche, 1st Baron la Zouche of Ashby married **0.<u>110111011011011110001</u>100** Eleanor de Segrave

Robert = son of

Generation 25

0.<u>110111011011011110001</u>111 Sir Robert de Holland married **0.<u>110111011011011110001</u>110 Eizabeth de Salmesbury**

First Drummond 21-28 Scotland

Generation 21

0.1101110110111101110 Annabella Drummond (1350 Stobhall, Cargill, Perth, Scotland -1401 Scone Palace, Scotland) married 1367 **0.1101110110111101111 King Robert III of Scotland** (1340-1406) **See Stewart** [We're also descended from her brother Sir John Drummond, 12th of Lenox]

daughter of

Generation 22

0.1101110110111011101 Sir John Drummond 11th of Lennox (1318-1373) and **0.1101110110111011100 Mary Montifex AKA Mary Montifichet** (b. 1325), daughter of **0.110111011011110111001 William de Montifex**

John = son of

Generation 23

0.110111011011110111011 Sir Malcolm Drummond 10th Thane of Lennox (b. after 1295 d. 1346) **0.110111011011110111010 Margaret de Graham. See Second Graham**

son of

Generation 24

0.1101110110111101110111 Sir Malcolm Drummond 9th Thane of Lennox (b. after 1270 d. 1325) married **0.1101110110111101110110 Margaret Graham** (b. before 1279)

son of

Generation 25

0.1101110110111101110111 Sir John Drummond, 8th Thane of Lennox (b. after 1240 d. 1301) married **0.1101110110111101110110 Elena Stewart**

son of

Generation 26

0.11011101101111101110111111 Sir Malcolm Drummond, 7th Thane of Lennox (b. after 1209 d. 1278)

son of

Generation 27

0.1101110110111101110111111 Malcolm Beg Drummond, 6th Thane of Lennox (b. afater 1169 d. 1259) married **0.1101110110111101110111110 Ada of Lennox**

son of

Generation 28

0.110111011011111011101111111 Sir Malcolm Drummond, 5th Thane of Lennox (b. before 1153 d. 1200)

Holstein-Ploen 22-24 Germany

Generation 22

0.1101110110111111010110 Agnes of Holstein married **0.1101110110111111010111 Count Christian V of Oldenburg,** became count 1398 (b. before 1347 d. 1423) **See Oldenburg**

daughter of

Generation 23

0.110111011011111110101101 Gerhard IV, Count of Holstein-Ploen (c. 1277-1323)married **0.110111011011111110101100 Anastasia of Wittenberg**

son of

Generation 24

0.1101110110111111101011011 Gerhard II, Count of Holstein-Ploen (1254-Oct. 28,1312) married **0.1101110110111111101011010 Ingeborg of Sweden, See Second Sweden 24**

Brunswick 22-36 Germany, Italy

Generation 22

0.1101110110111111010100 Katharina Elisabeth of Brunswick (1385-after 1423) married **0.1101110110111111010101 Count Gerhard VI of Holstein. See Schauenburg**

daughter of

Generation 23

0.110111011011111110101001 Magnus II, Duke of Brunswick-Luneburg (1324-1373) married **0.110111011011111110101000 Catherine of Anhalt-Bernburg**

son of

Generation 24

0.1101110110111111101010011 Magnus the Pious, Duke of Brunswick-Luneburg (d. 1369) married

0.1101110110111111101010010 Sophie of Brandenburg

son of

Generation 25

0.11011101101111110101000111 Albert II, "the Fat", Duke of Brunswick-Luneburg (1268-1318) married

0.11011101101111110101000110 Rixa of Mecklengurg-Werle

son of

Generation 26

0.110111011011111110101001111 Albert the Tall, Duke of Bruswick-Luneberg (1236-1279)

son of

Generation 27

0.1101110110111111101010011111 Otto the Child, first Duke of Bruswick-Luneburg (d. 1252)

son of

Generation 28
0.110111011011111010100111111 William of Winchester AKA
William Longsword, AKA William of Luneburg (April 11, 1184-Dec.
13, 1213) married **0.110111011011111010100111110 Helen**
daughter of **0.110111011011111010100111101 King Valdemar I of
Denmark. See Denmark**
William = son of
Generation 29
0.11011101101111101010011111111 Henry the Lion, Duke of
Saxony and Bavaria married **0.11011101101111101010011111110
Matilda,** Duchess of Saxony. **See First Saxony**
son of
Generation 30
0.1101110110111111010100111111111 Henry X, Duke of Bavaria
married **0.110111011011111010100111111110 Gertrude of
Supplinburg. See Supplinburg**
son of
Generation 31
0.1101110110111111010100111111111 Henry IX, Duke of Bavaria
(1075-Dec. 13, 1126) married **0.110111011011111010100111111110
Wulfhild Billung of Saxony** (1072-Dec. 29, 1126)
son of
Generation 32
0.1101110110111111010100111111111 Welf I Duke of Bavaria (c.
1035/1040-1101) married **0.110111011011111010100111111110
Judith of Flanders** (1030/1035 -1095)
[We are also descended from Welf I by way of Welf II, another son of
his]
Generation 33
0.110111011011111010100111111111 Alberto Azzo I, Margrave
of Milan (d. 1029)

son of

Generation 34

0.110111011011111101010011111111111 Oberto II, Margrave of Milan (d. after 1014) married

0.110111011011111101010011111111110 Railend

son of

Generation 35

0.110111011011111101010011111111111 Oberto I, Margrave of Milan (d. 975) (d. Oct. 15, 975), founder of the Obertenghi family, Count of Milan from 951

son of

Generation 36

0.110111011011111101010011111111111 Adalbert, Margrave of Milan (AKA Obertenghi or Adalbertnii) (970-1018/1029) Frankish nobility who settled in Lombardy

Second Graham 23-26 Scotland

Generation 23

0.110111011011110111010 Margaret de Graham married
0.110111011011110111011 Sir Malcolm Drummond 10th Thane of Lennox (after 1295-1346) **See Second Drummond**

daughter of

Generation 24

0.110111011011110111010101 Sir Patrick de Graham (d. 1296) and
0.110111011011110111010 Annabelle Graham daughter of
0.110111011011110111010101 Robert Graham, 4th Earl of Strathearn (d. before 1244)

son of

Generation 25

0.11011101101111011101011 David Graham (d. 1237) lived at Kincardine, Aberdeenshire, Scotland married **0.11011101101111011101010 Agnes (?)**

son of

Generation 26

0.110111011011110111010111 Gilbert Graham, 3rd Earl of Strathearn (b. circa 1150 d. circa 1223) married **0.110111011011110111010110 Maud d'Aubigny** (d. after 1210) **See D'Aubigny**

Bruce or Brus 23-30 Scotland

Generation 23

0.110111011011011110111110 Marjorie Bruce (1296-1316) married **0.110111011011011110111111 Walter Stewart,** 6th High Steward of Scotland (d. 1326) **See Second Stewart**

daughter of

Generation 24

0.11011101101101111011101 King Robert I of Scotland AKA Robert the Bruce (July 11, 1274-June 7, 1329) reigned 1306-1329 married **0.11011101101101111011100 Isabella of Mar** (c. 1277-1296)

son of

Generation 25

0.1101110110110111110111011 Robert de Brus, 6th Lord of Annandale and Earl of Carrick (July 1243-March 1304) participated in the Ninth Crusade married **0.1101110110110111110111010 Marjorie**, Countess of Carrick

son of

Generation 26

0.110111011011011101110111 Robert de Brus, 5th Lord of
Annandale (c. 1215-1295) married **0.110111011011011101110110
Isabella de Clare** (Nov. 21226-July 10, 1264) daughter of
0.110111011011011101110111011011101 Gilbert de Clare, 4th Earl of
Hertford
son of

Generation 27

0.11011101101101111011101111 Robert de Brus, 4th Lord of
Annandale (c. 1195-1232) married **0.11011101101101111011101110
Isobel of Huntingdon (1199-1251) See Huntingdon**
son of

Generation 28

0.1101110110110111101110111111 Willam de Brus, 3rd Lord of
Annandale (d. 1212) married **0.1101110110110111101110111110
Christina Mac Uhtred**
son of

Generation 29

0.110111011011011101110111111 Robert de Brus, 2nd Lord of
Annandale (d. 1194) married **0.11011101101101111011101111110
Euphemia**, daughter of **0.11011101101101111011101111101 William
le Gros**, 1st Earl of Albermarle
son of

Generation 30

0.110111011011011101110111111 Robert de Brus, 1st Lord of
Annandale (c. 1078-May 11, 1141)

Plantagenet 23-35 England, France

Generation 23

0.110111011011011101111100010 Joan "the Fair Maid of Kent", (1328-
1385) granddaughter of Edward I of England and mother of Richard

II of England married (1) **0.110111011011011100011 Thomas Holland,** 1st Earl Earl of Kent (c. 1314-Dec. 26, 1360) military commander during the Hundred Years' War. married (2) 1361 Edward the Black Prince **See Beaufort, Holland**

Joan = daughter of

Generation 24

0.1101110110110111000111 Edmund of Woodstock, 1st Earl of Kent (Plantagenet) (Aug. 5, 1301-March 19, 1330 executed for treason) married **0.1101110110110111000110** Margaret Wake, (c. 1297-Sept. 29, 1349) 3rd Baroness Wake, descendant of Llywelyn "the Great," Prince of Gwynedd, **See Wake**

Edmund = son of

Generation 25

0.110111011011011110001111 King Edward I of England "Longshanks" (June 14, 1229-July 7, 1307) reigned 1272-1307) married 1299 **0.110111011011011100110 Margaret of France** (1282-Feb. 14, 1317), daughter of **0.1101110110110111001101 King Philip III of France** married **0.1101110110110111001100 Maria of Brabant See Capet**

Edward = son of

Generation 26

0.110111011011011110001111 Henry III, King of England (Plantagenet) (1207-1272) reigned 1216-1272) married **0.110111011011011110001110 Eleanor of Provence** (c. 1223-1291) daughter of **0.1101110110110111000111101 Ramon Berenguer IV,** Count of Provence (1198-1245) and **0.1101110110110111000111100 Beatrice of Savoy** (1206-1266)) **See Provence**

Henry = son of

Generation 27

0.1101110110110111000111111 John I, "Lackland," King of England (Plantagenet) [Magna Carta] (1166-1216) married

0.110111011011011111000111110 Isabella of Angoulême (1187-1246) daughter of **0.1101110110110111110001111101 Aymer Taillefer**, Count of Angouleme

John = son of

Generation 28

0.1101110110110111110001111111 Henry II, King of England (Plantagenet) (1133-1189) reigned 1154-1189) married **0.1101110110110111110001111110 Eleanor of Aquitaine** (1122-1204) daughter of **0.11011101101101111100011111101** William X, Duke of Aquitaine and **0.11011101101101111100011111100** Aenor de Châtellerault **See Normandy, First Saxony, Champagne, Aquitaine, Beaufort**

Henry = son of

Generation 29

0.11011101101101111100011111111 Geoffrey V the Handsome Count of Anjou and Maine by inheritance, and Duke of Normandy by conquest 1144 (Plantagenet) (Aug. 24, 1113-Sept. 7 1151) married **0.11011101101101111100011111110 Empress Matilda** (1102-1110), briefly (contested) the first female ruler of England in 1141 (widow of Henry V Holy Roman Emperor) **See Normandy**

Geoffrey = son of

Generation 30

0.110111011011011111000111111111 Fulk V of Anjou AKA Fulk the Younger, (1089/1092-Nov. 13, 1143) Count of Anjou 1109-1129 and King of Jerusalem 1131-1143 went on Crusade in 1120 married (1) Eremburga of La Fleche, daughter of Elias I of Maine married (2) **0.110111011011011111000111111110 Matilda**, daughter of **0.110111011011011111000111111101 Gervais, Lord of Chateau-du-Loir**

[We are also descended from the marriage of Fulk V to Erembruga through their son Geoffrey V Count of Anjou and Maine]

Fulk = son of

Generation 31

0.11011101101101111000111111111 **Fulk IV** AKA le Réchin (1043-1109) Count of Anjou married **0.1101110110110111100011111111110** **Bertrade de Monfort,** who later deserted her husband and bigamously married King Philip I. she was the daughter of **0.1101110110110111100011111111101** **Simon of Monfort**

Fulk = son of

Generation 32

0.11011101101101111000111111111 **Geoffrey II** Count of Gatinais AKA Aubri married **0.1101110110110111100011111111110** **Ermengarde of Anjou** (1018-March-1076), daughter of **0.1101110110110111100011111111101** **Fulk III the Black**, Count of Anjou married Hildegarde of Sundgau

Geoffrey = son of

Generation 33

0.11011101101101111000111111111 **Hugues du Perche** (tenth century) married **0.1101110110110111100011111111110** **Beatrice to Macon**, daughter of **0.1101110110110111100011111111101** **Aubry II de Macon**

son of

Generation 34

0.11011101101101111000111111111 **Fulcuich** (Fulcois), Count of Mortagne married **0.1101110110110111100011111111110** **Melisende,** daughter of **0.1101110110110111100011111111101** **Hugues**, Viscount of Chateaudun md, Hildegarde of Perche.

son of

Generation 35

0.11011101101101111000111111111 **Rotrou,** Seigneur de Nogent married **0.1101110110110111100011111111110** **Hildegarde de Mortagne et Perche**

Hainault 23-29 Belgium

<u>Generation 23</u>

0.1101110110110111100110 Philippa of Hainaut (1314-1369) married **0.1101110110110111100111 King Edward III of England** (Nov. 13, 1312-June 21, 1377) reigned 1327-1377 **See Plantagenet** daughter of

<u>Generation 24</u>

0.110111011011011111001101 William I Count of Hainault (1286-1337) married 1305 **0.110111011011011111001100 Jeanne of Valois** (1292-1342) **See Valois**

son of

<u>Generation 25</u>

0.1101110110110111100110111 John II of Avesnes, Count of Holland (1247-Aug. 22, 1304) married **0.1101110110110111100110110**

Philippa of Luxembourg (1252-1311)

son of

<u>Generation 26</u>

0.1101110110110111100110111 John I of Avesnes, Count of Hainaut (1218-1257) married **0.1101110110110111100110110 Adelaide of Holland** AKA Aleide (Aleidis) van Holland (c. 1230-April 9, 1284)

son of

<u>Generation 27</u>

0.110111011011011110011011111 Bouchard IV of Avesnes married **0.110111011011011110011011110 Margaret II** Countess of Flanders and Hainault (1202-1280) **See Baldwin of Constantinople**

son of

<u>Generation 28</u>

0.1101110110110111100110111111 James of Avesnes (1152-Sept. 7, 1191) lord of Avesnes, Conde and Leuze; participated in the Third Crusade as leader of a detachment of French, Flemish, and Frisian soldiers which arrived in the Holy Land in 1189; died there at the

Battle of Arsuf in 1191 married **0.110111011011011100110111110
Adela of Guise** daughter of **0.110111011011011100110111101
Bernard of Guise**

James = son of

Generation 29

0.110111011011011100110111111 Nicholas d'Oisy, Lord of
Avesnes (1130-1170) married **0.110111011011011100110111110
Matilda de la Roche**

Valois and Capet 24-40 France

Generation 24

0.110111011011011110011100 Jeanne of Valois (1292-1342) married
1305 **0.110111011011011110011101 William I Count of Hainault**
(1286-1337) **See Hainault**

Jeanne = daughter of

Generation 25

0.11011101101101111110011001 Charles of Valois (1270-1325)
married **0.11011101101101111110011000 Marguerite of Anjou and
Maine** (1273-1299)

their son became Philip VI King of France

their nephews became Louis X, Philip V, and Charles IV, kings of
France

Charles = son of

Generation 26

 **0.11011101101101111110011001 King Philip III "the Bold" of
France** (Capet) (1245-1285) married **0.11011101101101111110011000
Isabella of Aragon** (1247-1271) **See Aragon** Philip appears in
Dante's *Divine Comedy.*

son of

Generation 27

0.110111011011011111100110011 King Louis IX of France (Capet)
Saint Louis of the Crusades (1214-1270), reigned 1226-1270 married
1234 **0.110111011011011111100110010 Marguerite of Provence**
(1221-1295) (sister of Eleanor, wife of Henry III King of England)
Louis = son of

Generation 28

0.11011101101101111001100111 King Louis VIII of France (Capet)
(1187-1226) married **0.11011101101101111001100110 Blanche of
Castile** (1188-1252) **See Castile** [We are also descended from Louis
VIII by another line]
son of

Generation 29

**0.1101110110110111110011001111 King Philip Augustus II of
France** (Capet) (1165-1223) reigned 1180-1223) married
0.1101110110110111110011001110 Isabelle of Hainaut (1170-1190)
son of

Generation 30

0.110111011011011111100110011111 King Louis VII King of France
AKA "the Younger" (Capet) (1120-1180) married
0.110111011011011111100110011110 Adela of Champagne (1140-
1206) daughter of **0.11011101101101111001100111101 Theobald II
of Champagne** and **0.11011101101101111001100111100 Matilda of
Carinthia** (= third wife)
Louis = son of

Generation 31

0.1101110110110111110011001111111 King Louis VI of France
(Capet) (1081-1127) married 1115
0.1101110110110111110011001111110 Adelaide of Savoy AKA
Adelaide of Maurienne (1092-1154) daughter of

0.110111011011011110011001111101 Humbert II of Savoy and
0.110111011011011110011001111100 Gisela of Burgundy
Louis = son of
<u>Generation 32</u>
0.110111011011011110011001111111 King Philip I of France
(Capet) (1053-1108) reigned 1060-1108) married
0.110111011011011110011001111110 Bertha of Holland (1055-
1094), daughter of **0.110111011011011110011001111101 Floris I,**
Count of Holland and **0.110111011011011110011001111100**
Gertrude of Saxony, the daughter of
0.110111011011011110011001111111001 Bernard II, Duke of
Saxony, **See Antioch**
Philip = son of
<u>Generation 33</u>
0.111011011011110011001111111 King Henry I of France (Capet)
(1008-1060) married **0.110111011011011110011001111110 Anne of**
Kiev AKA Anna Yaroslavna (between 1024 and 1032 – 1075)
daughter of **0.110111011011011110011001111101 Yaroslav I King**
of Kiev and **0.110111011011011110011001111100 Ingegerd**
Olofsdotter. See Kiev
Henry = son of
<u>Generation 34</u>
0.111011011011110011001111111 King Robert II of France
(Capet) (972–1031) (Capet) reigned 996-1031 married
0.111011011011110011001111110 Constance of Arles (973–1032)
daughter of **0.111011011011110011001111101 William I, count**
of Provence
Robert = son of
<u>Generation 35</u>
0.111011011011110011001111111111 King Hugh Capet of France
(940-996) married **0.111011011011110011001111110 Adele AKA**

Adelaide of Aquitaine AKA Adelaide of Poitiers (c. 945 or 952 –
1004) daughter of **0.11101101101111001100111111111101 William III
of Aquitaine** married 935 **0.11101101101111001100111111111100
Adele of Normandy** b. 912

Hugh = son of

Generation 36

0.11101101101111001100111111111111 Hugh "the Great," Duke of
France (d. 956) married **0.11101101101111001100111111111110
Hedwige of Saxony** (c. 910-965) daughter of
11101101101111001100111111111101 Henry I "the Fowler," Duke
of Saxony married **11101101101111001100111111111100 Matilda of
Ringelheim AKA Saint Matilda or Saint Mathilda.** In *The Divine
Comedy* Dante meets the soul of Duke Hugh in Purgatory, lamenting
the avarice of his descendants.

Hugh = son of

Generation 37

0.11101101101111001100111111111111 Robert I (866-923), king of
West Francia married (2) 895 **0.11101101101111001100111111111110
Béatrice of Vermandois** (880 – after 931) daughter of
0.11101101101111001100111111111101 Herbert I of Vermandois
(c. 848/850 – 907)) **See Vermandois**

Robert = son of

Generation 38

0.11101101101111001100111111111111 Robert IV "the Strong"
AKA Rupert d. 866, Margrave in Neustria (now central France)
married **0.11101101101111001100111111111110 Adelaide or
Adalais** daughter of **0.11101101101111001100111111111101 Hugh
or Hugo**, Count of Tours and Sens (780-837) during the reign of
Charlemagne; he was probably a son of Count Haicho of the House
of the Etichonen.

Robert = son of

Generation 39

0.111011011011110011001111111111111 Robert III (800-834),
Count of Worms and Rheingau married
0.111011011011110011001111111111110 Waldrada of Worms (b.
801) daughter of **0.111011011011110011001111111111101 Adrian**
Count of Orleans and **0.111011011011110011001111111111100
Waldrada of Autun,** daughter of
0.111011011011110011001111111111001 Adalhelm of Autun
Robert = son of

Generation 40

0.111011011011110011001111111111111 Robert II of Hesbaye (d.
807) Frankish nobelman, Count of Worms, Rheingau, and Hesbaye

Hohenzollern 20-36 Germany

Generation 20

0.11011101101111110100 Dorothea of Brandenburg (1430/1431-
1495), AKA Dorothea of Hohenzollern AKA Dorothy Achilles.
married **0.11011101101111110101 King Christian I** (1426-1481)
King of Denmark 1448-1481, Norway 1450-1481 and Sweden 1457-
1464, also Count of Oldenburg and Delmenhorst **See Oldenburg**
daughter of

Generation 21

0.1101110110111111101001 John "the Alchemist," Margrave of
Brandenburg-Kulmbach, (1406-1464) married
0.1101110110111111101000 Barbara of Saxe-Wittenberg (1405-
1465), daughter of **0.110111011011111101010001 Rudolf III Duke of
Saxe-Wittenberg**
John = son of

Generation 22

0.110111011011111101010011 Frederick I Margrave of Brandenburg
and Nuremberg (1371-1440) married **0.110111011011111101010010**
Elisabeth of Bavaria-Landshut (1383-1442) **See Bavaria**

son of

<u>Generation 27</u>

0.110111011011111110100111 Frederick V, Burgrave of Nuremberg (b. before 1333 d. Jan. 1398) married **0.110111011011111110100110 Elisabeth of Meissen** (1329-1375)

son of

<u>Generation 28</u>

0.11011101101111101001111 John II, Burgrave of Nuremberg (c. 1309-1357) married **0.11011101101111101001110 Elisabeth of Henneberg-Schleusingen**

Frederick = son of

Generation 29

0.1101110110111111010011111 Frederick IV, Burgrave of Nuremberg (1287-1332) married **0.1101110110111111010011110 Margarete of Gorz**

son of

<u>Generation 30</u>

0.11011101101111110100111111 Frederick III Burgrave of Nuremberg (c. 1220-1297) married **0.11011101101111110100111110 Helene of Saxony,** daughter of **0.11011101101111101001111101 Albert II Duke of Saxony** and **0.11011101101111101001111100 Helene of Braunschweig**

Frederick = son of

<u>Generation 31</u>

0.110111011011111101001111111 Conrad I Burgrave of Nuremberg and Count of Zollern of the House of Hohenzollern (c. 1186-1261) married **0.110111011011111101001111110 Adelheid of Frontenhausen**

son of

Generation 32

0.110111011011111010011111111 Frederick I Burgrave of
Nuremberg and Count of Zollern (b. before 1139 d. after 1200)
married **0.110111011011111010011111110 Sofie of Raabs**
son of

Generation 33

0.110111011011111010011111111 Count Frederick II of Zollern
(d. 1142 or after 1145)
son of

Generation 34

0.110111011011111010011111111 Frederick I Count of Zollern
(d. before 1125) married **0.110111011011111010011111110**
Udihild of Urach-Dettingen
son of

Generation 35

0.110111011011111010011111111111 Burkhard I Lord of the
House of Hohenzollern (b. before 1025 killed as part of a feud in
1061) married **0.110111011011111010011111111110 Anastasia von
Rheinfelden**
son of

Generation 36

? **0.110111011011111010011111111111 Friedrich of Sulichgau**
married ?**0.110111011011111010011111111110 Irmentrud of
Nellenburg**

Bavaria-Landshut 22-32 Germany, France
Generation 22
0.110111011011111010010 Elisabeth of Bavaria-Landshut (1383-
1442) married **0.110111011011111010011 Frederick I** Margrave of
Brandenburg and Burgrave of Nuremberg (1371-1440)
daughter of

Generation 23

0.110111011101111110100101 Frederick, Duke of Bavaria (1339-1393) married **0.110111011101111110100100 Maddelena Visconti**

son of

Generation 24

0.110111011011111101001011 Stephen II, Duke of Bavaria married 1328 **0.110111011011111101001010 Elisabeth of Sicily AKA Isabel of Aragon** (1310-1349)

daughter of

Generation 25

0.110111011011111101001011 Eleanor of Anjou AKA Eleanor of Naples (1289-1341) married 0.110111011011111101001011 Frederick III, King of Sicily

daughter of

Generation 26

0.110111011011111110100101101 Charles II "the Lame," King of Naples and Sicily, King of Jerusalem, Prince of Salerno (1254-May 5, 1309) married **0.110111011011111110100101100 Mary of Hungary** (1257-1323) **See Second Hungary**

son of

Generation 31

0.110111011011111101001011011 Charles I of Anjou, King of Sicily (1226/1227-Jan. 7, 1285) married **0.110111011011111101001011010 Beatrice of Provence** (1229-Sept. 23, 1267)

son of

Generation 32

0.110111011011111101001011011 Louis VIII (Sept. 1187-Nov. 8, 1226) the Lion, King of France (Capet) married **0.110111011011111101001011010 Blanche of Castile. See Castile**

[We are also descendants of Louis VIII through another line.]

Second Sweden 24-29 Sweden

Generation 24

0.110111011011111101011010 Ingeborg of Sweden (1263-1292) married **0.110111011011111101011011 Gerhard II, Count of Holstein-Ploen** (1254-Oct. 28, 1312) **See Holstein-Ploen** daughter of

Generation 25

0.11011101101111111010110101 Valdemar I, King of Sweden (1239-1302) married **0.11011101101111111010110100 Sophia of Denmark**, daughter of **0.11011101101111110101101001 Eric IV, King of Denmark. See Second Denmark** Valdemar = son of

Generation 26

0.11011101101111110101101011 Birger Magnusson AKA Birger Jarl, founder of Stockholm (1210-1266) married **0.11011101101111110101101010 Ingeborg Eriksdotter of Sweden**, daughter of **0.11011101101111110101101011 King Eric X of** Sweden married **0.11011101101111110101101010 Ricvheza of Denmark** Birger = son of

Generation 27

0.11011101101111110101101010 Lady Ingrid Ylva, "The White Witch" (1180-1250) married **0.11011101101111110101101011 Magnus Minneskold** (d. 1210)

Wake 24-40 England, Wales

Generation 24

0.110111011011011111000110 Margaret Wake, (c. 1297-Sept. 29, 1349) 3rd Baroness Wake, descendant of Llywelyn "the Great," Prince of Gwynedd married **0.110111011011011111000111 Edmund of Woodstock**, 1st Earl of Kent (Plantagenet) (1301-1330 executed

for treason) Their daughter Joan of Kent was the first English
princess of Wales. **See Plantagenet**

Margaret = daughter of

<u>Generation 24</u>

**0.110111011011011110001101 John Wake, First Baron Wake of
Liddell** (1268-1300) married **0.110111011011011110001100 Joan de
Fiennes** daughter of **0.11011101101101111100011001 William de
Fenes married 0.11011101101101111100011000 Blanche de Brienne**

John = son of

<u>Generation 25</u>

0.110111011011011110001011 Baldwin Wake, Lord of Bourne (d.
1282) married **0.110111011011011110001010 Hawise de Quincy**

Hawise de Quincy = daughter of

<u>Generation 26</u>

**0.110111011011011111000110110 Elen ferch Llywelyn AKA Helen
of North Wales** (1207-1253) married

0.110111011011011111000110111 Sir Robert de Quincy son of **Saer
de Quincy** (1155-1219) one of the leaders of the baronial rebellions
against King John

Elen = daughter of

<u>Generation 27</u>

**0.110111011011011110001101111 Llywelyn ap Iorwerth, Prince of
North Wales AKA Llywelyn "the Great"** (1173-1240) reigned
1218-1240 married **0.110111011011011110001101110 Joan, Lady of
Wales**, daughter of **0.11011101101101111100011011101 King John of
England See Plantagenet**

Llywelyn = son of

<u>Generation 28</u>

**0.1101110110110111100011011111 Iorwerth ab Owain Gwynedd
or Iorwerth Drwyndwn** (1145-1174)

son of

Generation 29

0.110111011011011110001101111111 Owain Gwynedd, King of Gwynedd (1100-1170) married **0.110111011011011110001101111110 Gladys ferch Llywarch**, daughter of

0.110111011011011110001101111101 Llywarch ap Trahaeran. Owain was the father of Madoc Gwynedd who purportedly sailed to America in 1170.

Owain = son of

Generation 30

0.110111011011011110001101111111 Gruffydd ap Cynan (1055-1137) married **0.110111011011011110001101111110 Angharad ferch Owain**, daughter of **0.110111011011011110001101111101 Owain ab Edwin**

Gruffydd = son of

Generation 31

0.110111011011011110001101111111 Cynan ab Iago (1014-1063) married **0.110111011011011110001101111110 Raignaillt**, daughter of **0.110111011011011110001101111101 Olaf of Dublin**, son of **0.110111011011011110001101111011 King Sigtrygg Silkbeard King of Dublin**

Cyan = son of

Generation 32

0.110111011011011110001101111111 Iago ab Idwal ap Meurig, King of Gwynedd (d. 1039)

son of

Generation 33

0.110111011011011110001101111111 Idwal ap Meurig (d. 996)

son of

Generation 34

0.110111011011011110001101111111 Meurig ab Idwal (d. 986)

son of

Generation 35

0.110111011011011110001101111111111 Idwal Foel ap Anarawd King of Gwynedd (d. 942)

son of

Generation 36

0.1101110110110111100011011111111111 Anarawd ap Rhodri, King of Gwynedd (d. 916)

son of

Generation 37

0.1101110110110111100011011111111111 Rhodri or Roderick "the Great" (820-878)

son of

Generation 38

0.1101110110110111100011011111111111 Merfyn Frych, King of Gwynedd (reigned 825-844) married
0.1101110110110111100011011111111110 Nest ferch Cadell daughter of **0.1101110110110111100011011111111101 Cadell ap Elisedd, King of Powys**

Merfyn = son of

Generation 39

0.1101110110110111100011011111111111 Gwriad married
0.1101110110110111100011011111111110 Ethyllt ferch Cynan daughter of Cynan Dindaethwy, king of Gwynedd.

son of

Generation 40

0.1101110110110111100011011111111111 Elidyr

Capet 24-25 France

Generation 24

0.11011101101101110001110 Marguerite of France (Capet) (1282-1317) married **0.11011101101101110001111 King Edward**

I of England "Longshanks" (1229-1307) reigned 1272-1307. **See Plantagenet**

daughter of

Generation 25

0.1101110110110111100011101 King Philip III "the Bold" of France (Capet) (1245-1285), reigned 1270-1285 married 1274 .
0.1101110110110111100011100 Maria of Brabant (1254-1321) **See Brabant Family** [Philip also married Isabella of Aragon (1247-1271) and by that marriage had Charles of Valois from whom we are also descended.] Philip appears in Dante's Divine Comedy. Dante does not name Philip directly, but refers to him as "the small-nosed" and "the father of the Pest of France." **See Valois, See Aragon**

Castile 25-38 Spain, Italy

Generation 25

0.1101110110110111110011110 Eleanor of Castile (1241-1290) married **0.1101110110110111110011111 Edward I, King of England** (Plantagenet) (1239-1307) reigned (1272-1304) **See Plantagenet** daughter of

Generation 26

_**0.1101110110110111100111101 Fernando III, King of Castile and Leon** married **0.1101110110110111100111100 Jeanne, Countess of Ponthieu**

son of

Generation 27

0.1101110110110111001111011 Alfonso IX of Leon (1171-1230)
0.1101110110110111001111010 Berengaria of Castile

son of

Generation 28

0.1101110110110111110011110111 Ferdinand II of Leon (c. 1137-Jan. 22, 1188) married **0.1101110110110111110011110110 Urraca of Portugal**

son of

Generation 29

0.110111011011011110011110111 Alfonso VII of Leon and Castile (1105-1157) married **0.110111011011011110011110110 Berenguela of Barcelona**

son of

Generation 30

0.11011101101101111001111011111 Raymond, Count of Galicia (1070-1107) married **0.11011101101101111001111011110 Urraca, Queen of Leon and Castile. See Jimenez**

son of

Generation 31

0.1101110110110111100111101111111 William I "the Great," Count of Burgundy (1020-1087) married **0.1101110110110111100111101111110 Stephanie**

son of

Generation 32

0.11011101101101111001111011111111 Renaud I, Count of Burgundy (986-1057) married **0.11011101101101111001111011111110 Alice of Normandy**

son of

Generation 33

0.110111011011011110011110111111111 Otto-William, Count of Burgundy (955/62-1026) married **0.110111011011011110011110111111110 Ermentrude de Roucy**

son of

Generation 34

0.110111011011011110011110111111111 Adalbert II of Ivrea
(932/936-971/975) married **0.110111011011011110011110111111110 Gerberga of Macon**

son of

Generation 35

0.11011101101101111100111101111111111 Berengar II (900-966)
married **0.11011101101101111100111101111111110 Willa of Tuscany**
son of

Generation 36

0.11011101101101111100111101111111111 Adalbert I Margrave of Ivrea (d. after Feb. 28, 929) married
0.11011101101101111100111101111111110 Gisela of Friuli
son of

Generation 37

0.11011101101101111100111101111111111 Anscar I Margrave of Ivrea (860-902)
son of

Generation 38

0.11011101101101111100111101111111111 Amadeus of Oscheret
(790-867)

Brabant 25-33 Belgium, France

Generation 25

0.11011101101101111100011100 Maria of Brabant (1254-1321,
Murel) married 1274 **0.11011101101101111100011101 King Philip
III "the Bold" of France** (Capet) (1245-1285), reigned 1270-1285.
Philip appears in Dante's Divine Comedy
daughter of

Generation 26

0.11011101101101111000111001 Henry III, Duke of Brabant (1230-1261) married **0.11011101101101111000111**000 Adelaide of Burgundy, daughter of **0.11011101101101111000111000**1 Hugh IV, Duke of Burgundy

Henry = son of

Generation 27

0.110111011011011110001110011 Henry II, Duke of Brabant (1207-, 1248) married **0.11011101101101111000111001**0 Marie of Hohenstaufen (1201-1235) **See First Hohenstaufen**

Generation 28

son of

0.1101110110110111110011100111 **Henry I "the Courageous" Duke of Brabant** (1165-1235) married 1179 **0.110111011011011111000110011**0 **Mathilde of Boulogne** (AKA Mathilde of Flanders), daughter of

0.11011101101101111000111001101 **Matthew of Alsace** married **0.1101110110110111100011100110**0 **Marie of Boulogne,** daughter of **0.11011101101101111000111001100**1 **King Stephen of England** married **0.11011101101101111000111001100**0 **Matilda I, Countess of Boulogne**

Henry = son of

Generation 29

0.11011101101101111000111001111 **Godfrey III of Leuven,** Duke of Lower Lotharingia and Landgrave of Brabant married **0.1101110110110111100011100111**0 **Margaret of Limbug**

son of

Generation 30

0.110111011011011110001110011111 **Godfrey II,** Count of Leuven and Landgrave of Brabant (1110-1142) married **0.11011101101101111000111001111**0 **Lutgarde of Sulzbach**

son of

Generation 31

0.110111011011011110001110011111 Godfrey I "the Bearded", "the Courageous" or "the Great," Landgrave of Brabant and Count of Burssels and Leuven, Duke of Lower Lorraine, and Margrave of Antwerp (1060-1139) married **0.110111011011011110001110011110 Ida of Chiny**

son of

Generation 32

0.11011101101101111000111001111111 Henry II, Count of Louvain married **0.11011101101101111000111001111110 Adela**

son of

Generation 33

0.110111011011011110001110011111111 Lambert II Count of Louvain (d. 1054) married **0.110111011011011110001110011111110** Oda of Verdun. Pope Stephen IX was her maternal uncle.

son of

Generation 34

0.1101110110110111100011100111111111 Lambert I Count of Louvain (950-1015) married **0.1101110110110111100011100111111110 Gerberga of Lower Lorraine** (975-1019) daughter of **0.1101110110110111100011100111111101 Charles,** Duke of Lower Lorraine, who was son of **0.1101110110110111100011100111111011 King Louis IV of France** married **0.1101110110110111100011100111111010 Gerberga of Saxony**

son of

Generation 35
0.110111011011011110001110011111111111 Reginar III Count of
Hainault (920-973) married
0.110111011011011110001110011111111110 Adela
son of

Generation 36
0.110111011011011110001110011111111111 Reginar II, Count of
Hainault (890-932) married
0.110111011011011110001110011111111110 Adelaide of Burgundy
son of

Generation 37
0.110111011011011110001110011111111111 Reginar, Duke of
Lorraine (850-915) married
0.110111011011011110001110011111111110 Hersinda
son of

Generation 38
0.110111011011011110001110011111111111 Gilbert, Giselbert, or
Giselbertus, Frankish noble in what would become Lotharingia,
eighth century

Second Capet 25-26
Generation 25
0.11011101101101110011101 King Philip IV of France (1268-
1314) married **0.11011101101101110011100 Joan I of Navarre** (d.
1305) **See Navarre**
son of

Generation 26
**0.11011101101101110011001 King Philip III "the Bold" of
France** (1245-1285), reigned 1270-1285
married **0.11011101101101110011000 Isabella of Aragon** (1247-
1271) **See Valois, Aragon**

Navarre 25-36

<u>Generation 25</u>

0.110111011011011110011100 Joan I of Navarre (d. 1305) married
0.110111011011011110011101 King Philip IV of France (1268-
1314) **See Second Capet**

daughter of

<u>Generation 26</u>

0.1101110110110111100111001 Henry I of Navarre (1244-1274)
married **0.1101110110110111100111000 Blanche of Artois**

son of

<u>Generation 27</u>

0.1101110110110111001110011 Theobald I, King of Navarre
(1234-1253) married **0.1101110110110111001110010 Margaret of
Bourbon**

son of

<u>Generation 28</u>

0.110111011011011110011100111 Theobald III, Count of
Champagne (1179-1201) married **0.110111011011011110011100110
Blanche of Navarre**

son of

<u>Generation 29</u>

0.110111011011011110011001111 Henry I "the Liberal," Count of
Champagne, Second Crusade (1127-1181) married
**0.110111011011011110011001110 Marie of France. See
Champagne**

son of

<u>Generation 30</u>

0.110111011011011110011001111 Theobald "the Great," Count
of Blois, Chartres, Champagne and Brie (1090-1152) married
0.110111011011011110011001110 Matilda of Carinthia

son of

Generation 31
0.11011101101101111001110011111 **Stephen, Count of Blois,** First
Crusade (c. 1045-May 19, 1102) married
0.11011101101101111001110011110 **Adela of Normandy**
son of
Generation 32
0.110111011011011110011100111111 **Theobald III,** Count of Blois
(1012-1089) married **0.110111011011011110011100111110**
Garsinde du Maine
son of
Generation 33
0.1101110110110111100111001111111 **Odo II,** Count of Blois (985-
1037) married **0.1101110110110111100111001111110** **Ermengarde**
of Auvergne
son of
Generation 34
0.11011101101101111001110011111111 **Odo I of Blois** (c. 950-996)
married **0.11011101101101111001110011111110** **Bertha of**
Burgundy
son of
Generation 35
0.110111011011011110011100111111111 **Theobald I of Blois**
(before 913-977) married **0.110111011011011110011100111111110**
Luitgard of Vermandois
son of
Generation 36
0.1101110110110111100111001111111111 **Theobald "the Elder"**
(890-940) married **0.1101110110110111100111001111111110**
Richildis

Provence 26-29 France, Spain

Generation 26

0.110111011011011110011110 Eleanor of Provence (c. 1223-1291) married **0.110111011011011110011111 Henry III, King of England** (Plantagenet) (1207-1272) reigned 1216-1272.
daughter of

Generation 27

0.1101110110110111001111101 Ramon Berenguer IV(1198-1245) Count of Provence married **0.1101110110110111001111100 Beatrice of Savoy** (1206-1266) [We are also descended from them by way of their daughter Beatrice of Provence]
son of

Generation 28

0.11011101101101111001111011 Alfonso II (1180-Feb. 1209) Count of Provence married **0.11011101101101111001111010 Garsenda II** (1180-1242) Countess of Forcalquier, daughter of Rainou of Sabran married Garsenda of Forcalquier
son of

Generation 29

0.110111011011011110011111 0111 Alfonso II "the Troubadour" of Aragon (1157- 1196) married **0.110111011011011110011111 0110 Sancha of Castile** (1154/55-1208) [We are also descended from them by way of their son Peter II of Aragon]

Second Saxony 26-33 Germany

Generation 26

0.110111011011111101011010010 Jutta of Saxony (d. 1250) married **0.110111011011111101011010001 King Eric IV "Ploughpenny" of Denmark** 1216-1250)
daughter of

Generation 27

0.110111011011111101011010100101 Albert I, Duke of Saxony (1175-1260) married **0.110111011011111101011010100100 Agnes of Thuringia**, daughter of **0.110111011011111101011011001001 Hermann I,** Landgrave of Thuringia. **See Thuringia**

Albert = son of

Generation 28

0.110111011011111101011011001011 Bernard III, Duke of Saxony (1134-1212) married **0.110111011011111101011011001010 Brigitte of Denmark**

son of

Generation 29

0.110111011011111101011010010111 Albert "the Bear," First Margrave of Brandenburg (1100-1170) married **0.110111011011111101011010010110 Sophie Winzenburg**

son of

Generation 30

0.110111011011111101011010010111 Otto, Count of Ballenstedt (1070-1123) married **0.110111011011111101011010010111110 Eilika of Saxony**

son of

Generation 31

0.110111011011111101011010010111111 Adalbert II, Count of Ballenstedt (1030-1076/1083) married **0.110111011011111101011010010111110 Adelaide of Weimar-Orlamunde**

son of

Generation 32

0.1101110110111111010110100101111111 Esico of Ballenstedt (d. 1060) progenitor of the House of Ascania married **0.110111011011111101011010010111110 Matilda of Swabia**

son of

Generation 33

0.110111011011111101011010010111111 Adalbert of Ballenstedt (b. 970) married **0.110111011011111101011010010111110 Hidda**

Second Denmark 25-35 Denmark, Sweden

Generation 25

0.1101110110111111010110100 Sophia of Denmark married **0.1101110110111111010110101 King Valdemar I of Sweden** (1239-1302)

daughter of

Generation 26

0.11011101101111110101101001 King Eric IV "Ploughpenny" of Denmark (1216-1250) married **0.11011101101111110101101001 0 Jutta of Saxony** (d. 1250) **See Second Saxony**

son of

Generation 27

0.11011101101111110101101001 1 King Valdemar II "the Conqueror" of Denmark (1170-1241) married **0.11011101101111110101101001 0 Princess Berengária of Portugal, See Portugal**

Valdemar = son of

Generation 28

0.110111011011111101011010 0111 King Valdemar I of Denmark (1131-1182) married **0.110111011011111101011010 0110 Sophia Valadarsdattir,** a Varangian princess [We're also descended from his daughter Helen]

son of

Generation 29

0.110111011101111110101101001111 Canute Lavard (1090-1131)

0.110111011101111110101101001110 Ingeborg of Kiev, See Second Kiev

son of

Generation 30

0.11011101110111111101011010011111 King Eric I "Evergood" of Denmark (1060-1103) married

0.11011101110111111101011010011110 Boedil Thurgotsdatter

son of

Generation 31

0.1101110111011111110101101001111111 King Sweyn II Estridsson of Denmark married **0.110111011101111110101101001111110 Gunhild Sveinsdotter**

son of

Generation 32

0.1101110111011111110101101001111111 Ulf Thorgilsson married **0.110111011101111110101101001111110 Estrid Margarete Svendsdatter**

son of

Generation 33

0.11011101110111111101011010011111111 Thorgil Styrbjornsson Sparkling

son of

Generation 34

0.110111011101111110101101001111111111 Styrbjorn the Strong (d. 985) married **0.110111011101111110101101001111111110 Thyra Haraldsdotter of Denmark**

son of

Generation 35

0.110111011101111110101101001111111111 King Olof II Bjornsson of Sweden (d. 975) married
0.110111011101111110101101001111111110 Ingeborg Thrandsdotter

Aragon 26-40 Spain

Generation 26

0.1101110110110111100110001 Isabella of Aragon (1247-1271) married **0.1101110110110111100110001 King Philip III "the Bold" of France** (Capet) (1245-1285), reigned 1270-1285. Philip appears in Dante's Divine Comedy. Dante does not name him directly, but refers to him as "the small-nosed" and "the father of the Pest of France." daughter of

Generation 27

0.110111011011011110011000111 King James I of Aragon, "the Conqueror" (1208-1276) almost a Crusader married
0.11011101101101111001100000 Violant or Yolanda (1212-1253) daughter of **0.110111011011011110011000001 Andrew II of Hungary**
James = son of

Generation 28

0.1101110110110111100110011 Peter II of Aragon (1174-1213) married **0.11011101101101111001100001 Marie of Montpellier** (1182-1213) **See Montpellier**
son of

Generation 29

0.110111011011011110011000111 Alfonso II of Aragon "the Chaste" or "the Troubadour" (1157-1196) reigned 1162 to 1196 married **0.11011101101101111001100110 Sancha of Castile** (1154-1208) daughter of **0.110111011011011110011000101 King Alfonso**

VII of Castile by his second queen
0.1101110110110111100110001100 Richeza of Poland (1140-1185)
the daughter of **0.1101110110110111100110001100 1 Vladislav II,
Duke of Silesia**. [We are also descended from another son of Alfonso
II of Aragon, Alfonso II Count of Provence]
Alfonso = son of
Generation 30
0.1101110110110111100110001111 Ramon Berenguer IV, Count of
Barcelona (1113-1162) Crusader married
0.1101110110110111100110001110 Peronila of Aragon (1135-1174)
son of
Generation 31
0.11011101101101111001100011111 King Ramiro II of Aragon
(1075-1157) reigned 1134-1137 married
0.11011101101101111001100011110 Agnes (d. 1160), daughter of
0.110111011011011110011000111101 William IX, Duke of
Aquitaine
Ramiro = son of
Generation 32
**0.110111011011011110011000111111 King Sancho Ramirez of
Aragon and Navarre** (1042-1094) married
0.110111011011011110011000111110 Felicia of Roucy, daughter of
0.110111011011011110011000111110 Hilduin III, Count of Roucy
Sancho = son of
Generation 33
0.1101110110110111100110001111111 King Ramiro I of Aragon
(1007-1063) married Aug. 22, 1036
**0.1101110110110111100110001111110 Gisberga AKA Emesinde of
Bigorre**, daughter of **0.11011101101101111001100011111101
Bernard Roger of Bigorre** (962-1034) Count of Couserans, son of
0.11011101101101111001100011111011 Roger I of Carcassonne

Ramiro = son of

Generation 34

**0.110111011011011110011000111111111 King Sancho III Garces
"the Great" of Navarre** (d. 1035) mated with **Sancha de Aybar**
son of

Generation 35

**0.110111011011011110011000111111111 King Garcia Sanchez II
"the Tremulous" of Pamploma,** which was later called the
Kingdom of Navarre and the County of Aragon (d. 1004) married
0.110111011011011110011000111111110 Jimena Fernandez,
daughter of **0.110111011011011110011000111111101** the Count of
Cea

Garcia Sanchez = son of

Generation 36

**0.110111011011011110011000111111111 King Sancho II of
Pamplona** (after 935-994) reigned 970-994 married
0.110111011011011110011000111111110 Urraca Fernandez,
daughter of **0.110111011011011110011000111111100 Sancha,**
daughter of **0.110111011011011110011000111111001 Sancho I of
Pamplona**

Sancho = son of

Generation 37

**0.110111011011011110011000111111111 King Garcia Sanchez I
of Pamplona** (later called Navarre) (c. 919-970) married
0.110111011011011110011000111111110 Andregota, daughter of
0.110111011011011110011000111111101 Galindo Aznarez II,
Count of Aragon (d. 922), son of
0.110111011011011110011000111111011 Aznar Galindez II,
Count of Aragon reigned 867-893 married
0.110111011011011110011000111111010 Oneca, daughter of
0.110111011011011110011000111111110101 King Garcia Iniguez

of **Pamplon**a (d. 882), son of
0.1101110110110111100110001111111110101 King Inigo Arista of Pamplona (790-851)
Garcia Sanchez = son of
<u>Generation 38</u>
0.1101110110110111100110001111111111 King Sancho I of Pamplona (860-925) reigned 905 to 926 married
0.1101110110110111100110001111111110 Toda Azarez (885-after 970)
Sancho = son of
<u>Generation 39</u>
0.1101110110110111100110001111111111 King Garcia Jimenez or Garcia II of Pamplona married
0.1101110110110111100110001111111110 Dadildis de Pallars
son of
<u>Generation 40</u>
0.1101110110110111100110001111111111 Jimeno of Pamplona

D'Aubigny 26-30 England
<u>Generation 26</u>
0.11011101101110111010110 Maud d'Aubigny (d. after 1210) married **0.11011101101110111010111 Gilbert Graham,** 3rd Earl of Strathearn (1150-1223) **See Second Graham**
daughter of
<u>Generation 27</u>
0.110111011011110111010101101 William d'Aubigny, 3rd Earl of Arundel (b. before 1193), embarked on crusade of 1218 married
0.110111011011110111010101100 Mabel of Chester
son of

Generation 28
0.110111011011110111011011 William d'Aubigny, 2nd Earl of Arundel (before 1150-1193) married after 1173
0.110111011011110111011010 Matilda de St. Hilary du Harouet son of

Generation 29
0.1101110110111101110110110111 William d'Aubigny, 1st Earl of Arundel (before 1126-1176) married 1138
0.1101110110111101110110110110 Adeliza de Louvain son of

Generation 30
0.11011101101111011101011101111 William d'Aubigny Lord of the Manor of Buckenham, Norfolk (before 1110-1139) married
0.11011101101111011101011101110 Maud le Bigod daughter of
0.11011101101111011101011011101 Roger le Bigod (before 1071-1107) married **0.11011101101111011101011011100 Alice de Tosny,** daughter of **0.110111011011110111010110111001 William de Tosny,** Lord of Belvoir

Second Hungary 26-46 Hungary

Generation 26
0.1101110110111111010010110110 Mary of Hungary (1257-1323) married **0.1101110110111111010010110111 Charles II, "the Lame", King of Naples and Sicily, King of Jerusalem, Prince of Salerno** daughter of

Generation 27
0.11011101101111110100101011001 Stephen V, King of Hungary, Dalmatia, Croatia, Rama, Serbia, Galicia, Lodomeria, Cumania, and Bulgaria, also Duke of Styria (1239-1272) married **0.11011101101111110100101011000 Elizabeth the Cuman,** daughter of **0.11011101101111110100101100001 Köten** (d.1241). Köten was a

Cuman–Kipchak chieftain (*khan*) and military commander active in the mid-13th century. He forged an alliance with the Kievan Rus against the Mongols but was ultimately defeated by them at the Kalka River. After the Mongol victory in 1238, Köten led 40,000 "huts" to Hungary, where he became an ally of the Hungarian king and accepted Catholicism but was nonetheless assassinated by the Hungarian nobility.

Stephen = son of

Generation 28

0.110111011011111010010110011 Bela IV, King of Hungary and Croatia and Duke of Styria (1206-1270) married

0.110111011011111010010110010 Maria Laskarina daughter of

0.110111011011111010010110010 Maria Laskarina daughter of
0.110111011011111010010110010 **Theodore I Laskaris (1175-1221) first emperor of Nicaea,** married

0.110111011011111010010110010 Anna Angelina

son of

Generation 29

0.1101110110111111010010110011 Andrew II the Jerosolimitan, King of Hungary, Crusader (1177-1235) married

0.1101110110111111010010110010 Gertrude of Merania

son of

Generation 30

0.1101110110111111010010110011 Bela III, King of Hungary, AKA Caesar Alexius of the Byzantine Empire (1148-1196 married

0.1101110110111111010010110010 Agnes of Antioch. See Antioch

son of

Generation 31

0.110111011011111010010110011111 Geza II, King of Hungary (1130-1162) married **0.110111011011111010010110011110 Euphrosyne of Kiev**

son of

Generation 32

0.110111011011111101001011001111 King Bela II "the Blind" of Hungary (1110-1141) married

0.110111011011111101001011001111110 Helena of Raska

son of

Generation 33

0.1101110110111111010010110011111111 Almos, Prince of Hungary (1070-1127) married **0.110111011011111101001011001111110 Predslava. See Second Kiev**

son of

Generation 34

0.1101110110111111010010110011111111 Geza I of Hungary (c. 1049-1077) married **0.1101110110111111010010110011111110 Sophia**

son of

Generation 35

0.11011101101111110100101100111111111 Bela I of Hungary (c. 1015-1063) married **0.11011101101111110100101100111111110 Richez or Adelaide of Poland** (1013-1075) daughter of **0.11011101101111110100101100111111101 Mikeszko II Lambert** married **0.11011101101111110100101100111111100 Richeza of Latharingia**

son of

Generation 36

0.1101110110111111010010110011111111111 Vazul (before 997-1031)

son of

Generation 37

0.110111011011111101001011001111111111 Michael of the House of Arpad (after 960-995 or 997)

son of

Generation 38

**0.110111011011111101001011001111111111111 Taksony, Grand
Prince of the Hungarians** (around 931-early 970s)

son of

Generation 39

0.11011101101111110100101100111111111111 Zoltan (880 or 903-
950)

son of

Generation 40

0.1101110110111111010010110011111111111111 Arpad (845-907)
head of the confederation of the Magyar tribes

son of

Generation 41

0.1101110110111111010010110011111111111111 Almos (820-895)
first head of the loose federation of Hungarian tribes

son of

Generation 42

0.110111011011111101001011001111111111111111 Ugyek (second
half of 8th century-first half of 9th century) married
0.110111011011111101001011001111111111111110 Emese daughter
of **0.110111011011111101001011001111111111111101 Duke
Eunedubelianus** By legend, Emese was impregnated by a turul bird
(a bird of prey). The bird appeared to her in a dream and told her that
her descendants would be glorious kings, hence the name of her son
"Almos" which means "the Dreamt One." The turul is a national
symbol of Hungarians.

Ugyek = descendant of

Generation Unknown

Csaba AKA Ernak by legend ancestor of the Arpad dynasty

son of

Generation Unknown
Attila the Hun (406-453)
son of
Generation Unknown
Mundzuk
Baldwin of Constantinople 27-40 Flanders
Generation 27
0.1101110110110111001101110 Margaret II Countess of Flanders
and Hainault (1202-1280) married **0.1101110110110111001101111
Bouchard IV of Avesne**
daughter of
Generation 28
**0.110111011011011110011011101 Emperor Baldwin I of
Constantinople** (1172-1205) also known as Baldwin VI Count of
Hainault and Baldwin IX Count of Flanders, Crusader married
0.110111011011011110011011100 Marie of Champagne (1174-
1204). **See Champagne**
In the Fourth Crusade the Crusaders conquered Constantinople and
made Baldwin emperor.
son of
Generation 29
0.1101110110110111100110111011 Baldwin V Count of Hainault,
AKA Baldwin VIII Count of Flanders and Baldwin I Margrave of
Namur (1150-1195) married **0.1101110110110111100110111010
Margaret** Countess of Flanders
son of
Generation 30
0.11011101101101111001101110111 Baldwin IV Count of Hainault
(1108-1171) married **0.11011101101101111001101110110 Alice of
Namur**
Baldwin = son of

Generation 31

0.1101110110110111100110111011111 Baldwin III Count of Hainault (1088-1120)

Baldwin = son of

Generation 32

0.110111011011011110011011101111 Baldwin II Count of Hainault (1056-1098?) married **0.110111011011011110011011101110 Ida of Leuven**

Baldwin = son of

Generation 33

0.11011101101101111001101110111111 Baldwin VI Count of Flanders (1030-1070) married

0.11011101101101111001101110111110 Richilde, Countess of Mons and Hainault

son of

Generation 34

0.110111011011011110011011101111111 Baldwin V Count of Flanders (d.1067) married **0.110111011011011110011011101111110 Adele Capet** AKA Adela the Holy, daughter of

0.110111011011011110011011101111101 King Robert II "the Pious" of France and **0.110111011011011110011011101111100 Constance of Arles**

Baldwin = son of

Generation 35

0.1101110110110111100110111011111111 Baldwin IV "the Bearded," Count of Flanders_(980-1035) = son of

Generation 36

0.1101110110110111100110111011111111 Arnulf II Count of Flanders (960-988) married

0.1101110110110111100110111011111110 Rozala of Lombardy. See Lombardy

son of

Generation 37

0.1101110110110111100110111011111111111 Baldwin III of Flanders (940-962) married

0.1101110110110111100110111011111111110 Matilda of Burgundy son of

Generation 38

0.11011101101101111001101110111111111111 Arnulf I "the Great," Count of Flanders (890-965)

son of

Generation 39

0.11011101101101111001101110111111111111 Baldwin II Count of Flanders (875-918) married

0.11011101101101111001101110111111111110 Aelfthryth (d. 929) daughter of King Alfred "the Great" of England **See Wessex** son of

Generation 40

0.11011101101101111001101110111111111111 Baldwin I of Flanders (830-879) married

0.11011101101101111001101110111111111110 Judith, daughter of **0.11011101101101111001101110111111111101 Charles the Bald, Holy Roman Emperor**

First Hohenstaufen 27-33 Germany

Generation 27

0.11011101101101111000111001 0 Marie of Hohenstaufen (1201-1235) married **0.11011101101101111000111001 1 Henry II,** Duke of Brabant (1207-1248)

daughter of

Generation 28

0.110111011011011110001110101 Philip King of Germany and Duke of Swabia (1177-1208) married

0.110111011011011110001110100 Irene Angelina

son of

Generation 29

0.11011101101101111000111001011 Frederick I Barbarossa King of Germany and Holy Roman Emperor (1155-1190) married

0.11011101101101111000111001010 Beatrice I, Countess of Burgundy (1143-1184)

Frederick = son of

Generation 30

0.110111011011011110001110010111 Frederick II "the One-Eyed" Duke of Swabia (of the Hohenstaufen dynasty) (1090-1147) married

0.11011101101101111000111001010 Judith of Welf or Guelph (d. 1130) **See Welf or Guelph**

son of

Generation 31

0.110111011011011110001110010111 Frederick I Hohenstaufen, Duke of Swabia (1050-1105) married

0.110111011011011110001110010110 Agnes of Germany (1072-1143), daughter of **0.11011101101101111000111001101 Henry IV, Holy Roman Emperor** married

0.110111011011011110001110010110 Bertha of Savoy (1051-1087)

Frederick = son of

Generation 32

0.110111011011011110001110010111 Frederick von Büren married **0.110111011011011110001110010110 Hildegard von Bar-Moussen**

Portugal 27-33 Portugal, France

Generation 27

0.1101110110111111010110100110 Princess Berengaria of Portugal
married **0.1101110110111111010110100111 King Valdemar II "the
Conqueror" or "the Victorious" of Denmark** (1170-1241) **See
Second Denmark**

daughter of

Generation 28

0.110111011011111101011010100101 King Sancho I of Portugal
(1154-1212) married **0.110111011011111101011010100100 Dulce of
Aragon**, daughter of **0.110111011011111101011010001001 Ramon
Berenguer IV,** Count of Barcelona **See Aragon**

Sancho = son of

Generation 29

**0.110111011011111101011010001011 Afonso I Henriques, King of
Portugal** (1109-1185) married **0.110111011011111101011010001010
Maud of Savoy** (1125-1158)

son of

Generation 30

0.1101110110111111010110100101 11 Henry of Burgundy, Count of
Portugal married **0.110111011011111101011010010110 Teresa of
Leon,** Countess of Portugal daughter of
0.110111011011111101011010010110 King Alfonso VI of León

Henry = son of

Generation 31

0.110111011011111101011010010111 Henry of Burgundy married
0.110111011011111101011010010110 Beatrix of Barcelona

son of

Generation 32

0.110111011011111101011010001011111 Robert I, Duke of Burgundy
married **0.110111011011111101011010010111110 Helie of Semur**

son of

Generation 33

0.110111011011111101011010010111111 Robert II, King of France
(972-1031) married **0.110111011011111101011010010111110**
Constance of Arles, [We are also descended from Robert II through another line]

Thuringia 27-32 Germany

Generation 27

0.110111011011111101011010100100 Agnes of Thuringia (1205-
1246) married **0.110111011011111101011010100101 Albert I,** Duke of
Saxony. **See Second Saxony**

daughter of

Generation 28

0.110111011011111101011010010001 Hermann I, Landgrave of
Thuringia (d. 1217). He figures in Richard Wagner's *Tannhäuser*.

son of

Generation 29

0.110111011011111101011010010011 Louis II, Landgrave of
Thuringia (*the Hard*) married **0.110111011011111101011010010010**
Judith of Hohenstaufen. See Second Hohenstaufen

son of

Generation 30

0.110111011011111101011010100100111 Louis I, Landgrave of
Thuringia married **0.110111011011111101011010100100110 Hedwig of**
Gudensberg

son of

Generation 31

0.110111011011111101011010010011111 Ludwig der Springer
married **0.110111011011111101011010010011110 Adelhel of Stade**,
daughter of **0.110111011011111101011010010011101 Lothair Udo**

II, Margrave of the Nordmark married
0.11011101101111110101101001001100 Oda of Werl
Ludwig = son of
<u>Generation 32</u>
0.11011101101111110101101001001111 Ludwig der Bartige (d.
1056 or 1080) married **0.11011101101111110101101001001110**
Cecilia of Sangerhausen

Montpellier 27-34 France

<u>Generation 27</u>
0.11011101101101111001100001 Marie of Montpellier (1182-1213)
married **0.11011101101101111001100011 Peter II of Aragon** (1174-
1213) **See Aragon**
Marie = daughter of
<u>Generation 28</u>
 0.11011101101101111001100001111 William VIII of Monpellier (d.
1202) married **0.11011101101101111001100110 Eudokia Komnene**
(1150 or 1152-1203) **See Komnene**
son of
<u>Generation 29</u>
 0.11011101101101111001100011111 William VII of Monpellier
married **0.11011101101101111001100011110 Matilda of Burgundy**,
daughter of **0.11011101101101111001100011101 Hugh II,** Duke of
Burgundy, who was son of **0.11011101101101111001100011011**
Eudes I of Burgundy (1058-1103) reigned 1079 to 1103 a Crusader,
who was son of **0.11011101101101111001100011101111 Henry of**
Burgundy (1035-1071), who was son of
0.11011101101101111001100011101111 Robert I Duke of Burgundy
(1011-1076), son of **0.11011101101101111001100011101111 King**
Robert II of France
William = son of

Generation 30

0.110111011011011110011000111111 William VI of Montpellier (d. after 1161) married **0.110111011011011110011000111110 Sibylle**
son of

Generation 31

0.110111011011011110011000111111 William V of Montpellier (1075-1121) Crusader married **0.110111011011011110011000111110 Ermessende**, daughter of **0.110111011011011100110001111101 Peter,** Count of Mauguio
William = son of

Generation 32

 0.110111011011011110011000111111 William IV of Montpellier (d. 1068) married **0.110111011011011110011000111110 Ermengarde** daughter of **0.110111011011011110011000111101 Raymond I** Count of Melgueil
William = son of

Generation 33

0.110111011011011110011000111111 William III Lord of Montpellier married **0.110111011011011110011000111110 Beliardis**
son of

Generation 34

0.110111011011011110011000111111111 William II Lord of Montpellier

Huntingdon 27-33 Scotland
Generation 27

0.110111011011011110111011110 Isabella or Isobel of Huntingdon (1199-1251) married **0.110111011011011110111011111 Robert Bruce, 4th Lord of Annandale. See Bruce or Brus**
daughter of

Generation 28

0.110111011011011110111011111 David of Scotland, 8th Earl of Huntingdon (1144-1219) married **0.110111011011011110111011110 Maud of Chester**, daughter of **0.110111011011011110111101110111101 Hugh de Kevlioc,** 3rd Earl of Chester

David = son of

Generation 29

0.110111011011011110111011111 Henry of Scotland, 3rd Earl of Huntingdon and Northampton and Earl of Northumberland (1114-June 12, 1152) married **0.110111011011011110111011110 Ada de Warenne**, daughter of **0.110111011011011110111011101111101 William de Warenne,** 2nd Earl of Surrey and

0.110111011011011110111011101111100 Elizabeth de Vermandois

Henry = son of

Generation 30

0.110111011011011110111011111111 King David I of Scotland, Prince of the Cumbrians and King of the Scots (Alpin dynasty) reigned 1124-1153 married **0.110111011011011110111011101111110 Maud**, 2nd countess of Huntingdon (1074-1130) daughter of **0.110111011011011110111011111101 Waltheof II,** Earl of Northumbria and Huntingdon (beheaded 1075) married **0.110111011011011110111011111100 Judith of Lens**

David = son of

Generation 31

0.110111011011011110111011111111 Malcolm III King of Scotland (1031-1093) (defeated Macbeth) married **0.110111011011011110111011111110 Saint Margaret** (1045-1093) daughter of **0.110111011011011110111011111101 Prince Edward the Exile** (1016-1057), who was the son of **0.110111011011011110111011111110 11 King Edmund Ironside of**

England (988/993-1016) who unsuccessfully tried to fend off the Danish invasion by King Canut

Malcolm = son of

Generation 32

0.11011101101101111011101111111111 King Duncan I of Scotland (1001-1040) reigned 1034-1040 (murdered by Macbeth)

son of

Generation 33

0.11011101101101111011101111111111 Crinan of Dunkeld AKA Grimus, Mormaer of Atholl, Lay Abbot of Dunkeld (975-1045) killed in battle at Dunkeld

married **0.11011101101101111011101111111110 Bethoc of Scone** daughter of **0.11011101101101111011101111111101 King Malcolm II of Scotland** (954-1034) **See Alpin**

Champagne 28-30 France

Generation 28

0.11011101101101111001101111100 Marie of Champagne (1174-1204) married **0.11011101101101111001101111101 Emperor Baldwin I of Constantinople** (1172-1205) also known as Baldwin VI Count of Hainault and Baldwin IX Count of Flanders. In the Fourth Crusade the Crusaders conquered Constantinople and made Baldwin emperor. **See Baldwin of Constantinople**

Marie = daughter of

Generation 29

0.11011101101101111001101111001 Henry I, Count of Champagne (1127-1181) married **0.11011101101101111001101111000 Marie of France** (1145-1198) poet, patron and probably lover of Chrétien de Troyes author of Arthurian romances

Marie = daughter of

Generation 30

0.110111011011011111001101110011 King Louis VII of France
(1120-1180) and **0.110111011011011111001101110010 Eleanor of
Aquitaine** (1122-1204) **See Aquitaine, Normandy, First Saxony,
Beaufort, Plantagenet, France** [We are also descended from
Eleanor of Aquitaine by her marriage with King Henry II of England
and by way of their son King John]

Komnene 28-33 Byzantine Empire

Generation 28

0.11011101101101111001100110 Eudokia Komnene (1150 or 1152-
1203) married **0.1101110110110111100110001111 William VIII of
Montpellier** (d. 1202) **See Montpelier**
daughter of

Generation 29

 0.110111011011011110011000110 1 Isaac Komnenos (1113-after
1154) married **0.1101110110110111100110001100 Irene
Diplosynadene**
son of

Generation 30

**0.11011101101101111001100011011 Byzantine Emperor John II
Komnenos** (Sept. 13, 1087-April 8, 1143) reigned 1118 to 1143
married **0.11011101101101111001100011010 Piroska of Hungary
AKA Saint Irene** (1088-1134) daughter of
**0.11011101101101111001100011010 1 King Ladislaus I of
Hungary** (1040-1095) **See Hungary**
John = son of

Generation 31

**0.110111011011011110011000110111 Byzantine Emperor Alexios I
Komnenos** (1048-1118) reigned 1081 to 1118 married

0.1101110110110111110011000110110 Irene Doukaina (1066-1123 or 1133) **The Doukas Family**

son of

<u>Generation 32</u>

0.11011101101101111100110001101111 Ioannis Komnenos (1015-1067) married **0.110111011011011111100110001101110 Anna Dalassena** (1025-1102), daughter of

0.11011101101101111001100011011101 Alexius Charon married **0.11011101101101111001100011011100 Adriana Dalassena**

Ioannis = son of

<u>Generation 33</u>

0.11011101101101111001100011011111 Manuel Erotikos Komnenos (955/960-1020), an officer of Emperor Basil II

Denmark 28-36 Denmark, Sweden

<u>Generation 28</u>

0.110111011011111101010011111110 Helen of Denmark (1180-1233) married **0.110111011011111101010011111111 William of Winchester** (1184-1213) AKA William Longsword, AKA William of Luneburg. **See Brunswick**

Helena = daughter of

<u>Generation 29</u>

0.110111011011111101010011111101 King Valdemar I of Denmark (1131-1182) married **0.110111011011111101010011111100 Sophia of Minsk** (1157-1182) daughter of

0.110111011011111101010011111001 Volodar of Minsk married **0.110111011011111101010011111009 Richeza of Poland**. Volodar was son of **0.110111011011111101010011111110011 Gleb Vseslavich of Minsk** (d. 1119) and **0.110111011011111101010011111110010 Princess Yaropolkovna of Minsk.**

Valdemar = son of

Generation 30
0.110111011011111101010011111011 Canute Lavard (1090-1131)
married **0.110111011011111101010011111010 Ingeborg of Kiev. See
Kiev**
son of
Generation 31
**0.11011101101111110101001111110111 Eric I (Evergood) of
Denmark** (1060-1103) married
0.11011101101111110101001111110110 Boedil Thurgotsdatter
son of
Generation 32
0.1101110110111111010100111110111 King Sweyn II Estridsson
married **0.1101110110111111010100111110110 Gunhild
Sveinsdotter**
son of
Generation 33
0.110111011011111101010011111011111 Ulf Thorgilsson married
**0.110111011011111101010011111011110 Estrid Margarete
Svendsdatter**
son of
Generation 34
**0.11011101101111110101001111101111111 Thorgil Styrbjornsson
Sparkling**
Thorgil = son of
Generation 35
0.11011101101111110101001111101111111 Styrbjorn "the Strong"
(d. 985) married **0.11011101101111110101001111101111110 Thyra
Haraldsdotter of Denmark**
son of

Generation 36

0.110111011011111101010011111011111111 King Olof II Bjornsson of Sweden married **0.110111011011111101010011111011111110 Ingeborg Thrandsdotter**

Kiev 29-37 Ukraine

Generation 29

0.11011101101111110101001111010 Ingeborg of Kiev married **0.11011101101111110101001111011 Canute Lavard** (1090-1131) **See Denmark**

daughter of

Generation 30

0.110111011011111101010011111101011 Mstislav I Vladimirovich "the Great" of Kiev (1076-1132) married **0.110111011011111101010011111101000 Christina Ingesdotter,** daughter of **0.11011101101111110101001111101001 King Inge I of Sweden.**

Mstislav = son of

Generation 31

0.110111011011111101010011111101011 Prince Vladimir II Monomakh of Kiev (1053-1125) married **0.110111011011111101010011111101010 Gytha of Wessex,** daughter of **0.110111011011111101010011111010101 King Harold II of England. See Second Wessex**

Vladimir = son of

Generation 32

0.11011101101111110101001111101011 Prince Vsevolod I of Kiev (1030-April 13 1093) married **0.11011101101111110101001111101010 Anastasia of Byzantium** (d. 1067), probably daughter of **0.11011101101111110101001111010101 Emperor Constantine IX**

Monomachos son of **0.110111011011111101010100111110101011 Theodosios Monomachos**

Vselvolod = son of

Generation 33

0.110111011011111101010011111010111 Prince Yaroslav I "the Wise" of Kiev (978-1054) married

0.110111011011111101010100111110101110 Ingegerd Olafsdottir (1001-1050) daughter of **0.110111011011111101010100111110101011101 King Olof Skolkonung, of Sweden** (980-1022). **See Sweden 34** [We are also descended from their daughter Anne of Kiev and from their son Izaslav]

Yaroslav = son of

Generation 34

0.110111011011111101010100111110101111 Prince Saint Vladimir I "the Great" (958-1015) married

0.110111011011111101010100111110101110 Anna Porphyrogenita (March 13, 963-1011) daughter of

0.110111011011111101010100111101011101 Romanos II, Byzantine Emperor (938-March 15 963) **See Macedonian and Amorian** [We are also descended from their daughter Maria Dobroniega]

son of

Generation 35

0.110111011011111101010011111010111111 Prince Sviatoslav I of Kiev (943-March 972)) mated with

0.110111011011111101010011111010111110 Malusha, his housekeeper

son of

Generation 36

0.110111011011111101010011111010111111 Prince Igor of Kiev (ruled 912-945) married **Saint Olga of Kiev** (890-969)

son of

<u>Generation 37</u>
0.11011101101111110101001111101011111111 Rurik (824-879)

Second Poland 29-42 Poland

<u>Generation 29</u>
0.110111011011011110011000110 Sancha of Castile (1154-1208)
married **0.110111011011011110011000111 Alfonso II of Aragon
"the Chaste" or " the Troubadour"** (1157-1196) reigned 1162 to
1196 [We are also descended from Alfonso II Count of Provence,
another son of Alfonso II of Aragon] **See Aragon**
Sancha = daughter of
<u>Generation 30</u>
0.11011101101101111001100011 King Alfonso VII of Castile
(1105-1157) by his second queen,
0.11011101101101111001100011001100 Richeza of Poland (1140-1185)
Richeza = the daughter of
<u>Generation 31</u>
0.110111011011011110011001001 Vladislav II (1105-1159) Duke
of Poland married **0.1101110110110111110011000110010 Agnes of
Babenberg,** daughter of **0.1101110110110111100110001100101
Margrave Leopold II of Austria** and half-sister of King Conrad III
of Germany
Vladislav = son of
<u>Generation 32</u>
0.110111011011011110011000110101 Boleslaw III "Wrymouth"
(Aug. 20, 1086-Oct. 28, 1138) a duke of Lesser Poland, Silesia and
Sandomierz married **0.1101110110110111110011000110010 Zbyslava
of Kiev** (1085/1090-1114) **See Second Kiev**
Boleslaw = son of

Generation 33

0.1101110110110111100110001100110011 Vladislav I Herman (1044-1102) Duke of Poland married **0.1101110110110111100110001100110010 Judith**, daughter of **0.1101110110110111100110001100101 Vratislaus of Bohemia**

Vladislav = son of

Generation 34

0.110111011011011110011000110001100111 Casimir I "the Restorer," Duke of Poland **(1016-1058)** married

0.110111011011011110011000110001100110 Maria Dobroniega (1012-1087), daughter of **0.110111011011011110011000110001100101 Prince Vladimir "the Great" of Kiev. See Kiev**

Casimir = son of

Generation 35

0.1101110110110111100110001100111 Mieszko II, Duke of Poland (990-1034) married **0.1101110110110111100110001100110 Richeza of Lotharingia** (995/1000-1063) **See Lotharingia**

son of

Generation 36

0.1101110110110111100110001100111111 Boleslaw I "the Brave," Duke of Poland (967-1025) married

0.1101110110110111100110001100111110 Emnnilda of Lusalia

son of

Generation 37

0.11011101101101111001100011001111111 Mieszko I (930-992) Poland's first Christian ruler married

0.11011101101101111001100011001111110 Dobrawa of Bohemia

son of

Generation 38

0.110111011011011110011000110011111111 Siemomysl (d. 950/960) Duke of Poland

son of

0.1101110110110111100110001100111111111 Lestek (870/880-930/940) Duke of Poland

son of

0.1101110110110111100110001100111111111 Siemowit, Duke of Poland in the 9th century

son of

0.1101110110110111100110001100111111111 Plast the Wheelwright married
0.1101110110110111100110001100111111110 Rzepicha

son of

0.1101110110110111100110001100111111111 1 Choscisko

Second Hohenstaufen 29-32 Germany

0.11011101101111101011010010010 Judith of Hohenstaufen (1133-1191) married **0.11011101101111101011010010011 Louis II "the Hard,"** Landgrave of Thuringia **See Thuringia**

daughter of

0.1101110110111110101101001001011 Frederick II, Duke of Swabia married **0.1101110110111110101101001001001 Agnes of Saarbrucken. See Saarbrucken**

son of

Generation 31

0.1101110110111111010110100100101011 Frederick I, Duke of Swabia (1050-before 1105) married

0.1101110110111111010110100100101010 Agnes of Germany son of

Generation 32

0.1101110110111111010110100100010111 Frederick von Buren (fl. 1053) married **0.1101110110111111010110100100010110 Hildegard of Egisheim**

First Saxony 29-30 Germany, England

Generation 29

0.1101110110111111010100111110 Matilda, Duchess of Saxony (1156-1189) married **0.1101110110111111010100111111 Henry the Lion,** Duke of Saxony (1129/1131-1195) **See Brunswick** Matilda = daughter of

Generation 30

0.1101110110111111010100111101 King Henry II of England (1133-1189) **See Plantagenet** married 1152

0.1101110110111111010100111100 Eleanor of Aquitaine (1124-1204) **See Normandy, First Saxony, Champagne, Aquitaine, Beaufort, France, Plantagenet**

Normandy 29-40 England, France, Norway

Generation 29

0.1101110110110111001101110011 King Henry II of England (Plantagenet) (1133-1189) married

0.1101110110110111001101110010 Eleanor of Aquitaine (1122-1204) daughter of **0.110111011011011110011011100101 William X, Duke of Aquitaine** married **0.110111011011011110011011100100**

Aenor de Châtellerault. See First Saxony, Champagne, Aquitaine, Beaufort, France, Plantagenet

Henry = son of

<u>Generation 30</u>

0.110111011011011110011011100110 Empress Matilda (1102-1110), briefly (contested) the first female ruler of England in 1141 (widow of Henry V Holy Roman Emperor) married

0.110111011011011110011011100111 Geoffrey V "the Handsome" Count of Anjou and Maine by inheritance and Duke of Normandy by conquest (Plantagenet) (1113-1151) **See Plantagenet**

Matilda = daughter of

<u>Generation 31</u>

0.11011101101101111001101110011101 King Henry I of England "Beauclerc" (1068-1135) married

0.11011101101101111001101110011100 Matilda of Scotland (1080-1118) daughter of Malcolm III King of Scotland, who was the son of Duncan I, King of Scotland, who was murdered by Macbeth

Henry = son of

<u>Generation 32</u>

0.110111011011011110011011100110011 William I "the Conqueror," King of England (1027-1087) married 1053

0.110111011011011110011011100110010 Matilda of Flanders (c. 1031-1083) daughter of **0.1101110110110111100110111001100101 Count Baldwin V of Flanders** married

0.1101110110110111100110111001100100 Adela Capet (1000-1079), daughter of **0.11011101101101111001101110011010011 Robert II "the Pious", King of France, See First Flanders**

William = son of

Generation 33

0.110111011011011110011011100110111 Robert I "The Magnificent" (1000-1035), Duke of Normandy and his mistress **0.110111011011011110011011100110110** Herleve (1003-1050) son of

Generation 34

0.1101110110110111100110111001101111 Richard II "the Good" (963-1027), Duke of Normandy (d. 1026) married **0.1101110110110111100110111001101110 Judith de Rennes** (982-1017) daughter of **0.1101110110110111100110111001101100 Conan I of Brittany** (927-992)

Richard = son of

Generation 35

0.1101110110110111100110111001101111 Richard I "the Fearless" (933-996), Duke of Normandy married **0.1101110110110111100110111001101110 Gunnor** (936-1031) son of

Generation 36

0.110111011011011110011011100110111111 William I "Longsword" (893- 942), Second Duke of Normandy married **0.110111011011011110011011100110111110 Sprota** son of

Generation 37

0.1101110110110111100110111001101111111 Rollo (860-932) founder and first ruler of the Viking principality that became Normandy married **0.1101110110110111100110111001101111119 Poppa** [We are also descended from Rollo's daughter Gerloc AKA Adele who married William III of Aquitaine] son of

Generation 38

0.110111011011011110011011100110111111111 Rognvald Eysteinsson, Earl of More in Western Norway, and founder of the Earldom of Orkney in the Norse Sagas

son of

Generation 39

0.110111011011011110011011100110111111111 Eystein Ivarsson (b. 788) a "petty" king of Norway married 819 **0.110111011011011110011011100110111111110 Ascrida Rognvaldsdatter See Early Norwegian Kings**

Eystein = son of

Generation 40

0.110111011011011110011011100110111111111 Halfdan "the Old" legendary king, ancestor of many lineages.

Jimenez 30-38

0.110111011011011110011110111110 Urraca "the Reckless" Queen of Leon, Castile, and Galicia (1081-1126) the first European queen to reign in her own right married

0.110111011011011110011110111111 Raymond, Count of Galicia (1070-1107)

See Castile

daughter of

Generation 31

0.110111011011011110011110111101 Alfonso VI, King of Leon and Castile (1040-1190) married **0.110111011011011110011110111100 Constance of Burgundy**

son of

Generation 32

0.110111011011011110011110111011 Ferdinand I "the Great" King of Leon (1015-1065) married

0.110111011011011110011110111010 Sancha of Leon

son of

Generation 33

0.110111011011011110011110111101111 Sancho III King of Pamplona and Navarre (992-1035) married

0.110111011011011110011110111101110 Muniadona of Castile

son of

Generation 34

0.1101110110110111100111101111101111 Garcia Sanches II King of Pamplona and Count of Aragon (d. 1000) married

0.1101110110110111100111101111101100 Jimena Fernandez

son of

Generation 35

0.11011101101101111001111011111011111 Sancho II King of Pamplona and Count of Aragon (938-994) married

0.11011101101101111001111011111011110 Urraca Fernandez

son of

Generation 36

0.110111011011011110011110111101111111 Garcia Sanchez II, King of Pamplona (919-970) married

0.110111011011011110011110111101111110 Andrego Galindez

son of

Generation 37

0.1101110110110111100111101111011111111 Sancho I, king of Pamplona (860-925) married

0.1101110110110111100111101111011111110 Toda Azarnez

son of

Generation 38

0.110111011011011110011110111101111111 Garcia Jimenez, king of part of Pamplona married

0.110111011011011110011110111101111110 Dadildis de Pallars

Hungary 30-43 Hungary *Attila the Hun*

Generation 30

0.1101110110110111001100011010 Piroska of Hungary AKA Saint Irene (1088-1134) married

0.1101110110110111001100011011 Byzantine Emperor John II Komnenos (1087-1143) **See Komnene**

daughter of

Generation 31

0.110111011011011110011000110101 King Ladislaus I of Hungary (1040-1095) married **0.110111011011011110011000110100 Adelaide of Rheinfelden**

Ladislaus = son of

Generation 32

0.110111011011011110011000110101 King Bela I "the Champion" of Hungary (1015-1063) married **0.110111011011011110011000110101 0 Richeza or Adelaide of Poland**

son of

Generation 33

0.110111011011011110011000110101 11 Vazul AKA Vaszoly (before 997-1031 or 1032)

son of

Generation 34

0.110111011011011110011000110101 01111 Michael (after 960-997), member of the House of Arpad

son of

Generation 35

0.110111011011011110011000110101111 Taksony, Grand Prince of the Hungarians (931-early 970s)

son of

Generation 36

0.1101110110110111100110001101011111 Zoltan AKA Zolta, Grand Prince of the Hungarians (903-950) married

0.1101110110110111100110001101011110 daughter of

0.1101110110110111100110001101011111101 Menumorut

son of

Generation 37

0.11011101101101111001100011010111111 Arpad, founder of the Country of Hungary and founder of the Arpad dynasty (845-907)

son of

Generation 38

0.110111011011011110011000110101111111 Almos, first head of the confederation of Hungarian tribes (820-895)

son of

Generation 39

0.110111011011011110011000110101111111 Ugyek AKA Elod (second half of the 8th century-first half of the 9th century), a Scythian, married **0.1101110110110111100110001101011111110 Emese**

Ugyek = descendant of

Generation Unknown

Csaba AKA Ernak by legend ancestor of the Arpad dynasty

son of

Generation Unknown

Attila the Hun (406-463)

son of

Generation Unknown
Mundzuk

Saarbrucken 30-32 Germany

Generation 30
0.11011101101111110101101001001001 Agnes of Saarbrucken
married 1132 **0.11011101101111110101101001001001 Frederick II,**
Duke of Swabia. See Second Hohenstaufen
daughter of
Generation 31
0.11011101101111110101101001001001 Frederick I, Count of
Saarbrucken (d. 1135) married
0.11011101101111110101101001001000 Gisela of Lorraine Family
of Lorraine
son of
Generation 32
0.11011101101111110101101001001011 Siegbert I, Count of
Saarbrucken

Supplinburg 30-33 Germany

Generation 30
0.11011101101111110101001111110 Gertrude of Supplinburg
married **0.11011101101111110101001111111 Henry X,** Duke of
Bavaria (1108-1139) **See Brunswick**
daughter of
Generation 31
 0.11011101101111110101001111101 Lothair III, Holy Roman
Emperor (1075-1137) married
0.11011101101111110101001111100 Richenza of Northeim
son of

Generation 32

0.110111011101111110101001111111011 Gebhard of Supplinburg
(d. 1075) Saxon count in the Eastphalian Harzgau and
Nordthuringgau married **0.110111011101111110101001111111010**
Hedwig of Formbach
son of
Generation 33

0.110111011101111110101001111110111 Bernhard, Count of
Supplinburg (d. 1069) married
0.110111011101111110101001111110110 Ida of Querfurt, niece of
Saint Bruno of Querfurt

Aquitaine 30-39 France

<u>**Generation 30**</u>
0.110111011011011110011011100010 Eleanor of Aquitaine (1122-
1204) married **0.110111011011011110011011100011 King Louis VII**
of France (1120-1180) **See Normandy, First Saxony 29**, and
Champagne 28
Eleanor = daughter of
Generation 31
0.110111011011011110011011100101 William X, Duke of Aquitaine
(1099-1137) married **0.110111011011011110011011100100 Aenor de**
Châtellerault (1103-1130) daughter of
0.110111011011011110011011001001 Viscount Aimery I of
Chattellerault married **0.110111011011011110011011001000**
Dangereuse de L'Isle Bouchard (d. 1151)
William = son of
Generation 32
0.110111011011011110011011001011 William IX "the
Troubador," Duke of Aquitaine and Gascony and Count of Poitu

(1071-1126) one of the leaders of the Crusade of 1101 married **0.11011101101101111001101110010 Philippa of Toulouse** Willliam = son of
Generation 33
0.110111011011011110011011100101111 William VIII of Aquitaine (1025-1086) married **0.110111011011011110011011100101110 Hildegarde of Burgundy**, daughter of **0.11011101101101111001101110010101 Robert I (Capet) of Burgundy**, son of **0.1101110110110111100110111001011011 King Robert II of France** [We are also descended from William by other lines]
William = son of
Generation 34
0.1101110110110111100110111001011111 William V of Aquitaine (969-1030) married **0.1101110110110111100110111001011110 Agnes of Burgundy**, daughter of **0.11011101101101111001101110010111011 Otto-William,** Duke of Burgundy, son of **0.1101110110110111100110111001011011 Adalbert, King of Italy** married **0.110111011011011110011011100101110 Gerberga of Macon**
William = son of
Generation 35
0.11011101101101111001101110010111 William IV of Aquitaine (937-994) married **0.1101110110110111100110111001011110 Emma**, daughter of **0.11011101101101111001101110010111101 Theobald I of Blois**
William = son of
Generation 36
0.110111011011011110011011100101111 William III "the Towhead" of Aquitaine (915-963) married **0.110111011011011110011011100101110** Gerloc AKA Adele,

daughter of **0.1101110110110111100110111100101111101 Rollo of Normandy** [We are also descended from Rollo's son William I Longsword]

William = son of

Generation 37

0.1101110110110111100110111100101111111 Ebalus Manzer, Count of Poitu and Duke of Aquitaine (870-935) married

0.1101110110110111100110111100101111110 Emiliene

son of

Generation 38

11011110011011100101111111111 Rainulf II of Aquitaine (850-890)

son of

Generation 39

110111100110111001011111111111 Rainulf I, Count of Poitiers and Duke of Aquitaine (820-866) married

11011110011011100101111111110 Bilichild of Maine. Ranulf I, is the 32nd Great-Grandfather of Queen Elizabeth II

Welf or Guelph 30-37 Germany

Generation 30

0.110111011011011110001110010101 Judith of Welf or Guelph (d. 1131) married **0.110111011011011110001110010101 Frederick II " the One-Eyed,** Duke of Swabia (1090-1147) **See First Hohenstaufen**

daughter of

Generation 31

0.110111011011011110001110010101 Henry IX "the Black," Duke of Bavaria from the House of Welf or Guelph (d. 1126) married

0.110111011011011110001110010100 Wilfhild, daughter of

0.11011101101101111000111001001 Magnus, Duke of Saxony,

son of **0.110111011011011110001110010100111 Ordulf** and
0.110111011011011110001110010100110 Wulfhild of Norway
Henry = son of
<u>Generation 32</u>
0.11011101101101111000111001011001011 Welf I, Duke of Bavaria
("Welf IV" in Welf genealogy) (d. 1101) first member of the Welf
branch of the **House of Este**; joined the Crusade of 1101 and died
while returning home married
0.11011101101101111000111001011001010 Judith of Flanders, daughter
of **0.110111011011011110001110010110010101 Baldwin IV,** Count of
Flanders
Welf = son of
<u>Generation 33</u>
0.11011101101101111000111001011001011 Alberto Azzo II of Este
(997-1097), Margrave of Milan and Liguria, Count of Gavello and
padua, Rovigo, Unigiana, Monselice, and Montagnana; around 1073
he made a castle at Este his residence from which the House of Este
takes its name married around 1035
0.11011101101101111000111001011001010 Chuniza of Altdorf,
daughter of **0.110111011011011110001110010101101 Welf II** Count
of Altdof married **0.110111011011011110001110010101100 Imiza of
Luxembourg. See Second Welf or Guelf**
[We are also descended from Alberto Azzo by way of his son Fulco]
Alberto = son of
Generation 34
**0.110111011011011110001110010101111 Alberto Azzo I, Margrave
of Milan** (d. 1029)
son of
<u>Generation 35</u>
0.110111011011011110001110010101111 Oberto II married
0.110111011011011110001110010101110 Railend

son of
Generation 36
0.110111011011011110001110010101111111 Oberto I, Count Palatine
of Italy and Count of Milan (d. 975), founder of the Obertenghi
family
son of
Generation 37
**0.110111011011011110001110010101111111 Margrave Adalbert of
Mainz**, Frankish noble who settled in Lombardy

Antioch 30-35 Antioch, France

Generation 30
0.11011101101111110100101011001110 Agnes of Antioch married
**0.11011101101111110100101011001111 Bela III, King of Hungary,
AKA Caesar Alexius of the Byzantine Empire** (1148-1196) **See
Second Hungary**
Agnes = daughter of
Generation 31
0.11011101101111110100101100011100 Constance of Antioch (1127-
1163) married **0.11011101101111110100101100011101 Raynald of
Chatillon, Prince of Antioch,** Crusader
Constance = daughter of
Generation 32
0.11011101101111110100101100111001 Bohemond II, Prince of
Taranto and of Antioch, Crusader (1108-1130) married
0.11011101101111110100101100111000 Alice of Jerusalem (1110-
after 1151). **See Rethel 32**
Bohemond = son of
Generation 33
0.11011101101111110100101100111011 Bohemond I of Antioch
(1054-1111) Crusader married

0.110111011011111101001011001110010 Constance of France (1078-1125)

son of

Generation 34

0.110111011011111101001011001110011 Robert Guiscard de Hauteville (1015-1095) count of Apulia and Calabria married **0.110111011011111101001011001110110 Alberada of Buonalbergo**. Robert conquered southern Italy and Sicily.

son of

Generation 35

0.110111011011111101001011001110011 Tancred of Hauteville (980-1019) married **0.110111011011111101001011001110110 Fressenda**

Doukas 31-34 Byzantine Empire

Generation 31

0.110111011011011110011000110110 Irene Doukaina (1066-1123 or 1133) married **0.110111011011011110011000110111 Byzantine Emperor Alexios I Komnenos** (1048-1118) **See Komnene**

daughter of

Generation 32

0.110111011011011110011000110110 Andronikos Doukas (d. Oct. 14, 1077) married **0.110111011011011110011000110110 Maria of Bulgaria, See Bulgaria**

son of

Generation 33

0.110111011011011110011000110110 John Doukas, Caesar (d. 1088) married **0.110111011011011110011000110110 Eirene Pegonitissa**

son of

Generation 34
0.110111011011011011001100011011011 Andronikos Doukas, a Paphlagonian nobleman who may have served as governor of the theme of Moesia

First Lorraine 31-34 France

Generation 31
0.110111011011111101011010010001000 Gisela of Lorraine married **0.110111011011111101011010010001001 Frederick I,** Count of Saarbrucken (d. 1135). **See Saarbrucken**
daughter of
Generation 32
0.110111011011111101011010010010001 Theodoric II AKA Thierry II, Duke of Lorraine (d. 1115) married **0.110111011011111101011010010010000 Gertrude of Flanders**
son of
Generation 33
0.110111011011111101011010010010011 Gerhard, Duke of Lorraine (1030-1070) and **0.110111011011111101011010010010010 Hedwig de Namur,** daughter of
0.110111011011111101011010010010101 Albert I, Count of Namur and **0.110111011011111101011010010010100 Ermengarde,** daughter of
0.110111011011111101011010010010001001 Charles, Duke of Lower Lorraine. **See Second Lorraine**
Gerard = son of
Generation 34
0.110111011011111101011010010010111 Gerard de Bouzonville, Count of Metz married **0.110111011011111101011010010010110 Gisela,** possibly a daughter of

463

0.110111011011111101011010010010001101 Thierry I, Duke of Upper Lorraine

First Flanders 31-41 Flanders
Generation 31
0.1101110110110111001101110011010 Matilda of Flanders (1031-1083) married 1053 **0.1101110110110111001101110011011 William "the Conqueror," King of England** (1027-1087) **See Normandy**
daughter of
Generation 32
0.110111011011011110011011100110101 Baldwin V Count of Flanders (d. 1067) married **0.110111011011011110011011100110100 Adela Capet** (1000-1079), daughter of
0.110111011011011110011011001101001 Robert II "The Pious", King of France
Baldwin = son of
Generation 33
0.110111011011011110011011001101011 Baldwin IV "the Bearded," Count of Flanders (980-1035) married
0.110111011011011110011011001101010 Ogive of Luxembourg
son of
Generation 34
0.11011101101101111001101110011010111 Arnulf II, Count of Flanders (961-988) married
0.11011101101101111001101110011010110 Rozala of Lombardy
son of
Generation 35
0.11011101101101111001101110011010101111 Baldwin III of Flanders (940-962) married
0.11011101101101111001101110011010101110 Matilda of Burgundy

Baldwin = son of

Generation 36

0.1101110110110111100110111001101011111 Arnulf I "the Great,"
Count of Flanders (890-965)

son of

Generation 37

0.1101110110110111100110111001101011111 Baldwin II, Count of
Flanders (875-918) married

0.1101110110110111100110111001101011110 Aelfthryth (d. 929),
daughter of **0.110111011011011110011011100110101111101 King
Alfred "the Great" of England. See Alfred**

Baldwin = son of

Generation 38

**0.1101110110110111100110111001101011111 Baldwin I "Iron
Arm" of Flanders** (830-879) married

0.1101110110110111100110111001101011110 Judith of Flanders
(844-870) **See Holy Roman Emperors**

Baldwin = son of

Generation 39

0.1101110110110111100110111001101011111111 Odoacer

son of

Generation 40

**0.11011101101101111001101110011010111111111 Enguerrand delle
Flandre**

son of

Generation 41

0.11011101101101111001101110011010111111111 Liederik

Dublin 31-35 Ireland

<u>Generation 31</u>

0.1101110110110111100011011111110 **Raignaillt of Dublin** married **0.110111011011011110001**1011111111 **Cynan ab Iago** (1014-1063)

See Wake

daughter of

<u>Generation 32</u>

0.1101110110110111100011011111111101 Olaf of Dublin

Olaf = son of

<u>Generation 33</u>

0.110111011011011110001101111111011 King Sigtrygg Silkbeard, King of Dublin married **0.110111011011011110001101111111010 Sláine,** daughter of **0.110111011011011110001101111110101 Brian Boru, High King of Ireland,** Founder of the O'Brien Dynasty

Sigtrygg = son of

<u>Generation 34</u>

0.1101110110110111100011011111110111 **Olaf or Amlaib Cuaran, King of York and Dublin** married **0.110111011011011110001**1011111110110 **Gormflaith,** (960-1030) daughter of **0.110111011011011110001**10111111101101 **Murchad mac Finn, King of Leinster.** She later married Brian Boru, Emperor of the Irish.

Olaf or Amlaib = son of

<u>Generation 35</u>

0.1101110110110111100011011111110111 **1 Sitriuc Caech or Sigtrygg** (d. 927)

Rouen 32-37 France

<u>Generation 32</u>

0.110111011011011111100111111111100 Agnes d'Evreux (b. 1030) married **0.110111011011011111100111111111101 Simon I de Monfort** (1025-1087) **See Beaufort**

daughter of

<u>Generation 33</u>

0.11011101101101111001111111111001 Richard, Count of Evreux (1015-1067) married **0.11011101101101111001111111111000 Godechildis**

son of

<u>Generation 34</u>

0.1101110110110111100111111111110011 Robert II, Archbishop of Rouen and Count of Evreux (989-1037) married **0.1101110110110111100111111111110010 Harleve of Rouen**

son of

<u>Generation 35</u>

0.110111011011011110011111111100111 Richard I Duke of Normandy (942-996) married **0.110111011011011110011111111100110 Gunnor**

son of

<u>Generation 36</u>

0.11011101101101111001111111111001111 William Longsword, Count of Rouen (893-942) married **0.11011101101101111001111111111001110 Sprota**

son of

<u>Generation 37</u>

0.110111011011011110011111111110011111 Rollo, Count of Rouen, first ruler of Normandy, a Viking (911-933) married **0.110111011011011110011111111110011110 Poppa of Bayeux**

Monfort 32-35 France

0.1101110110110111100111111111101 Simon I de Monfort (1025-1087) married (2) **0.1101110110110111100111111111100 Agnes d'Evreux** (b. 1030) **See Rouen**

son of

Generation 33

0.1101110110110111100111111111011 Amaury I de Monfort (d. 1053) married **0.1101110110110111100111111111010 Bertrade**

son of

Generation 34

0.1101110110110111100111111111110111 Guillaume de Montfort of Hainaut (before 990-before 1053)

son of

Generation 35

0.1101110110110111100111111111101111 Amaury, Count of Valenciennes (d. after 973)

Bulgaria 32-36 Bulgaria

Generation 32

0.1101110110110111100110001101100 Maria of Bulgaria married **0.1101110110110111100110001101101 Andronikos Doukas** (d. 1077) **See Byzantine**

daughter of

Generation 33

0.1101110110110111100110001101001 Troian of Bulgaria,

son of

Generation 34

0.1101110110110111100110001101100011 Emperor Ivan Vladislav of Bulgaria reigned 1015-1018

son of

Generation 35

0.1101110110110111100110001101100111 Aron of Bulgaria
son of
Generation 36
0.1101110110110111100110001101100111 Comita Nikola, Duke of
Sofia married **0.110111011011011110011000110011001110 Ripsimia
of Armenia** (911-969) **See Armenia**

Second Wessex 32-54 England

Generation 32

0.11011101101111110101001111101010 Gytha of Wessex, married
**0.11011101101111110101001111110101 Prince Vladimir Monomakh
of Kiev** (1053-1125) **See Ukraine**
Gytha = daughter of
Generation 33
**0.11011101101111110101001111010101 King Harold II of
England [Harold Godwinson]** (1022-1066) mated with
0.11011101101111110101001111010100 Edith Swanneck (1025-
1086)
son of
Generation 34
0.110111011011111101010011111101011 Godwin, Earl of Wessex
(990-1053) married **0.110111011011111101010011111101010
Gytha Thorkelsdottir**, daughter of
0.110111011011111101010011111010101 Throgil Sprakling
Godwin = son of
Generation 35
0.110111011011111101010011111101111 Wulnoth Cild, Thegn of
Sussex (983-1015)
son of

Generation 36

0.110111011011111101010011111010101111 Aethelmaer

son of

Generation 37

0.11011101101111110101001111101011111 Aethelward "the Historian"

Aethelward = son of

Generation 38

0.1101110110111111010100111101010111111 Eadric of Washington, Wessex

Eadric = son of

Generation 39

0.1101110110111111010100111101010111111 Aethelfrith (900-927), Ealdorman of Wessex AKA Aethelfrith of Mercia

son of

Generation 40

 0.110111011011111101010011111010101111111 Aethelhelm (859-893), Ealdorman of Wiltshire married

0.1101110110111111010100111110101011111110 Aethelgyth of Mercia

Aethelhelm = son of

Generation 41

 0.1101110110111111010100111110101011111111 Ethelred II (837-871), King of Wessex, brother of Alfred "the Great"

Ethelred = son of

Generation 42

0.11011101101111110101001111101010111111111 Ethelwulf of Wessex (AKA Aethelwulf) (800-858) King of Wessex (839-856) married **0.1101110110111111010100111110101011111110 Osburga** (810-855) [We are also descended from this pair in another way as well.]

son of

Generation 43

0.110111011011111101010011111010101111111111 Egbert, King of Wessex (770-839) married

0.110111011011111101010011111010101111111110 Redburga

Egbert = son of

Generation 44

0.110111011011111101010011111010101111111111 Ealhmund, King of Kent

Ealhmund = son of

Generation 45

0.110111011011111101010011111010101111111111 Eafa (730) married **0.110111011011111101010011111010101111111110 Kentish princess**

Eafa = son of

Generation 46

0.110111011011111101010011111010101111111111 Eoppa (b. 706)

Eoppa = son of

Generation 47

0.110111011011111101010011111010101111111111 Ingild of Wessex (672-718)

Ingild = son of

Generation 48

0.110111011011111101010011111010101111111111 Coenred (b. 640)

Coenred = son of

Generation 49

0.110111011011111101010011111010101111111111 Ceolwald

Generation 50

Ceolwald = son of

0.110111011011111101010011111010101111111111111111 Cutha
Cathwulf (b. 592)
Cutha = son of
<u>Generation 51</u>
0.110111011011111101010011111010101111111111111111
Cuthwine (d. 592)
Cuthwine = son of
<u>Generation 52</u>
0.110111011011111101010011111010101111111111111111
Ceawlin, King of Wessex (c. 535-592), reigned 560-592
Ceawlin = son of
Generation 53
0.110111011011111101010011111010101111111111111111
Cynric, King of Wessex (c. 495-560), reigned 534-560
Cynric = son of
Generation 54
0.110111011011111101010011111010101111111111111111
Cerdic, King of Wessex reigned 519-534

Rethel 32-37

<u>Generation 32</u>
 0.11011101101111110100101100111000 Alice of Jerusalem (1110-
after 1151) married **0.11011101101111110100101100111001**
Bohemond II, Prince of Taranto and of Antioch, Crusader (1108-
1130) See Antioch 30
daughter of
<u>Generation 33</u>
 0.11011101101111110100101100111 0001 Baldwin II, Count of
Edessa and King of Jerusalem (1075-1131) Crusader married
0.11011101101111110100101100111 0000 Morphia of Melitene (d.
1127). **See Second Armenia 33**

son of
Generation 34
 0.110111011011111101001011001110011 Hugh I, Count of Rethel
(1040-1118) married **0.1101110110111111010010110011100010**
Melisende of Crecy
son of
Generation 35
 0.110111011011111101001011001110001 11 Manasses III, Count of
Rethel (1022-1065 or 1080) married
0.110111011011111101001011001110001 10 Judith of Lorena
son of
Generation 36
0.110111011011111101001011001110001111 Manasses II, Count of
Rethel married **0.110111011011111101001011001110001110 Dada**
son of
Generation 37
0.110111011011111101001011001110001 1111 Manasses of Omont
married **0.110111011011111101001011001110001 1110 Castricia**

Second Welf or Guelf 33-39 Germany

Generation 33
0.110111011011101111000111001010110 Kunigunde or Chuniza of
Altdorf, married **0.110111011011101111000111001010111 Alberto**
Azzo II of Este (997-1097), Margrave of Milan and Liguria, Count
of Gavello and padua, Rovigo, Unigiana, Monselice, and
Montagnana **See Estes**
daughter of
Generation 34
0.110111011011011110001110010101101 Welf II Count of Altdof
(960-1030) Swabian count married
0.110111011011011110001110010101100 Imiza of Luxembourg

(990/1000-1056) daughter of

**0.110111011011011110001110010101011001 Frederick of
Luxembourg** (965-1019) married

0.110111011011011110001110010101011000 Ermentrude of Gleiberg

Welf II = son of

Generation 35

0.110111011011011110001110010101011011 Rudolf II, Count of
Altdorf (d. 990) married **0.110111011011011110001110010101011010
Ita of Ohningen** daughter of

0.110111011011011110001110010101 10101 Conrad I, Duke of
Swabia

son of

Generation 36

0.110111011011011110001110010101 10111 Rudolf I, Count of
Altdorf married **0.110111011011011110001110010101 10110
Siburgis**

son of

Generation 37

0.110111011011011110001110010101101111 Henry Count of the
Wolden Wagon married **0.110111011011011110001110010101101110
Atha von Hohenwart**

son of

Generation 38

son of

0.110111011011011110001110010101011111 Eticho, Count of
Ammergau married **0.110111011011011110001110010101011110
Egila**

Generation 39

son of

0.110111011011011110001110010101101111 11 Welf I Swabian
nobleman (d. before 876)

Second Lorraine 33-39 Belgium, France

<u>Generation 33</u>

0.110111011011111101011010100100100010 Hedwig de Namur married **0.110111011011111101011010100100100011 Gerhard,** Duke of Lorraine (c. 1030-April 14, 1070) **See First Lorraine**
daughter of

<u>Generation 34</u>

0.11011101101111110101101001001000100 Ermengarde married **0.11011101101111110101101001001000101 Albert I,** Count of Ermengarde = daughter of

<u>Generation 35</u>

0.1101110110111111010110100100100010001011 Charles, Duke of Lower Lorraine (953-993)
son of

<u>Generation 36</u>

0.110111011011111101011010010010010001011 Louis IV, King of France (920-954) married
0.110111011011111101011010010010010001010 Gerberga of Saxony (913-984) **See Third Saxony**
son of

<u>Generation 37</u>

0.110111011011111101011010010010001011111 Charles III "the Simple" or "the Straightforward," King of France (879-929) and **0.110111011011111101011010010010001011110 Eadgifu of England**, daughter of
0.1101110110111111010110100100100010111101 King Edward "the Elder." See Third Wessex
Charles = son of

<u>Generation 38</u>

0.1101110110111111010110100100100010111111 Louis "the Stammerer" (846-879) married

0.110111011101111110101101001001000101110 Adelaide of Paris
See Toulouse
son of
Generation 39
0.110111011101111110101101001001000101111 Charles "the
Bald," Holy Roman Emperor (823-877) married
0.110111011101111110101101001001000101110 Ermentrude of
Orleans (823-869) [We are descended from Charles the Bald by
another line as well]

Alpin 33-58 Scotland

Generation 33
0.110111011011011101110111111110 Bethoc of Scone married
0.110111011011011101110111111111 Crinan of Dunkeld AKA
Grimus, Mormaer of Atholl, Lay Abbot of Dunkeld (975-1045)
killed in battle at Dunkeld **See Huntingdon**
Bethoc = daughter of
Generation 34
0.110111011011011101110111111101 Malcolm II, King of
Scotland (954-1034)
son of
Generation 35
0.110111011011011101110111111011 Kenneth II, King of
Scotland (954-995)
son of
Generation 36
0.110111011011011101110111110111 Malcolm I, King of
Scotland (900-954)
Malcolm = son of

Generation 37

0.11011101101101111011101111111111101111 Donald II, King of Scotland (d. 900)

Donald = son of

Generation 38

0.110111011011011110111011101111111111011111 Constantine I AKA Causantin mac Cinaeda, King of the Picts (d. 877)

son of

Generation 39

0.1101110110110111101110111011111111110111111 Kenneth I mac Alpin, King of Scotland (810-858) conqueror of the Picts, first king of the Scots

son of

Generation 40

0.11011101101101111011101110111111111101111111 Alpín mac Echdach

Alpin = son of

Generation 41

0.110111011011011110111011101111111111011111111 ?Eochaid mac Áeda Find

son of

Generation 42

0.1101110110110111101110111011111111110111111111 Áed Find (Áed the White) AKA Áed mac Echdach (before 736–778), King of Dál Riata (in western Scotland).

son of

Generation 43

0.11011101101101111011101110111111111101111111111 Eochaid mac Echdach, King of Dál Riata (in western Scotland) reigned 726-733.

son of

Generation 44

0.110111011011011110111011111111101111111111 Eochaid mac Domangairt, King of Dál Riatad (in western Scotland)

son of

Generation 45

0.110111011011011110111011111111011111111111 Domangart mac Domnaill, King of Dál Riata (in western Scotland) (d. 673)

son of

Generation 46

0.110111011011011110111011111111101111111111111 Domnall Brecc AKA Donald "the Freckled," King of Dál Riata (in western Scotland) (d. 642)

son of

Generation 47

0.1101110110110111101110111111111011111111111111 Eochaid Buide, King of Dál Riata, (in western Scotland), reigned around 608-629. ("Buide" refers to the colour yellow, as in the colour of his hair.)

son of

Generation 48

0.11011101101101111011101111111110111111111111111 Áedán mac Gabráin, King of Dál Riata (in western Scotland) from c. 574 onwards.

son of

Generation 49

0.110111011011011110111011111111101111111111111111 Gabrán mac Domangairt, King of Dál Riata (in western Scotland) in the middle of the 6th century.

son of

Generation 50

0.1101110110110111101110111111111011111111111111111 ? Dungal

son of

Generation 51

0.110111011011011101110111111111101111111111111111 Fergus Mór mac Eirc, legendary founder of Scotland

son of

Generation 52

0.110111011011011101110111111111101111111111111111 Eirc

son of

Generation 53

0.110111011011011101110111111111101111111111111111 Eochaid Muinremuir

son of

Generation 54

0.110111011011011101110111111111101111111111111111 Oengusa Fir

son of

Generation 55

0.110111011011011101110111111111101111111111111111 Feideilmid

son of

Generation 56

0.110111011011011101110111111111101111111111111111 Oengusa

son of

Generation 57

0.110111011011011101110111111111101111111111111111 Feideilmid

son of

Generation 58

0.110111011011011101110111111111101111111111111111 Cormaicc, Wikipedia lists the generations from Erc to Cormaicc in the Fergus Mor mac Eirc article and says this comes from a Middle

Irish genealogy of the kings of Alba [The Book of Lismore], which lists an additional 46 generations

Second Armenia 33-34

<u>Generation 33</u>
0.110111011011111101001011001110000 Morphia of Melitene (died 1127) married
0.110111011011111101001011001110001 Baldwin II, Count of Edessa and King of Jerusalem (1075-1131) Crusader
daughter of
<u>Generation 34</u>
0.110111011011111101001011001100001 Gabriel of Melitene, Armenian general (died 1102)

Macedonian and Amorian 34-40 Byzantine Empire

<u>Generation 34</u>
0.110111011011111101010011110101110 Anna Porphyrogenita (963-1011) married **0.110111011011111101010011110101111 Saint Vladimir I "the Great," Prince of Kiev** (958-1015) **See Kiev**
daughter of
<u>Generation 35</u>
0.110111011011111101010011110101101 Romanos II, Byzantine Emperor, Macedonian Dynasty (938-963) married
0.110111011011111101010011110101100 Theophano
son of
<u>Generation 36</u>
0.110111011011111101010011111010111011 Constantine VII, Byzantine Emperor, Macedonian Dynasty (913-959) married
0.110111011011111101010011111010111010 Helena Lekapene
son of

Generation 37

0.11011101101111110101001111101011110111 Leo VI the Wise, Byzantine Emperor, Macedonian Dynasty (886-912) married **0.11011101101111110101001111101011110110 Zoe Karbonopsina** officially son of

Generation 38

Basil I, Byzantine Emperor, Macedonian Dynasty (811-886) reputedly son of **0.11011101101111110101001111101011101111 Michael III "the Drunkard," Byzantine Emperor, Amorian Dynasty** (840-867) Michael = son of

Generation 39

0.11011101101111110101001111101011011111 Theophilos, Byzantine Emperor, Amorian Dynasty (812-842) married **0.11011101101111110101001111101011011110 Theodora** son of

Generation 40

0.110111011011111101010011111010111011111 Michael II "the Stammerer," Byzantine Emperor, Amorian Dynasty (770-829) married **0.110111011011111101010011111010111011110 Thekla.** Michael was born in Amorium, Phyrgia. His family belonged to the Judeo-Christian sect of Athinganoi whose members had adopted the Jewish faith and rituals.

First Sweden 34-36 Sweden

Generation 34

0.11011101101111110101001111101011110 Ingegerd Olafsdottir married **0.1101110110111111010100111110101110 Yaroslav I the Wise** (978-1054) **See Kiev**
Ingegerd Olfsdatter = daughter of

Generation 35

0.11011101101111110101001111101011101 King Olof Skotkonung of Sweden (980-1022) married

0.11011101101111110101001111101011100 Estrid or Astrid of the Obotrites (979-1035)

son of

Generation 36

0.11011101101111110101001111010111011 Eric "the Victorious," King of Sweden (945-995) married

0.11011101101111110101001111010111010 Sigrid the Haughty

Lotharingia 35-40 Germany

Generation 35

0.11011101101101111001100011001110 Richeza of Lotharingia (995/1000-1063) married **0.11011101101101111001100011001111 Mieszko II Lambert, King of Poland** (990-1034) **See Second Poland**

Richeza = daughter of

Generation 36

0.11011101101101111001100011001101 Ezzo of Lotharingia (c. 955-March 21, 1034) Count Palatine married

0.11011101101101111001100011001100 Mathilda of Germany (979-1025) **See Second Holy Roman Emperors**

son of

Generation 37

0.11011101101101111001100011001111011 Herman I "the Slender" (d. 996) Count Palatine of Lotharingia married

0.11011101101101111001100011001111010 Heylwig of Dillingen

son of

Generation 38

0.110111011011011110011000110011101 Erenfried II (d. 970), a Lotharingian nobleman married

0.110111011011011110011000110011101 Richwara of Zulpichgau

(probably) son of

Generation 39

0.1101110110110111100110001100111011111 Eberhard I, Count of Bonngau

son of

Generation 40

0.1101110110110111100110001100111011111 Erenfried I of Maasgau married **0.110111011011011110011000110011101110 Adelgunde of Burgundy** (860-902) daughter of

0.110111011011011110011000110011101101 Conrad II, Duke of Transjurane Burgundy, Count of Auxerre married

0.110111011011011110011000110011101100 Judith of Frioul

Second Holy Roman Emperors 36-39

Generation 36

0.11011101101101111001100011001100 Mathilda of Germany (979-1025) married **0.11011101101101111001100011001101 Ezzo of Lotharingia** (955-1034) Count Palatine **See Lotharingia**

Mathilda = daughter of

Generation 37

0.11011101101101111001100011001001 Otto II "the Red" (955-983) Holy Roman Emperor married

0.11011101101101111001100011001000 Theophanu (955-991) daughter of **0.11011101101101111001100011001110001 Constantine Skleros** of a Byzantine noble family married

483

0.110111011011011111001100011001110000 Sophia Phokaina of a Byzantine noble family from Cappadocia

Otto = son of

<u>Generation 38</u>

0.110111011011011111001100011001110011 Otto I "the Great" (912-973) married **0.110111011011011111001100011001110010 Saint Adelaide of Italy** (931-999) daughter of

0.110111011011011111001100011001110101 Rudolph II of Burgundy (880-937) married

0.110111011011011111001100011001110100 Bertha of Swabia

Otto = son of

<u>Generation 39</u>

0.110111011011011111001100011001110111 Henry the Fowler (876-936) married **0.110111011011011111001100011001110110 Saint Mathilda** (c. 894/897-968)

[We are also descended from their daughter Gerberga]

Armenia 36-47 Armenia

<u>Generation 36</u>

0.110111011011011111001100011011001110 Ripsimia of Armenia (911-969) married **0.110111011011011111001100011011001111 Comita Nikola,** Duke of Sofia (906-968) **See Bulgaria**

daughter of

<u>Generation 37</u>

0.110111011011011111001100011011001110 1 King Ashot II Bagratuni of Armenia (reigned 914-929) married **0.110111011011011111001100011011001110 0 Marie of Artsakh**

son of

<u>Generation 38</u>

0.110111011011011111001100011011001110 11 King Smbat I (850-912/914)

Generation 39

**0.110111011011011110011000110110011110111 Ashot I "the Great"
King of Armenia** (820-890) oversaw the beginning of Armenia's
second golden age, married
0.110111011011011110011000110110011110110 Katranide
son of

Generation 40

**0.110111011011011110011000110110011101111 Smbat VIII "the
Confessor"** (reigned 852-855) married
0.110111011011011110011000110110011101110 Hripsime
son of

Generation 41

**0.110111011011011110011000110110011101111 Ashot Msaker
AKA Ashot IV Bagratuni, Prince of Armenia** (reigned 790-826)
son of

Generation 42

**0.110111011011011110011000110110011101111 Smbat VII,
presiding prince of Arab-ruled Armenia** (reigned 751-775)
son of

Generation 43

**"0.110111011011011110011000110110011101111111 Ashot III
Bagratuni AKA Ashot "the Blind,"** presiding prince of Armenia
(690-762)
grandson of

Generation 45

**0.1101110110110111100110001101100111011111111 Varaztirots II
Bagratuni, presiding prince of Armenia** (590-645)
son of

Generation 46

0.110111011011011110011000110110011101111111111 Smbat IV Bagratuni, Marzban of Hyrcania and of Persian Armenia, (d. 617)

son of

Generation 47

0.110111011011011110011000110110011101111111111111 Manuel or Manvel Bagratuni (b. 530)

Lombardy 36-40 Italy, *Charlemagne*

Generation 36

0.11011101101101111001101110111111110 Rozala of Lombardy (950-1003) married **0.11011101101101111001101110111111111 Arnulf II Count of Flanders** (961-988). Rozala later married King Robert II of France **See First Flanders**

Rozala = daughter of

Generation 37

0.11011101101101111001101110111111101 Berengar II of Italy (c. 900-Au. 4, 966) married **0.11011101101101111001101110111111100 Willa of Tuscany**.

Berengar = son of

Generation 38

0.11011101101101111001101110111111111011 Adalbert I Margrave of Ivrea (d. 929) married **0.11011101101101111001101110111111111010 Gisela of Friuli** daughter of **0.1101110110110111100110110111111110101 King Berengar I of Italy** (845-924) married **0.1101110110110111100110110111111110100 Gertila of Spoleto** (860-915), Bergengar I was son of **0.11011101101101111001101110111111101011 Berhard Duke of Friuli** (808-866) married

0.1101110110110111100110111011111111101010 Gisela, daughter of
0.1101110110110111100110111011111111010101 Louis the Pious
(821-874) Holy Roman Emperor and son of
0.1101110110110111100110111011111111101011 Charlemagne
(742- 814)
Adalbert = son of

Generation 39
**0.1101110110110111100110111011111111110111 Anscar I, Margrave
of Ivrea** (860-902)
son of

Generation 40
**0.1101110110110111100110111011111111101111 Count Amadeus of
Oscheret** (790-867)

Third Saxony 36-40 Germany

Generation 36
0.1101110110111111010110100100100010110 Gerberga of Saxony
(913-984) married **0.1101110110111111010110100100100010111
Louis IV of King France** (920-954) **See Second Lorraine**
daughter of

Generation 37
**0.1101110110111111010110100100100010110 Henry the Fowler,
king of Germany** (876-936), and
**0.1101110110111111010110100100100010110 Saint Matilda of
Ringelheim** (894-968) [We are also descended from their son Otto I
"the Great," Holy Roman Emperor]
son of

Generation 38
**0.1101110110111111010110100100100010110 Otto I "the
Illustrious,"** Duke of Saxony married

0.110111011011111101011010010010001011000 Hedwig of Franconia

son of

Generation 39

0.110111011011111101011010010010001011011 Liudolf, Duke of Saxony (805-866) married

0.110111011011111101011010010010001011010 Oda, daughter of

0.110111011011111101011010010010001011010 Billung married

0.110111011011111101011010010010001011010 Aeda

Liudolf = son of

Generation 40

0.110111011011111101011010010010001011011 Graf Brun Bruhart married **0.110111011011111101011010010010001011010 Gisla von Verla**

Second Kiev 37-40 Ukraine

Generation 37

0.110111011011111101001011001111110 Predslava of Kiev married

0.110111011011111101001011001111111 Almos, Prince of Hungary (1070-1129) **See Second Hungary**

daughter of

Generation 38

0.110111011011111101001011001111101 Sviatopolk II Iziaslavich, Prince of Kiev (1050-1130) [We are also descended from another daughter of his, Zbyslava]

Sviatopolk = son of

Generation 39

0.110111011011111101001011001111011 Iziaslav I, Prince of Kiev (1024-1078) married

0.110111011011111101001011001111010 Gertrude of Poland, See Poland

son of

Generation 40

0.11011101101111110100101100111110111 Yaroslav the Wise (978-1054) married **0.11011101101111110100101100111110110 Ingegerd Olofsdotter** daughter of

0.11011101101111110100101100111110101 Olof Skolkonung [We are also descended from Yaroslav's son Vsevolod I]

Third Wessex 37-40 *Alfred "the Great"*

Generation 37

0.11011101101111110101101001001000010110 Eadgifu of Wessex (d. after 951) married **0.11011101101111110101101001001000010111 Charles III, the Simple or the Straightforward, King of France** (Sept. 17, 879-Oct. 7, 929) **See Second Lorraine** daughter of

Generation 38

0.11011101101111110101101001001000101101 Edward the Elder (870s-924) king of the Anglo-Saxons married

0.11011101101111110101101001001000101100 Aeifflaed Edward = son of

Generation 39

0.11011101101111110101101001001000101011 Alfred "the Great," Saxon King of England (Wessex) (849-899) married **0.11011101101111110101101001001000101010 Ealhswith** (852-905), daughter of **0.110111011011111101011010010010001011010101 Aethered Mucil, Ealdorman of the Gaini**

Alfred = son of

Generation 40

0.11011101101111110101101001001000010110111 Ethelwulf, King of Wessex (AKA Aethelwulf) (800-858) married **0.11011101101111110101101001001000010110110 Osburga** (810-855) **See First Wessex for earlier ancestors**

Vermandois 38-48 France, Italy, *Charlemagne*

Generation 38

0.1110110110111100110011111111111110 Béatrice of Vermandois
(880–931) married **0.1110110110111100110011111111111111 Robert I**
King of West Francia (866–923) **See Valois, See Antioch**

Beatrice = daughter of

Generation 39

0.1110110110111100110011111111111101 Herbert I, Count of
Vermandois, Lord of Senlis, Peronne and Saint Quentin (848-907)
married **0.1110110110111100110011111111111100 Bertha de Morvois**

son of

Generation 40

0.1110110110111100110011111111111011 Pepin, 1st Count of
Vermandois, Lord of Senlis Peronne and Saint Quentin (b. 815)

son of

Generation 41

0.1110110110111100110011111111110111 Bernard, King of Italy
(797-818) married **0.1110110110111100110011111111110110**
Cunigunda

son of

Generation 42

0.1110110110111100110011111111101111 Pepin, "Carloman",
King of Italy (777-810) married
0.1110110110111100110011111111101110 Bertha

son of

Generation 43

0.1110110110111100110011111111011111 Charlemagne, Holy
Roman Emperor (742-814) married
0.1110110110111100110011111111011110 Hildegarde of
Vinzgouw

son of

Generation 44

0.111011011011110011001111111111110111111 Pepin the Short, King of the Franks (d. 768) married

0.111011011011110011001111111111110111110 Bertrada of Laon son of

Generation 45

0.1110110110111100110011111111111101111111 Charles Martel, "the Hammer", Mayor of the Palace of Austrasia, commander of the European armies that defeated the Moors at the Battle of Tours in 732 (688-741) married

0.1110110110111100110011111111111101111110 Rotrude son of

Generation 46

0.11101101101111001100111111111111011111111 Pepin II of Herstal (635-714) mated with

0.11101101101111001100111111111111011111110 Alpaida son of

Generation 47

0.111011011011110011001111111111110111111111 Ansegisel married **0.111011011011110011001111111111110111111110 Saint Begga** (615-693) **See Saint Begga** son of

Generation 48

0.1110110110111100110011111111111101111111111 Saint Arnulf of Metz (582-640) married

0.1110110110111100110011111111111101111111110 Saint Doda (b. around 584) **See Saint Doda 46**

Toulouse 38-47 France

Generation 38

0.110111011011111101011010010010001011110 Adelaide of Paris (853-901) married **0.110111011011111101011010010010001011111 Louis "the Stammerer" King of Western Francia** (Nov. 1, 846-April 10, 879) **See Second Lorraine**

Adelaide = daughter of

Generation 39

0.110111011011111101011010010010001011101 Adalard of Paris, Count of Paris and Count Palatine (830-890)

Adalard = son of

Generation 40

0.110111011011111101011010010010001011101 1 Wulfhard of Flavigny married **0.110111011011111101011010010010001011101 0** Suzanne of Paris

Suzanne = daughter of

Generation 41

0.110111011011111101011010010010001011101 1 Beggo, Count of Toulouse (d. 816) married

0.110111011011111101011010010010001011101 0 Alpais or Amaudru

Beggo = son of

Generation 42

0.110111011011111101011010010010001011101 11 Gerard I of Paris married **0.110111011011111101011010010010001011101 10 Rotrude**

Rotrude = daughter of

Generation 43

0.110111011011111101011010010010001011101 111 Carloman, Mayor of the Palace (713-754)

son of

Generation 44

0.1101110110111111010110100100100010111011111 Charles "The Hammer" Martel (688-741) Mayor of the Palace of Austrasia and King or Duke of the Franks, won the Battle of Tours in 732, halting Muslim expansion in Europe married

0.1101110110111111010110100100100010111011110 Rotrude of Treve (690-724) daughter of

0.1101110110111111010110100100100010111011101 Saint Leutwinus, Count and Bishop of Treves **See Treve**

Generation 45

0.1110110110111100110011111111111011111111 Pepin II of Herstal (635-714) mated with

0.1110110110111100110011111111111011111110 Alpaida son of

Generation 46

0.1110110110111100110011111111110111111111 Ansegisel married **0.1110110110111100110011111111110111111110 Saint Begga** (615- 693) **See Saint Begga**

son of

Generation 47

0.1110110110111100110011111111101111111111 Saint Arnulf of Metz (582-640) married

0.1110110110111100110011111111101111111110 Saint Doda (b. 584)

See Saint Doda

Holy Roman Emperors 38-46 *Charlemagne*

Generation 38

0.110111011011011110011011100110101111110 Judith of Flanders (844-870) married **0.110111011011011110011011100110101111111 Baldwin I "Iron Arm" of Flanders. See First Flanders 31**

Judith = daughter of

Generation 39

0.110111011011011110011011100110101111101 Charles the Bald, Holy Roman Emperor (823-877) married

0.110111011011011110011011100110101111100 Ermentrude of Orleans (823-869)

son of

Generation 40

0.110111011011011110011011100110101111011 Louis "the Pious" AKA Louis I "the Fair" (778-840) **Holy Roman Emperor and King of the Franks** (813-840 married

0.110111011011011110011011100110101111010 Judith of Bavaria (805-843) daughter of

0.1101110110110111100110111001101011111101 Count Welf and

0.1101110110110111100110111001101011111100 Hedwig, Duchess of Bavaria

Louis = son of

Generation 41

0.1101110110110111100110111001101011111111 Charlemagne Holy Roman Emperor (747-814) married

0.1101110110110111100110111001101011111110 Hildegarde (758-783) **See Bavaria**

son of

Generation 42

0.11011101101101111001101110011010111111 Pepin or Pippin AKA Pepin the Younger or Pepin III (714-768), Mayor of the Palace of Austrasia and King of the Franks married

0.11011101101101111001101110011010111110 Bertrada of Laon (720-783) daughter of

0.110111011011011110011011100110101111011101 Caribert, Count of Laon, who was son of

0.11011101101101111001101110011010111110111010 Bertrada of Prium

Pepin = son of

<u>Generation 43</u>

0.11011101101101111001101110011010111110111111 Charles "The Hammer" Martel (688-741) Mayor of the Palace of Austrasia and King or Duke of the Franks, won the Battle of Tours in 732, halting Muslim expansion in Europe. married

0.11011101101101111001101110011010111110111110 Rotrude of Treve (690-724) daughter of

0.11011101101101111001101110011010111110111101 St. Leutwinus, Count and Bishop of Treves **See Treve 43**

Charles = son of

<u>Generation 44</u>

0.110111011011011110011011100110101111101111111 Pepin of Herstal AKA Pepin II or Pepin the Middle (635-616) Mayor of the Palace of Austrasia, and of Neustria and Burgundy married

0.110111011011011110011011100110101111101111110 Alpaida son of

<u>Generation 45</u>

0.1101110110110111100110111001101011111101111111 Ansegisel (602-662) married

0.1101110110110111100110111001101011111101111110 Saint Begga (615-693) **See Saint Begga** [We are also descended from Ansegisel's brother Saint Clodulf]

Ansegisel = son of

<u>Generation 46</u>

0.11011101101101111001101110011010111111011111111 Saint Arnulf of Metz (582-640) married

0.11011101101101111001101110011010111111011111110 Saint Doda (b. 584) **See Saint Doda**

Early Norwegian and Swedish Kings 39-100
Beowulf, Odin, Zeus

Generation 39

0.110111011011011110011011100110111111110 Ascrida Rognvaldsdatter married

0.110111011011011110011011100110111111111 Eystein Ivarsson (b. 788) a "petty" king of Norway **See Normandy**

Ascrida = daughter of

Generation 40

0.11011101101101111001101110011011111111101 Ragnvald or Rognvald "the Mountain-High" Olafsson king of Vestfold in what is today Norway.

son of

Generation 41

0.110111011011011110011011100110111111111101 Olaf Gudrødsson, or as he was named after his death **Olaf Geirstad-Alf**, was a legendary Norwegian king of the House of Yngling from the *Ynglinga Saga*. (Brother of Halfdan the Black).

son of

Generation 42

0.1101110110110111100110111001101111111111011 Gudrød the Hunter was a semi-legendary king in south-east Norway, during the early Viking Age.

Gudrød = son of

Generation 43

0.11011101101101111001101110011011111111110111 Halfdan the Mild of the House of Yngling, King of Romerike and Vestfold in what now is Norway married

0.11011101101101111001101110011011111111110110 Liv daughter of

0.110111011011011110011011100110111111111101101 King Dag of Vestmar

496

Halfdan = son of

Generation 44

**0.11011101101101111001101110011011111111101111 Eystein
Halfdansson, King of Romerike and Vestfold** in what is now
Norway married

0.11011101101101111001101110011011111111101110 Hild daughter
of **0.11011101101101111001101110011011111111011101 Erik
Ragnarsson, King of Romerike and Vestfold**

Eystein = son of

Generation 45

**0.11011101101101111001101110011011111111011111 Halfdan
Hvitbeinn "Whiteshanks,"** a mythical petty king in Norway of the
House of Yngling (described in Ynglinga Saga, written in the 1220s
by Snorri Sturluson) married

0.11011101101101111001101110011011111111011110 Asa daughter
of **0.11011101101101111001101110011011111110111101 Eystein,
King of Oppland and Hedmark**

Halfdan = son of

Generation 46

**0.11011101101101111001101110011011111110111111 Olaf "Tree
Feller"** or Olof Tratalja of the House of Yngling. Sacrificed to Odin
by the Swedish settlers in Värmland because of a famine.

son of

Generation 47

**0.11011101101101111001101110011011111110111111 Ingjald III,
King of Sweden** married

**0.11011101101101111001101110011011111110111110 Gauthild
Algautsdottir** (7th century), daughter of

**0.11011101101101111001101110011011111111011111101 Algaut,
Geatish King of West Gotaland** according to the Heimskringla.
Snorri Sturluson relates that he was burnt to death by his son-in-law,

the Swedish king Ingjald Ill married

0.110111011011011110011011100110111111111011111100 unknown, daughter of

0.110111011011011110011011100110111111110111111001 Olof the "Sharp-Sighted," King of Nerike

Ingjald = son of

Generation 48

0.110111011011011110011011100110111111111011111111 King Onund or Anund of Sweden, House of Yngling. His name meant "Winning Ancestor."

son of

Generation 49

0.110111011011011110011011100110111111110111111111 King Ingvar Harra of Sweden,

House of Yngling (d. early 7th century). Fell in battle in Estonia son of

Generation 50

0.110111011011011110011011100110111111101111111111 King Eysteinn AKA Östen of

Sweden, House of Yngling (d. 600)

son of

Generation 51

0.110111011011011110011011100110111111101111111111111 King Eadgils of Sweden, House of

Yngling (6th century). Mentioned in *Beowulf.*

son of

Generation 52

0.110111011011011110011011100110111111110111111111111 King Ohthere or Ottar of

Sweden, House

of Scylfings (early 6th century). Mentioned in *Beowulf.*

son of

Generation 53

0.1101110110110111100110111001101111111101111111111111 King Egill or Ongentheow of

Sweden. House of Scylfings (d. 515). Mentioned in *Beowulf*.

son of

Generation 54

0.1101110110110111100110111001101111111101111111111111 King On or Aun the Old of Sweden

son of

Generation 55

0.1101110110110111100110111001101111111101111111111111111

King Jorund of Sweden

son of

Generation 56

0.110111011011011110011011100110111111110111111111111111

King Yngvi of Sweden

son of

Generation 57

0.1101110110110111100110111001101111111101111111111111111

King Alaric of Sweden

son of

Generation 58

0.1101110110110111100110111001101111111101111111111111111

King Agne of Sweden

son of

Generation 59

0.1101110110110111100110111001101111111101111111111111111

King Dag of Sweden, who understood the language of birds. He had a sparrow which flew to different countries and brought him news ("a little bird told me")

son of

Generation 60

0.110111011011011110011011100110111111110111111111111111111

1 King Dyggvi of Sweden

son of

Generation 61

0.110111011011011110011011100110111111110111111111111111111

11 King Domar of Sweden

son of

Generation 62

0.110111011011011110011011100110111111110111111111111111111

111 King Domalde of Sweden

son of

Generation 63

0.110111011011011110011011100110111111110111111111111111111

1111 King Visbur of Sweden

son of

Generation 64

0.110111011011011110011011100110111111110111111111111111111

11111 King Vanlande of Sweden

son of

Generation 65

0.110111011011011110011011100110111111110111111111111111111

111111 King Sveigde of Sweden

son of

Generation 66

0.110111011011011110011011100110111111110111111111111111111

1111111 King Fjölner of Sweden

son of

Generation 67
**0.110111011011011110011011100110111111110111111111111111111111
11111111 Yngve Frey, god and sovereign of the Swedes**
son of
Generation 68
**0.110111011011011110011011100110111111110111111111111111111111
111111111 Njord of Noatum, god and sole sovereign of the Swedes**
married
**0.110111011011011110011011100110111111110111111111111111111111
111111110 Skadi** a goddess or a jötunn, a non-human creature,
perhaps like a troll
Generation 69
**0.110111011011011110011011100110111111110111111111111111111111
1111111111 Odin, king of the gods** married
**0.110111011011011110011011100110111111110111111111111111111111
1111111110 Frigg**
According to *The Saga of the Ynglings* by Snorri Sturlson, Odin is
son of
Generation 70
**0.110111011011011110011011100110111111110111111111111111111111
11111111111 Bür, father of all other gods**, and of
**0.110111011011011110011011100110111111110111111111111111111111
11111111110 Bestia**, the daughter or granddaughter of a jötunn
named Böjborn. (A jötunn is a class of creature like a troll.)

According to *The Prose Edda* by Snorri Sturlson:
Generation 69
**0.110111011011011110011011100110111111110111111111111111111111
1111111111 Odin** married
0.110111011011011110011011100110111111110111111111111111111111

1111111110 Frigida AKA Frigg. "Each member of his family is divine". (That includes us).

son of

<u>Generation 70</u>

0.11011101101101111001101110011011111111011111111111111111 11111111111 Voden

son of

<u>Generation 71</u>

0.11011101101101111001101110011011111111011111111111111111 111111111111 Friallaf AKA Fridleif

son of

<u>Generation 72</u>

0.11011101101101111001101110011011111111011111111111111111 1111111111111 Fin

son of

<u>Generation 73</u>

0.11011101101101111001101110011011111111011111111111111111 11111111111111 Gudolf

son of

<u>Generation 74</u>

0.11011101101101111001101110011011111111011111111111111111 111111111111111 Jat

son of

<u>Generation 75</u>

0.11011101101101111001101110011011111111011111111111111111 1111111111111111 Biaf AKA Bjar

son of

<u>Generation 76</u>

0.11011101101101111001101110011011111111011111111111111111 11111111111111111 Skjaldun AKA Skjold

son of

Generation 77

**0.1101110110110111100110111001101111111011111111111111111
1111111111111111111 Heremod**

son of

Generation 78

**0.1101110110110111100110111001101111111011111111111111111
1111111111111111111 Itrmann**

son of

Generation 79

**0.1101110110110111100110111001101111111011111111111111111
1111111111111111111**

Acnar

son of

Generation 80

**0.1101110110110111100110111001101111111011111111111111111
1111111111111111111 Athra**

son of

Generation 81

**0.1101110110110111100110111001101111111011111111111111111
1111111111111111111 Bedrig**

son of

Generation 82

**0.1101110110110111100110111001101111111011111111111111111
1111111111111111111 Seskef**

son of

Generation 83

**0.1101110110110111100110111001101111111011111111111111111
1111111111111111111 Magi**

son of

Generation 84

0.110111011011011110011011100110111111110111111111111111111111111111111111111111111 Moda

son of

Generation 85

0.110111011011011110011011100110111111110111111111111111111111111111111111111111111 Vingerif

son of

Generation 86

0.110111011011011110011011100110111111110111111111111111111111111111111111111111111 Vige

son of

Generation 87

0.110111011011011110011011100110111111110111111111111111111111111111111111111111111 Eiridi

son of

Generation 88

0.110111011011011110011011100110111111110111111111111111111111111111111111111111111 Lordi

son of

Generation 89

0.110111011011011110011011100110111111110111111111111111111111111111111111111111111 Tror AKA Thor married **0.110111011011011110011011100110111111110111111111111111111111111111111111111111110 Sif**. Tror was raised in Thrace by Loricos, whom he murdered together with his wife. He then ruled in Thrace and later travelled north where he met and married the prophetess Sif.

son of

Generation 90

0.11011101101101111100110111001101111111101111111111111111111 11111111111111111111111111111110 Troan married
0.11011101101101111100110111001101111111101111111111111111111 11111111111111111111111111111111 Munon AKA Mennon
daughter of

Generation 91

0.11011101101101111100110111001101111111101111111111111111111 11111111111111111111111111111101 King Priam of Troy AKA of Asgard
according to Homer and Greek myth

Generation 91

0.11011101101101111100110111001101111111101111111111111111111 11111111111111111111111111111011 King Priam of Troy married
0.11011101101101111100110111001101111111101111111111111111111 11111111111111111111111111111010 Hecuba
son of

Generation 92

0.11011101101101111100110111001101111111101111111111111111111 11111111111111111111111111110111 King Laomedon of Troy
son of

Generation 93

0.11011101101101111100110111001101111111101111111111111111111 11111111111111111111111111101111 Ilus, founder of the city of Troy
son of

Generation 94

0.11011101101101111100110111001101111111101111111111111111111 11111111111111111111111111011111 Tros, founder of the kingdom of Troy
son of

Generation 95
0.1101110110110111100110111001101111111011111111111111111111111111111111111111111111111110111111 **Erichthonius**
son of
Generation 96
0.1101110110110111100110111001101111111011111111111111111111111111111111111111111111111111101111111 **Dardanus,** founder of the city of Dardania
son of
Generation 97
0.11011101101101111001101110011011111111011111111111111111111111111111111111111111111111011111111 **Zeus,** king of the gods according to Hesiod and Greek myth:
Zeus = son of
Generation 98
0.11011101101101111001101110011011111111011111111111111111111111111111111111110111111111 **Cronus** mated with
0.110111011011011110011011100110111111101111111111111111111111111111111110111111110 **Rhea**
son of
Generation 99
0.1101110110110111100110111001101111111101111111111111111111111111111111101111111111 **Uranus** mated with
0.110111011011011110011011100110111111101111111111111111111111111111111111111101111111111110 **Gaia (his mother)**
son of
Generation 100
0.1101110110110111100110111001101111111101111111111111111111111111111111110111111111110 **Gaia**

First Wessex 39-52 *Alfred "the Great"*

Generation 39

0.1101110110110111100110110111111111110 Aelfthryth (d. 929)
married **0.1101110110110111100110110111111111111 Baldwin II
Count of Flanders** (875-918) **See Baldwin of Constantinople**
Aeltfhryth = daughter of

Generation 40

**0.1101110110110111100110110111111111101 Alfred "the Great,"
Saxon King of England** (Wessex) (849-899), married
0.1101110110110111100110110111111111100 Ealhswith (852-
905), daughter of **0.1101110110110111100110110111111111001**
Aethered Mucil, Ealdorman of the Gaini (see Anglo-Saxon
Chronicles)
son of

Generation 41

**0.110111011011011110011011101111111111011 King Ethelwulf of
Wessex** (795-858) married
0.110111011011011110011011101111111111010 Osburga
son of

Generation 42

**0.110111011011011110011011101111111110111 King Egbert of
Wessex,** first king of England (d. 839)
son of

Generation 43

**0.110111011011011110011011101111111101111 Ealmund of
Kent** (745-827)
son of

Generation 44

**0.110111011011011110011011101111111011111 Eafa the West
Saxon** (married **0.110111011011011110011011101111111011110**

507

daughter of **0.110111011011011110011011101111111111110111100**
Aethelbert II of Kent

Eafa = son of

Generation 45

0.110111011011011110011011101111111111110111111 Eoppa (b, 706)
married Kentish princess

son of

Generation 46

0.110111011011011110011011101111111111101111111 Ingild of
Wessex (672-718)

Ingild = son of

Generation 47

0.110111011011011110011011101111111111011111111 Cenred of
Wessex (b. 640)

Cenred = son of

0.110111011011011110011011101111111111110111111111 Ceolwald
of Wessex

Generation 48

Ceolwald = son of

0.110111011011011110011011101111111111101111111111 Cutha
Cathwulf of Wessex (b. 592)

Cutha Cathwulf = son of

Generation 49

0.110111011011011110011011101111111111011111111111
Cuthwine of Wessex

son of

Generation 50

0.110111011011011110011011101111111111101111111111111 Cealwin
of Wessex (d. 593)

Cealwin = son of

Generation 51

0.110111011011011110011011101111111111101111111111111 Cynric of Wessex, king of Wessex 534-560

Cynric = son of

Generation 52

0.110111011011011110011011101111111111101111111111111 Cerdic of Wessex (d. 534) ruled as King of Wessex 519-534 = leader of the first group of West Saxons to come to England in 495. He and his son are portrayed in the movie *King Arthur* as killed in battle by King Arthur and Sir Lancelot.

Poland 39-42 Poland

Generation 39

0.1101110110111111010010110011111010 Gertrude of Poland married **0.1101110110111111010010110011111011 Iziaslav I, Prince of Kiev** (1024-1078) **See Second Kiev**

Gertrude = daughter of

Generation 40

0.110111011011111101001011001111110101 Mieszko II Lambert, King of Poland (990-1034) married **0.110111011011111101001011001111110100 Richeza of Lotharingia**

son of

Generation 41

0.11011101101111110100101100111111101011 Bolesaw I, "the Brave", King of Poland (967-1025) married **0.11011101101111110100101100111111101010 Enmilda**

son of

Generation 42

0.1101110110101111101001011001111111010111 Mieszko I, King of Poland married **0.1101110110101111101001011001111111010110 Dobrawa** (940-977) **See Bohemia**

Bavaria 41-42 Germany, Charlemagne

Generation 41

0.1101110110101101110011011100110101111110110 Hildegarde (758-783) married

0.1101110110101101110011011100110101111110111 Charlemagne, Holy Roman Emperor (747-814) **See Vermandois**

Hildegarde = daughter of

Generation 42

0.1101110110101101110011011100110101111101101 Count Gerold of Vinzgau (725-799) Margrave of the Avarian March and Prefect of Bavaria married

0.1101110110101101110011011100110101111101100 Emma of Alamannia (730-789) **See Alamannia**

Bohemia 42 Bohemia

Generation 42

0.1101110110101111101001011001111111010110 Dobrawa (940-977) married **0.1101110110101111101001011001111111010111 Mieszko I, King of Poland See Second Poland**

Dobrawa = daughter of

Generation 43

0.1101110110101111101001011001111110101101 Boleslaus I, "the Cruel", Duke of Bohemia (d. 967) married **0.1101110110101111101001011001111110101100 Biagota.** Boleslaus was a brother of "Good King Wenceslaus" and killed Wenceslaus to get his throne.

Boleslaus = son of

Generation 44

0.110111011101111110100101100111111101011011 Vratislaus I, Duke of Bohemia (888-921) married

0.110111011101111110100101100111111101011010 Drahomira son of

Generation 45

0.110111011101111110100101100111111101011011 Borivoj I, Duke of Bohemia married

0.110111011101111110100101100111111101011010 Saint Ludmila (c. 860-921) daughter of

0.110111011101111110100101100111111101011011 Slavibor a Sorbian prince, reigned 859-894

Alamannia 42-45 Germany

Generation 42

0.110111011011011110011011100110101111110110 Emma of Alamannia (730-789) married

0.110111011011011110011011100110101111110110 Count Gerold of Vinzgau (725-799) Margrave of the Avarian March and Prefect of Bavaria **See Bavaria**

Emma = daughter of

Generation 43

0.110111011011011110011011100110101111110110 Hnabi or Nebi (c. 710-c. 788) Alemannic duke married

0.110111011011011110011011100110101111110110 Hereswind

Hnabi = son of

Generation 44

0.110111011011011110011011100110101111110110 Huoching

Huoching = ? son of

Generation 45

0.1101110110110111100110111001101011111101100111 Duke Gotfrid or Godefroy (d. 709) Duke of Alemannia in Bavaria

Treve 43-46 France

Generation 43

0.1101110110110111100110111001101011111011110 Rotrude of Treve (690-724) married

0.1101110110110111100110111001101011111011111 Charles "the Hammer" Martel (688-741) Mayor of the Palace of Austrasia and King or Duke of the Franks, won the Battle of Tours in 732, halting Muslim expansion in Europe. **See Vermandois**

Rotrude = daughter of

Generation 44

0.1101110110110111100110111001101011111110111101 Saint Leudwinus, Count and Bishop of Treves and Trier (660-722) married **0.1101110110110111100110111001101011111110111100 Willigard of Bavaria**

Leudwinus = son of

Generation 45

0.110111011011011110011011100110101111110111011 Warinus, Count of Poitier (638-677) married

0.110111011011011110011011100110101111110111010 Gunza of Treves,

son of

Generation 46

Bodilon Count of Poitier (d. 677) **married Sigrada of Alsace.** She was from the Syagrii family of Gallo-Roman patricians

Saint Begga 45-47 France

son of

Generation 48

0.110111011011011110011011100110101111101111110011

Ansbertus. Gallo-Roman senator married

0.110111011011011110011011100110101111101111110010

Blithilde of Cologne (538-603) daughter of

0.110111011011011110011011100110101111101111100101

Charibert I who married

0.110111011011011110011011100110101111101111100100

Ingoberga

?Ansbertus = son of

Generation 49

0.110111011011011110011011100110101111101111100111

Ferreolus of Rodz (born around 485), Gallo-Roman senator of Narbonne married

0.110111011011011110011011100110101111101111100110 Dode

son of

Generation 50

0.110111011011011110011011100110101111101111001111

Tonantius Ferreolus (440-517) a Gallo-Roman senator

son of

Generation 51

0.110111011011011110011011100110101111101111110011111

Tonantius Ferreolus (390-475) praetorian prefect of Gaul, instrumental in organizing Gaul in defense against invasion of Attila married

0.110111011011011110011011100110101111101111110011101

Papianilla (b. 415), niece of Emperor Avitus (395-457) son of Tonantius = son of an unnamed daughter of

Generation 53
0.1101110110110111100110111001101011111011111001111101
Afranius Syagrius (345-382), consul in 382, originated in Lyon

Saint Doda 46-52 France, Rome

Generation 46
**0.110111011011011110011011100110101111101111110 Saint
Doda** (b.584) married
**0.110111011011011110011011100110101111101111111 Saint
Arnulf of Metz** (582-640) **See Vermandois**
Doda = daughter of
Generation 47
0.1101110110110111100110111001101011111101111111101 Arnoald
(560-611) married
0.1101110110110111100110111001101011111101111111100 Oda
son of
Generation 48
0.110111011011011110011011100110101111101111111011
Ansbertus, a Senator married
0.110111011011011110011011100110101111101111111010 Blithilde
(538-603) daughter
of **0.1101110110110111100110111001101011111101111111110101**
Chlothar I, King of the Franks (497-561) married
0.1101110110110111100110111001101011111101111111110100
Waldrada, a Lombard princess **See Merovingian**
Ansbertus = son of
Generation 49
0.110111011011011110011011100110101111101111111110111
Ferreolus, Senator of Narbonne (b. 470 or 475)
married **0.110111011011011110011011100110101111101111111110110**
Saint Dode, daughter of

0.110111011011011110011011100110101111110111111101101 King Chloderic of the Ripuarian Franks (d. 509) King Chloderic was son of

0.110111011011011110011011100110101111110111111011011 Sigobert the Lame (d. 509) king of the Franks in the area of Zulpich and Cologne

Ferreolus = son of

Generation 50

0.110111011011011110011011100110101111110111111101111 Tonantius Ferreolus (440 or 450-511 of after 517) Roman Senator who lived in Narbonne married

0.110111011011011110011011100110101111110111111101110 Industria of Narbonne daughter of

0.110111011011011110011011100110101111110111111011101 Flavius Probus, Roman Senator who married

0.110111011011011110011011100110101111110111111011100 Eulalia

Tonantius Ferreolus = son of

Generation 51

0.110111011011011110011011100110101111110111111011111 Tonantius Ferreolus (390-475) Praetorian Prefect of Gaul, instrumental in organizing Gaul for defense against invasion of Attila the Hun, married

0.110111011011011110011011100110101111110111111110111110 Papianilla (born 415) niece of Emperor Avitus (395-457), reigned 455- 456

Tonantius = son of

Generation 52

0.110111011011011110011011100110101111110111111110111111 Ferreolus a Roman senator married unnamed daughter of Afranius Syagrius (345-382) consul in 382

Merovingian 48-56 France *Clovis*

Generation 48

0.11011101101101111001101110011010111111011111111010 Blithilde
(538-603) married
0.11011101101101111001101110011010111111011111111011
Ansbertus a Senator (505 or 535-570 or 611) **See Ancient Rome,**
See Saint Doda
? Blithilde = daughter of
Generation 49
0.11011101101101111001101110011010111111011111110101 Chlota
r I, King of the Franks (497-561) married
0.11011101101101111001101110011010111111011111110100
Waldrada, a Lombard princess, daughter of
0.11011101101101111001101110011010111111011111101001
Wacho King of the Lombards, reigned 510-539 married
0.11011101101101111001101110011010111111011111101000
Ostrogotha or Austrigusa. Wacho was son of
0.11011101101101111001101110011010111111011111111010011
Unchis
Clothar = son of
Generation 50
0.11011101101101111001101110011010111111011111111101011 Clovis
(466-511) married
0.11011101101101111001101110011010111111011111111101010 Saint
Clotilde (475-545)
Clovis = son of
Generation 51
0.11011101101101111001101110011010111111011111111010111
Childeric I (440-481) married
0.11011101101101111001101110011010111111011111111010110
Queen Basina of Thuringia (438-477)

Childeric was son of

Generation 52

0.11011101101101111001101110011010101111110111111110101111

Merovech AKA Meroveus or Merovius (411-457) Semi-legendary founder of the Merovingian dynasty of the Salian Franks (although either Childeric I, his supposed son, or Clovis I, his supposed grandson, may in fact be the founder), which later became the dominant Frankish tribe. He is said to be one of several barbarian warlords and kings that joined forces with the Roman general Aetius against the Huns under Attila in the Battle of the Catalaunian Plains, .

Generation 53

0.11011101101101111001101110011010101111110111111101011111

Chlodio (395-448) Chlodio was son of

Generation 54

0.110111011011011110011011100110101011111101111111010111111

Theodemer, a Frankish king.

Generation 55

0.1101110110110111100110111001101010111111011111110101111111

Richomeres (d. 393) married

0.1101110110110111100110111001101010111111011111110101111110

Ascyla. Richomere was Roman consul in 384. Supreme commander in the Eastern Empire 388-393. Uncle of General Arbogast. son of

Generation 56

0.1101110110110111100110111001101010111111011111110101111111

Teutomer, French general in service to Rome

Second Merovingian 48-55 *Clovis*

Generation 48

0.11011101101101111001101110011010101111101111110010

Blithilde of Cologne (538-603) married

0.110111011011011110011011100110101111101111110011

Ansbertus. Gallo-Roman senator

daughter of

Generation 49

0.110111011011011110011011100110101111101111110101

Charibert I, Merovingian King of Pars (c. 517-Dec. 567) married

0.110111011011011110011011100110101111101111110100

Ingoberga

son of

Generation 50

0.110111011011011110011011100110101111101111110001011

Clothar I, King of the Franks (500-561)

son of

Generation 51

0.1101110110110111100110111001101011111101111110010111

Clovis I, first King Franks (c. 466-Nov. 511) married

0.1101110110110111100110111001101011111101111110010110

Saint Clotilde (474-June 3, 541) converted to Roman Catholicism

daughter of

Generation 52

0.1101110110110111100110111001101011111101111110010111

Chilperic II, King of Burgundy (450-493) married

0.1101110110110111100110111001101011111101111110010110

Caretena

Chilperic = son of

Generation 53

0.110111011011011110011011100110101111101111110010111111

Gondioc (c. 420-473) In 451, he joined forces with Flavius Aetius against Attila, King of the Huns (our ancestor), in the Battle of the Catalaunian Plains.

son of

Generation 54

0.1101110110110111100110111001101011111101111110010111111
Gundahar AKA Gunther, King of Burgundy (d. 437) married
0.1101110110110111100110111001101011111101111110010111110
Brunhild. Gunther was defeated by the Roman general Flavius
Aetius, who destroyed Gundahar's kingdom with the
help Hunnish mercenaries the following year, resulting in Gundahar's
death. The historical Gundahar's death became the basis for a
tradition in Germanic heroic legend in which the legendary Gunther
met his death at the court of Attila the Hun (also our ancestor). Both
he and Brunhild appear in in the German *Nibelungenlied*, the Old
Norse *Poetic Edda* and *Volsunga Saga*, and in Wagner's operatic *Ring*
cycle.

Generation 55

0.1101110110110111100110111001101011111101111110010111111
Gibicca, King of Burgundy (c. 407)

www.ingramcontent.com/pod-product-compliance
Lightning Source LLC
Chambersburg PA
CBHW072136100125
20242CB00036B/531